CRITICAL CONVERSATIONS IN HIGHER EDUCATION

Editor
René Pellissier

Critical Conversations in Higher Education

Published by AFRICAN SUN MeDIA under the SUN PReSS imprint
Place of publication: Stellenbosch, South Africa

All rights reserved

Copyright © 2025 AFRICAN SUN MeDIA and René Pellissier

The editor and the publisher have made every effort to obtain permission for and acknowledge the use of copyrighted material. Refer all enquiries to the publisher.

No part of this book may be reproduced or transmitted in any form or by any electronic, photographic or mechanical means, including photocopying and recording on record, tape or laser disk, on microfilm, via the internet, by email, or by any other information storage and retrieval system, without prior written permission by the publisher.

Views reflected in this publication are not necessarily those of the publisher.

First edition 2025

978-0-6398892-2-1 (print)
978-0-6398892-3-8 (eBook)
https://doi.org/10.52779/9780639889238

Set in Minion Pro 11/13

Cover design, typesetting and production by AFRICAN SUN MeDIA

This publication can be ordered from:
orders@africansunmedia.co.za
Takealot: bit.ly/2monsfl
Google Books: bit.ly/2k1Uilm
Amazon Kindle: amzn.to/2ktL.pkL
JSTOR: https://bit.ly/3udc057
africansunmedia.store.it.si (eBooks)

Visit africansunmedia.co.za for more information.

Contents

Acknowledgements   1

Foreword   3

SECTION 1: Conversations about Pedagogy   5

  1 Avoiding human deepfakes: A learning and care-centred approach to learning in higher education   7
Hanelie Adendorff, Nicoline Herman, and Dalene Joubert

  2 Peer-assisted learning as a pedagogical strategy for decolonising higher education in the Global South   31
Sharon Margaretta Auld

  3 Digitally transforming the teaching of numeracy: Exploring trends within a South African private higher education institution   57
Dominique Marié Nupen and Jayseema Jagernath

SECTION 2: Conversations about Teaching and Learning   79

  4 Creating residential undergraduate experiences that meet the needs of students   81
Chris Mayer

  5 A vernacular reframing of professionalism: Ubuntu in the education of the next generation of professionals   95
Lionel Green-Thompson, Ann George, and Mantoa Mokhachane

  6 Homo umoyanus not homo neoliberalus: Socio-moral subjectivity for a transformed higher education   117
Shahieda Jansen

SECTION 3: Conversations about Innovation and Technology   143

  7 Incorporating generative AI into academia: Implications for a disruptive pedagogy   145
Jerome D. Kiley

  8 Employability of graduates: Introducing dual higher education (DHE) as an innovative model in higher education in South Africa   163
Antoinette Smith-Crous

SECTION 4: Conversations about Strategy and Policy   185

9 Academic citizenship and effective governance: Nurturing a nation's future   187
Ayansola Olatunji Ayandibu

10 It's 2025: Are our higher education models still valid?   201
René Pellissier

11 Unmasking neoliberalism: Exploring the dark side of leadership in a South African higher education institution   211
Lizl Steynberg and Jan P. Grundling

12 Beyond tokenistic civically engaged curriculum design and delivery   229
Rika Swanzen

13 Transformative dynamics in South African higher education: An economic lens on student and staff transformation   263
Leigh Neethling

14 Universities as economic drivers   289
Eugene Cloete

Contributing Authors   305
Authors Bios   311

ACKNOWLEDGEMENTS

This book is the product of a collective effort by a diverse group of scholars, practitioners, and thought leaders who are deeply invested in the future of higher education in South Africa. We extend our heartfelt gratitude to each of the contributing authors for their courage, insight, and commitment to challenging the status quo and imagining a more inclusive, just, and responsive higher education landscape.

We are grateful to our respective institutions for providing the academic space and support necessary for this work to come to life. Special thanks to the Cape Higher Education Consortium (CHEC) for its vision, coordination, and sustained support throughout this project.

We acknowledge the students, staff, communities, and activists whose lived experiences, critical questions, and persistent demands for transformation continue to inspire and shape this discourse. Your voices echo through every chapter.

A sincere thank you to the reviewers and editors who provided thoughtful feedback and helped sharpen the clarity, coherence, and relevance of this volume.

Finally, we dedicate this book to all those working tirelessly within and beyond the higher education sector to make higher education a place of meaning, care, and possibility.

FOREWORD

René Pellissier

Reimagine higher education in an era of disruption and transformation. Higher education in South Africa stands at a critical juncture. Confronted by widening inequality, the digital revolution, systemic injustices, and shifting global and local expectations, universities are being called to radically rethink their purpose, structures, and practices. This book is a response to that call.

Bringing together diverse scholarly voices from across the country and even internationally, the chapters in this volume interrogate the philosophical, structural, pedagogical, and economic foundations of higher education. They examine what it means to be a university in the 21st century, and how higher education institutions might reimagine themselves as engines of social transformation, ethical leadership, and inclusive development.

The early chapters set the philosophical tone, raising urgent questions about the authenticity of learning in an era of AI-generated content and the role of peer-assisted, critical pedagogy in post-apartheid South Africa. These chapters call for more engaged, responsive, and relational approaches to teaching and learning. Further contributions explore how digital tools, such as generative AI, are reshaping assessment and pedagogy, and how models, like dual higher education and service-learning, can address the employability crisis facing graduates. At the heart of these discussions lies a deeper critique of the university's traditional elitist models and a call for decolonised, community-rooted curricula. Several chapters place a spotlight on ethical and institutional transformation. Leadership in the academy is scrutinised, especially in the context of neoliberal pressures that promote toxic managerialism and the commodification of knowledge. Through reflective autoethnography and data-driven analysis, contributors expose how institutional cultures can perpetuate harm and marginalisation unless deeply reformed.

Crucially, this book extends beyond critique. It presents hopeful alternatives grounded in *ubuntu*, personhood, civically engaged curriculum design, and academic citizenship. Universities are shown not just as knowledge producers, but as vital contributors to national governance, social justice, and economic resilience. The economic role of universities is also a central theme. Several chapters examine higher education's impact on inequality, transformation, and economic development, both as employers and as drivers of innovation. Drawing on empirical data and case studies, contributors show how universities can help rebuild economies, but only if they shift away from outdated business models and toward more inclusive, sustainable approaches.

Taken together, this book offers a compelling narrative. The transformation of higher education cannot be a technical fix; it must be a radical reimagining. It must centre ethical leadership, social justice, inclusion, and the lived realities of both staff and students. It must reckon with the legacies of colonialism and Apartheid, while also embracing the possibilities of technological innovation and collaborative governance.

This book is intended for scholars, practitioners, students, and institutional leaders who are grappling with the future of higher education in South Africa and beyond. It does not offer easy answers. Rather, it opens critical conversations, shares innovative practices, and invites bold experimentation. Above all, it calls on universities to become spaces of care, creativity, and courage in a rapidly changing world.

SECTION 1

Conversations about Pedagogy

CHAPTER 1

Avoiding human deepfakes: A learning and care-centred approach to learning in higher education

Hanelie Adendorff, Nicoline Herman, and Dalene Joubert

Abstract

Artificial intelligence (AI) in the landscape of higher education (HE) is disruptive, not only by exposing existing inadequacies, but by raising deeper questions about whether transformative student learning has ever been fully realised. Despite attempts to the contrary, it can be argued that higher education practice often cultivates calculative, rather than critical, thinking (Zournazi, 2022). In this chapter, we contend that an overemphasis on calculative thinking risks hollowing out the learning process, leaving graduates who resemble deepfake versions of AI chatbots – technically adept but lacking critical depth. In response, we propose a learning- and care-centred paradigm for HE, inspired by Zournazi's interpretation of Heidegger's 'building, dwelling, caring'. Expanding on Heidegger's concept of the clearing, we frame learning as a process of grappling – an approach that fosters deep engagement rather than mere proficiency. By reimagining education through a 'care-full' lens, we seek to move beyond calculative thinking and toward a system that prioritises transformation over transaction. Through this exploration, we aim to deepen our understanding of the current context, and contribute to a broader conversation about the evolving purpose and practices of higher education in the age of AI.

Introduction

Higher education (HE) finds itself caught in a troubling dissonance. While it promises to provide transformative learning experiences, neoliberal institutions are ill-equipped to fulfil them. The rise of generative AI (GenAI) has only deepened this paradox. A lot has been written about the potential threat of GenAI tools to the integrity of the assessments intended to measure and report on students' learning (Sullivan et al., 2023). However, these concerns assume that our current teaching-learning-assessment (TLA) approaches can and do lead to transformative learning characterised by changed viewpoints, frames of reference

(Friedman, 2022), and 'structures of assumptions' (Mezirow, 1997: 5). But what if this is not the case (see, for example Barnett, 2004; Halupa, 2017; Hodge, 2015; LaCapra, 1998; Land, 2006; Wheaton, 2020)?

Inspired by Zournazi's (2022) work on how we 'create and think with technologies' in HE, we draw on Heidegger's philosophy to explore underlying concerns about the impact of GenAI on education. We argue that current HE practices, shaped by industrial, compliance-based models, often neglect the role of care in learning, thereby resulting in an education system more likely to produce human deepfakes[1] – technically adept but lacking critical depth – than being spaces that allow for the transformation of the learner. The term 'deepfake' is typically applied to digitally manipulated synthetic versions of humans, often with the intent to cause harm. We invert this term to describe graduates who have been shaped by an education system that prioritises efficiency over meaning and delivers graduates with machine-like abilities or what Heidegger calls 'calculative thinking'. We propose that centring care in TLA practices can potentially reclaim education as a deeply human endeavour by resisting this mechanisation of learning.

Rather than focussing on the practical challenges associated with GenAI in HE, we situate it as a conceptual and philosophical provocation, one that compels us to reconsider the fundamental nature of education, learning, and care in a digital age. The question of how these conceptual shifts might translate into practice is one we leave open for future research.

Heidegger, technology, and higher education

While few would dispute technology's ubiquity in our lives (Harvard *Business Review*, 2014; Smith, 1991), Heidegger (1977b) argues that modern technology, distinct from the ancient techne, has become an uncontrollable force that shapes our lives (Dreyfus & Spinosa, 2003; Waddington, 2005). For Heidegger, the risk imposed by technology is not in the outward trappings of it, but in its ability to fundamentally alter the essence of who we are. Modern technology, he holds, reduces everything, including humans, to mere 'standing reserves' – resources to be ordered, positioned, and exploited for their use-value. It constrains how we interpret the world, and results in seeing everything through a lens of utility and availability (Waddington, 2005). Technology is therefore not merely a tool, but a way of interpreting the world (Lee & Hu-Au, 2021) that leads to a mode of thinking focused on productivity, results, and efficiency (Huttunen & Kakkori, 2022). This 'calculative thinking' approach considers or values everything in the world around us, including humans, in terms of what we can get out of it or them. Calculative thinking is thus always on the move and restless; it never stops to reflect (Heidegger, 1966).

---

[1] The term 'deepfake' refers to an image or recording that has been convincingly altered and manipulated to misrepresent someone as doing or saying something that was not actually done or said (Merriam Webster, https://www.merriam-webster.com/dictionary/deepfake)

We see this manifest in the language and practices in the modern workplace, including universities (Gibbs, 2010; Thomson, 2001 & 2003). Examples include an increased emphasis on concepts such as human resource management, efficiency optimisation, and technological determinism, rooted in performativity (Gibbs, 2020). Viewed through a lens of productive utility, employees become resources to be managed and optimised. Similarly, nature is reframed as a stock of resources to be extracted and exploited for their utility. Social relations, such as human interactions and connections, are turned into data sources to be leveraged by technological systems. Heidegger holds that this way of thinking results in human experience being continuously reshaped and delimited by the ordering logic of what he calls technological 'enframing' (Thomson, 2001) which fundamentally alters our perception and lived experience of the world.

The problem is that this kind of technological and calculative thinking is increasingly visible in HE, with some even arguing that it has become the only kind of thinking in the modern world (Huttunen & Kakkori, 2022) Examples of the impact of enframing on higher education are ample, i.e., seeing students through the lens of standardised testing and performance metrics (Dasein, 2018; Williamson, 2019). Adhering to 'notion[s] of serviceability, conduciveness, usability and manipulability' (Gibbs 2010: 283) and restrictive predetermined outcomes or a narrow focus on job readiness (Dasein, 2018) are all examples of a system that values calculative thinking instead of transformative learning.

Heidegger's critique of the increasing dominance of modern technology has profound implications for how we think about TLA practices. Dasein (2018), for example, contends that the increasing focus on assessment and 'the culture of efficiency' in education is in direct opposition to, and overshadowing, approaches which prioritise the human in the TLA process. Hodge (2015: ix) opens his volume on Heidegger with the words: 'Heidegger could see that modern education was in the grips of a business "paradigm" and argued that it needed to be more than an institution of knowledge transformation.'

The tensions caused by this means-to-an-end enframing became starkly apparent to one of the authors, Hanelie, during a conversation with a group of STEM colleagues. In her own words:

'Bemoaning the strong focus on efficiency, speed, and productivity in the learning context, I mentioned a desire that students would be less product driven, less focussed on the pursuit of a degree, that they would take time to explore, to try, to fail, to try again, to change course, even – to figure out what they deeply care about and who they are. While I did not expect this to sit comfortably with everyone in the group, I was a little taken aback when it was rather unceremoniously dismissed and labelled as "bourgeois". Though keenly aware of the burden of cost and promise involved in access to higher education, especially in a developing country such as ours, I had failed to comprehend the depth of the technological enframing. I couldn't shake a profound sense of loss. Both viewpoints stemmed from a position of care. My colleagues deeply cared about the costs of students failing familial expectations of provision, while I deeply cared about students' learning not being merely a means to an end, irrespective of how noble that end. I wanted students to experience more than the academic treadmill. I wanted room for them to explore the magical woods of academia before leaving the assembly line, that was so mercilessly shaping them into workplace assets.'

It is against this backdrop of the tensions inherent in the current higher education system, and exacerbated by easily accessible GenAI tools, that we would like to reconsider HE. The rise of AI tools does not only disrupt traditional models of skills acquisition; it also challenges how we care for learning and learners. Institutions' punitive approaches to AI – focusing on detection, deterrence, and punishment – ignore the deeper care-related responsibilities of education. Rather than addressing the root causes of students' reliance on AI, such approaches reinforce a transactional, compliance-driven ethos. By framing AI as a threat to academic integrity rather than an opportunity to rethink pedagogy, institutions risk further entrenching calculative thinking. Care, as both an ethical commitment and a pedagogical practice, offers an alternative. It invites us to create learning environments where students feel supported, valued, and empowered to engage deeply and critically with their education, rather than merely navigating it as a series of transactions.

We contend that the rise of AI tools is not presenting us with a new problem in HE; it is highlighting the fault lines that are already there. Although the question of GenAI in HE is a practical one, we think it also calls for a deeper philosophical inquiry into the essence of higher education and the nature of TLA itself. For example, how should we rethink our current HE approach to avoid a future filled with human deepfakes? How do we heed Heidegger's call for a different, more mindful, and reflective approach to technology to avoid its dehumanising consequences (Thomson, 2001)?

We argue that current higher education practice, steeped in neoliberal approaches (Burke & Larmar, 2021; Boughey & McKenna, 2021; Grealy & Laurie, 2019), where learning is organised on the basis of efficiency 'rather than the time needed to develop pedagogical principles that are transformative and meaningful for teachers and students' (Zournazi, 2022: 153), is at odds with the higher aspiration of learning that transforms.

HE as a clearing in the contemporary woods

In *Basic writings: from Being and time (1927) to The task of thinking (1964)*, Heidegger (1977a) introduces the notion of a clearing, drawn from the metaphor of a forest path opening up to a clearing in the woods, to describe a space where truth unfolds and things become intelligible. The clearing thus signifies the opening that allows for revelation (Sallis, 2017; Sheehan, 2014). While the concept of the clearing can be challenging to grasp, and has been interpreted in various ways, it offers a valuable perspective on how we encounter the world and make meaning of our experiences. The clearing represents an openness that is essential for understanding, as it allows entities, concepts, and even the nature of humans to emerge and become intelligible. For Sheehan (2014: 267) the clearing is about 'mak[ing] meaningfulness possible' and 'holding open the "space" for discursive intelligibility.' It is about transformation, not just about 'knowing something, getting the answer to a question, no matter how profound that question might be' (ibid: 273).

The South African author Dalene Matthee's novel *Toorbos* (2003) (the English translation is titled *Dreamforest* (2006)) is an almost haunting tale about the impact of technology on the being of 'forest people' in Knysna during the early 20th century. There is a scene in which Karoliena Kapp, the protagonist, stumbles upon a clearing of sorts at the edge of the forest, described as an almost magical place filled with red lilies – the garden of the elephants and the heart of the forest. The wonder of the moment is nearly tangible in Matthee's writing: 'Her eyes look, but it is too much to see! The beauty is too sharp. Each lily is a little red cup surrounded with the greenest bush. If this really is the elephants' garden, then they had chosen the smartest hiding place for it. This is a secret garden where something wants to make her quietly turn around and sneak off so that no elephant would ever know that she was there.' In Karoliena's stumbling upon the clearing, and in her wandering through the woods, there is not only wonder – there is a revelation too, about herself, who she is, and where she belongs; about others and their place, and about the world. And, as in many a story, there is transformation.

This leads us to question whether there is still space for this kind of wonder and becoming in our higher education practices – unscripted moments akin to Matthee's forest clearing or the exciting journey of mathematical discovery portrayed in Paul Robertson's *An Elegant Solution* (2013). In Robertson's telling of Leonhard Euler's 18th century intellectual journey, there is no sign of the stale mathematics of many modern classrooms.

When we asked a number of GenAI tools if one could conceive of HE as a Heideggerian clearing, they all felt that it was a stretch too far. They explained that Heidegger's clearing represents spontaneous, unpredictable moments of revelation, outside of human control. They added that Heidegger is focused on ontology and fundamental aspects of existence and is thus more abstract, poetic, and metaphysical. HE, they suggested, by contrast, consists of formalised systems with measurable outcomes, covering specialised domains of knowledge. Is this data-sourced picture of HE accurate? Has HE become a production facility for assembling human calculators; a space for counting, computing, and controlling?

Heidegger, himself saw the university as a clearing. In his 1945 deposition before the commission on the de-Nazification of Freiburg University, translated by Allen and Axiotis, he argues that 'the university emerges as a clearing in which the relation between teacher and student takes on different shapes and forms' (Heidegger, 2002: 35). In the address, he attempts to dismantle the idea of the teachers as moulds into whose image students should be fashioned, referring to education as violence, and stating that the dominant approach at that time was that of students being 'beaten into an image, fashioned as if he [sic] were a drachma coin to be put into circulation' (ibid).

Viewing HE as a space of clearings instead shifts the focus away from standardised outcomes and toward a more holistic understanding of education. In this regard, Dasein (2018:157) argues that the clearing 'offers a way out of the enframing', admitting that the 'way out is indistinct and thus difficult, but is nonetheless a way out: there is – has to be – a path to the clearing.' We need to remember, however, that 'we do not produce the clearing. It produces us as the kind of human beings that we are' (Dreyfus, 1997: 270). From this perspective, HE is no longer just about acquiring knowledge or skills, but also about what the world is and how we fit into the world, uncovering who we are as individuals. This view of higher education thus challenges conventional paradigms and invites a re-evaluation of the fundamental purpose and essence of education. It encourages us to reconsider what it means to truly learn and grow, not just in terms of external achievements but as a transformative journey toward self-discovery and understanding. Is there still scope for higher education to be a transformative space where individuals have the opportunity to come to a different and deeper understanding of themselves and the world around them? A Heideggerian approach to HE in the age of AI would demand that we resist seeing education as mere information transfer and instead cultivate spaces where students can engage in meaning-making – where they are cared for as thinking beings rather than as economic outputs.

To unpack this, we use the causal layered analysis methodology.

Uncovering what is beneath

Causal layered analysis (CLA) originates from futures studies and foresight work, offering a means to explore the deeper causes and worldviews underlying a problem and to envision alternative futures. Developed by Sohail Inayatullah, CLA deconstructs different levels of causality recognising 'that the future is constructed from the root narratives of the present' (Milojević, 2005: 221, in Haigh, 2016). Understanding these underlying myths and worldviews is essential to shaping the future (Haigh, 2016: 169).

CLA examines issues through four layers:

1. Litany: The public surface-level description of the issue – how the issue is commonly framed in the media, reports, and policy discourse.
2. System: The underlying social, economic, political causes or systems that give rise to or perpetuate the issue at the litany level.
3. Worldview: The ideological narratives, belief systems, and paradigms that justify and sustain these systems.
4. Myth/Metaphor: The unconscious, archetypal stories that underpin how the issue is understood.

This approach enables us to critically consider the HE landscape in relation to concerns about GenAI and TLA.

Litany

HE is often marked by tensions between its realities, actions, and ideals (Ramboarisata, 2022). At the litany level, it faces increasing class sizes, diminishing financial resources, staff burn-out, and troubling student success statistics (Boughey & McKenna, 2021; Urbina-Garcia, 2020: 563). These realities are in conflict with HE's promise of transformative educational experiences and graduates capable of positively shaping and serving society.

These tensions are especially visible in the domain of learning outcomes. Rather than fostering dialogue-rich environments, embracing the grappling inherent to genuine growth, and cultivating caring relationships, university education often reduces learning to predetermined, discrete, and measurable outcomes. The cognitive domain, with its focus on rationality, is often disproportionally prioritised (Lynch, 2010). This, in turn, translates into assessment approaches that favour calculable, easily measurable products, such as formulised essays and contained calculations, while overlooking the complexities of affective learning, such as collaboration and professional conduct.

Amidst these challenges, we see uncertainty and anxiety around GenAI's impact on learning with a myriad of media articles on platforms like *University World News* and *The Conversation*, voicing these fears (see Sullivan et al., 2023). The student author of 'I'm a Student. You Have No Idea How Much We're Using ChatGPT. No professor or software could ever pick up on it' (Terry, 2023) asks pertinent questions about what learning is and where it happens, while McKenna et al (2023) suggest that 'ChatGPT is the push higher education needs to rethink assessment.' On their blogs, respected HE educators, such as Ethan Mollick ('One Useful Thing')[1] and Maha Bali ('Reflecting allowed')[2], have also extensively engaged with AI's implications for HE.

---

[1] Available at https://www.oneusefulthing.org
[2] Available at https://blog.mahabali.me/bio/

Systems

Analyses at the structural level (Burke & Larmar, 2021; Boughey & McKenna, 2021; Grealy & Laurie, 2019) reveal that HE systems' quality assurance, accountability, and data-driven decision-making, and by implication control, accountability, and numbers, can be translated into sources for data analytics. Urbina-Garcia's (2020) review of 28 papers on academics' mental health notes that 'the university environment is triggering high levels of stress and burnout and low levels of well-being for academics' (Urbina-Garcia, 2020: 563) and that the impact of HE's culture of audit, accountability, and performativity 'could importantly reduce productivity' (ibid: 570).

Ramboarisata (2022: 33) notes a tension between 'the romantic discourse of ethics, social responsibility and sustainability' and the lived experience of academics in a 'culture of audit, accountability and performativity.'

Dasein's (2018) PhD thesis speaks to this in critiquing standardised testing, grades, and rigid curricula as indicators of an increasing focus on measuring humanity rather than fostering it. While HE's economic accountability to society justifies some level of standardisation, Zournazi (2022) warns that 'efficiency-obsessed HE structures widen the gap between students and lecturers, reducing meaningful engagement.'

It is within this context of an education framed by the need to measure and account for everything (Grealy & Laurie, 2019) whilst doing more with less (Kinman, 2014) that the ready availability of GenAI tools pose pertinent risks, such as 1) undetectable AI-abuse, destroying the integrity of HE assessment systems, and 2) over-reliance on AI, undermining learning and setting graduates up for failure, especially against always available, increasingly powerful, and possibly easier to manage AI tools.

Counting what is convenient rather than creating spaces for personal and intellectual becoming might result in graduates leaving the HE system with transcripts full of credits, but lacking the critical wisdom, empathetic capacity, and experience to be positive forces for change that the world so desperately needs.

Worldviews and existing metaphors

The picture above portrays a HE system that is still largely built on a modernist ethic of justice whilst promising the products of a post-modernist ethic of care. An ethic of justice, as a necessary means of ensuring 'fair and equitable treatment of all people' (Brook 1987: 370), often has one of three foci, namely principles, purposes, or results (French & Weis, 2000). It is thus concerned with verifiability and reliability in decision making, based on universal rules and principles. In HE TLA it prioritises predetermined outcomes, measurable assessment criteria, data, and rule-based decision making as a means of ensuring fairness.

While an ethic of justice has its merits, an overreliance on this approach alone can lead to a dehumanising and reductionist experience for both students and lecturers (Botes, 2000: 1072), for example, critiques justice-driven models in professional fields, noting that rigid principles fail to accommodate the complexity of human experience and can result in patients feeling depersonalised. In pedagogy, this worldview reduces academics and students to 'technicians', boxed into established procedures, codes of practice, and guidelines rather than individuals who can think for themselves (Veck, 2014: 452–453). If what is easily quantifiable and standardised is prioritised, we risk losing sight of the transformative potential of education – a potential that can only be fully realised through personal relationships and an ethic of care. In powerful words, often attributed to Albert Einstein (Toye, 2014: 29), 'not everything that counts can be counted.'

An ethic of care, on the other hand, recognises that learning is a deeply personal and relational process, one that cannot be adequately captured by rigid metrics or predetermined outcomes. It acknowledges the inherent complexity and contextuality of human experiences, and the need for nurturing environments that foster genuine dialogue, empathy, and mutual understanding.

Despite the care-rhetoric, often present in HE, its practices reflect an underpinning worldview rooted in modernity, valuing objectivity, universality, and control. Ultimately, HE requires an approach that integrates the principles of fairness and accountability from an ethic of justice with the relational, context-sensitive, and holistic perspectives of an ethic of care.

Metaphor – the story

Various metaphors have been used to describe contemporary HE. Barnes (1928), Wheaton (2020), and Luke (2023), spanning a period of almost a century, have likened HE to a factory where knowledge is produced and quality controlled. In this view of HE, student throughput takes centre stage and students are treated as products to be processed according to standardised specifications. Rigid curricula, one-size-fits-all assessments, and mass lectures aim for industrialised consistency and throughput, not individualised growth and transformative learning. Efficiency, market forces, and economic imperatives are often drives for pedagogy (Zournazi, 2022: 153) in this neoliberalist approach (Burke & Larmar, 2021) with deviation from the predetermined path seen as a wasteful inefficiency that should be minimised.

Another metaphor, sometimes used to describe HE, is that of a shop (Bok, 2009). In this conception, students are consumers or clients purchasing credits, grades, and ultimately a degree. The 'shop' encourages pragmatism and efficiency over curiosity and exploration. This transactional view of education runs counter to its higher ideals. If knowledge is a means to an end, and HE is the shop selling that means, who can blame students for enlisting all the support they could get, including that offered for free by powerful GenAI assistants?

These metaphors – the factory and the shop – reflect the priorities of systematisation, measurement, and control that arise from the ethic of justice perspective dominating HE. Both reduce the richness of learning to an industrial process or an impersonal transaction, and they leave little room for stumbling upon the 'unexpected clearings' that allow true learning and transformation to take place. Transformative and meaningful learning for both students and lecturers, however, demands a slower approach, with space for learning to think with technology (Zournazi, 2022) – a legacy of modernist rationality that values efficiency, data, and measurable outcomes. If our educational efforts produce this mindset, we have cause for concern. AI tools then pose a threat to teaching, learning, and assessment in higher education, as they encourage students to become mere imitations of AI chatbots, practising calculative thinking while mimicking transformative learning.

From this analysis, it becomes clear that the core issue with AI in higher education is the prevalence of calculative thinking, a remnant of the modernist focus on rationality, efficiency, data, calculations, and measurable outcomes, amongst others. If we are encouraging students to be deepfake versions of AI chatbots, practising calculative thinking while mimicking a transformed learning experience, we do indeed have cause for concern with AI tools posing a very real threat to HE TLA.

Learning that transforms

Seeing HE as a space for clearings, in the Heideggerian sense, implies a transformation on a deeper, more existential level, where it cannot be faked or mimicked. As explained by Sheehan (2014: 273), and quoted earlier in this chapter, Heidegger's philosophy is 'not just about knowing something'; it is instead about a true transformation of the self. By necessity, this kind of transformation requires being confronted with different ways of knowing, being, doing, and thinking (Mezirow, 2000). Taylor (2008: 11) explains that 'without experiences to test and explore new perspectives, it is unlikely that learners will fully transform.' In this section, we first explore what this kind of learning is before looking at the roles that dialogue and grappling as learning tools could play in its formation.

Transformative learning theory, originally conceived by Mezirow (with works dating from 1978–2008), requires change at a deeper level. It challenges, changes, and transforms 'problematic frames of reference' in a learner, to make these frames and ways of knowing more 'inclusive, open, reflective, and emotionally able to change' (Mezirow 2003: 58). Frames of reference are comprised of both 'points of view' and 'habits of mind' (Friedman, 2022: 2). Both of these, as well as their relation to each other, need to be altered to change a frame of reference, and result in transformative learning (Friedman 2022: 7). Inspired by Friedman

(2022: 8) and a critical conversation with Anthropic's GenAI tool Claude, an example of this transformative learning process within the spheres of economics and sustainability could play out as follows: an old habit of mind (e.g. 'protecting the environment is too costly and restrictive for businesses') and a new point of view (e.g. 'given sustainability and the innovation it spurs, businesses can potentially thrive by adopting eco-friendly practices') can lead to the adoption of only a new habit of mind (e.g. 'although important, environmentally good practices are too expensive to be applied widely') or a new frame of reference (e.g. 'environmental protection and economic growth go hand-in-hand'). Friedman (2022: 2) explains that transformative learning is 'neatly described as occurring in the moment when a point of view transforms not only the habit of mind, but the entire frame of reference.'

Problematising this 'neat' definition of transformative learning and arguing for a more 'inclusive' definition, Illeris (2014: 162) highlights that transformative learning implies a change in identity as these elements are 'substantial parts of the identity.' Transformative learning therefore calls for a transformation of the student to someone who thinks and does differently. Links between learning (or knowing) and the learner's identity (or being) have long been recognised (see also Wortham, 2006; Vygotsky, 1934/1987; Bakhtin, 1981). Boughey and McKenna (2021), for example, also argue that learning in higher education in the South African context involves a profound transformation of the individual to a different way of knowing and being, or becoming a 'different knower.'

Two ways in which such transformative change can be brought about are 1) critical reflections, dialogues, and interactions with others (Mezirow, 2000; Taylor, 2008), and 2) grappling that challenges the student to delve deeper (Taylor, 2008).

Dialogue and critical reflection

Although not initially part of his conceptualisation of transformative learning, Mezirow included some of the more social aspects of learning, such as the necessity for learning through dialogue, in his later works (see Illeris, 2014). Mezirow (2003: 60) highlights two critical adult learning capabilities needed to participate fully in what he calls 'critical-dialectical discourse', namely 'critical self-reflection' and 'reflective judgement'. These terms refer to the ability to evaluate the assumptions on which 'interpretations, beliefs, habits of mind and points of view are based' (Hyde 2021: 376).

Critical-dialectical discourse, in turn, involves the 'uniquely adult capacity' for developing the ability to engage in discourse that leads to the evaluation of the assumptions supporting our unique feelings, beliefs, and values (Mezirow, 2003: 60). Mezirow (2003: 59) explains that: 'Discourse involves topics referred to from the point of view of a particular frame of reference. Justification of a proposition must be assessed in relation to the particular frames of reference applied.' Cynically, he points out that the only alternative options that he can foresee to critical-dialectical discourse are 'the appeal to tradition, an authority figure, or the use of force' (Mezirow, 2003: 60).

In essence, Mezirow argues that these abilities to evaluate differing assumptions and viewpoints through discourse are crucial for making meaning of experiences, and for participating in transformative, rational dialogue. He views these elements as the foundational capabilities for adult learning and perspective transformation to take place. Critical-dialectical discourse, manifested in genuine human interactions with diverse viewpoints, offers a means of prioritising this kind of grappling with different perspectives and ideas.

The outputs of GenAI tools could potentially count among these different viewpoints, if these are treated with the necessary level of scepticism and awareness of the limitations of the tools. With GenAI tools to an extent threatening to standardise and homogenise communication and information to an American and Western narrative (Shwartz, 2024), in turn potentially limiting exposure to diverse perspectives, protecting spaces for transformative learning becomes increasingly important. With the further educational 'threat' of GenAI running the risk of taking over students' learning, we would like to explore the importance of learning as grappling as an essential part of the learning process.

Learning as grappling and grappling as learning

In contemporary educational theory the concept of grappling as an essential part of learning is also not new, and one idea that it can link with is the 'productive struggle' in learning. Originally associated with teaching mathematics, particularly in middle and high school (Warshauer 2011: 8–10), the 'productive struggle' refers to the intellectual effort students expend to make sense of challenging, difficult concepts that are within their reasonable capabilities (Hiebert & Grouws, 2007).

To assist in framing this idea of 'struggling' in an encouraging manner, we propose rebranding the concept to 'grappling' or 'grappling as learning'. Despite its origins in secondary education, the concept has also been applied to TLA in higher education. It has been utilised in the fields of quantitative literacies in HE, science, engineering, and geography teaching and learning (Mhakure et al., 2019; Park et al., 2022; Hsu et al., 2023; Zeybek, 2016) and it is often linked with the transformative process, including identity changes, that comes about when grappling while learning. We therefore believe that the connection between grappling and learning can be applied to higher education TLA across various disciplines, because all fields of study inherently have elements where students can productively grapple as they are confronted with ideas and perspectives that are foreign to them. We would like to extend this concept to also include the idea of grappling with different voices or perspectives.

Grappling as learning occurs when students' prior knowledge is inadequate to fully grasp a new concept or task, requiring them to restructure and integrate their existing understanding in more powerful ways (Rahman, 2023). Problems and tasks should challenge students to extend their understanding yet remain within reasonable reach if given sufficient effort and support (Warshauer, 2015). This process of grappling is considered positive and productive when it provides opportunities for students to delve deeper into conceptual understanding and to confront their own perspectives, rather than simply seeking correct solutions (Warshauer 2015; Roble, 2017). Grappling as learning, especially from the perspective of critical-dialectical discourse, includes interacting with others, amongst which are more knowledgeable others in the learning situation (Vygotsky 1987: 86; Bates 2022: 118; Taylor, 2008). It is in these spaces of learning where students are exposed to a multiplicity of voices creating spaces where learning that challenges, changes, and transforms can happen.

It is also within these spaces where Zournazi's (2022: 153) genuine learning, which 'has the characteristic of attunement and taking time that opens out to a more meditative thinking or response to the world', can be cultivated. That is, if we afford the time and space for students to build on and dwell in knowledge (Zournazi 2022), we might just open the opportunities for them to stumble upon the unexpected clearings in the metaphorical HE forest and ultimately avoid something of the feared negative impact of GenAI on learning.

The teacher's role in this context then becomes that of creating an environment conducive to grappling as learning (Rahman, 2023). This implies offering suitably challenging opportunities, while providing timely feedback, and sequencing guiding questions to navigate impasses (Barlow, 2018; Warshauer, 2015; Mhakure et al., 2019). It also requires the cultivation of a dialogue-rich environment where students are exposed to the often differing viewpoints of others and where they have the opportunity to critically reflect on and engage with these viewpoints in order to expand their own habits of mind and frames of reference, as described by Mezirow (2003: 62–63).

It is, however, important to note that 'learning as grappling' is by definition an uncomfortable experience for students, especially if past experiences have prioritised the more easily definable outcomes of calculative thinking. Illeris (2014: 159), for example, explains that when working with adult learners (such as students in HE), transformative learning is especially challenging because these students need a strong, internal motivation to undergo the challenges and changes required by this more demanding form of learning. This motivation cannot be instilled or created; it should be activated within the individual (Illeris, 2014). In addition, students often experience discomfort or resist deep learning strategies, even when new technologies are utilised and 'exciting' projects are proposed (McLay et al., 2023). Creating these kinds of deeply challenging learning environments therefore requires a deeply 'care-full' approach.

A care-full approach to higher education

Teaching and learning, especially of the kind described above, should be a personal endeavour (Noddings, 2012). However, when efficiency is the prevailing discourse, as many argue is the case in contemporary HE (Burke & Larmar, 2021; Boughey & McKenna, 2021; Dasein, 2018; Gibbs, 2020; Grealy & Laurie, 2019; Huttunen & Kakkori, 2022; Zournazi, 2022), it can lead to students feeling de-personalised. And when such feelings are associated with a lack of care and trust, it could result in or be perceived as an absence of central elements of care listed by Noddings (2012: 771): 'listening, dialogue, critical thinking, reflective response, and making thoughtful connections among the disciplines and to life itself.'

The factory and shop metaphors from earlier in this chapter highlight the same issue. Neither of these describe a place of care. Heidegger, in fact, warns that technological enframing changes the nature of care. In the words of Gibbs (2010: 397), 'others are encountered as the means and resource to an end.' Within this context, Brown's (2018: 43) assertion, with reference to the work of Antonio Damasio, highlights Heidegger's and Botes' concerns and warnings in more ways than one: 'We are not necessarily thinking machines. We are feeling machines that think.' Lynch (2010) goes as far as calling 'carelessness' a hidden doxa of higher education, and labels the absence of outcomes addressing affect and care a 'serious deficit' in our curricula.

We need to reimagine HE as a care-full space where students can stumble upon unexpected clearings as they engage in learning as grappling and grappling as learning. Heeding the call of authors such as Tronto (2017: 39), Motta and Bennet (2018), and Zournazi (2022: 154), to name but a few, a care-full (Herman et al., 2018; Motta & Bennet, 2018) approach towards transformative learning is becoming even more important as the trappings of technological enframing multiplies in the age of AI.

Care has been described as 'a species activity that includes everything that we do to maintain, continue, and repair our "world" so that we can live in it as well as possible. That "world" includes our bodies, our selves, and our environment, all of which we seek to interweave in a complex, life-sustaining web' (Fisher & Tronto, 1990: 40). It involves both reason and emotion as well as the cognitive and the affective; it is concerned with others and calls for an ontology in which people are understood relationally (Dison, 2018; Moen et al., 2020). Tronto (1993) holds that care is a moral value as well as the basis of societal achievement and postulates that those who see themselves as connected to others, would mostly act from a position of care. An ethic of care is thus flexible and adaptable to different contexts and includes attitudes, behaviours and practices (Tronto, 2013: 19).

Such a care-full approach in education would imply a commitment to embrace the whole student as human being (Motta & Bennet, 2018) and not reducing them to products on a conveyor belt, empty heads to be filled, data points on a spreadsheet, consumers of knowledge, or clients in a shop. Such a care-full approach would thus aim for holistic, contextual and needs-based development and involves compassion and attention, while striving to maintain harmonious relationships with students who are seen as individual human beings.

Veck (2014: 457), drawing on Hart et al (2004), reminds us that this opportunity to respond to the needs of our students and to guide them in their transformative learning journey is not just a responsibility, but also a gift – gifted to us by the students themselves.

A care-full approach is usually in direct contrast to a care-less approach (Lynch, 2010). It is posited (Moen et al., 2020) that a care-less approach to education originates from the Kantian view of scholarly work, within which learners are autonomous, rational, logical, thinking people whose relationality is not regarded as central to their being. This somewhat resembles the famous words of Descartes, 'I think, therefore I am.' From this perspective, education is separated from emotional thought and feeling. A certain level of 'blindness to the centrality of nurturing for the preservation and self-actualization of the human species' exists within such care-less spaces (Lynch, 2010: 61). Drawing from the work of Gardner (1983, 1999), Lynch (2010) further highlights that current educational thinking mostly emphasises the development of logical intelligence and abstract reasoning, and continues that 'knowledge is reduced to the status of an adjective in the service of the economy' (ibid: 62). And so are people. Dasein points out that personalisation 'enacted by Big Data is really the opposite of person-centred self-actualisation and freedom to learn because it actively, and continually, constructs the person by categorizing both their performance and identity according to externally prescribed norms' (Dasein, 2018: 195).

The care-less cultivation of 'calculative' thinking coupled with the fear around the use of AI, in a justice-driven context, can lead to a focus on the surveillance and 'catching out' of students. By contrast, in a care-full environment, the focus would be on cultivating honesty in support of HE's purpose of transformative learning and its quest for scientific truth. While institutional structures often constrain such an approach – through rigid accountability metrics, efficiency imperatives, and policy inertia – a care-full ethos resists these forces not by dismantling them entirely, but by creating counterpoints within existing spaces of learning.

The HE system, with a focus on an ethic of justice on the one hand, and the promises and expectations of a transformative learning experience rooted in an ethic of care on the other, often results in and encourages a kind of 'doublethink' as described by Orwell (1949). We thus posit that finding a way forward in the age of AI demands that we consider how to balance these two ethics.

A new metaphor

Earlier in this chapter, when unpacking the 'education as transaction' metaphor, we mentioned authors who have likened HE to a factory or a shop, and concluded that both of these ways of seeing HE reduce the richness of learning and leave little to no room for stumbling upon the 'unexpected clearings' that allow true learning and transformation to take place. Recognising that 'narrative is one of the primary modes of knowing for humans', and that 'framing of new and reframing of old narratives' (Milojević & Inayatullah, 2015: 152) is key to a better future, we will now proceed to offer what we hope might be a more compelling metaphor or 'deep story' (Inayatullah, 2009) for HE. Milojević and Inayatullah (2015), quoting Goddard (1951: 208), hold that 'the destiny of the world... is determined less by the battles that are lost and won than by the stories it loves and believes in.'

The approach to HE we have presented in this chapter, where students grapple to learn whilst confronted with ideas and perspectives that challenge them, reminds one of the so-called hero's journey (Farmer, 2018; Denmeade, 2017; Simpson & Coombes, 2001). In the hero's journey[3], the protagonist in the story needs to heed the call to leave the familiar to embark on a journey into the unknown. Similarly, students who arrive in HE have to leave behind their familiar 'ordinary world' for a voyage similarly replete with challenges, opportunities, triumphs, and setbacks, mirroring the archetypal elements of narrative storytelling. The hero's journey thus vividly depicts the epic, human scale of what higher education should aspire to provide – a deeply personal, emotional, and existential journey. As in many good stories, the crux of the academic story lies in the protagonist's internal transformation and not in the more obvious and visible external trials. From this perspective, the academic journey is not just a quest for knowledge, but a profound voyage of personal growth, transformation, and achievement.

Whilst the hero's journey is often thought of as a solitary quest, it is in fact shaped by interactions with others along the route. It is a developing conversation between the protagonist and an array of characters they meet along the way. Building on this metaphor, we see HE lecturers, mentors, and peers as the characters that guide the hero through challenges and tests. Each of these social encounters provides an opportunity for growth as it challenges the hero to grapple with new ideas and confront their own preconceptions, enabling them to develop a deeper understanding of themselves and the world around them.

It is here, amidst a care-full introduction to a variety of perspectives, that grappling becomes learning and learning becomes grappling. It is amidst ideas

---

[3] This is a common narrative structure and archetype that has been observed in many myths, legends, and stories across various cultures, as outlined by Joseph Campbell in his book *The Hero with a Thousand Faces* (1949). Recent research has shown that it might yield psychological benefit to frame your life story as a hero's journey (Haupt, 2023).

and opinions that challenge us that we learn to confront our own perspectives and positions, and it is in this confrontation that we might occasionally stumble upon unexpected clearings. It is here that students learn who they are and what they care about, and it is here that we need to tread care-fully in carving out a space for academic clearings. Prioritising transformative learning through a care-full approach, this kind of HE space leaves little room for students to act as, become, or be treated as human deepfakes.

Like Karoliena Kapp, in *Toorbos/Dreamforest*, we need to be both guides to and wanderers in the academic woods, knowing it well enough to help others find a way, whilst remaining open to stumbling upon unexpected clearings ourselves. Finally, it is here, when we care enough to allow learning to become dwelling again, that we might just escape the enframing power of AI as an industrialising curator of the academic forest.

Seeing ourselves and our students as the protagonists of our own adventures, journeying through the magical woods of academia while conquering challenges, might just make room for a worldview in which the occasional stumbling into unexpected clearings is not a distraction, but a delight – a transformative moment.

AI use declaration

We have used generative AI tools such as Claude, ChatGPT, and Pi as brainstorming partners, proofreaders and critical friends, whilst always keeping in mind their limitations and biases, and not relying on their outputs as sources of information. We often challenged their 'perspectives' on their own usefulness in HE TLA. We referred to these tools outright wherever their outputs were relevant to our argument.

References

Bakhtin, M. (1981). Discourse in the Novel. Holquist, M. & Emerson, C. (trans.). In Holquist, M. (ed.) *The Dialogic Imagination: Four Essays*. Austin: University of Texas Press.

Bali, M. (undated). *Reflecting Allowed*. Available at: https://blog.mahabali.me/bio/. Date accessed: 2 May 2024.

Barnes, H.E. (1928). The Educational Factory for Mass Production. *Current History (1916-1940)*, 27(4): 478–488.

Barnett, R. (2004). The Purposes of Higher Education and the Changing Face of Academia. *London Review of Education*, 2(1).

Bates, A.W. (2022). *Teaching in a digital age* (third edition). Available at: https://pressbooks.bccampus.ca/teachinginadigitalagev3m/.

Bodenheimer, G. & Shuster, S.M. (2020). Emotional labour, teaching and burnout: Investigating complex relationships. *Educational Research*, 62(1): 63–76.

Bok, D. (2009). *Universities in the Marketplace: The Commercialization of Higher Education*. Princeton: Princeton University Press.

Botes, A. (2000). A comparison between the ethics of justice and the ethics of care. *Journal of Advanced Nursing*, 32(5): 1071–1075. https://doi.org/10.1046/j.1365-2648.2000.01576.x.

Boughey, C. & McKenna, S. (2021). *Understanding higher education: Alternative perspectives*. Cape Town: African Minds.

Brown, B. (2018). *Dare to Lead: Brave Work. Tough Conversations. Whole Hearts.* London: Vermilion.

Burke, K. & Larmar, S. (2021). Acknowledging another face in the virtual crowd: Reimagining the online experience in higher education through an online pedagogy of care. *Journal of Further and Higher Education*, 45(5): 601–615. https://doi.org/10.1080/0309877X.2020.1804536.

Campbell, J. (1949/2008). *The Hero with a Thousand Faces*. New World Library: Joseph Campbell Foundation.

Dasein, B.M. (2018). Freedom to learn for the 21st century (education as if people mattered). [Unpublished doctoral dissertation] Birmingham: University of Birmingham.

'Deepfake'. (2024). Mirriam-Webster.com. Available at: https://www.merriam-webster.com/dictionary/deepfake. Date accessed: 2 May 2024.

Denmeade, N.C. (2017). The hero's learning journey. *World Journal of Science, Technology and Sustainable Development*, 14(2/3): 155–171. https://doi.org/10.1108/WJSTSD-06-2016-0042.

Dison, A. (2018). Development of students' academic literacies viewed through a political ethics of care lens. *South African Journal of Higher Education*. 32(6): 65–82. https://doi.org/10.20853/32-6-2657.

Dreyfus, H.L. (1997). Heidegger on gaining a free relation to technology. In Shrader-Frechette, K. & Westra, L. (ed.) *Technology and Values*. Lanham: Rowman & Littlefield Publishers, 41–55.

Dreyfus, H. L. & Spinosa, C. (2003). Further Reflections on Heidegger, Technology, and the Everyday. *Bulletin of Science, Technology & Society*, 23(5): 339–349. https://doi.org/10.1177/0270467603259868.

Farmer, R. (2018). The Hero's Journey in Higher Education: A Twelve Stage Narrative Approach to the Design of University Modules. *Innovative Practice in Higher Education*, 3(3).

Fisher, B. & Tronto, J. (1990). Toward a feminist theory of caring. In Abel, E.K. & Nelson, M. (ed.) *Circles of Care: Work and Identity in Women's Lives*. Albany: SUNY Press, 35–62.

French, W. & Weis, A. (2000). An Ethics of Care or an Ethics of Justice. *Journal of Business Ethics*, 27(1/2): 125–136. Accessed at: http://www.jstor.org/stable/25074369.

Friedman, J. (2022). How a New Learning Theory can Benefit Transformative Learning Research: Empirical Hypotheses. *Frontiers in Education* , 7. https://doi.org/10.3389/feduc.2022.857091.

Gibbs, P. (2010). Heidegger: Time, work and the challenges for higher education. *Time & Society*, 19(3): 387–403.

Gibbs, P. (2020). Martin Heidegger (1889–1976): Higher Education as Thinking. In Barnett, R. & Fulford, A. (ed.) *Philosophers on the University: Reconsidering Higher Education*. Cham: Springer, 123–135.

Goddard, H.C. (1951). *The Meaning of Shakespeare*. Chicago: The University of Chicago.

Grealy, L. & Laurie, T. (2019). Higher degree research by numbers: Beyond the critiques of neo-liberalism. In Peseta, T., Barrie, S. & McLean, J. (ed.) *Academic Life in the Measured University: Pleasures, Paradoxes and Politics*. Routledge, 6–19.

Halupa, C. (2017). Are students and faculty ready for transformative learning. In Spector, M., Lockee, B. & Childress, M. (ed.) *Learning, Design, and Technology: An International Compendium of Theory, Research, Practice, and Policy*. Cham: Springer, 1–24.

Hart, S., Dixon, A., Drummond, M. J. & McIntyre, D. (2004). *Learning Without Limits*. Berkshire: Open University Press.

Harvard Business Review. (2014). Technology and Human Vulnerability. Available at: https://hbr.org/2003/09/technology-and-human-vulnerability. Date accessed: 12 April 2024.

Haupt, A. (2023). Want to Give Your Life More Meaning? Think of It As a 'Hero's Journey'. *Time Magazine*. Available at: https://time.com/6304708/heros-journey-psychology/. Date accessed: 12 April 2024.

Heidegger, M. (1977a). *Basic writings: from Being and time (1927) to The task of thinking (1964)*. San Francisco: Harper Colling Publishers.

Heidegger, M. (1977b). *The Question Concerning Technology, and Other Essays*. Lovitt, W. (trans.). New York: Garland Publishing, 9–24.

Heidegger, M. (1966). *Discourse on Thinking: A Translation of Gelassenheit*. Anderson, J.M. & Freund, E.H. (trans.). New York: Harper & Row.

Heidegger, M. (2002). Heidegger on the art of teaching. Allen, V. & Axiotis, A.D. (trans.). In Peters, M.A. (ed.) *Heidegger, Education, and Modernity*. Oxford: Rowman & Littlefield. 27–45.

Held, V. (2006). *The Ethics ofCcare: Personal, Political, and Global*. New York: Oxford University Press.

Herman, N., Bitzer, E. & Leibowitz, B. (2018). Professional learning for teaching at a research-intensive university: The need for a 'care-full' environment. *South African Journal of Higher Education*, 32(6): 99–116. https://doi.org/10.20853/32-6-2647.

Hiebert, J. & Grouws, D.A. (2007). The Effects of Classroom Mathematics Teaching on Students' Learning. In Lester, F. (ed.) *Second Handbook of Research on Mathematics Teaching and Learning*. Charlotte, NC: Information Age, 371–404.

Hodge, S. (2015). *Martin Heidegger: Challenge to Education*. Cham: Springer.

Hsu, P.S., Lee, E.M. & Smith, T.J. (2023). Exploring non-dominant youths' engineering identity through productive struggle in a making summer program. *Educational technology research and development*, 72: 83–107. https://doi.org/10.1007/s11423-023-10299-w.

Huttunen, R. & Kakkori, L. (2022). Heidegger's critique of the technology and the educational ecological imperative. *Educational Philosophy and Theory*, 54(5): 630–642. https://doi.org/10.1080/00131857.2021.1903436.

Hyde, B. (2021). Critical Discourse and Critical Reflection in Mezirow's Theory of Transformative Learning: A Dialectic Between Ontology and Epistemology (and a Subtext of Reflexivity Mirroring My Own Onto-Epistemological Movement. *Adult Education Quarterly*, 71(4): 373–388. https://doi.org/10.1177/07417136211003612.

Illeris, K. (2014). Transformative Learning and Identity. *Journal of Transformative Education*, 12(2): 148–163. https://doi.org/10.1177/1541344614548423.

Inayatullah, S. (2009). Causal layered analysis: An integrative and transformative theory and method. In Glenn, J. & Gordon, T (ed.) *Futures Research Methodology—Version 3*. Washington DC: The Mellennium Project.

Kinman, G. (2014). Doing more with less? Work and wellbeing in academics. *Somatechnics*, 4(2): 219–235. https://doi.org/10.3366/soma.2014.0129.

LaCapra, D. (1998). The University in Ruins? *Critical Inquiry*, 25(1): 32–55. https://doi.org/10.1086/448907.

Land, R. (2006). Paradigms Lost: Academic Practice and Exteriorising Technologies. *E-Learning and Digital Media*, 3(1): 100–110. https://doi.org/10.2304/elea.2006.3.1.100.

Lee, J.J. & Hu-Au, E. (2021). E3XR: An Analytical Framework for Ethical, Educational and Eudaimonic XR Design. *Frontiers in Virtual Reality*, 2: 697–667. https://doi.org/10.3389/frvir.2021.697667.

Luke, J. (2023). Closing the factory: Reimagining higher education as commons. In Cronin, C., Czerniewicz, L. & Onokpite, L.E. (ed.) *Higher Education for Good: Teaching and Learning Futures*. Available at: https://books.openbookpublishers.com/10.11647/obp.0363/.

Lynch, K. (2010). Carelessness: A hidden doxa of higher education. *Arts and Humanities in Higher Education*, 9(1): 54–67. https://doi.org/10.1177/1474022209350104.

Matthee, D. (2003). *Toorbos*. Tafelberg Publishers: Cape Town.

Matthee, D. (2006). *Dreamforest*. Penguin Group: Johannesburg.

McKenna, S., Dixon, D., Oppenheimer, D., Blackie, M. & Illingworth, S. (2023). ChatGPT is the push higher education needs to rethink assessment. *The Conversation*. 12 March. Available at: https://theconversation.com/chatgpt-is-the-push-higher-education-needs-to-rethink-assessment-200314. Date accessed: 2 May 2024.

McLay, K.F., Thomasse, L. & Reyes, V.C. (2023). Embracing discomfort in active learning and technology-rich higher education settings: sensemaking through reflexive inquiry. *Educational technology research and development*, 71: 1161–1177. https://doi.org/10.1007/s11423-023-10192-6.

Mezirow, J. (1997). Transformative Learning: Theory to Practice. *New directions for adult and continuing education*, 74: 5–12. https://doi.org/10.1002/ace.7401.

Mezirow, J. (2000). Learning to think like an adult. In Mezirow, J. & associates (ed.) *Learning as Transformation: Critical Perspectives on a Theory in Progress*. San Francisco, CA: Jossey-Bass, 3–33.

Mezirow, J. (2003). Transformative Learning as Discourse. *Journal of Transformative Education*, 1: 58–63. https://doi.org/10.1177/1541344603252172.

Mhakure, D., Jaftha, J., Rughubar-Reddy, S. & Manzini, M. (2019). Exploring undergraduate students' productive struggles in a quantitative literacy course: Implications for the development of tutoring. *South African Journal of Higher Education*, 33(3): 45–64. https://doi.org/10.20853/33-3-3073.

Milojević, I. & Inayatullah, S. (2015). Narrative foresight. *Futures*, 73: 151–162. https://doi.org/10.1016/j.futures.2015.08.007.

Moen, K.M., Westlie, K., Gerdin, G., Smith, W., Linnér, S., Philpot, R., Schenker, K. & Larsson, L. (2020). Caring teaching and the complexity of building good relationships as pedagogies for social justice in health and physical education. *Sport, Education and Society*, 25(9): 1015–1028. https://doi.org/10.1080/13573322.2019.1683535.

Mollick, E. (undated). One Useful Thing. Available at: https://www.oneusefulthing.org. Date accessed: 2 May 2024.

Motta, S.C & Bennet, A. (2018). Pedagogies of care, care-full epistemological practice and 'other' caring subjectivities in enabling education. *Teaching in Higher Education*, 23(5): 631–646. https://doi.org/10.1080/13562517.2018.1465911.

Noddings, N. (2012). The caring relation in teaching. *Oxford Review of Education*, 38(6): 771–781. https://doi.org/10.1080/03054985.2012.745047.

Orwell, G. (1949). *Nineteen Eighty-Four*. London: Secker & Warburg.

Park, J., Starrett, E., Chen, Y. & Jordan, M.E. (2022). Facilitating productive struggle in science education: The possible benefits of managing scientific uncertainty during sensemaking. In Chinn, C., Tan, E., Chan, C., & Kali, Y. (ed.) *Proceedings of the 16th International Conference of the Learning Sciences – ICLS 2022. International Society of the Learning Sciences*: 1117–1120. Available at: https://repository.isls.org//handle/1/8423.

Ramboarisata, L. (2022). Post-pandemic responsible management education: an invitation for a conceptual and practice renewal and for a narrative change. *Journal of Global Responsibility*, 13(1): 29–41.

Rahman, Z.G. (2023). Pre-Service Mathematics Teachers' Experience with Productive Struggle. *The Educational Forum*, 87(2): 112–130. https://doi.org/10.1080/00131725.2022.2072033.

Robertson, P. (2013). *An Elegant Solution*. Bethany House Publishers.

Roble, D.B. (2017). Communicating and valuing students' productive struggle and creativity in calculus. *Turkish Online Journal of Design Art and Communication*, 7(2): 255–263. https://doi.org/10.7456/10702100/009.

Sallis, J. (1981/2017). Into the Clearing. In Sheehan, T. (ed.) *Heidegger: The Man and the Thinker*. New York: Routledge, 107–116.

Sheehan, T. (2014). What, after all, was Heidegger about? *Continental Philosophy Review*, 47: 49–274. https://doi.org/10.1007/s11007-014-9302-4.

Shwartz, V. (2024). Artificail intelligence needs to be trained on culturally diverse datasets to avoid bias. *The Conversation*. 13 February. Available at: https://theconversation.com/artificial-intelligence-needs-to-be-trained-on-culturally-diverse-datasets-to-avoid-bias-222811. Date accessed: 20 April 2024.

Simpson, J. & Coombes, P. (2001). Adult learning as a hero's journey: Researching mythic structure as a model for transformational change. *Queensland Journal of Educational Research*, 17(2): 164–177.

Smith, G.B. (1991). Heidegger, technology and postmodernity. *The Social Science Journal*, 28(3): 369–389.

Sullivan, M., Kelly, A. & McLaughlan, O. (2023). ChatGPT in higher education: Considerations for academic integrity and student learning. *Journal of Applied Learning and Teaching*, 6(1). https://doi.org/10.37074/jalt.2023.6.1.17.

Taylor, E.W. (2008). Transformative learning theory. In Merriam, S.B. (ed.) *Third Update on Adult Learning Theory: New Directions for Adult and Continuing Education*. San Francisco: Jossey-Bass, 5–15.

Terry, O.K. (2023). I'm a Student. You Have No Idea How Much We're Using ChatGPT. No professor or software could ever pick up on it. *The Chronicle of Higher Education*. 12 May. Available at: https://www.chronicle.com/article/im-a-student-you-have-no-idea-how-much-were-using-chatgpt?sra=true&cid=gen_sign_in. Date accessed: 2 May 2024.

Thomson, I. (2001). Heidegger on Ontological Education, or: How We Become What We Are. *Inquiry*, 44(3): 243–268. https://doi.org/10.1080/002017401316922408.

Thomson, I. (2003). Heidegger and the Politics of the University. *Journal of the History of Philosophy*, 41(4): 515–542. https://doi.org/10.1353/hph.2003.0069.

Toye, F. (2014). Measuring research impact: 'Not everything that can be counted counts, and not everything that counts can be counted'. *British Journal of Pain*, 9(1): 29–41. https://doi.org/10.1177/2049463714565569.

Tronto, J. (2017). There is an alternative: *homines curans* and the limits of neoliberalism. *International Journal of Care and Caring*, 1(1): 27–43. https://doi.org/10.1332/239788217X14866281687583.

Tronto, J.C. (1993). *Moral Boundaries. A Political Argument for an Ethic of Care*. New York and London: Routledge.

Tronto, J.C. (2013). *Caring Democracy. Markets, Equality, and Justice*. New York: New York University Press.

Urbina-Garcia, A. (2020). What do we know about university academics' mental health? A systematic literature review. *Stress and Health*, 36(5): 563–585. https://doi.org/10.1002/smi.2956.

Veck, W. (2014). Inclusive pedagogy: ideas from the ethical philosophy of Emmanuel Levinas. *Cambridge Journal of Education*, 44(4): 451–464. https://doi.org/10.1080/0305764X.2014.955083.

Vygotsky, L.S. (1934/1987). Thinking and speech. In Rieber, R.W. & Carton, A.S. (ed.) *The collected works of L.S. Vygotsky, Volume 1: Problems of general psychology.* New York: Plenum Press.

Waddington, D.I. (2005). A Field Guide to Heidegger: Understanding 'The Question Concerning Technology'. *Educational Philosophy and Theory,* 37(4): 567–583. https://doi.org/10.1111/j.1469-5812.2005.00141.x.

Warshauer, H.K. (2015). Productive struggle in middle school mathematics classrooms. *Journal of Mathematics Teacher Education* 18(4): 375–400. https://doi.org/10.1007/s10857-014-9286-3.

Warshauer, H.K. (2011). The role of the productive struggle in middle school mathematics. [Unpublished doctoral dissertation] Austin: University of Texas.

Wheaton, A. (2020). Shift happens; moving from the ivory tower to the mushroom factory. *Higher Education Research & Development,* 39(1): 67–80. https://doi.org/10.1080/07294360.2019.1670145.

Williamson, B. (2019). Policy networks, performance metrics and platform markets: Charting the expanding data infrastructure of higher education. *British Journal of Educational Technology,* 50(6): 2794–2809. https://doi.org/10.1111/bjet.12849.

Wortham, S. (2006). *Learning Identity: The Joint Emergence of Social Identification and Academic Learning.* Cambridge University Press.

Zeybek, Z. (2016). Productive struggle in a geometry class. *International Journal of Research in Education and Science,* 2(2): 396–415. https://doi.org/10.21890/IJRES.86961.

Zournazi, M. (2022). Building Dwelling Caring – Some reflections on the future of learning. *CriSTaL,* 13(1) (Special Issue). https://doi.org/10.14426/cristal.v10iSI.544.

CHAPTER 2

Peer-assisted learning as a pedagogical strategy for decolonising higher education in the Global South

Sharon Margaretta Auld

Abstract

Introduction – Students are key stakeholders in higher education, yet their perspectives are often overlooked in curriculum development. The #RhodesMustFall and #FeesMustFall movements in South Africa amplified student voices, demanding transformation and decolonisation in universities. This study explores peer-assisted learning (PAL) as a collaborative and inclusive alternative to traditional educator-led instruction, aligning with calls for a more participatory higher education system.
Methodology – Taking an action research design and employing focused group discussions, needs analysis and questionnaires containing both open-ended and closed questions. The author and seven postgraduate psychology students collaborate with the undergraduates and academic staff to expand a community psychology module, addressing academic and campus life challenges.
Findings and new insights – Results indicate that PAL creates an inclusive space, allowing students and educators to engage as equals while developing context-specific, proactive knowledge. Findings advocate for integrating PAL into university curricula, fostering student-centred education that aligns with broader higher education transformation efforts.
Keywords: collaborative learning; critical theory; decoloniality; peer-assisted learning; third space.

Introduction and background

Students constitute a vital cohort of stakeholders whose perspectives often go unnoticed in the traditional realm of curriculum development and educational innovation (Tamburro, 2013; Amosun et al., 2018; Watkins et al., 2018; Maine & Wagner, 2021). Provocatively, these voices demanded to be heard in the South African student protests of 2015 and 2016, known as #RhodesMustFall and #FeesMustFall. These movements propelled the discourse on transformation and decolonisation of higher education into the mainstream, rendering it socially relevant (Becker, 2017; Meda, 2020; Hlatshwayo & Shawa, 2020).

#RhodesMustFall initially emerged from student dissatisfaction with the prevalence of colonial culture and imperialist symbols in South African higher education institutions (HEIs) (Costandius et al., 2018; Maine & Wagner, 2021). As additional issues surfaced, #RhodesMustFall evolved into the #FeesMustFall movement. Here, #FeesMustFall primarily protested against rising tertiary education fees, advocating for fee reductions and free higher education (Maine & Wagner, 2021). Additional concerns included the need for decolonised curricula, the underrepresentation of black South African scholars, concerns about teaching and learning quality, staff outsourcing, and the urgent need for student accommodation solutions (Costandius et al., 2018; Hlatshwayo & Shawa, 2020; Meda, 2020; Maine & Wagner, 2021). A key outcome of these protests was the opportunity for students to engage in discussions about what a decolonised higher education system should entail and how to implement it – opening up the possibility of mitigating against Eurocentric biases (Oelofsen, 2015; Amosun et al., 2018; Maine &Wagner, 2021).

Focusing on this key outcome, it is crucial to maintain students' voices at the forefront of the decolonial project in the Global South. Engaging with students in ways which enable them to actively contribute to reshaping the higher educational landscape is essential (Távara & Moodley, 2017; Maine & Wagner, 2021). To this end, peer-assisted learning (PAL) is put forward as a means of prioritising student voices – assisting students and educators in developing progressive understandings which are deeply rooted in their specific socio-political contexts (Bugaj et al., 2019; Rollmann et al., 2023; Rawson & Rhodes, 2022). Utilising PAL as a critical pedagogical strategy, students are viewed as not merely recipients of knowledge but as active participants in their own educational journey (Bugaj et al., 2019). Going further, in terms of a decolonial project, this strategy attempts to bring students and educators together as an academic community which, while different in many ways, shares common values, beliefs, activities, and practices. Importantly, PAL seeks an alternative to traditional top-down interventions that often uphold certain identities as dominant and others as subordinate. The aim of using PAL as a critical pedagogical strategy within the decolonial project, then, is twofold: firstly, to assess the challenges that this community faces, and secondly, to empower the community to mitigate against these challenges.

To situate this study, the chapter begins with a discussion of the need to decolonise higher education and the usefulness of a critical pedagogical approach to this endeavour. This is followed by an overview of PAL and its relationship to critical pedagogy. The practical implementation of PAL in the context of a postgraduate psychotherapeutic programme is then given. Finally, the results of the study are explored in terms of its decolonial potential. This encompasses an examination of how PAL can potentially contribute to the ongoing discourse on the evolution of higher education in an era marked by unprecedented socio-political complexity and the pressing need for education that is not just informative but deeply transformative.

Decolonising education

As a result of South African psychology's deep colonial and apartheid roots, its decolonisation is crucial for democratic education, research, and practice (Auld, 2022a, 2022b, & 2023b). Colonialism and apartheid have shaped psychology, and, conversely, the discipline has been complicit in perpetuating these abusive systems (Dudgeon & Walker, 2015; Long, 2016; Adams et al.,, 2017; Maine & Wagner, 2021). Case in point, psychology colluded with the apartheid regime by organising people into racial groupings and categorising black South Africans as inferior. In this way, psychology legitimised colonialism and apartheid, and contributed to widespread abuse (Kessi, 2017).

More recently, neoliberalism has significantly impacted curriculum development and educational innovation. Long (2016), for example, highlights how post-apartheid South Africa adopted neoliberal ideologies as a prerequisite for the country's reintegration into the global community. As a result, neoliberalism has infiltrated politics, economics, and higher education, causing individualism and free-market capitalism to be placed at the core of theory, research, and practice (Long, 2016; Chiodo et al., 2014). This has led to higher education becoming commercialised and commodified, with students as passive consumers of information, and their success depending on their ability to reproduce 'banked' information as accurately as possible (Mbembe, 2016; Freire, 2018). Today, South African HEIs still persist in promoting engagement with Eurocentric ideals of excellence, instructing students to conform to the norms of the middle classes within a capitalist neoliberal framework (Maldonado-Torres, 2017).

A review of the literature highlights that, under the guise of neoliberalism, the relationship between traditional psychology and colonialism has continued to influence regulations related to what constitutes 'best' professional practice, as well as curriculum development processes (Maine & Wagner, 2021; Dudgeon & Walker, 2015; Barnes, 2018; Chilisa, 2017; Zinga & Styres, 2019). For example, Dudgeon and Walker (2015) point out how the vast amount of traditional psychological theory, research, and practice in the Global South still contributes to the reproduction of individualistic, universalistic, and decontextualised notions of human behaviour. Importantly, these scholars suggest that traditional psychology's tendency toward individualism can be seen as an enduring legacy of colonisation and the dominance of positivism. This contrasts sharply with African cultures, where the individual is not viewed in isolation but as part of a larger collective that includes family, community, and ancestors. Thus, contrary to Eurocentric positivistic thought, sociocentric knowledge examines subjective reality by considering how it is embedded in socio-political norms and values.

Going further, Ratele et al (2020) highlight how traditional psychology often perpetuates a divide between thinking and feeling, positioning emotions as the antithesis of rational knowledge. However, emotions are inherently tied to social, political, cultural, ethical, and everyday contexts. Failing to acknowledge and engage with emotions like powerlessness, vulnerability, discomfort, and privilege can reinforce injustice and inequality. Ultimately, as scholars such as Barnes (2018), Chilisa (2017), and Zinga and Styres (2019) point out, when the researcher turns a blind eye (Steiner, 1985) in the name of scientific neutrality and ignores reflection on dominant power structures, cultural racism ensues. To decolonise psychology in the Global South, then, we must shift the focus away from the individual as the sole centre of analysis and knowledge. This change is necessary to avoid overlooking the significant impact of the social, economic, and political contexts within which people are situated.

Given the perpetuation of cultural racism in traditional psychological education, research, and practice, questions have been raised as to why we should even contemplate its decolonisation and transformation. Ratele et al (2020), for example, ask 'Why not simply discard it?' Well, drawing on Ivey (2013), dismissing psychology due to its Eurocentric origins and cultural biases perpetuates problematic essentialised cultural notions. As opposed to discarding psychology, I advocate questioning how socio-political influences impact psychological education, research, and practice. In other words, we need to view psychology as embedded in history, culture, and politics; psychology exists in a field of power relations (Massey, 2005). Ratele et al (2020) concur, emphasising the importance of bringing awareness to the realities, norms, beliefs, and policies of the societies we live and work in, to enable researchers, students, practitioners, and educators to ask more meaningful questions and engage more effectively with the complexity of lived experience.

To develop a transformative approach to psychological knowledge production, then, disrupting both capitalist neoliberal agendas and Eurocentric epistemic dominance, an integration of critical theory with decoloniality may prove useful. However, weaving together these perspectives is not without its inherent tensions. Critical theory, rooted in the Frankfurt School (including scholars such as Horkheimer (1972); Adorno (1997); Marcuse (1970); Habermas (2018)), critiques capitalist ideology, systemic oppression, and power structures, yet remains largely Eurocentric in its intellectual foundations. Decoloniality, on the other hand, led by scholars from the Global South (such as Quijano (2000); Mignolo (2012); Maldonado-Torres (2017); Ndlovu-Gatsheni (2019)), seeks to dismantle colonial knowledge hierarchies, reclaim indigenous epistemologies, and reject Western universality. The challenge lies in bridging these two approaches without reinforcing colonial academic dominance or ignoring the contributions of critical theory to social transformation.

Grappling with ways to address this challenge, the work of Butler (1990), Frosh et al (2002), Grosfoguel (2009), and Haraway (1988) may prove useful. To elaborate, taking a poststructuralist perspective, Butler (1990) explores intersectionality, examining how systems of inequality (entrenched in factors like gender, race, ethnicity, sexual orientation, disability, and class) intersect to generate unique dynamics and outcomes. Going further, Haraway (1988), from a feminist perspective, challenges the notion of disembodied subjectivity that champions objectivity and neutrality as 'best practice'. Instead, she advocates for an embodied subjectivity, prompting reflection on how our positioning within prevailing social narratives and discourses influences our observations; from a decolonial perspective, then picks up on such positioning and contends that we express ourselves within the constraints of existing socio-political power relations; from a psychosocial perspective, then emphasises that our place within these hierarchies defines the range of experiences available to us. Thus, drawing from Grosfoguel (2009) and Frosh et al (2002), we need to challenge the illusion of neutral, objective knowledge and shift toward a relational, context-driven epistemology that disrupts dominant ideologies and fosters epistemic plurality. A key strategy for achieving this, therefore, may lie in situated reflexivity, where both educators and students critically reflect on how their positionality within prevailing social narratives and discourses shapes their observations and understanding of knowledge

A personal connection to such an endeavour is evident in my background. I was born in Northern Ireland during 'The Troubles', a period marked by deep societal divisions based on religion and nationality. Later, I pursued my clinical psychology education in South Africa, a nation grappling with profound divisions primarily along racial and resource-access lines. In both countries, these divisions significantly influenced various aspects of personal identity, such as residence, education, activities, language use, career aspirations, friendships, and even choices of love and marriage partners.

As an immigrant in South Africa, my complex positioning within the socio-political norms of both the Global South and Global North often leaves me feeling in a 'no-man's land'. Being simultaneously an insider and outsider in different social narratives has prompted me to critically examine how my contexts have shaped my identity. This intricate and paradoxical positioning has led me to understand that subjectivity is deeply influenced by sociocultural power differentials and socio-political hierarchies. The significance of these power dynamics becomes more apparent when viewed through the lens of individual experience. Recognising how our personal subjectivity is moulded by the often-overlooked socio-political power dynamics in our upbringing underscores our inability to separate ourselves from these influences. This realisation underscores the importance of considering how such factors impact education, research, and practice. Acknowledging the impact of socio-political worldviews, therefore, may hold the key to addressing the historical legacies of segregation and oppression. The objective of decolonising psychology is to establish culturally inclusive postgraduate psychotherapy programmes that equip practitioners to effectively work with diverse populations, fostering greater equity and effectiveness in mental healthcare while dismantling historical marginalisation and stigmatisation.

Going forward, taking a decolonial stance in psychological education necessitates, first and foremost, engagement in critical self-reflection in order to develop awareness of how such taken-for-granted socio-political norms and values shape each of us – both student and educator. I have explored strategies for such reflection in earlier work. For instance, educator autoethnography followed by student autoethnography – as forms of research-based self-study – are two such critical pedagogical strategies which can help us gain personal understanding of the impact that taken-for-granted socio-political norms and values, unconscious processes, defenses, affective experience – and the complexity of identity – on our lives. However, following these initial moves, we need further pedagogical approaches which encourage both educators and students to critically engage with their positionality in order to disrupt Eurocentric academic norms, and to foster a more pluralistic, inclusive, and socially embedded learning environment. Opening up possibilities, Segalo and Cakata (2017), Naude (2019), and Távara and Moodley (2017) advocate for the development of approaches that accommodate multiple voices in the decolonial project, dismantling the perception that only Eurocentric forms of teaching and learning are effective and viable.

PAL and critical pedagogy

A traditional approach to teaching and learning places the educator at the centre of all learning practices, utilising direct instruction and lecture-based lessons to communicate different topics to students. With this approach the educator is seen as the sole authority in the classroom. Unfortunately, such an approach often leads to students being treated as passive recipients of information. In effect, it promotes 'banking' knowledge and does not encourage active engagement or the development of student voices and perspectives (Freire, 2018). A traditional approach, therefore, does not foster reflection on, or questioning of, the inherent biases in the content of lectures or classroom resources (Tovani & Moje, 2017). This prevents the students and educators from developing what Freire (2018) terms 'critical consciousness'. As a result, students and educators struggle to question the very nature of the knowledge they are presented with (or are presenting) and have difficulty forming their own interpretations of the resources they encounter.

In sharp contrast, a critical approach advocates for the classroom operating on democratic principles, with students and educators working together, learning from one another to discover new knowledge. From a critical perspective, knowledge and skills should be acquired through active engagement with supportive others (Topping & Ehly, 2001). A critical approach also acknowledges that education cannot be divorced from the broader fabric of society. This approach advocates that the strategies we employ as educators must strive to reflect the intricate interplay of institutional and socio-political dynamics. In this way, the approach offers the potential for all voices within the academic community to be heard. It follows that, to truly decolonise and transform higher education, we must embrace pedagogical strategies that promote the development of multiple voices as well as self-reflexivity (Fassett & Warren, 2007) in order to encourage both students and educators to critically examine their beliefs, biases, and perspectives in the context of their HEI and broader socio-political frameworks (Freire & Ramos, 1970).

With such a decolonial project in mind, cultural-historical activity theory (CHAT) explores the relationship between what people think and feel, and what they do. The theory draws from Vygotsky's (1978) sociocultural learning framework and emphasises that learning must be seen as mediated by culture, while being simultaneously shaped by individual agency. Vygotsky illustrates the impact of such social mediation by introducing the concept of the zone of proximal development. He defines this concept as a 'gap between the current developmental stage achieved through independent problem-solving and the potential level of development reached through problem-solving with adult guidance or collaboration with more proficient peers' (Vygotsky, 1978). Through the zone of proximal development, therefore, Vygotsky's work draws attention to how learners are influenced by their social interactions, particularly with more knowledgeable others.

Going further, Vygotsky's work has been developed into a second generation of CHAT by scholars such as Leont'ev (1981), Il'enkov (1977), and Davydov (1988). Their work is an attempt to advance the complex interplay of individual, institutional, and socio-political dynamics. Here, Leont'ev (1981), for example, shifts the focus from individual subjects to groups, highlighting the distinction between individual action and collective activity, and making the activity itself (rather than the individual) the unit of analysis (Hirsh, 2020). Leont'ev's colleague, Il'enkov (1977) introduces Marxist dialectics to this second generation of the theory, highlighting internal contradictions as the driving force for learning and change. Davydov (1988), influenced by Il'enkov's ideas, then further translates dialectical learning concepts into classroom-based strategies, encouraging active learner engagement and progressive movement from the abstract to the concrete via learning actions. Ultimately, therefore, bringing these scholars work together, this second generation of CHAT emphasises cultural awareness and active learning, contrasting with traditional education's emphasis on passive information acquisition.

Taking a further step towards a platform for multiple voices and perspectives, Engeström (2001) extends Leont'ev's (1981) Il'enkov (1977), and Davydov's (1988) second generation of CHAT to organisational learning, bringing about the development of a third generation of CHAT known as expansive learning theory. This evolution is driven by an increased awareness of the impact of cultural diversity on task accomplishment. To elaborate, with the third generation of CHAT, cultural diversity is seen as resulting in varied approaches to tasks, as well as influencing how tasks are defined, perceived, and related to other activities. This generation of CHAT also offers a means of integrating individual and social analyses, acknowledging that while individuals have differing capacities for activities – such as cooking or composing music – these abilities are shaped by environmental factors – such as available tools or instruments – and the rules governing behaviour – for example, as in the case of a musical performance (Cole, 1988; Griffin & Cole, 1984). Engeström (1987) also highlights that learning occurs both vertically and horizontally. While vertical learning encompasses gaining knowledge and understanding through accumulating experience over time, horizontal learning involves boundary crossing. Here, learning occurs by navigating between different contexts and activities in order to solve problems in novel ways (often applying knowledge and tools/instruments acquired in one context to address issues in another) (Engeström et al., 1995). Put another way, horizontal learning involves awareness of the variety of possible resources available to tackle problems rather than profound knowledge of a specific area. Sometimes, this process leads to 'knotworking', or collaborative efforts where separate threads of activity are interconnected to solve problems (Hirsh, 2020). With knotworking no single party (for example, neither students nor educators) dominates. Rather, all parties are accountable for the activity through interaction involving coordination, cooperation, and reflective communication. Herein lies the opportunity to create a democratic learning environment where all voices are heard. To explain, according to Gutierrez (2008), such learning environments can be realised when each party (students and educators) collaboratively build a 'third space' in which they each contribute knowledge and experience. Thus, this expansive learning theory harnesses the diversity of cultural backgrounds, multiple voices, discourses, and knowledge held by both students and educators in order to facilitate learning.

Looking at the 'third space' from a postcolonial perspective, Bhabha (1994) argues that cultural identity is not fixed but emerges dynamically in spaces of interaction between different cultural groups. His conceptualisation of the third space challenges binary understandings of identity (e.g., coloniser/colonised, self/other) and highlights how meaning is negotiated through hybridity. Bhabha's understanding of the third space provides a powerful lens for understanding decolonial transformation in higher education by challenging colonial binaries and creating hybrid spaces where marginalised epistemologies and dominant academic traditions interact to produce new, inclusive knowledge formations. Bhabha's conceptualisation, therefore, can allow for hybrid pedagogies such as those which blend critical theory, indigenous epistemologies, and student experiences. Such hybrid pedagogies can enable decolonial curriculum reform through the integration of local histories, languages, and ways of knowing into knowledge development rather than relying on Eurocentric academic canons (ibid). Such a conceptualisation opens up the possibility of dialogical learning environments where students and educators can co-create knowledge, rather than reproducing colonial hierarchies. Ultimately, in such spaces, critical pedagogy and decolonial thought have the potential to merge and, thereby, to challenge Eurocentric dominance in teaching and research.

Drawing on the third generation of CHAT and Bhabha's conceptualisation of the third space, PAL as a hybrid pedagogy offers the potential for students and educators to share knowledge, experiences, and their understanding of their worlds (Bugaj et al.,, 2019; Rollmann et al.,, 2023; Rawson & Rhodes, 2022). With such a strategy, students would be not just seen as receivers of knowledge, but also as creators of knowledge; both the source and agents of their own learning (Bugaj et al.,, 2019). In other words, PAL has the potential to empower students to see themselves and their educators as part of an academic community that has diverse perspectives and abilities, and such diversity opens up an abundance of resources. In this way, PAL seeks to foster a culture where people of different backgrounds can interact with understanding, respect, and appreciation for one another's cultural values, perspectives, skills, and insights.

Drawing this argument together, PAL, as hybrid pedagogy seeks to transform the structures and practices of education to better reflect and promote the values of democracy, human rights, justice, equity, and respect for diversity and difference. Importantly, PAL does not prescribe particular content or knowledge but rather uses critical awareness as its primary tool for change (Rawson & Rhodes, 2022). PAL, therefore, has the potential to help educators and students develop a critical consciousness that can be used to challenge existing power structures. It also helps develop understanding of how these structures are connected to broader social, political, economic, environmental, and cultural contexts (Rollmann et al.,, 2023). In so doing, PAL potentially provides a framework for reflection on what teaching and learning means and can mean. This framework is critical as it can enable both students and educators to reflect on how taken-for-granted socio-political attitudes, norms, and values shape identity, as well as the ways in which HEIs may perpetuate certain forms of oppression.

In order to explicate how the PAL strategy can potentially enable students and educators to collaboratively build a 'third space' where each mutually benefits from the other, I will now explore the practical implementation of PAL within the context of a postgraduate psychotherapeutic programme.

Procedure

This study employed an action research design using focused group discussions, needs analysis, and questionnaires containing both open-ended and closed questions to explore:

1. the usefulness of PAL in developing a third space for students to become

active participants in their own educational journeys,
2. for student voices to be heard within higher education, and
3. for students to see themselves and their educators as part of an academic community that, while having diverse perspectives, share common values, beliefs, and practices.

Ethical clearance for this study was granted by The Independent Institute of Education's Ethics Committee (Reference: R.000132[REC]), ensuring compliance with ethical research standards. All participants provided informed written consent for the use of their data and photographic images in this chapter.

Population

This study focused on seven postgraduate students (facilitators) enrolled in a community psychology module with an educator (the author). As part of this module the facilitators and educator reflected on the psychological, socio-political, and economic impact of the global COVID-19 pandemic, devastating regional floods, and social unrest on the academic community. Discussions then coalesced around the potential usefulness of PAL in addressing challenges faced. To determine the viability of this idea, undergraduate students and educators were asked to take part in an anonymous and voluntary needs analysis to determine challenges faced and receptiveness to a PAL strategy. All respondents were supportive of a PAL strategy.

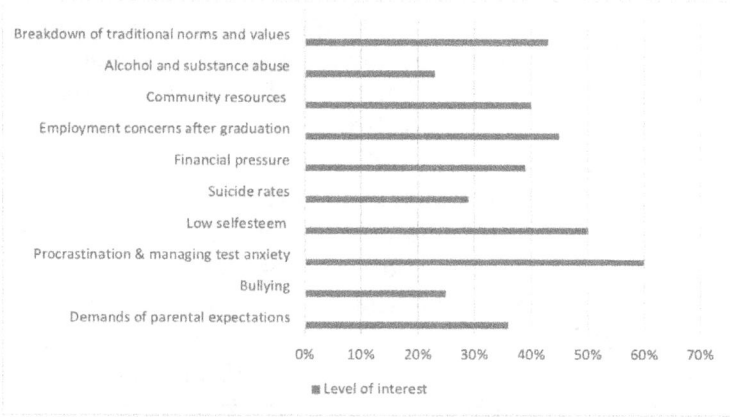

GRAPH 2.1: Range of reported challenges faced by campus community in 2023

The majority of respondents (60%) highlighted support for stress management PAL sessions targeted at procrastination and test anxiety. A study was therefore initiated aimed at empowering the campus community to meet these challenges.

PAL study

The following steps were followed in conducting the study:

1. All members of the academic community (both students and educators) were invited to participate in stress management and study skills PAL sessions on a voluntary basis. At these sessions a total of 92 participants voluntarily took part in a pre- and post-strategy questionnaire.
2. The PAL strategy was held over four morning sessions. Each session was 50 minutes in duration and ran two weeks before formative tests and assessments were scheduled. At each session, seven facilitators (post-graduate students), one educator acting as supervisor (the author), and +/- 25 participants (students and educators) were in attendance.
3. All sessions were led by the facilitators. Each session included engagement and discussion of various aspects of stress, stress management, time management, study skills, and ways to counter procrastination. In the discussions, participants were encouraged to talk about possible stressors, brainstorm coping strategies, and receive support from their peers. Facilitators also shared their own coping strategies.
4. The learning objectives are summarised in Table 2.1 below along with Bloom's taxonomy of learning classification levels (Bloom & Krathwohl, 2020).

TABLE 2.1: Summary of learning objectives from implementing the PAL strategy

Learning objectives	Bloom's taxonomy
Participants develop the necessary knowledge to understand the basic underlying causes of procrastination.	Level 1: Remembering Level 2: Understanding
Participants gain the necessary knowledge to understand the basic stress reaction.	Level 1: Remembering Level 2: Understanding
Participants are able to identify their own stressors.	Level 1: Remembering Level 2: Understanding Level 3: Applying Level 4: Analysing
Participants are able to identify various techniques for studying and time management.	Level 1: Remembering Level 2: Understanding Level 3: Applying

5. A detailed outline of the content of each session is shown in Table 2.2 below:

TABLE 2.2: Outline of the stress management and study skills development PAL strategy

Content	Details	Duration
Welcome and introductions:	Introduction of facilitators and participants. The facilitators could explore the following with the group: i. The reason for the group. i. Expectations of the group process in terms of the format and sequence of events. i. Outline the rules for group participation.	5 min
Overview:	Discussion of the key issues related to test and exam anxiety on campus. The facilitators encourage the participants to reflect on, and explore, this challenge in terms of the impact of taken-for-granted socio-political and economic norms and values.	10 min
Skills development:	Discussion of some skills which might be useful in overcoming this challenge.	10 min
Group brainstorming	Reflection of personal experience of test and exam anxiety and ways of overcoming it.	15 min
Closure	i. Allow participants to summarise or make final comments. ii. Develop a plan of action in collaboration with the other participants, for example, agreeing to keep in contact and draw on one another for peer support.	10 min

6. Any participant in need of further support was identified by the facilitators and referred to the appropriate counselling and social support services.

Data collection

The data comprised the pre- and post-strategy questionnaires completed by both participants and facilitators, as well as focused group discussions with facilitators.

Data analysis

1. Closed-ended responses

Both the pre- and the post-PAL questionnaires contained six dichotomous (Yes/No) questions and one Likert-type question. The pre-strategy Likert-type question assesses baseline perceptions of traditional educator-led support while the post-strategy contained a comparative question evaluating how students perceive PAL versus didactic lectures. These comparative dichotomous and Likert-type questions are summarised in Table 2.3.

TABLE 2.3: Summary of comparative questions in pre- and post-PAL questionnaires

	Pre-PAL questionnaire	Post-PAL questionnaire
Q1	Do you feel that PAL will benefit you in coping with test and exam anxiety? Yes/No	Do you feel that PAL benefited you in coping with test and exam anxiety? Yes/No
Q2	Do you understand what is meant by procrastination? Yes/No	Do you now understand what is meant by procrastination? Yes/No
Q3	Do you understand what is meant by stress? Yes/No	Do you now understand what is meant by stress? Yes/No
Q4	Can you identify your own stressors? Yes/No	Can you now identify your own stressors? Yes/No
Q5	Do you have knowledge of study techniques? Yes/No	Do you now have knowledge of study techniques? Yes/No
Q6	Do you have knowledge of time management? Yes/No	Do you now have knowledge of time management? Yes/No

Data for the six dichotomous questions was analysed using descriptive statistics. The mean pre-test score for each of the six comparative questions was compared with the mean post-test score for each. The differences between the two scores were then calculated and expressed as a percentage. These differences are interpreted in the following section.

Results

a) For the participants

The changes in perceived benefit of PAL (Q1), understanding of procrastination (Q2), understanding of stress (Q3), ability to identify own stressors (Q4), knowledge of study techniques (Q5), knowledge of time management (Q6), and usefulness of PAL over didactic lecturing in conveying this knowledge (Q7) are summarised in Table 2.4 and Graph 2.2 below.

TABLE 2.4: Summary of differences in scores for comparative dichotomous questions pre- and post-strategy

Learning objective	Pre-initiative	Post-initiative	Difference	Percentage improvement
Benefit of PAL	52	92	40	43%
Understanding of procrastination	40	85	45	49%
Understanding of stress	52	88	36	39%
Identification of own stressors	46	89	43	46%
Knowledge of study techniques	38	73	35	38%
Knowledge of time management	27	75	48	52%

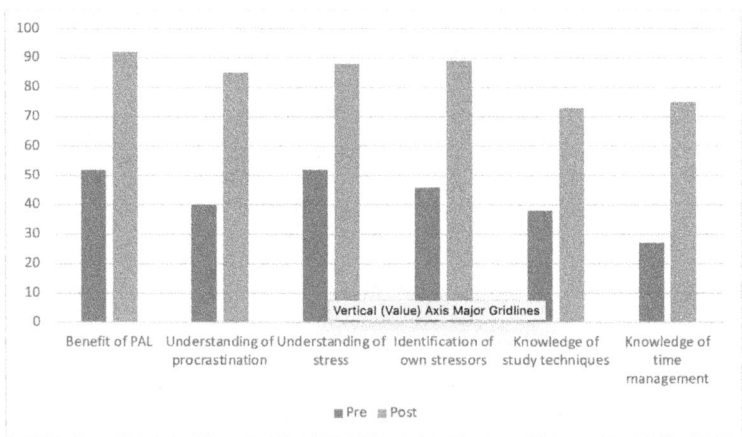

GRAPH 2.2: Differences in scores of comparative dichotomous questions pre- and post-debrief

The above table and graph suggest that gains were experienced by the participants in terms of their understanding of procrastination and stress, as well as the identification of stressors, knowledge of study techniques, and time management.

The pre-strategy Likert-type question aimed to assess participants' perceptions of the effectiveness of educator-led sessions in helping them navigate academic challenges. The responses were as follows:

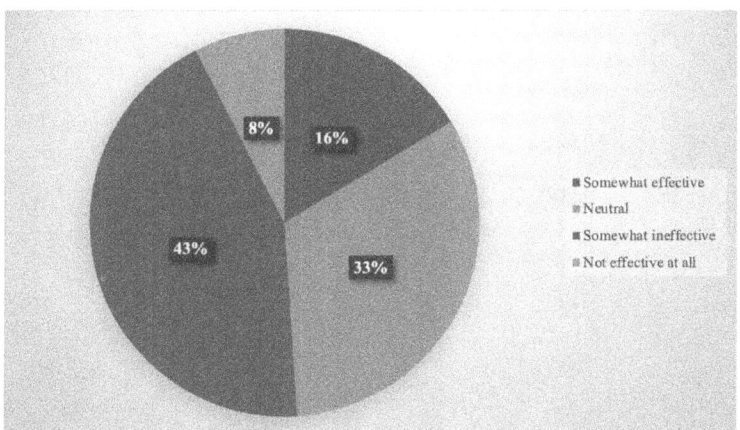

GRAPH 2.3: Participants' perceptions of the effectiveness of educator-led sessions pre-strategy

The post-strategy Likert-type question assessed how participants perceived the effectiveness of PAL compared to traditional educator-led sessions after participating in PAL. The responses were as follows:

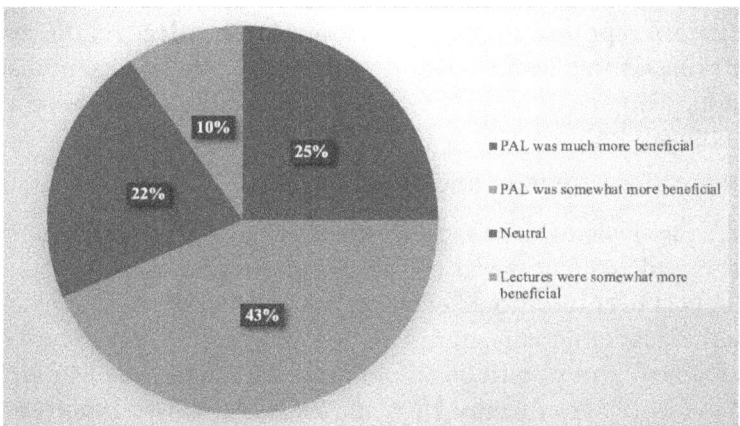

GRAPH 2.4: Participants' perceptions of effectiveness of PAL compared to traditional educator-led sessions post-strategy

Before PAL, 43% of participants found educator-led sessions somewhat effective, whereas after PAL, only 10% preferred lectures over PAL.

b) For the facilitators

In terms of the facilitators, all seven postgraduate psychology students felt they benefited from the strategy, with the majority (78%) feeling they had developed a wide range of skills and resources.

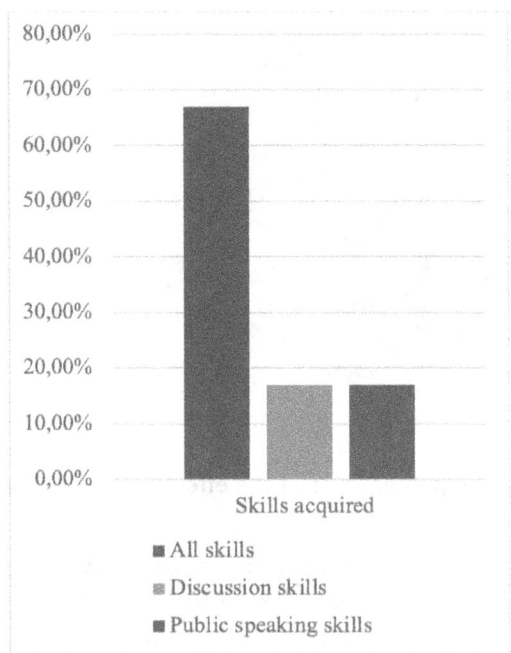

GRAPH 2.5: Perceived range of skills acquired by facilitators

The facilitators reported improved communication, leadership, and public speaking skills, as well as the ability to think critically, engage in discussions, engage in social interactions, gain a sense of community, and develop a practical understanding of PAL.

2. **Open-ended responses and focused groups**

A thematic analysis of the responses to open-ended questions from both participants and facilitators was conducted to explore the possible advantages of peer support over traditional educator support in addressing the challenges faced by the academic community. Open-ended responses were collected through focused groups and questionnaires. The data were transcribed and reviewed to identify key themes. Thematic analysis followed Braun and Clarke's (2006) six-step approach, focusing on how participants perceived PAL in comparison to educator support.

Results

a) For the participants
Thematic coding of participants responses emphasised the relatability and accessibility of peer support in overcoming academic and emotional challenges.

Key themes included:

- Reduced power dynamics: Participants reported feeling more comfortable asking questions and discussing academic difficulties with peers than with lecturers.
- Emotional and academic support: Participants felt that peer mentors provided more relatable academic guidance and emotional reassurance than educators alone, particularly in managing test anxiety and adapting to post-pandemic learning.
- Practical study strategies over theoretical instruction: Students found that peer-led discussions offered concrete, experience-based study strategies rather than abstract academic advice.
- Stronger sense of community and belonging: Participants felt that PAL created a collaborative and inclusive environment, helping students and educators reintegrate into campus life after disruptions caused by COVID-19, socio-political unrest, and floods.

b) For the facilitators
Facilitators' thematic coding focused on both their observations of student and educator engagement and learning outcomes, as well as their own learning and development as postgraduate psychology students.

Key themes included:

- Increased participant engagement: Facilitators felt that students were more active participants in their learning when guided by peers, as opposed to passive recipients of educator-led instruction.
- Bridging the knowledge gap more effectively: Facilitators felt that peers explained concepts in ways that were more relatable and easier to understand, breaking down difficult topics without the formal barriers of their perceptions of educator-student interactions.
- Development of independent learning skills: Facilitators felt that PAL encouraged collaborative problem-solving, helping both facilitators and participants become more self-sufficient students, rather than

relying on educators alone for solutions.
- Sustained support beyond the classroom: Unlike educators, who were perceived as having limited availability, peer mentors were perceived as being able to provide ongoing, informal support, making academic help more accessible and flexible to participants – providing a sense of an academic community.
- Bridging the gap between theory and practice: PAL was felt to allow the facilitators to apply community psychology concepts to real-life university challenges, making learning more meaningful to them.
- Development of leadership and teaching skills: Postgraduate students saw themselves not just as facilitators but as mentors, enhancing their own understanding of community psychology.

Some verbatim comments made by the facilitators in focused group discussions which highlight these themes included:
- 'We could talk about topics students are interested in talking and learning about.'
- 'It was amazing to be able to facilitate constructive discussions.'
- 'I felt we were really building a sense of community.'
- 'This initiative provides a safe space to learn about relevant and sensitive topics.'
- 'We were able to provide appropriate resources to those who needed it.'

These verbatim comments highlight the sense of empowerment, learning, and collaboration which appeared to have been achieved through the PAL strategy.

Findings from the thematic analysis of open-ended responses and focused groups suggests that peer support was felt by both participants and facilitators to be more effective than educator-led support alone in helping students navigate the challenges of campus life. Participants and facilitators felt that PAL provided a safe, more relatable, and emotionally supportive space, fostering academic confidence, community building, and self-directed learning. Findings also suggest that, while lectures were perceived to be of some use, participants valued peer guidance for tackling the practical and emotional hurdles of university life.

Discussion

FIGURE 2.1: PAL in action
(Auld, 2023a)

Drawing on Haraway's (1988) concept of situated knowledge and Grosfoguel's (2009) critique of epistemic racism, this PAL approach to test-anxiety management creates a transformative third space where academic well-being can be renegotiated beyond colonial binaries. Rather than merely critiquing neoliberal, high-stakes assessment cultures (critical theory) or replacing Western psychological models of anxiety with indigenous alternatives (decoloniality), PAL fosters a hybrid learning space that reshapes emotional and academic resilience as a shared, co-constructed experience. In this space, PAL enables students and educators to engage in epistemic disobedience by resisting the assumption that Western psychological models of stress are the only valid approaches to academic well-being. It dismantles institutional gatekeeping, ensuring that marginalised understandings of mental resilience – including *ubuntu*-based collectivism, indigenous healing traditions, and alternative coping strategies – are central to student support rather than merely added as supplementary resources.

Decolonial scholars (such as Segalo & Cakata (2017); Naude (2019); Távara and Moodley (2017)) advocate for educational approaches that accommodate multiple voices, rejecting the notion that academic success and well-being must conform to Euro-American models. PAL fosters such a space for intercultural dialogue, where students and educators from diverse backgrounds share coping mechanisms, perspectives on academic pressure, and culturally rooted approaches to stress management. Thus, PAL is not merely a peer-support tool but a decolonial intervention, addressing the tensions between critical theory and decoloniality by shifting academic well-being from passive institutional services to active, student-led transformation. It redefines learning success beyond Eurocentric individualism, creating a more democratic academic environment where emotional resilience and diverse perspectives are valued as integral to knowledge production.

Conclusion

As the decolonisation movement gains momentum, it is crucial to prioritise student voices in reshaping education (Segalo & Cakata, 2017; Távara & Moodley, 2017; Naude, 2019). This PAL study addresses the lack of literature on collaboration and curriculum transformation in the Global South by developing a 'third space' for engaging with diverse perspectives, fostering mutual learning, and creating a context-specific understanding of the challenges faced. In so doing, PAL seeks to empower students and educators by providing them with the necessary tools to critically engage with their own histories, cultures, and experiences. Importantly, this is not done in order to create uniformity or conformity but rather as a means of challenging oppressive structures that have been historically embedded into educational systems and practices (ibid).

In the Global South, histories and statuses are always transfused with racial and cultural superiorities and inferiorities. These intersect with stark socio-political realities such as racism, economic subjugation, and gender discrimination, to name a but few (Ratele et al.,, 2020). By championing collaboration, PAL fosters the creation of a third space (Gutierrez, 2008) in which power dynamics and resistance may be enacted, allowing for acknowledgement and reflection on such socio-political disparities. Within this third space, empathic facilitation can enable participants to recognise that they bring their own histories and statuses into each discussion (accompanied by intersecting racial, cultural, economic, gender, and sexual inequalities). Thus, through collaboration, the PAL study attempts to bring awareness to, engagement with, and momentum towards, dismantling power dynamics inherent in traditional pedagogical approaches. This enables students and educators to view themselves as an academic community with common values, beliefs, activities, and practices. In so doing, PAL allows the academic community to feel heard and to learn on equal terms, fostering context-specific, forward-looking, proactive knowledge, and developing more comprehensive and nuanced relationships, understandings, and skills (Perkins, 2008). As a result, students and educators can contribute towards making their HEI more culturally inclusive and free of Western biases.

The PAL approach also ensures that student voices are at the forefront of the decolonial project. In so doing, it assists students in developing progressive understandings which are deeply rooted in their specific socio-political contexts (Bugaj et al.,, 2019; Rollmann et al.,, 2023; Rawson &Rhodes, 2022). As students are both facilitators and participants, PAL allows for informal and empathetic communication through a shared social role, enabling students to become active participants in their own educational journeys (Ten Cate & Durning, 2007; Lockspeiser et al.,, 2008; Bugaj et al.,, 2019). The development of shared understanding makes it easier for students to communicate with one another, creating a collaborative and empathetic learning environment. Such collaboration is further enhanced by including not only students, but also educators in the PAL study. Here, learning occurs by navigating between the academic community's varying contexts and life experiences. This opens the opportunity to meet the challenges of test and exam anxiety in new and innovative ways, expanding the resources of both students and educators (Engeström et al.,, 1995). Also, as Engeström (1987) and Gutierrez (2008) point out, when both students and teachers are in a learning relationship with one another, classrooms become spaces where everyone learns about themselves. PAL achieves this by harnessing the diversity in cultural backgrounds, discourses, and knowledge held by both parties in order to facilitate learning.

Recommendations for future research include exploring the usefulness of PAL on an ongoing basis within HEIs in the Global South. Here, continued investigation could identify the potential influence of PAL on transforming and decolonising higher education, helping address issues of social justice and equity by promoting student engagement in developing regions. Sustained investigation of the impact of PAL over time could lead to a more thorough comprehension of its efficacy. This would involve challenging existing power structures within HEIs and promoting alternative ways of knowing. The PAL could also be used as a tool for self-reflection and self-assessment within HEIs. This would enable individuals to identify their own biases and prejudices, which may then be addressed through further transformational educational strategies. On top of this, PAL could be used to facilitate conversations about diversity, inclusion, and social justice within HEIs, thereby promoting a more inclusive environment for all students and educators.

References

Adams, G., Gómez Ordóñez, L., Kurtiş, T., Molina, L. E. & Dobles, I. (2017). Notes on decolonizing psychology: from one Special issue to another. *South African Journal of Psychology,* 47(**4**), 531–541.

Amosun, S.L., Naidoo, N. & Maart, S. (2018). Addressing change in physiotherapy education in South Africa. *South African Journal of Physiotherapy,* 74(1), 1–4.

Auld, S. (2022a). Autoethnography as a Pedagogical Tool for Developing Culturally Situated Psychotherapeutic Practice. *Critical Arts,* 36(3), 8–27.

Auld, S. (2022b). Role-play as a Pedagogical Strategy to Assist Postgraduate Psychology Students Engage with the Social Embeddedness of Trauma. *Critical Arts*, **36(5)**, 1–20.

Auld, S. (2023a). Peer Assisted Learning Image. Durban North: The IIE's Varsity College.

Auld, S. (2023b). Transforming students' perceptions of selfhood through pedagogical theatre strategies. *The Independent Journal of Teaching and Learning,* 18(1), 132–149.

Barnes, B.R. (2018). Decolonising research methodologies: Opportunity and caution. *South African Journal of Psychology,* 48(3), 379–387.

Becker, A. (2017). Rage, loss and other footpaths: Subjectification, decolonisation and transformation in higher education. *Transformation in Higher Education,* 2(0), 1–7.

Bloom, B.S. & Krathwohl, D.R. (2020). *Taxonomy of Educational Objectives, The Classification of Educational Goals, Book 1: Cognitive Domain.* Longman.

Bugaj, T. J., Blohm, M., Schmid, C., Koehl, N., Huber, J., Huhn, D., Herzog, W., Krautter, M. & Nikendei, C. (2019). Peer-assisted learning (PAL): skills lab tutors' experiences and motivation. *BMC Medical Education,* 19(353), 1–14.

Butler, J. (1990). *Gender trouble : Feminism and the subversion of identity.* New York, NY: Routledge.

Chilisa, B. (2017). Decolonising transdisciplinary research approaches: an African perspective for enhancing knowledge integration in sustainability science. *Sustainability Science,* 12, 813–827.

Chiodo, L.N., Sonn, C.C. & Morda, R. (2014). Implementing an Intercultural Psychology Undergraduate Unit: Approach, Strategies, and Outcomes. *Australian Psychologist,* 49, 181–192.

Cole, M. (1988). Cross-cultural research in the sociohistorical tradition. . *Human Development,* 31(3), 137–157.

Costandius, E., Nell, I., Alexander, N., Mckay, M., Blackie, M., Malgas, R. & Setati, E. (2018). #FeesMustFall and decolonising the curriculum: Stellenbosch University students' and lecturers' reactions. *South African Journal of Higher Education,* 32(2), 65–85.

Davydov, V.V. (1988). *Problems of Developmental Teaching: the Experience of Theoretical and Experimental Psychological Research : Excerpts.* Armonk, North Castle, NY: M.E. Sharpe.

Dudgeon, P. & Walker, R. (2015). Decolonising Australian Psychology: Discourses, Strategies, and Practice. *Journal of Social and Political Psychology,* 3(1), 276–297.

Engeström, Y. (2001). Expansive Learning at Work: Toward an activity theoretical reconceptualization. *Journal of Education and Work,* 14, 133–156.

Engeström, Y. (1987). *Learning by Expanding: An Activity-Theoretical Approach to Developmental Research.* Cambridge: Cambridge University Press.

Engeström, Y., Engeström, R. & Kärkkäinen, M. (1995). Polycontextuality and boundary crossing in expert cognition: Learning and problem solving in complex work activities. *Learning and Instruction,* 5(4), 319–336.

Fassett, D. & Warren, J. (2007). Critical Communication Pedagogy. Thousand Oaks, California: Sage publications.

Freire, P. (2018). *Pedagogy of the Oppressed.* New York: Bloomsbury publishing USA.

Freire, P. & Ramos, M.B. (1970). *Pedagogy of the Oppressed.* New York: Herder & Herder.

Frosh, S. (1999). What is outside discourse. *Psychoanalytic Studies,* (1).

Frosh, S., Phoenix, A. & Pattman, R. (2002). *Young masculinities: Understanding boys in contemporary society.* Basingstoke, Palgrave.

Griffin, P., & Cole, M. (1984). Current activity for the future: The Zo-ped. *New Directions for Child and Adolescent Development,* 23, 45–64.

Grosfoguel, R. (2009). A decolonial approach to political-economy: Transmodernity, border thinking and global coloniality. *Kult,* 6, 10–38.

Gutierrez, K. (2008). Developing Sociocritical Literacy in the Third Space. *Reading Research Quarterly,* 43(2).

Haraway, D. 1988. Situated Knowledges: The Science Question in Feminism and the Privilege of Partial Perspective. *Feminist Studies,* 14(3), 575–599.

Hirsh, K. (2020). Expansive Learning, Third Spaces, and Culturally Sustaining Pedagogy. *LIS Scholarship Archive.*

Hlatshwayo, M.N. & Shawa, L.B. (2020). Towards a critical *re*-conceptualization of the purpose of higher education: the role of Ubuntu-Currere in re-imagining teaching and learning in South African higher education. *Higher Education Research & Development,* 39(1), 26–38.

Il'Enkov, È. (1977). *Dialectical Logic: Essays on Its History and Theory.* Moscow: Progress Publishers.

Ivey, G. (2013). Unconscious meaning and magic: Comparing psychoanalysis and African indigenous healing. *Psychodynamic Psychotherapy in South Africa: Contexts, theories and applications,* 141–168.

Kessl, S. (2017). Community social psychologies for decoloniality: an African perspective on epistemic justice in higher education. *South African Journal of Psychology,* 47(4), 506–516.

Leont'ev, A. (1981). *Problems of the Development of the Mind.* Moscow: Progress Publishers.

Lockspeiser, T.M., O'sullivan, P., Teherani, A. & Muller, J. (2008). Understanding the experience of being taught by peers: the value of social and cognitive congruence. *Advances in Health Sciences Education,* 13(3), 361–372.

Long, W. (2016). *On the Africanization of psychology.* Sage Publications UK: London, England.

Maine, K. & Wagner, C. (2021). Student voices in studies on curriculum decolonisation: A scoping review. *Psychology in Society,* **61(61)**, 27–53.

Maldonado-Torres, N. (2017). Frantz Fanon and the decolonial turn in psychology: From modern/colonial methods to the decolonial attitude. *South African Journal of Psychology,* 47, 432–441.

Massey, D. 2005. *For Space.* Sage Publications.

Mbembe, A.J. (2016). Decolonizing the university: New directions. *Arts and Humanities in Higher Education,* 15(1), 29–45.

Meda, L. (2020). Decolonising the curriculum: Students' perspectives. *Africa Education Review,* 17(2), 88–103.

Naude, P. (2019). Decolonising knowledge: Can *Ubuntu* ethics save us from coloniality? *Journal of Business Ethics,* 159(1), 23–37.

Oelofsen, R. (2015). Decolonisation of the African mind and intellectual landscape. *Phronimon,* 16(2), 130–146.

Perkins, D. (2008). Beyond understanding. In Land, R., Meyer, J.H.F. & Smith, J. (ed.) *Threshold Concepts within the Disciplines.* Rotterdam: Sense Publishers.

Ratele, K., Malherbe, N., Cornell, J., Day, S., Helman, R., Makama, R., Titi, N., Suffla, S. & Dlamini, S. (2020). Elaborations on (a) Decolonising Africa (n)-centred Feminist Psychology. *Psychology in Society,* **59(1)**, 1–19.

Rawson, R. & Rhodes, C. (2022). Peer-Assisted Learning Online: Peer Leader Motivations and Experiences. *Journal of Peer Learning,* 15(1), 32–47.

Rollmann, I., Lauter, J., Kuner, C., Herrmann-Werner, A., Bugaj, T. J., Friederich, H.-C. & Nikendei, C. (2023). Tutors' and Students' Agreement on Social and Cognitive Congruence in a Sonography Peer-assisted-learning Scenario. *Medical Science Educator,* **33**, 1–9.

Segalo, P. & Cakata, Z. (2017). A psychology in our own language: Redefining psychology in an African context. *Psychology in Society,* **54(54)**, 29–41.

Steiner, J. (1985). Turning a blind eye: The cover up for Oedipus. *International Review of Psycho-Analysis,* 12(2), 161–172.

Tamburro, A. (2013). Including decolonization in social work education and practice. *Journal of Indigenous Social Development,* 2(1), 1–16.

Távara, G. & Moodley, S. (2017). Decolonising the academy: praxis and participation: Response to 'Community social psychologies for decoloniality: An African perspective on epistemic justice in higher education' by Shose Kessi. *South African Journal of Psychology,* 47(4), 517–519.

Ten Cate, O. & Durning, S. (2007). Dimensions and psychology of peer teaching in medical education. *Medical teacher,* 29(6), 546–552.

Topping, K.J. & Ehly, S.W. (2001). Peer Assisted Learning: A Framework for Consultation. *Journal of Educational and Psychological Consultation,* 12(2), 113–132.

Tovani, C. & Moje, E.B. (2017). *No more telling as teaching: less lecture, more engaged learning.* Heinemann.

Vygotsky, L.S. (1978). *Mind in Society: the Development of Higher Psychological Processes.* Harvard University Press.

Watkins, M., Ciofalo, N. & James, S. (2018). Engaging the struggle for decolonial approaches to teaching community psychology. *American Journal of Community Psychology,* 62(3), 319–329.

Zinga, D. & Styres, S. (2019). Decolonizing curriculum: Student resistances to anti-oppressive pedagogy. *Power and Education,* 11(1), 30–50.

CHAPTER 3

Digitally transforming the teaching of numeracy: Exploring trends within a South African private higher education institution

Dominique Marié Nupen and Jayseema Jagernath

Abstract

Digital technologies are revolutionising teaching and assessment strategies within higher education (HE). Yet, trends within traditionally challenging numeracy modules are largely unexplored. Utilising Bloom's Digital Taxonomy and constructivist principles, this study explores the use of technology by lecturers within commerce-related qualifications offered by a South African Private Higher Education Institution (PHEI).

Using an interpretivist exploratory research design, qualitative semi-structured interviews were employed to collect comprehensive data on technology-driven teaching and assessment strategies. Participants were selected using non-probability purposive sampling. Thematic analysis was used to identify reoccurring themes, patterns, innovations, and effective strategies for promoting student success in the digital age.

This study contributes meaningful insights into digitally enabled teaching and assessment strategies in HE numeracy subjects for enhanced student success within South African PHEIs. Findings will interest various academic stakeholders, including lecturers, academic managers, educational technologists, and teaching and learning specialists.

Keywords: blended learning; digital teaching strategies; digital technology; higher education; numeracy.

Introduction and background

The global trend of digital transformation (DT), driven by the Fourth Industrial Revolution (4IR) technologies, is one of the most significant forces shaping educational strategies and practices today. As these digital technologies continue to evolve, primary sources of knowledge are shifting, and higher education institutions (HEIs) are rapidly adapting their approaches to knowledge dissemination and pedagogy (Amin & Mirza, 2020; Bucăța & Tileagă, 2024).

Between the 1990s and early 2000s, the transition from Web 1.0, characterised by static, read-only content, to Web 2.0, which enabled interactive and collaborative engagement, saw both educators and students transformed into active creators of knowledge (Alaghbary, 2021). Learning evolved from passive consumption to personalised engagement with information (Acikgul Firat & Firat, 2021). Later in the 2000s, Web 3.0 introduced personalised searches, machine learning algorithms, and virtual three-dimensional technologies, enhancing how information is processed and understood by bringing it to life (Miranda et al., 2014; Rangaro et al., 2023). Knowledge and the educational experience have become more accessible, dynamic, and personalised to individual learning needs.

In South Africa's higher education (HE) sector, Web 2.0 and Web 3.0 digital learning technologies are the primary drivers of change in teaching and learning (T&L). Changes in T&L strategies are not necessarily altering the foundational theoretical concepts that are taught in higher education institutions (HEIs). Rather, they are transforming how educators deliver these concepts and how students receive and engage with the content (Pettersson, 2021), giving way to knowledge co-creation and networked collaboration (Gierl, 1997; Li et al., 2014). This shift fosters active participation and encourages students to contribute to the learning process. One-way information delivery is becoming obsolete, giving way to knowledge co-creation and networked collaboration. The DT of the HE sector, together with the opportunities for new T&L strategies presented by 4IR technologies, must be proactively addressed by educators. To fully leverage these technologies, adapted T&L frameworks and strategies must be developed and implemented (Abalkheel, 2022; Alaghbary, 2021). Recognising this need, Churches (2008) adapted the well-recognised educational scaffolding framework known as Bloom's Revised Taxonomy into Bloom's Digital Taxonomy (Alaghbary, 2021; Wedlock & Growe, 2017). Bloom's Digital Taxonomy maintains the original six thinking skills descriptors. It builds on these descriptors to incorporate digital cognitive objectives or digital tools and provides guidance on applying digital technologies in educational settings (Churches, 2008; Zawedde, 2014).

While Bloom's Digital Taxonomy helps educators link cognitive skill levels to digital tools, it does not provide insights into context-specific adjustments needed for T&L approaches driven by the 4IR. In South Africa, successful DT in HE requires educators to effectively integrate digital learning tools within their teaching practice in a way that aligns with both institution strategies and subject-specific needs. The relevance of digital learning tools in HE, therefore, rests upon two key pillars. The first pillar is ensuring that Bloom's Digital Taxonomy is applied to institutional T&L strategies. The second is integrating digital tools effectively into subject-specific knowledge and skills development (Amin & Mirza, 2020). The value of digital tools is, therefore, determined by their ability to support both institutional T&L principles and student cognitive development, culminating in enhanced learning within the relevant subject (Alenezi, 2023; Scheel et al., 2022).

Achieving the first pillar of digital learning tool relevance in HE requires educators to have a strong understanding of how digital technologies align with institutional T&L principles. A commonly cited theoretical foundation for Bloom's Digital Taxonomy is constructivism (Anderson & Dron, 2012; Corbett & Spinello, 2020; Siemens, 2005). Social constructivism, in particular, emphasises learner-centred approaches, whereby students actively construct their knowledge rather than being passive participants in their learning journey (Fosnot & Perry, 1996; Saleem et al., 2021). The digital technologies of Web 2.0 and Web 3.0 facilitate this approach by enabling shared and active engagement with the content (Mohammed & Kinyo, 2020).

In addition to understanding technology within the context of institutional T&L principles, the second pillar of digital tool relevance relies on educators to appropriately integrate these tools within subject-specific learning processes. In South African HE, numeracy-based subjects, such as accounting, financial management, economics, and statistics, are a major focus due to their mathematical demands and impact on student success (Haleem et al., 2022). While evolutions in digital technologies offer enhanced learning opportunities, there are significant challenges to their effective implementation within numeracy subjects (Clark-Wilson et al., 2014; Faloye & Ajayi, 2021). Research on best practices for structuring, sequencing, and scaffolding technology in numeracy HE remains limited (Abalkheel, 2022; Alaghbary, 2021). Additionally, clear guidelines for effectively applying Bloom's Digital Taxonomy to integrate digital tools into numeracy education at the HE level are insufficient (Abalkheel, 2022; Alaghbary, 2021; Mattar, 2018). Addressing these gaps is essential if the role of DT in improved learning outcomes within HE numeracy subjects is to be realised and optimised.

This study aimed to bridge the research gap in the application of digital technologies for enhancing T&L in numeracy subjects within HE in the context of the 4IR. By identifying key themes related to the application of Bloom's Digital Taxonomy in selected numeracy modules and within the constructivist learning environment of a South African Private Higher Education Institution (PHEI), this research provides insights into the practical use of digital tools for T&L. It also offers recommendations to support educators in leveraging digital technologies more effectively, ultimately enhancing student success in the digital age.

Frameworks for digital transformation in South African higher education

The importance of a structured approach towards the inclusion of technology within the South African HE sector is reflected in multiple global, regional, and country-level goals and frameworks. At the global level, DT in HE supports several sustainable development goals (SDGs), including SDG 4: Quality education, SDG 9: Industry, innovation and infrastructure, and SDG 10: Reduce inequality within and among countries (UNESCO, 2021). These SDGs emphasise the role of digital learning tools in promoting inclusive, equitable, and innovative learning environments.

Regionally, DT in HE aligns with Agenda 2063 and the Southern African Development Community Vision 2050, which promote quality education and innovation as drivers of Africa's socio-economic development (African Union, 2024; Southern African Development Community, 2020; UNESCO, 2021). At the national level, South Africa's National Development Plan 2030 underscores the role of education in developing future-ready graduates equipped with the skills necessary for a technology-driven economy (Republic of South Africa, undated b). Within the post-apartheid educational landscape, the integration of digital learning technology is particularly significant in addressing historical disparities, promoting skills development, and aligning educational practices with industry needs. However, DT in HEIs extends beyond simply implementing technology. It requires the collective commitment of stakeholders, including educators, policymakers, industry leaders, and students, who are willing to restructure traditional processes, champion change, and drive innovation amid technological disruption (Díaz-García et al., 2022).

Challenges to digital transformation across South African higher education

Educators in HEIs play a crucial role in developing future-ready graduates, fostering new skills, advancing societal research, and contributing to the achievement of the SDGs. Positioned at the forefront of DT in South African HE, they are responsible for preparing technology-enabled citizens and leaders for an increasingly digital workforce. However, several complex challenges often impede the effective integration of digital technology in T&L. One of the most pressing challenges is the inadequacy of digital infrastructure in South African HEIs. Outdated or insufficient infrastructure often cannot meet the specifications required for the effective use of digital tools in education. In addition, the digital divide exacerbates inequities in access to digital resources. This divide disproportionately affects under-resourced communities, making it particularly difficult to implement 4IR technologies within these settings (Assan & Thomas, 2012; Masenya, 2021). Another critical factor influencing DT in South African HE is the digital proficiency of educators. The successful implementation of digital technologies into their teaching practice requires significant and structured changes in pedagogy (Adekola et al., 2017; Nyathi & Joseph, 2024). Emerging technologies, such as artificial intelligence (AI), offer new opportunities for educators to make quick but meaningful T&L changes, as well as to introduce complexities such as requirements for advanced digital infrastructure, ethical considerations, and upskilling to ensure effective use of these tools (Zawacki-Richter et al., 2019). Finally, financial constraints associated with DT in HE must be addressed. Both HEIs and students face significant challenges in financing the adoption and maintenance of advanced digital technologies (Jaffer et al., 2007; Sithole & Mbukanma, 2024). Recognising the magnitude of these resource challenges, the South African government has prioritised 4IR adoption through initiatives such as the Presidential Commission on the 4IR and the 4IR Project Management Office. These entities have been tasked with facilitating the integration of new technologies, infrastructure development, and digital skills training across various sectors, including HE (Republic of South Africa, undated a). However, many of these government-funded initiatives are limited to public HEIs, leaving PHEIs to seek alternative funding models.

The challenges faced when integrating digital technologies into South African HEIs are significant. However, the successful integration of digital technologies in HE is essential for ensuring graduates are digitally proficient and prepared for the world of work. Given the transformative impact of HEIs in equipping students with digital skills, the adoption of digital technologies must be actively facilitated and supported among both educators and students (Benavides et al., 2020), harnessing the potential of DT for creating inclusive and future-ready learning environments.

The digital era and South African higher education

HEIs foster new skills, pioneer societal research, and contribute to realising sustainable development goals (SDGs). They develop the technology-enabled citizens and leaders of the future workforce. Globally, SDG 4: Quality Education confirms the central role of education in the future of our world (UNESCO, 2021). Regionally, the Southern African Development Community (SADC) includes education as key to Vision 2050 (UNESCO, 2021). Within a South African context, the pivotal role of access to relevant and quality education in the country's development is reflected in the National Development Plan (NDP) 2030 (South African Government, 2024). The integration of digital technology within HEIs in the post-apartheid South African context holds substantial promise for skills development and aligning educational practices with industry needs. However, DT of HEIs transcends mere technological implementation. It constitutes a comprehensive institutional overhaul involving processes and the collective commitment of all stakeholders to champion change amid disruptive forces (Díaz-García et al., 2022).

Several complex challenges impede this transformation. Among these challenges, the issue of inadequate and outdated infrastructure is prevalent. This infrastructure often cannot meet the specifications required for effectively utilising digital technologies. In addition, the digital divide exacerbates existing inequities and unequal access to digital resources among students (Assan & Thomas, 2023; Masenya, 2021). The digital proficiency of lecturers is another critical factor influencing the successful implementation of digital technologies, with changes required in pedagogy and curriculum development (Adekola et al., 2017). Integrating emerging artificial intelligence (AI) tools offers many opportunities to make these changes but also introduces new complexities, such as requirements for advanced digital infrastructure and training to ensure effective and ethical use of the tools (Zawacki-Richter et al., 2019). Finally, institutions and their students often face challenges in financing the adoption of advanced digital technologies (Jaffer et al., 2007).

The challenges to integrating digital technology into South African HEIs are significant. However, recognising the transformative impact HEIs play in developing digitally proficient graduates and facilitating the adoption of digital technology among lecturers and students is essential, aligning educational practices with industry and societal needs (Benavides et al., 2020).

Bloom's digital taxonomy: Integrating digital tools in higher education

Bloom's Taxonomy is a globally recognised framework used to structure learning content and objectives, as well as assessments, teaching strategies, and evaluations. Originally developed in 1950, the framework was revised in the 1990s, resulting in Bloom's Revised Taxonomy (Churches, 2008; Sneed, 2016). Bloom's Revised Taxonomy consists of six thinking skills levels, progressing from lower-order thinking skills (LOTS) to higher-order thinking skills (HOTS). These levels, arranged in ascending complexity, are remembering, understanding, applying, analysing, evaluating, and creating (Deller, 2022; Zawedde, 2014).

Recognising the increasing role of digital learning technologies, Churches (2008) introduced Bloom's Digital Taxonomy in the 2000s. This digital-era adaptation retains the original hierarchical thinking skill levels and cognitive verbs (Adams, 2015; Chandio et al., 2016; Churches, 2008; Currell, 2021) and integrates digital learning tools to provide valuable guidelines for educators in the digital era (Wedlock & Growe, 2017). As reflected in Table 3.1, Bloom's Digital Taxonomy acknowledges the fluidity of digital technologies, allowing for their adapted application across multiple thinking skill levels. This flexibility enables the use of digital tools to be contextualised to HEIs' T&L strategies and subject-specific learning outcomes.

TABLE 3.1: Key terms from Bloom's Digital Taxonomy
Source: Authors' compilation adapted from Churches (2008)

Level 1 Remembering	Revised Bloom	Recognising, Listing, Describing, Identifying, Retrieving, Naming, Locating, Finding
	Digital Bloom	Bullet pointing, Bookmarking, Social networking, Social Bookmarking, Searching/Googling
Level 2 Understanding	Revised Bloom	Interpreting, Summarising, Inferring, Paraphrasing, Classifying, Comparing, Explaining
	Digital Bloom	Advanced searching, Blog journaling, Categorising and Tagging, Commenting, Subscribing
Level 3 Applying	Revised Bloom	Carrying out, Using, Executing, Implementing, Showing, Exhibiting
	Digital Bloom	Running and operating, Playing, Uploading and sharing, Hacking, Editing
Level 4 Analyzing	Revised Bloom	Comparing, Organising, Deconstructing, Attributing, Outlining, Structuring, Integrating
	Digital Bloom	Mashing, Linking, Reverse-engineering, Cracking
Level 5 Evaluating	Revised Bloom	Checking, Hypothesising, Critiquing, Experimenting, Judging, Testing, Monitoring
	Digital Bloom	Blog commenting, Posting, Moderating, Collaborating, Networking, Testing, Validating
Level 6 Creating	Revised Bloom	Designing, Constructing, Planning, Producing, Inventing, Devising, Making
	Digital Bloom	Programming, Filming, Animating, Mixing, Directing, Producing, Blogging, Publishing

Bloom's Digital Taxonomy has been widely adopted in T&L (Wilson, 2021). However, it shares the common criticisms of Bloom's Revised Taxonomy. One common concern is the misinterpretation of the hierarchical structure, where educators overemphasise HOTS at the expense of LOTS (Soozandehfar & Adeli, 2016). In addition, the framework's linear structure does not fully reflect the interconnected, fluid, and iterative nature of learning (Rahman & Manaf, 2017; Sockett, 1971; Tutkun et al., 2012). The emergence of AI also presents a new dimension to Bloom's Digital Taxonomy, introducing both opportunities and challenges. When AI is used as a complementary tool, it can enhance engagement and learning across all cognitive levels. At the HOTS level, educators can easily generate problem-based scenarios, fostering personalised learning experiences where students can critique and refine AI-generated content (Gonsalves, 2024; Hmoud & Shaqour, 2024). However, educators share concerns about students' overreliance on generative AI, which may undermine their ability to critically analyse or engage with content, weakening HOTS development (Çela et al., 2024; Zhai et al., 2024). Further research is needed to determine how Bloom's Digital Taxonomy can be adapted to fully incorporate AI's potential and complexities, taking into consideration the rigidity of the current model.

Aligning digital tools to teaching and learning principles within a higher education institution

The application of Bloom's Digital Taxonomy must align with the HEI's T&L principles. There is a reciprocal relationship between the pedagogical approach and the incorporation of digital tools. The principles of the HEIs T&L philosophies, therefore, determine the selection and application of digital tools, while the technologies, in turn, enhance and amplify the institution's education objectives. This study focused on a PHEI with T&L practices rooted in constructivism. Figure 3.1 demonstrates how this philosophy may shape digital tools and how digital tools reinforce constructivist principles (Allen, 2022; Chand, 2024; Hein, 1991).

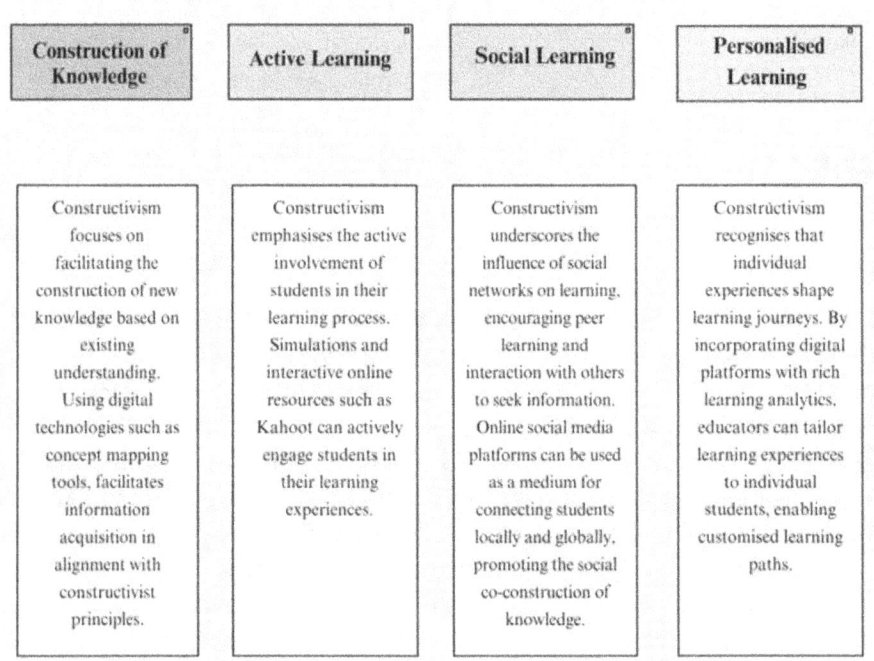

FIGURE 3.1: Linking digital tools and constructivism

Criticisms of constructivism include cognitive overload for students who struggle with self-directed learning, the lack of universality across educational disciplines and contexts, and a lack of clarity among educators about their role in a learner-driven educational model (Alanazi, 2016; Matthews, 2014; Osborne, 2015). The participating PHEI has, however, successfully implemented constructivism across faculties, supported by structured and ongoing T&L support.

Aligning digital learning tools to subject context within a higher education institution

The application of Bloom's Digital Taxonomy must align with the requirements of the content being taught. This study was centred around the use of digital technologies in numeracy education within a PHEI. Numeracy education, which includes subjects such as accounting, financial management, economics, and statistics, presents unique challenges due to its mathematical complexity. These challenges negatively impact student success rates within South African HE. Innovative and aligned T&L strategies are needed for improved engagement and comprehension (Makhathini et al., 2024).

The integration of digital technologies in numeracy education is particularly complex because of the highly technical and practical formula-driven nature of the content (Haleem et al., 2022). Insufficient digital capabilities among lecturers and students compound this complexity (Abalkheel, 2022). As a result, lecturer confidence and student engagement could decline, further impacting the use of digital tools for T&L. Despite the growing emphasis on technology-enabled learning in HE, there is limited research on the effective application of digital tools in numeracy education (Butler et al., 2022; Dalim et al., 2023).

Theoretical framework

This study is grounded in Bloom's Digital Taxonomy and constructivist learning theory. The participating PHEI employs Bloom's Revised Taxonomy and social constructivism as the foundation for its T&L philosophy. The theoretical framework, therefore, aligns with the institution's pedagogical context and globally recognised frameworks within HEIs (Amin & Mirza, 2020; Dziubaniuk et al., 2023; Manjunat & Kumar, 2023).

Research aim and methodology

The aim of this study was to identify trends in the application of digital tools for T&L in numeracy subjects within a South African PHEI. The research followed an interpretivist paradigm and employed an exploratory approach to gain a deeper understanding of technology-enabled T&L strategies in numeracy education. A qualitative research design was selected to facilitate in-depth data collection on digital learning practices within the participating PHEI (Creswell & Creswell, 2018; Kothari, 1990). To gather data, 15 semi-structured interviews were conducted with lecturers teaching numeracy modules in commerce-related Higher Certificate and Bachelor of Commerce qualifications at the PHEI. Respondents were selected using non-probability purposive sampling. In cases where respondents lecture across multiple modules or student groups, they were asked to select one module and group for the purposes of the study. Thematic analysis was used to identify trends in the use of digital technologies within numeracy education.

The study received ethical clearance from the Independent Institute of Education in accordance with institutional ethics review and approval procedures (R.000134). Respondents were afforded 24 hours post-interview to retract either the entire interview or specific segments thereof. This option was not exercised by any of the respondents. Data recording, handling, and storage processes adhered to the provisions of the Protection of Personal Information Act and complied with ethical research standards.

Results and discussion

A thematic analysis of the qualitative data yielded 377 unique codes. These codes were categorised according to five key themes: 1) T&L and digital tools; 2) Assessments and digital learning tools; 3) Lecturer sentiment towards using digital learning tools; 4) Perceived benefits of digital learning tools; and 5) Challenges to digital learning tool integration.

Teaching, learning, and the digital tools used within numeracy modules

Respondents were asked to identify the digital tools they use in their T&L practice and to reflect on how they have implemented these tools in the context of their T&L approach and numeracy content. The concept of 'digital tools in T&L practice' was purposefully left open to interpretation, allowing respondents to define these technologies based on their perceptions and experiences. Findings suggest that most respondents are still in the early stages of digital technology integration. The lecturers who include technology such as PDFs, PowerPoint, and Excel in their definition of digital technology use technology all the time. However, the lecturers who defined technology in terms of newer technologies stated that they made use of digital technologies 20 to 40% of the time.

The most widely used digital learning tool identified was Blackboard, the PHEI's Learning Management System (LMS), which was cited by 80% of respondents. This result was expected as Blackboard is a standard tool used by the institution for blended and online learning. However, lecturers have significant autonomy in how they integrate the LMS into their pedagogical practice. Respondents indicated that the LMS is used predominantly for communication with learners and dissemination of resources such as prerecorded videos to support a flipped classroom approach. Lecturers also use the platform for informal assessments, particularly auto-graded assessments integrated into their teaching. Microsoft applications such as Excel and PowerPoint (70%) were also cited as valued for their ability to demonstrate practical applications of academic content, simulate scenarios, and visually display the impact of a change in one variable on an entire calculation. Smart whiteboards and the Microsoft Whiteboard application were also noted as effective for teaching step-by-step approaches to numerical problem-solving, mitigating limitations associated with finite board space. However, the high cost of smart whiteboards was highlighted as a challenge, and tablet technology was identified as a more cost-effective alternative to consider.

Third-party online applications are predominantly being used for two key purposes: 1) supplementing and reinforcing numeracy content and 2) knowledge assessment. In terms of supplementing and reinforcing content, tools such as YouTube (80%) and Khan Academy (40%) are used to reinforce numeracy concepts during class discussions, complement course material, provide diverse theoretical insights, and support self-guided learning. Respondents noted a growing trend of students requesting that lecturers use TikTok as a method for summarising and explaining difficult concepts. However, lecturers are hesitant to shift too many learning resources to video platforms as they view these tools as being limited to specific numeracy concepts rather than supporting the higher-order cognitive engagement needed for complex concepts.

For knowledge assessment, Kahoot was the most popular third-party platform (46%). The platform is valued for its gamified approach to assessment, which enabled lecturers to administer engaging and entertaining quizzes and develop positive associations with assessment. The platform's automated marking system and instantaneous feedback were also noted as valuable for active learning.

AI tools such as Google Bard were noted for supplementing and reinforcing knowledge, as well as for assessing knowledge. These tools have been highly effective in improving students' comprehension and proficiency, particularly when building upon a solid foundational understanding of numeracy concepts. The AI tools were reported as fostering user-generated content, interactivity, and collaboration in a constructivist learning environment. They were not, however, deemed suitable for use when teaching foundational numeracy concepts. Respondents highlighted that these platforms often do not encourage critical thinking as they allow students to easily generate answers to complex calculations without critically engaging with the underlying theoretical processes involved in those calculations. This raises concerns about potential overreliance on AI, which could undermine students' ability to develop critical thinking skills. Other digital learning tools mentioned included Sage, an accounting platform prescribed by the PHEI, Canva for creating infographics and visually engaging content, and WhatsApp for personalised, asynchronous communication with students.

When asked to reflect on and evaluate their integration of digital technologies into T&L using Bloom's Digital Taxonomy, respondents noted the use of online quizzes such as Kahoot to reinforce content as aligning with 'Remembering'. Platforms such as YouTube, Google Bard, and Khan Academy assisted students by creating a deeper comprehension of content, aligning with 'Understanding', while tools such as Smart whiteboards, Canva, and Excel allowed students to use their numerical knowledge for solving practical scenarios, aligning with 'Applying'. Excel was occasionally used to analyse data and generate results, aligning with the cognitive level of 'Analysing'. A small number of respondents (24%) indicated very limited use of discussion forums on the LMS for peer-based discussion and feedback, aligning with 'Evaluating'. The application of digital tools aligned with the cognitive thinking level of 'Creating' was very limited. The trend that emerged, therefore, is that digital learning tools are predominantly employed for the LOTS of Remembering, Understanding, and Applying. Far fewer lecturers reported successfully applying these tools for learning at the HOTS levels of Analysing, Evaluating, and Creating.

Assessment and the digital learning tools used within numeracy modules

The use of digital learning tools for the assessment of knowledge is either informal or formal. Regarding informal assessments, all respondents are empowered by the participating PHEI to autonomously set and administer specific informal assessments within their numeracy module/s. These assessments are developed in response to specific student challenges, ranging from understanding basic numeracy concepts to applying formulas in calculations. As a result, informal assessment formats vary across different student groups, depending on specific learning needs.

Respondents predominantly use the PHEIs LMS (Blackboard) to administer informal assessments, ensuring accessibility and ease of use by using a platform already known to students. In addition, many assessments are set up as auto-graded tasks, meaning that submissions are marked by the system, students receive instant feedback on their performance, and grades are automatically transferred to the student gradebook. This provides significant benefits for students, particularly when 'tricky topics' in numeracy require specific feedback and support ahead of formal assessments. Blackboard is also used to individually track student engagement and the time taken to complete assessments.

Kahoot, again, emerged as a preferred third-party platform for informal quiz-based assessments. Lecturers reported that gamification increases student engagement and that Kahoot can be used to create a competitive atmosphere in class by awarding points to students for correct answers. Respondents highlighted the importance of using a tool, such as Kahoot, alongside the LMS because 'silent learners' and very introverted students tend to engage less effectively in the class-based setting than in self-paced assessments created in Blackboard.

While respondents acknowledged the advantages of digital technology for informal assessments, a unanimous reservation was expressed regarding its suitability for formal assessments. A major issue that was raised was the increased risk of unethical use of digital tools, such as AI, when students complete their assessments. Lecturers appreciated the application of digital tools for online marking and feedback but noted challenges in a developing country such as South Africa, which is often plagued by unreliable electricity supply. Respondents specifically noted this as a significant limitation of formal online, timed assessments. During electricity interruptions, network connectivity can be compromised, resulting in permanent data loss or data corruption. This negatively affects not only student submissions but also the online marking of assessments by lecturers. Respondents particularly noted that the risks associated with data loss are particularly concerning due to the complex nature of numeracy. Numeracy often requires that students scaffold solutions, meaning that losing an earlier solution can compromise the integrity of subsequent calculations. Sequential problem-solving also makes it difficult to recreate lost data, which creates student anxiety and negative assessment experiences.

Lecturer sentiment towards using digital learning tools in numeracy modules

The third theme in the data analysis explored lecturers' sentiments towards integrating digital tools into their teaching of numeracy-based subjects. Using a Likert scale, respondents were asked to indicate their current level of confidence in using digital technologies for T&L and assessment in numeracy subjects. The Likert scale had 'very confident' as the highest rate and 'not confident' as the lowest. Most respondents (68%) felt either confident or very confident in their ability to use digital tools for numeracy education. A smaller portion of the respondents (32%) indicated a low to moderate level of confidence, but all expressed a strong interest in training to enhance their digital skills, particularly in relation to tools designed specifically for numeracy education. A positive correlation was observed between respondents who rated themselves as having higher confidence levels and more frequent integration of digital tools into their teaching practice. Lecturers who rated themselves as having lower confidence levels were less inclined to integrate digital tools into their pedagogy.

Respondents emphasised the importance of intentionality when integrating digital technologies into T&L. Lecturers highlighted that purposeful and selective use of technology is crucial to ensure that the technology serves as a valuable enhancement rather than being incorporated arbitrarily. They also highlighted that such intentional use of technology in complex numeracy lessons is time-consuming and requires specific digital skills requiring training. Despite the increasing use of digital learning tools, there was a prevailing consensus that traditional face-to-face interactions and discussions remain the foundational elements of T&L within numeracy, with digital technology serving as a complementary aid rather than a replacement for direct lecturer-student engagement.

Digital learning tools were largely found to be suitable for supplementing or assessing aspects of numeracy education, such as specific theoretical concepts or short calculations. Respondents specifically highlighted that digital tools were helpful in assisting students with recall, which further aided their understanding and ability to apply knowledge to complex calculations. These tools were, however, deemed less suited to engaging students' HOTS. Aspects of numeracy education, such as complex, multi-step numerical calculations, were felt to be more aligned with more 'traditional' T&L approaches. Interestingly, respondents who indicated the use of digital technology at the HOTS levels indicated less frequent integration of digital tools. They noted that the integration of digital technology at these levels requires a deliberate integration to achieve intentional outcomes of the numeracy modules. This approach is often time-consuming, requiring advanced technological skills from both lecturers and students. While it was noted that there may well be more digitally advanced and suitable learning tools available, lecturers also struggle with the time it takes to find these tools and acquire the digital skills to use them effectively. From a sustainability perspective, respondents raised the adverse health effects of long hours spent in front of a digital device, including eye strain, back strain, and headaches.

Approaches to the integration of digital learning tools across Bloom's cognitive levels are also highly varied. Factors such as lecturer and student technological skills and time appear to largely determine integration strategies. These results emphasise the need for tailored approaches to effectively integrate digital tools into HE settings, with all digital technologies being strategically integrated into lesson planning. Importantly, respondents highlighted a trend of students disengaging when technology was either overused or not integrated appropriately.

Perceived benefits of integrating digital learning tools in numeracy education

Respondents were asked to highlight positive outcomes and achievements resulting from the integration of digital learning tools in their classrooms. Several noteworthy benefits were identified. These included an overall increase in confidence and empowerment among both students and staff, increased resourcefulness and digital skill development, improved accessibility to learning resources and informal assessments, increased engagement due to gamified learning materials, and heightened student participation. Digital technology emerged as a valuable enabler for teaching, contributing to a more dynamic numeracy-based educational environment.

Challenges experienced in digital learning tool integration in numeracy education

Respondents were asked to highlight and discuss any challenges that were faced when integrating digital tools into their pedagogical approaches. Several challenges were identified. Firstly, there are difficulties in teaching high application-based numeracy content online, with lecturers emphasising the necessity for in-person interaction to effectively demonstrate step-by-step problem-solving processes and encourage active student participation. Secondly, multiple challenges centred around infrastructure and access challenges arose. The respondents mentioned issues such as insufficient hardware, unreliable availability of electricity, poor connectivity and unstable internet connections, and limited participation when students neglect to bring digital devices to class. Thirdly, there are significant disparities in students' digital skills, with the same classes comprising some students who are unfamiliar with basic computer usage and others who are skilled users. This creates a challenge for lecturers who must not only find digital tools suitable for numeracy education but also tools that can create inclusivity of the varied demographics of students present in one class setting. Lastly, lecturers expressed concerns about the use of AI, specifically tools such as ChatGPT, and increasing student reliance on these tools to complete tasks without fully engaging with the learning process. An overreliance on AI tools could detrimentally impact students' authentic understanding of numeracy and, as a result, their preparedness for formal assessments and, ultimately, future employment. Solutions that are AI-generated are also believed to be increasing the extent of plagiarism.

Insights and implications for future research and practice within South African higher education

Four key trends were identified in the DT of T&L strategies in HE numeracy subjects. Firstly, regarding blended learning and pedagogical approaches, digital learning tools are being used to complement rather than replace traditional face-to-face teaching in numeracy education. The use of this technology is intended to enhance the appeal of fundamental knowledge acquisition, fostering greater engagement and commitment among students, and enhancing more traditional T&L strategies. Additionally, the HEI's T&L philosophy determines how technology is applied. In the context of this study, digital tools used for T&L must be integrated to complement constructivist teaching methodologies in which students and lecturers remain co-creators of the learning process. Digital learning tools are most commonly being used for the facilitation of LOTS in the participating PHEI, with the facilitation of HOTS still heavily reliant on lecturer guidance and face-to-face interaction. Blended learning models integrating digital technologies and traditional pedagogical strategies are emerging as the preferred approach to numeracy education. Future research is needed to identify strategies for intentional digital learning tool integration that balance technology tool use with interactive numeracy education in hybrid and online educational settings. Structured training for lecturers to strategically integrate digital learning tools is also needed.

Secondly, regarding student engagement, digital literacy, and career readiness, using digital technology plays a significant role in increased student engagement and the development of digital skills for future-ready graduates. Indeed, lecturers are intent on adequately preparing students for prospective careers, aligning technological skills with industry demands for career development within the 4IR. A growing digital skills divide among students means that lecturers are seeking pedagogical strategies that integrate digital tools effectively at various levels of digital skills, engage students at various levels of thinking skills, and effectively support student engagement and student employability. It is recommended that HEIs implement training programmes that enhance the digital skills of both lecturers and students that are globally aligned. Additionally, future research should explore the nexus between digital skills that both support student success in numeracy and are relevant to career development in the 4IR.

The third key trend is that effective digital integration in numeracy education is highly dependent on technological infrastructure, access to the various digital learning tools, and institutional readiness for the DT of numeracy education. In the resource-constrained South African HE context, strategies to address digital access and skills disparities are needed, as are offline-compatible learning tools to mitigate access issues. Institutional support programmes are needed to assist lecturers in identifying and integrating appropriate technologies in time-efficient, effective, and innovative ways. Support programmes should also assist both lecturers and students to work at varying digital skills levels, developing enhanced skills over time. A digital readiness tool for assessing readiness levels among students and lecturers, as well as at the institutional level, would be valuable. Additionally, research is needed to develop scalable, cost-effective digital solutions for the teaching of numeracy in South African HE.

Lastly, the fourth key trend relates to ethical AI use, assessment integrity, and digital challenges. There is a rapid evolution taking place in the use of generative AI in HE. AI can be used to personalise learning and support a deeper understanding of numeracy concepts, but concerns about student overreliance on AI solutions and vulnerabilities to poor academic integrity must be addressed. Digital learning tools are effective for informal assessments but less suitable for formal, high-stakes numeracy assessments requiring structured and complex problem-solving processes. Research into ethical AI integration and assessment models, as well as evolving HE policies and academic integrity frameworks governing the use of AI, will be of benefit. Bloom's Digital Taxonomy should also be updated to reflect the use of AI tools at different cognitive levels.

These four trends highlight strategic focus areas for South African PHEIs as they respond to the DT of numeracy education in the era of 4IR digital learning technologies. Educators aim to integrate technologies that can support student engagement with numeracy concepts on equal footing, regardless of prior experience and access to digital tools. Ultimately, strategies for the integration of digital learning tools in HE numeracy education aim to produce industry-ready graduates, well-equipped to navigate and contribute to countries, industries, and communities in the digital age.

Conclusion

This study identified trends in the integration of digital tools in the T&L of numeracy education within a South African PHEI, highlighting both opportunities and challenges in leveraging technology for teaching, learning, and assessment. The findings indicate that lecturers vary in the types of tools used. Some rely on basic or institutionally prescribed tools, while others are more adventurous, citing the use of more modern tools. Despite the types of tools identified, lecturers are using digital learning tools to engage students mostly in LOTS, indicating a gap in the ability of lecturers to use technology to encourage critical thinking skills and engage students in HOTS.

While the findings reflect positive lecturer sentiments on the potential benefits of technologies in numeracy education, lecturers also placed emphasis on significant challenges such as disparities in access to technology, concerns about plagiarism, and the need for a balanced approach to technology integration. This study highlights the critical need for focused support initiatives aimed at supporting lecturers with the integration of digital tools that are suited for T&L in numeracy education so they can engage students at the cognitive levels of Bloom's Digital Taxonomy while ensuring a constructivist approach. In addition, this study highlights the need for future research into the identification of digital learning tools that offer inclusive, equitable, and effective digital learning experiences to students studying numeracy subjects in South African HEIs.

References

Abalkheel, A. (2022). Amalgamating Bloom's Taxonomy and Artificial Intelligence to Face the Challenges of Online EFL Learning Amid Post-COVID-19 in Saudi Arabia. *International Journal of English Language and Literature Studies*, 11(1): 16–30. https://doi.org/10.18488/5019.v11i1.4409

Acikgul Firat, E. & Firat, S. (2021). Web 3.0 in Learning Environments: A Systematic Review. *Turkish Online Journal of Distance Education*, 22(1): 148–169.

Adams, N.E. (2015). Bloom's taxonomy of cognitive learning objectives. *Journal of Medical Library Association*, 103(3): 152–153. https://doi.org/10.3163/1536-5050.103.3.010.

Adekola, J., Dale, V. & Gardiner, K. (2017). Development of an institutional framework to guide transitions into enhanced blended learning in higher education. *Research in Learning Technology*, 25:1973. https://doi.org/10.25304/RLT.V25.1973.

African Union. (2024). *Goals & priority areas of Agenda 2063*. African Union. Available at: https://au.int/agenda2063/goals. Date accessed: 27 February 2025.

Alaghbary, G.S. (2021). Integrating technology with Bloom's Revised Taxonomy: Web 2.0-enabled learning designs for online learning. *Asian EFL Journal*, 28(2): 10–37.

Alanazi, A. (2016). A Critical Review of Constructivist Theory and the Emergence of Constructionism. *American Research Journal of Humanities and Social Sciences*, 2. https://doi.org/10.21694/2378-7031.16018.

Alenezi, M. (2023). Digital Learning and Digital Institution in Higher Education. *Education Sciences*, 13(1): 88. https://doi.org/10.3390/educsci13010088.

Allen, A. (2022). An Introduction to Constructivism: Its Theoretical Roots and Impact on Contemporary Education. *Journal of Learning Design and Leadership*, 1(1): 1–11.

Amin, H. & Mirza, M.S. (2020). Comparative study of knowledge and use of Bloom's digital taxonomy by teachers and students in virtual and conventional universities. *Asian Association of Open Universities Journal*, 15(2): 223–238. https://doi.org/10.1108/AAOUJ-01-2020-0005.

Anderson, T. & Dron, J. (2012). Learning Technology through Three Generations of Technology Enhanced Distance Education Pedagogy. *European Journal of Open, Distance and E-Learning*, 1.

Assan, T.E. & Thomas, R.K. (2012). Information and communication technology integration into teaching and learning: Opportunities and challenges for commerce educators in South Africa. *International Journal of Education and Development using Information and Communication Technology*, 8(2): 4–16.

Benavides, L.M.C., Arias, J.A.T., Serna, M.D.A, Bedoya, J.W.B. & Burgos, D. (2020). Digital Transformation in Higher Education Institutions: A Systematic Literature Review. *Sensors*, 20(11): 3291. https://doi.org/10.3390/s20113291.

Bucăța, G. & Tileagă, C. (2024). Digital Renaissance in Education: Unveiling the Transformative Potential of Digitization in Educational Institutions. *Land Forces Academy Review*, 29(1): 20–37. https://doi.org/10.2478/raft-2024-0003.

Butler, D., Giblin, F. & Kingston, M. (2022). *Numeracy and digital learning: Use of digital technologies as tools for numeracy development: A review of the literature.* Ireland: Department of Education.

Çela, E., Fonkam, M. & Potluri, R.M. (2024). Risks of AI-Assisted Learning on Student Critical Thinking: A Case Study of Albania. *International Journal of Risk and Contingency Management*, 12(1). https://doi.org/10.4018/IJRCM.350185.

Chand, S.P. (2024). Constructivism in Education: Exploring the Contributions of Piaget, Vygotsky, and Bruner. *International Journal of Science and Research*, 12(7): 274–278. https://doi.org/10.21275/SR23630021800(7): 274-278.

Chandio, T.M., Pandhiani, S.M. & Iqbal, R. (2016). Bloom's Taxonomy: Improving Assessment and Teaching-Learning Process. *Journal of Education and Educational Development*, 3(2): 203–221.

Churches, A. (2008). *Bloom's Digital Taxonomy.* Available at: http://burtonslifelearning.pbworks.com/w/file/fetch/26327358/BloomDigitalTaxonomy2001.pdf. Date accessed: 21 November 2023.

Clark-Wilson, A., Aldon, G., Cusi, A. & Goos, M. (2014). The challenges of teaching mathematics with digital technologies – The evolving role of the teacher. In Liljedahl, P., Nicol, C., Oesterle, S. & Allan, D. (ed.) *Proceedings of the 38th Conference of the International Group for the Psychology of Mathematics Education and the 36th Conference of the North American Chapter of the Psychology of Mathematics Education.* British Columbia: University of British Columbia. 87–116.

Corbett, F. & Spinello, E. (2020). Connectivism and leadership: Harnessing a learning theory for the digital age to redefine leadership in the twenty-first century. *Heliyon*, 6(1). https://doi.org/10.1016/j.heliyon.2020.e03250.

Creswell, J.W. & Creswell, J.D. (2018). *Research design: Qualitative, quantitative, and mixed methods approaches (5th edition).* Los Angeles: Sage Publications.

Currell, J. (2021). *Bloom's Taxonomy: What is it and how can you apply it in your classroom?* Available at: https://mathsnoproblem.com/blog/teaching-practice/apply-blooms-taxonomy-in-classroom. Date accessed: 21 September 2023.

Dalim, S.F., Aris, S.R.S., Hoon, T.S., Nadzri, F.A., Deni, S.M., Yahya, N. et al. (2023). Framework for Numeracy and Digital Skills Attributes in Higher Education. *Research in Social Sciences and Technology*, 8(3): 16–35. https://doi.org/10.46303/ressat.2023.18.

Díaz-García, V., Montero-Navarro, A., Rodriguez-Sánchez, J.-L. & Gallego-Losada, R. (2022). Digitalization and digital transformation in higher education: A bibliometric analysis. *Frontiers in Psychology*, 13. https://doi.org/10.3389/fpsyg.2022.1081595.

Dziubaniuk, O., Ivanova-Gongne, M. & Nyholm, M. (2023). Learning and teaching sustainable business in the digital era: a connectivism theory approach. *International Journal of Educational Technology in Higher Education*, 20(20).

Faloye, S.T. & Ajayi, N.A. (2021). Understanding the impact of the digital divide on South African students in higher educational institutions. *African Journal of Science Technology Innovation and Development*, 14(7): 1734–1744.

Fosnot, C.T. & Perry, R.S. (1996). Constructivism: a psychological theory of learning. In Fosnot, C.T. (ed.) *Constructivism: Theory, Perspectives, and Practice (first edition)*. New York: Teachers College Press, 8–33.

Gierl, M.J. (1997). Comparing Cognitive Representations of Test Developers and Students on a Mathematics Test with Bloom's Taxonomy. *The Journal of Educational Research*, 91(1): 26–32. https://doi.org/10.1080/00220679709597517.

Gonsalves, C. (2024). Generative AI's Impact on Critical Thinking: Revisiting Bloom's Taxonomy. *Journal of Marketing Education*. https://doi.org/10.1177/02734753241305980.

Haleem, A., Javaid, M., Qadri, M.A. & Suman, R. (2022). Understanding the role of digital technologies in education: A review. *Sustainable Operations and Computers*, 3: 275–285.

Hein, G.E. (1991). Constructivist learning theory. *International Committee of Museum Educators Conference*, 15–22 October, Jerusalem, Israel.

Hmoud, M. & Shaqour, A. (2024). AIEd Bloom's Taxonomy: A Proposed Model for Enhancing Educational Efficiency and Effectiveness. *The International Journal of Technologies in Learning*, 31(2): 111–128. https://doi.org/10.18848/2327-0144/CGP/v31i02/111-128.

Jaffer, S., Ng'ambi, D. & Czerniewicz, L. (2007). The role of ICTs in higher education in South Africa: One strategy for addressing teaching and learning challenges. *International Journal of Education and Development using ICT*, 3(4): 131–142.

Kothari, C.R. (1990). *Research Methodology: Methods and Techniques (second edition)*. New Delhi: New Age International Publishers.

Li, Y., Silver, E.A. & Li, S (ed.). (2014). Transforming professional practice in numeracy teaching. In Goos, M., Geiger, V. & Dole, S. (ed.) *Transforming Mathematics Instruction: Multiple Approaches and Practices*. Cham: Springer, 81–102.

Makhathini, L., Adam, J. & Akpa-Inyang, F. (2024). Examining the challenges of tertiary teaching and learning in the accounting discipline within KwaZulu-Natal, South Africa. *Research in Social Sciences and Technology*, 9(2): 261–280.

Manjunat, K. & Kumar, A. (2023). Applying Bloom's Revised Taxonomy on Information and Communication Technology skills of University Faculty Members. *International Journal of Management, Technology, and Social Sciences*, 8(1): 53–67. https://doi.org/10.47992/ijmts.2581.6012.0255.

Masenya, T.M. (2021). Digital Literacy Skills as Prerequisite for Teaching and Learning in Higher Education Institutions. *Mousaion: South African Journal of Information Studies*, 39(2). https://doi.org/10.25159/2663-659X/8428.

Mattar, J. (2018). Constructivism and connectivism in education technology: Active, situated, authentic, experiential, and anchored learning. *RIED: Revista Iberoamericana de Educación a Distancia*, 21(2): 201–213. https://doi.org/10.5944/ried.21.2.20055.

Matthews, M.R. (2014). Philosophical and Pedagogical Problems with Constructivism in Science Education. *Epistémologie et didactique de la physique: Le constructivisme en question*, 38: 40–55. https://doi.org/10.4000/trema.2823.

Miranda, P., Isaias, P. & Costa, C.J. (2014). E-learning and web generations: Towards Web 3.0 and e-learning 3.0. *4th International Conference on Education, Research and Innovation*. Singapore: IACSIT Press, 92–103. https://doi.org/10.7763/IPEDR.2014.V81.15.

Mohammed, S.H. & Kinyo, L. (2020). Constructivist theory as a foundation for the utilization of digital technology in the lifelong learning process. *Turkish Online Journal of Distance Education*, 21(4): 90–109. https://doi.org/10.17718/tojde.803364.

Nyathi, T. & Joseph, R.M. (2024). Empowering South African educators: Navigating the challenges of digital teaching and learning competencies. *SA Journal of Human Resource Management*, 22(1): 2591. https://doi.org/10.4102/sajhrm.v22i0.2591.

Osborne, J. (2015). Constructivism: Critiques. In Gunstone, R. (ed.) *Encyclopaedia of Science Education*. London: Springer Nature, 224–228.

Pettersson, F. (2021). Understanding digitalization and educational change in school by means of activity theory and the levels of learning concept. *Education and Information Technologies*, 26: 187–204. https://doi.org/10.1007/s10639-020-10239-8.

Rahman, S.A. & Manaf, N.F.A. (2017). A Critical Analysis of Bloom's Taxonomy in Teaching Creative and Critical Thinking Skills in Malaysia through English Literature. *English Language Teaching*, 10(9): 245–256. https://doi.org/10.5539/elt.v10n9p245.

Rangaro, M.S., Girish, P.H. & Tulsani, V. (2023). Web3 Technology: The New Beginning. *International Journal of Advanced Trends in Computer Science and Engineering*, 12(2): 68–72. https://doi.org/10.30534/ijatcse/2023/061222023.

Republic of South Africa (RSA). (undated a). *About the 4IR PMO*. Available at: https://www.dcdt.gov.za/4ir-pmo.html#:~:text=About%20the%204IR%20PMO&text='The%204th%20Industrial%20Revolution%20is,social%2C%20economic%20and%20political%20spheres. Date accessed: 27 February 2025.

Republic of South Africa (RSA). (undated b). *National Development Plan 2030*. Available at: https://www.gov.za/sites/default/files/gcis_document/201409/ndp-2030-our-future-make-it-workr.pdf. Date accessed: 27 March 2024.

Scheel, L., Vladova, G. & Ullrich, A. (2022). The influence of digital competences, self-organization, and independent learning abilities on students' acceptance of digital learning. *International Journal of Educational Technology in Higher Education*, 19(44). https://doi.org/10.1186/s41239-022-00350-w.

Siemens, G. (2005). Connectivism: A learning theory for the digital age. *International Journal of Instructional Technology & Distance Learning*, 2(1).

Sithole, V.L. & Mbukanma, I. (2024). Prospects and Challenges to ICT Adoption in Teaching and Learning at Rural South African Universities: A systematic review. *Research in Social Sciences and Technology*, 9(3): 178–193.

Sneed, O. (2016). *Integrating technology with Bloom's Taxonomy*. Available at: https://teachonline.asu.edu/2016/05/integrating-technology-blooms-taxonomy/. Date accessed: 26 September 2023.

Sockett, H. (1971). Bloom's Taxonomy: A philosophical critique. *Cambridge Journal of Education*, 1(1): 16–25. https://doi.org/10.1080/0305764710010103.

Soozandehfar, S.M.A. & Adeli, M.R. (2016). A Critical Appraisal of Bloom's Taxonomy. *American Research Journal of English and Literature*, 2: 1–9.

Southern African Development Community. (2020). *Vision 2050*. Available at: https://www.sadc.int/sites/default/files/2021-08/SADC_Vision_2050.pdf. Date accessed: 27 February 2025.

Tutkun, O.F., Guzel, D., Koroğlu, M. & İlhan, H. (2012). Bloom's Revised Taxonomy and critics on it. *The Online Journal of Counselling and Education*, 1(3): 23–30.

UNESCO. (2021). *Education for sustainable development – Learning to act for people and planet*. Available at: https://en.unesco.org/themes/education/sdgs/material. Date accessed: 28 March 2024.

Wedlock, B.C. & Growe, R. (2017). The Technology Driven Student: How to Apply Bloom's Revised Taxonomy to the Digital Generations. *Journal of Education & Social Policy*, 7(1): 25–34.

Wilson, L.O. (2021). *Anderson and Krathwohl Bloom's Taxonomy Revised: Understanding the new version of Bloom's Taxonomy*. Available at: https://quincycollege.edu/wp-content/uploads/Anderson-and-Krathwohl_Revised-Blooms-Taxonomy.pdf. Date accessed: 22 September 2023.

Zawacki-Richter, Marín, V.I., Bond, M. & Gouverneur, F. (2019). Systematic review of research on artificial intelligence applications in higher education – where are the educators? *International Journal of Educational Technology in Higher Education*, 16(39).

Zawedde, A. (2014). *Management of System Analysis and Design Knowledge: A Case for m-Learning*. Available at: https://www.researchgate.net/profile/Aminah-Zawedde/publication/269617172_Management_of_System_Analysis_and_Design_Knowledge_A_Case_for_m-Learning/links/548ff26d0cf214269f2642c5/Management-of-System-Analysis-and-Design-Knowledge-A-Case-for-m-Learning.pdf. Date accessed: 27 February 2025.

Zhai, C., Wibowo, S. & Li, L.D. (2024). The effects of over-reliance on AI dialogue systems on students' cognitive abilities: a systematic review. *Smart Learning Environments*, 11(28). https://doi.org/10.1186/s40561-024-00316-7.

SECTION 2

Conversations about Teaching and Learning

CHAPTER 4

Creating residential undergraduate experiences that meet the needs of students[4]

Chris Mayer

Abstract

Higher education institutions (HEIs) in the United States face many challenges. A declining population of high school graduates, high tuition costs, student loan debt, and scepticism regarding the value of higher education are some of these challenges. Highly selective residential HEIs are weathering the storm, and there has been significant growth in online education. The HEIs that are most in danger are less selective, residential HEIs. This chapter employs a theoretical approach to explore how these HEIs can survive and thrive by embracing specialised missions and student experiences that distinguish their residential experiences and the development they promote, offering a lower cost, and attracting those who are not inclined to pursue residential education. The chapter will offer ideas for strategies that address the challenges faced by less selective, residential HEIs.

Keywords: higher education; residential; enrolment; strategy; innovation.

Higher education institutions (HEIs) in the United States are facing significant challenges. Concern about the costs and the debt students incur is causing many potential students to not pursue undergraduate degrees, especially those from residential, four-year institutions. Also impacting HEIs is the belief that degrees do not improve employment prospects for those who earn them because many graduates experience underemployment. A report from the Burning Glass Institute and Strada Education Foundation found that 52% of graduates are underemployed a year after graduation, with 45% of graduates remaining underemployed a decade after graduation (Hanson, 2024). The report defines underemployment as 'the experience of four-year graduates who are employed in jobs that don't typically require a bachelor's degree' (Hanson, 2024). Underemployment often makes it difficult for people to pay back student loans. This impacts the majority of graduates as 61% of US students graduate with some type of debt related to their education (Hanson, 2024).

Even if student demand remained the same and was not negatively impacted by these factors, declining numbers of high school aged students

---
[4] The views in this article are those of the author and not the views of the United States Military Academy, United States Army, or United States Department of Defense.

means that HEIs are competing for a shrinking pool of applicants. There will be a 13% decrease of 18-year-olds from 2025 through 2041 (Mullin, 2024). Potential students also have many more options for higher education than they used to, which include flexible online programmes as well as employers who provide tuition assistance for employees, which causes them to choose online programmes or part-time programmes rather than residential undergraduate programmes. While these conditions impact all HEIs, they especially impact less selective, residential, primarily undergraduate HEIs (less selective HEIs). Thriving in this environment will require less selective HEIs to distinguish themselves in ways that are clear to students and highlight how they are different from other HEIs. This requires the less selective HEI sector to adopt a differentiation strategy, although it will look different at each HEI given its specific strengths and the needs of its potential students. Currently, many less selective HEIs are similar to one another with many seeking to become like highly selective HEIs by offering the types of programmes offered by highly selective HEIs. A differentiation strategy will require less selective HEIs to set aside the goal of becoming or looking like a highly selective HEI or other less selective HEIs. They will need to pursue changes that allow them to leverage their unique strengths and better serve potential students, especially those who are not able to find the types of programmes and experience they are seeking. Although focused on HEIs in the United States, insights in this chapter are relevant to less selective HEIs in South Africa and other countries.

Background

Through October 2023, 14 non-profit and 16 for-profit HEIs closed, which comes after 23 HEIs closed during 2022. The previous high for non-profit HEIs in a year was 13 (Sanchez, 2024). One expert, Rachel Burns, believes that declining enrolments are the cause: 'It's not corruption, it's not financial misappropriation of funds, it's just that they can't rebound enrolment' (Sanchez, 2024). As Sanchez reports, enrolment projections into the future are even more dire: 'By 2030, 449 colleges are expected to see a 25 percent decline in enrolment and 182 colleges are expected to see a 50 percent decline, according to an EAB analysis of federal enrolment data. By 2035, those numbers are expected to rise to 534 colleges expecting a 25 percent decline and 227 colleges expecting a 50 percent decline; by 2040, a total of 566 colleges are expected to see a 25 percent decline and 247 are expected to see a 50 percent decline, according to EAB's analysis.' Although this is based on declining numbers of high school students and assumes that HEIs address this gap by enrolling older students, it is still an issue. In addition to the declining population of high school students who typically enroll in residential HEI programmes, the US public is less confident in higher education and is sceptical that the cost of pursuing an undergraduate degree is worth it. In 2015, 57% of those surveyed had 'a great deal' or 'quite a lot' of confidence in higher education. That dropped to 36% in 2023 (Brenan, 2023).

Bryan Alexander categorises the multitude of ways that these challenges impact HEIs through five different categories. These categories are: 'closing colleges and universities; campuses cutting programmes and jobs; campuses cutting programmes but not laying off people yet; budget crises, no programme or people cuts announced yet; and institutions merging' (Alexander, 2024). Although highly selective HEIs are not immune, as demonstrated by the institutions Bryan mentions, these different struggles are especially threats to less selective HEIs.

Michael Horn makes this point as well. Horn, who with Clay Christensen suggested that 25% of colleges would close or merge during the mid 2020s and 2030s, argues that 'Not only will the top selective undergraduate programmes likely be OK, but they almost certainly won't be "disrupted" at all' (Horn, 2024). This is because 'Exclusive colleges and universities, particularly in the United States, thrive because they reject volume. In that they are quite similar to the luxury watch makers that have survived disruption by digital technologies. Their very value propositions are tied up in the fact that they are selective and small' (Horn, 2024). Highly selective HEIs do not require significant numbers of students, and their reputation will continue to attract students. It will be the less selective HEIs that are most at risk from the challenging environment. This will require them to reflect on how they are serving students and consider how they might change.

Business theory

In thinking about the value less selective HEIs offer potential students and how they market this value to them, it is helpful to consider concepts used to discuss business competitiveness. Although many in higher education resist applying business ideas to higher education, some of these ideas are relevant to higher education, especially at a time when there is such intense competition for students. This section highlights relevant business concepts and explains their importance for less selective HEIs, but first it is important to explain why a resistance to employing business concepts exists.

Many in higher education, especially faculty members, believe that HEIs should be solely or primarily focused on academic endeavors that include knowledge production and intellectual development. This makes supporting student goals such as career readiness or transforming their student experiences to meet the changing needs of students and employers counter to the purpose of higher education. Also counter to what some see as the purpose of higher education is the application of business concepts to HEIs. The use of business concepts suggests that HEIs are no different than businesses that have profit as their primary objective, and this is not aligned with the purpose of higher education. Despite these concerns, business concepts can be useful for less selective HEIs.

The jobs-to-be-done (JTBD) framework is applicable to HEIs in that it helps place the focus on what students are seeking by pursuing higher education. The JTBD framework includes a number of foundational principles that illustrate its central ideas. The first and primary principle is that 'people buy products and services to get a "job" done' (Ulwick, 2017). People possess a specific JTBD and then seek a product or service to complete the job. This means that the JTBD framework requires businesses to consider what job their product or service would perform for consumers as a guideline on designing the product or service. This is in line with another JTBD principle, 'success comes from making the "job", rather than the product or the customer, the unit of analysis', which further emphasises the importance of focusing on the job when considering developing a product or service (Ulwick, 2017). Finally, two of the principles address the importance of understanding the characteristics of the job that needs to be performed: 'A deep understanding of the customer's "job" makes marketing more effective and innovation far more predictable', and 'People want products and services that will help them get a job done better and/or more cheaply' (Ulwick, 2017). Effective marketing efforts rely upon an understanding of the job as well as the expectations of customers in terms of the importance they put on the quality and cost of the product or service.

One example of how a product or service fulfils customers' JTBD is the job of furnishing one's apartment quickly. Clay Christensen noted that when you mention this job to someone, 'over 95 percent of them say IKEA' (Gerdeman, 2016). IKEA has understood and effectively developed products that fulfil this JTBD. Joshua Kim offers another example provided by Clay Christensen: 'Christensen developed the Jobs to Be Done framework by considering why people buy milkshakes from fast food restaurants. His answer is that we "hire" milkshakes to do a "job". That job for morning commuters is to keep us entertained and stimulated during our drive to work. The thicker the milkshake and the narrower the straw the longer the milkshake does its job on our morning commute' (Kim, 2016). In terms of higher education, Kim notes that Christensen would say this about how higher education could use the JBTD framework: 'we should have a much clearer idea of the job that our students are hiring us to do' (Kim, 2016).

Christensen's insights are very helpful and demonstrates how less selective HEIs might employ the JTBD framework. Less selective HEIs should consider the different jobs their prospective students have compared to prospective students seeking admission to highly selective residential HEIs. Students pursuing degrees at less selective institutions typically have career readiness as their primary goal, which is in line with the primary reasons most US students pursue degrees across the higher education sector. This makes students' JTBD to secure meaningful work following graduation. Because students at less selective HEIs are typically from the region where the less selective HEI is located, the JTBD is often securing meaningful work in the region in which the HEI is located. This requires less selective HEIs to make connections with employers in the area to ensure students have internship opportunities, to provide channels for employer feedback on how HEIs are preparing their students for work, to ensure students are aware of employment opportunities in the areas, and to provide students an advantage when applying for their first post-graduation job.

Once the JTBD is understood, less selective HEIs should adapt their educational offerings and experiences to fulfil those jobs; this will be essential if less selective HEIs are to survive and thrive in the competitive enrolment environment. As Ulwick notes, it is important to understand expectations related to quality, cost, and speed (Ulwick, 2017), and this is especially true for less selective HEIs seeking potential applicants. Those who might attend these HEIs might also consider online education, which offers a more flexible format that would allow them to work while taking a full load of courses or live at home and save the cost of living on campus. The key is understanding what job students might seek a less selective HEI to do. Once this is identified, less selective HEIs should tailor their student experience to fulfil those jobs.

Another idea that comes from business focuses on developing a strong identity as articulated through the concepts of differentiation strategy and cost strategy. A business that adopts a differentiation strategy 'attempts to convince customers to pay a premium price for its goods or services by providing unique and desirable features' (Kennedy et al., 2020). Unique and desirable features are essential given that cost is higher than other products or services. Examples of a firm with a successful differentiation strategy is FedEx, which communicates this strategy through its slogan, 'When it absolutely, positively has to be there overnight [that] highlights the commitment to a very speedy delivery that differentiates FedEx from competitors such as UPS or Canada Post' (Kennedy et al., 2020). Another example is Coleman camping gear that sells for a higher price but promises higher quality. Coleman stresses the importance of high-quality gear because 'If camping equipment such as sleeping bags, lanterns, and stoves fail during a camping trip, the result will be, well, unhappy campers' (Kennedy et al., 2020).

Consumers are willing to pay higher prices, but the perceived value of the product or service must be high and deemed worthwhile. This is why it is important to keep in mind that 'Successful use of a differentiation strategy depends on not only offering unique features but also communicating the value of these features to potential customers' (Kennedy et al., 2020). If customers do not recognise the unique features of a product, and if they do not accept that they are valuable and worth the additional cost, then a differentiation strategy fails. This is because 'The big risk when using a differentiation strategy is that customers will not be willing to pay extra to obtain the unique features that a firm is trying to build its strategy around' (Kennedy et al., 2020). Cheaper versions may be seen as 'good enough' for the job that the consumer is trying to get done; the additional quality or uniqueness may be judged superfluous. Another risk is that other businesses may be able to imitate a similar uniqueness for a lower cost. While this product may be seen as lower quality, enough consumers may be drawn to it to undermine a differentiation strategy. Finally, efforts to communicate these features could be ineffective, leading to a failure to attract enough customers.

Another strategy that creates a strong identity is cost leadership. To employ a cost leadership strategy is to offer 'products or services with acceptable quality and features to a broad set of customers at a low price' (Kennedy et al., 2020). One example of an effective cost leadership strategy is Little Debbie snacks, which offers its products at lower prices than other snacks. Little Debbie's strategy can be explained as follows: 'Most consumers today would view the quality of Little Debbie cakes as a step below similar offerings from Entenmann's, but enough people believe that they offer acceptable quality that the brand is still around eight decades after its creation' (Kennedy et al., 2020). Little Debbie satisfies the JTBD for many consumers who want a snack but do not want to pay a lot for it. What they are seeking is a snack that offers 'good enough' quality to satisfy their desire. Walmart is another example of employing a cost leadership strategy. Its 'advertising slogans such as "Always Low Prices" and "Save Money. Live Better" communicate Walmart's emphasis on price slashing to potential customers' (Kennedy et al., 2020). Walmart is not trying to compete with higher-end stores, but it is seeking to appeal to consumers seeking low prices.

One risk of a low-cost strategy is that consumers might equate low cost with quality that is so low that it does not fulfil the job-to-be-done. Another risk is that profit margins are very low given the low cost of the product or service, which requires firms to achieve high sales volumes to ensure they have enough to sustain business operations (Kennedy et al., 2020).

Both the differentiation strategy and cost strategy are applicable to higher education. HEIs can seek a differentiation strategy by offering a unique experience that promises a particular outcome that is valuable to prospective students. Less selective HEIs will likely need differentiation strategies that enable them to be distinctive and communicate their value compared with other options that prospective students have that include completing a degree online, completing it part time without the residential experience, and not pursuing a degree at all. It is especially important that the residential experience deliver value given the numerous options available to complete degrees without the cost associated with a residential experience. Low-cost strategies are also applicable. If a less selective HEI's cost is lower than similar HEIs and comparable to other options such as online degrees, and it is able to maintain and communicate acceptable quality, it can successfully employ a low-cost strategy.

Another business concept relevant to the focus of this chapter is the idea of nonconsumption, which is often discussed in the context of disruptive innovation. Nonconsumption is 'the phenomenon where would-be consumers, who would otherwise benefit from purchasing particular products or services, go without because none on the market are affordable, simple, or convenient' (Ojomo, 2016). Another way to describe this concept is: 'Nonconsumption is the inability of an entity (person or organisation) to purchase and use (consume) a product or service required to fulfil an important Job to Be Done. This inability to purchase can arise from the product's cost, inconvenience, and complexity, along with a host of other factors – none of which tend to be limitations for the rich, skilled, and powerful in society' (Ojomo, 2016). The idea of nonconsumption is not that a need for a product or service (a job-to-be-done) does not exist, but that there are a lack of products or services that fulfil this need due to their cost, quality, convenience, or the fact that what is available provides more than is needed to fulfil the need. Businesses can identify and target nonconsumers by addressing their needs in this way: 'Market-creating innovations target nonconsumption by transforming complicated and expensive products into products that are simple and affordable so many more people in society can access them' (Ojomo, 2016). These new products and services transform nonconsumers into consumers.

In terms of higher education, there are many groups of potential students who could qualify as nonconsumers. High school students who are graduating soon and who do not plan to apply or attend a HEI are one group of nonconsumers. An EAB report noted a 10% drop in high school students who plan to pursue higher education following graduation. Numerous reasons are given for this drop that include cost, concerns about the value of a degree, a strong job market, and public concerns about the culture of HEIs (Donaher et al., 2023: 18). Another possibility, which will be discussed below, is that these nonconsumers cannot find an HEI that reflects their identity. Another example of nonconsumers are people who have completed some higher education but who have not completed. In 2021, 40,4 million people had completed some college credits but had not attained a degree (National Student Clearinghouse Research Center, 2023). Convincing them to reenroll will take offering them programmes that meet their needs.

Examples of less selective HEIs employing these concepts

The section above highlights the applicability of the business concepts to HEIs, especially less selective ones. This section will provide examples of HEIs employing these concepts, both new HEIs and existing HEIs. Given all of the challenges facing HEIs and the number of closures, mergers, and budget cuts, it seems odd that there would be new HEIs opening. Yet in recent years a number of HEIs have been created, and most have distinctive identities that differentiate them from other HEIs. That is, they are employing differentiation strategies, cost strategies, and fulfil jobs-to-be-done that are not being fulfilled by other HEIs. Additionally, existing less selective HEIs have adopted some of these concepts in an effort to thrive in a challenging environment.

The Reverend Dennis Holtschneider, president of the Association of Catholic Colleges and Universities, comments on the closing of some Catholic HEIs while others opened. He describes how many Catholic HEIs were created to educate (immigrant populations in the North-East) have dropped significantly, leading many Catholic HEIs to struggle, while at the same time a number of new HEIs have emerged (Weissman, 2024). He proposes that to survive in the current higher education landscape, 'you have to pick a strategy that makes you different from the rest, and for all five of these [new HEIs], that's true. They're claiming very specific spaces… These are kind of new attempts to be very specific in the marketplace for a need they believe exists' (Weissman, 2024). His advice reflects the need for less selective HEIs to adopt differentiation strategies.

Catholic Polytechnic University (CPU) is one example (Weissman, 2024). Its mission is to 'promote the intersection of faith and science as seen through the lens of faithful Catholic teachings. Catholic Polytechnic is the fulcrum at the intersection of Faith and Science seeking to promote and combine a deep quest for scientific, tech, engineering and business expertise with the enduring truths of the Catholic faith' (Catholic Polytechnic University, 2024). CPU launched its first programme in September 2020, a cybersecurity certificate, and will enroll its first students in its Bachelor of Science and Master of Science computer science programmes in fall 2024 (Catholic Polytechnic University, 2024). CPU offers a distinctive experience where 'students, faculty and researchers do not compromise Catholic principles to conduct science and engineering research. Catholic Polytechnic will be a strong voice in a world that often suppresses religious expression' (Catholic Polytechnic University, 2024). CPU will certainly attract a unique set of students who are interested in conducting science and engineering research that aligns with the Catholic faith, and it remains to be seen whether this new HEI will attract learners in the numbers needed to sustain it, but it is an interesting example of an HEI that provides a unique experience in line with the differentiation strategy. It will certainly provide a unique experience that other HEIs are not capable of providing and may convince high school students who were considering not pursuing education to apply or who have completed some college and were not satisfied with their previous experience.

This is also true of Catholic trade schools that Weissman writes about. These schools are designed to offer 'a new path for students who don't want to take on crippling debt from traditional four-year colleges by training them in a skill, cultivating their faith, and doing it all affordably' (Bukuras, 2024). The Santiago Trade School's mission is: 'Built upon the solid foundations of work, study & friendship, Santiago Trade School forms young men into excellent Christian tradesmen. We are a community committed to the tough work of gaining practical jobsite wisdom as well as the spiritual wisdom that unites men to Christ' (Santiago Trade School, 2024). Students begin their day with prayer at the chapel and then complete trade instruction and religious activities throughout the day. This unique experience, which is also lower cost than comparable programmes, brings together two important JTBD for students: preparing them to secure employment and doing so in a way that strengthens their faith.

Another new Catholic trade school offers a similar approach. The Harmel Academy of the Trades, which describes itself as a 'residential, Catholic, post-secondary, trade school for men', has a similar mission that 'Helps students grow in holiness through a deeper relationship with Jesus Christ' while preparing 'students to be technical experts in their chosen trade' and equipping them 'with the skills and support to lead their future families' (Harmel Academy, 2024). Its curriculum includes a humanities component, which is described as 'humanities for men with bloody knuckles', along with traditional trade fields related to manufacturing and machining (Harmel Academy, 2024). This HEI, with more traditional humanities coursework, provides another experience that is unique and satisfies a JTBD of potential students. Given the number of Catholic HEIs that have closed over the past decade, the support of the Catholic Church for these new, less selective HEIs is surprising at first; however, they make sense given how they employ differentiation strategies, and in one case a low-cost strategy, to satisfy a JTBD.

Another new HEI that reflects a differentiation strategy and seeks to fulfil a JTBD for a specific population is Outer Coast, a two-year, less selective HEI in Sitka, Alaska. Outer Coast has a liberal arts identity, will enroll 20 students beginning fall 2024, and is placing particular emphasis on 'reaching Alaskan students, and especially Alaska Native Indigenous students and rural Alaskans for whom opportunities for access to higher ed are really limited' (Koenig, 2024). Outer Coast's programming reflects what is important to students in the region and includes requirements to speak the Tlingit language and study the Tlingit culture, and the culture of other Native Alaskans (Koening, 2024). The identity of Outer Coast reflects areas that have been neglected in the past. Sheldon Harris, the former HEI whose location Outer Coast uses, and the boarding school from which Sheldon Harris started, 'were founded to educate Alaska Native students as part of "a deeply assimilationist institution'" (Koening, 2024). Outer Coast offers an alternative that is more aligned with the residents in the area. By doing this, Outer Coast is differentiating itself from alternatives and addressing a job-to-be-done: provide an in-person, residential education that reflects the culture of the Tlingit culture and other Native Alaskans.

Existing HEIs have also adopted strategies to ensure survival. One example is Hampshire College. Hampshire College is a private liberal arts college that has existed for over five decades and can be classified as a less selective HEI. It was on the brink of closing but made some dramatic changes, one of which was changing its curriculum and committing to its mission, which is 'to foster a lifelong passion for learning, enquiry, and ethical citizenship that inspires students to contribute to knowledge, justice, and positive change in the world and, by doing so, to transform higher education' (Hampshire College, 2024). The curricular change involved 'doing away with majors and departments and instead offering curriculum focused on addressing the world's pressing issues, such as climate change and racial injustice' (McLean, 2024). This is an unusual approach for HEIs because its majors focus on problems rather than specific disciplines and offers students a lot more freedom designing their course of study than at other HEIs. A curriculum of this type attracts students who are interested in focusing their studies on the most critical issues facing society. Edward Wingenbach, president of Hampshire College, explained the importance of doing this: 'If we're going to be successful as an autonomous institution and reverse these financial challenges, it had to be by fundamentally committing to the mission and reinvigorating Hampshire's distinctiveness' (McLean, 2024).

Hampshire College employed a differentiation strategy and committed to fulfilling a very specific job-to-be-done, providing students opportunities to address issues that they care about. It took a much different approach from what other HEIs with similar characteristics were doing. It appears that this approach is paying off. Hampshire College experienced a 59,5% enrolment increase from fall 2021 to fall 2023, as well as a 82,7% application increase from fall 2020 to fall 2023 (McLean, 2024). This highlights how existing HEIs might address declining enrolment.

Gettysburg College is another existing less selective HEI that has implemented changes to address enrolment concerns and concerns about the return on investment of a degree. Although there are many reasons students pursue degrees, one survey notes that 51% 'say they enrolled in higher education for higher earning potential, 45 percent are looking to access better job benefits and 40 percent say their field of study requires a degree' (Mowreader, 2024). In recognition of this, Gettysburg College created a coherent co-curricular path to prepare students for their futures by creating five guided pathways: 'Creativity, Entrepreneurship and Innovation Pathway; Global Citizenship and Intercultural Fluency Pathway; Justice and Community Change Pathway; Leadership,

Teamwork and Collaboration Pathway; and Career Development Pathway' (Mowreader, 2024). Through pathway experiences and advising, students develop 'enduring skills that align with their passions and the expectations of tomorrow's employers' (Mowreader, 2024). Gettysburg College's new programme meets a JTBD of many potential students, which distinguishes it from other less selective HEIs.

Implications for higher education

Less selective HEIs would benefit from considering the business concepts mentioned in this chapter given the challenging environment they face. Although not mentioning these concepts explicitly, Colin Koproske captures the ideas behind them when he writes that HEIs must 'Ensure your strengths are relevant, distinctive, widely experienced by students, and provable' (Koproske, 2024). Ensuring institutional strengths are relevant is to know what JTBD potential students are seeking to complete and tailoring those strengths to fulfil that JTBD. Distinctive and provable relates to a differentiation strategy that provides a unique experience. The distinctiveness should not be a boutique programme within the HEI, but it should be part of the HEI's identity and widely available. Finally, an HEI's strengths must be successfully communicated to potential students.

This last point, about successful communication, highlights the importance of marketing. Rob Zinkan demonstrates the marketing gap that many HEIs display when creating new strategic plans. He notes: 'In our study, we found nearly two-thirds of plans (63 percent) lacked any formal market research. It's part of the reason why strategic plans include more planning – an internal concentration on items an institution can control – than strategy, a set of choices made knowing your position in a dynamic marketplace' (Zinkan, 2023). It is essential that less selective HEIs not only make changes aligned with the business concepts in this chapter but that they effectively communicate their identity to potential students.

References

Alexander, B. (2024). Starting 2024 with all kinds of academic cuts. *Bryan Alexander*. Available at: https://bryanalexander.org/economics/starting-2024-with-all-kinds-of-academic-cuts/. Date accessed: 12 March 2024.

Brenan, M. (2023). Americans' Confidence in Higher Education Down Sharply. *Gallup*, 11 July 2023. Available at: https://news.gallup.com/poll/508352/americans-confidence-higher-education-down-sharply.aspx. Date accessed: 23 January 2024.

Bukuras, J. (2024). New Catholic trade schools are sprouting up across the country – here are four. *Catholic World Report*, 2 January 2024. Available at: https://www.catholicworldreport.com/2024/01/02/new-catholic-trade-schools-are-sprouting-up-across-the-country-here-are-four/. Date accessed: 11 March 2024.

Castillo, E. & Welding, L. (2024). Tracking College Closures and Mergers. *Best Colleges*, 1 April 2024. Available at: https://www.bestcolleges.com/research/closed-colleges-list-statistics-major-closures/. Date accessed: 3 April 2024.

Catholic Polytechnic University. (2024). *Catholic Polytechnic University*. Available at: https://catholicpolytechnic.org/. Date accessed: 12 March 2024.

Donaher, L., Dodson, A., Koppenheffer, M. & Royall, P.K. (2023). Recruiting 'Gen P': 6 Insights into How the Pandemic Has Altered College Search Behavior from EAB's Survey of 20,000+ Students. *EAB*. Available at: https://chat.eab.com/Recruiting-Gen-P-Insight-Paper?aliId=eyJpIjoiY3pNVkx0eW1WNjFhQWxvUSIsInQiOiJGSzUyemdFWUlvSllxM1VMeFZIdUhBPT0ifQ%253D%253D. Date accessed: 1 March 2024.

Hanson, A., Salerno, C., Sigelman, M., de Zeeuw, M. & Moret, S. (2024). Talent Disrupted: College Graduates, Underemployment, and the Way Forward. Burning Glass Institute and Strada Education Foundation. Available at: https://www.burningglassinstitute.org/research/underemployment. Date accessed: 17 February 2025.

Hanson, M. (2024). Average Student Loan Debt for a Bachelor's Degree. *Education Data Initiative*. Available at: https://educationdata.org/average-debt-for-a-bachelors-degree Date accessed: 17 February 2025.

Gerdeman, D. (2016). What Job Would Consumers Want to Hire a Product To Do? *Working Knowledge: Business Research for Business Leaders*, 3 October 2016. Available at: https://hbswk.hbs.edu/item/clay-christensen-the-theory-of-jobs-to-be-done. Date accessed: 12 March 2024.

Hampshire College. (2024). *Mission and Vision*. Available at: https://www.hampshire.edu/hampshire-experience/mission-and-vision#:~:text=The%20mission%20of%20Hampshire%20College,so%2C%20to%20transform%20higher%20education. Date accessed: 13 March 2024.

Harmel Academy. (2024) *Curriculum*. Available at: https://www.harmelacademy.org/curriculum/ Date accessed: 13 March 2024.

Harmel Academy. (2024). *Why We Exist*. Available at: https://www.harmelacademy.org/why-we-exist/. Date accessed: 13 March 2024.

Horn, M. (2024). Selective Universities Won't Be Disrupted. *Forbes*, 2 April 2024. Available at: https://www.forbes.com/sites/michaelhorn/2024/04/02/selective-universities-wont-be-disrupted/?sh=49dadb0e4a38. Date accessed: 6 April 2024.

Kennedy, R., with Jamison, E, Simpson, J., Kumar, P., Ayenda, K., Kemp, A., Awate, K. & Manning, K. (2020). *Strategic Management*. University Libraries Virginia Tech. Available at: https://pressbooks.lib.vt.edu/strategicmanagement/. Date accessed: 3 March 2024.

Kim, J. (2016). The Jobs To Be Done Framework and 'Competing Against Luck'. *Inside Higher Ed*, 7 December 2016. Available at: https://www.insidehighered.com/blogs/technology-and-learning/jobs-be-done-framework-and-competing-against-luck Date accessed: 4 March 2024.

Koening, R. (2024). In Coastal Alaska, 2 Visions for the Future of Higher Education. *EdSurge*, 29 March 2024. Available at: https://www.edsurge.com/news/2024-03-29-in-coastal-alaska-2-visions-for-the-future-of-higher-education. Date accessed: 4 March 2024.

Koproske, C. (2024). Stand out to today's skeptical students in 3 steps. *EAB*, 13 March 2024. Available at: https://eab.com/resources/blog/strategy-blog/todays-skeptical-students/ Date accessed: 20 March 2024.

McLean, D. (2024). Back from the brink, Hampshire College is nearing financial viability. *Higher Ed Dive*, 20 March 2024. Available at: https://www.highereddive.com/news/hampshire-college-turnaround-closure-finances/710520/. Date accessed: 25 March 2024.

Mowreader, A. (2024). Survey: Why Students Enroll and Why They Persist. *Inside Higher Ed*, 23 February 2024. Available at: https://www.insidehighered.com/news/student-success/academic-life/2024/02/23/student-survey-gauges-importance-college-degree Date accessed: 20 March 2024.

Mullin, C. (2024). Teetering on the edge: The enrollment cliff nears as higher education hangs in the balance. *Lumina Foundation*. Available at: https://www.luminafoundation.org/news-and-views/teetering-on-the-edge-the-enrollment-cliff-nears-as-higher-education-hangs-in-the-balance/ Date accessed: 17 February 2025.

National Student Clearinghouse Research Center. (2023). *Some College, No Credential* Student Outcomes: Annual Progress Report – Academic Year 2021/22. *National Student Clearing House*. Available at: https://nscresearchcenter.org/some-college-no-credential/ Date accessed: 20 March 2024.

Ojomo, E. (2016). Nonconsumption is your fiercest competition–and it's winning. *Christensen Institute*, 27 July 2016. Available at: https://www.christenseninstitute.org/blog/non-consumption-is-your-fiercest-competition-and-its-winning/. Date accessed: 24 March 2024.

Ojomo, E. (2016). Targeting nonconsumption: The most viable path to growth. *Christensen Institute*, 8 October 2019. Available at: https://www.christenseninstitute.org/blog/targeting-nonconsumption-the-most-viable-path-to-growth/. Date accessed: 24 March 2024.

Sanchez, O. (2024). Experts predicted dozens of colleges would close in 2023 – and they were right. *Hechinger Report*, 12 January 2024. Available at: https://hechingerreport.org/experts-predicted-dozens-of-colleges-would-close-in-2023-and-they-were-right/. Date accessed: 15 January 2024.

Santiago Trade School. *Santiago Trade School*. Available from: https://www.santiagotradeschool.com/. Date accessed: 12 March 2024.

Santiago Trade School. (2025). *A Day at Santiago Trade School*. Available at: https://www.santiagotradeschool.com/a-day-at-sts. Accessed at: 12 March 2024.

Ulwick, T. (2017). What Is Jobs-to-be-Done? *jobs-to-be-done.com*, 28 February 2017. Available at: https://jobs-to-be-done.com/what-is-jobs-to-be-done-fea59c8e39eb#:~:text=JOBS%2DTO%2DBE%2DDONE%20THEORY%20is%20comprised%20of%20a,get%20a%20%E2%80%9Cjob%E2%80%9D%20done. Date accessed: 4 March 2024.

Weissman, S. (2024). A Rise in Hyperspecialized Catholic Colleges and Trade Schools. *Inside Higher Ed*, 8 February 2024. Available at: https://www.insidehighered.com/news/institutions/religious-colleges/2024/02/08/new-catholic-colleges-and-trade-schools-emerge. Date accessed: 12 March 2024.

Zinkan, R. (2023). Your Institution Is Only Distinctive If Others Take Notice. *Inside Higher Ed*, 6 December 2023. Available at: https://www.insidehighered.com/opinion/blogs/call-action/2023/12/06/how-marketing-leaders-can-help-institutions-distinguish. Date accessed: 1 April 2024.

CHAPTER 5
A vernacular reframing of professionalism: *Ubuntu* in the education of the next generation of professionals

Lionel Green-Thompson, Ann George, and Mantoa Mokhachane

Abstract

Professionalism exists when society permits a group of educated people to self-regulate, establishing a social contract that implies accountability for graduate health professionals. However, power asymmetries between healthcare professionals and communities limit community agency to hold professionals accountable, necessitating alternative frameworks prioritising interconnectedness. The calabash metaphor, embodying *ubuntu* principles through vernacular expressions of *letsema, lebollo, mbokodo,* and *ugqirha,* provides a framework for understanding professional development as community centred.

This chapter draws on a conceptual framework integrating social accountability and professional identity formation constructed through the synthesis of prior research on community expectations of healthcare professionals and student experiences during social upheaval. The framework was presented at a national workshop with 30 health professions educators who expressed their conceptualisations of Professional Identity Formation (PIF) using vernacular languages. Analysis of 24 workshop outputs identified three perspectives that inform professional development: Professional habitus, Identity formation, and Becoming.

The implication of this work is a focus on role modelling in higher education to enhance 'graduateness'. Social accountability, as a relationship between communities and higher education institutions, and *ubuntu* as the interconnectedness of people in a community, offers a vernacular framing of professionalism.

Keywords: professionalism; graduate attributes; power; advocacy; higher education.

Introduction

South Africa needs holistic graduates who are more than the sum of the knowledge they accumulate. Graduates must possess professionalism that capacitates them to act as local change agents and global citizens engaging in an increasingly uncertain and complex world.

Professionalism, as a graduate attribute, offers a heuristic to understand the nature of graduates from our higher-education system. Ballim (2022: 188) used the term 'graduateness' to describe the 'attributes and generic competencies of a graduate that amount to more than merely an ability to pass examinations'. Freire (1970) conceptualised education for the common good as a process which conscientises the learners through the transformative nature of the learning process. As a conscientising process, professionalism, as one part of professional identity formation (PIF) during the higher education experience, may facilitate the emergence of 'graduateness'.

This chapter explores the role of community and professionalism in the social contract implied in graduateness, drawing on research on social accountability (Green-Thompson, 2014), and professionalism and Professional Identity Formation (PIF) (Mokhachane et al., 2022; Mokhachane et al., 2023a; Mokhachane et al., 2023b). Green-Thompson (2014) used a grounded theory approach to listen to four rural and four urban communities in contextually located focus-group discussions. This work connected *ubuntu* to the expectations communities have of their doctors. Mokhachane applied a phenomenological approach to understanding the impact of social upheaval (#FeesMustFall) on the Professional Identity Formation (PIF) of graduating medical doctors. The metaphor of the calabash captured the sense of communal responsibility and the inherent contribution of *ubuntu* to students' experiences. Mokhachane's work on Professional Identity Formation (PIF) was presented and tested in a workshop at the 2023 Southern African Association of Health Educationalists conference. At the workshop, participants conveyed their conceptions of Professional Identity Formation (PIF) using vernacular and traditional expressions. Retrospective consent and ethics approval through the University of Cape Town Human Research Human Research Ethics Committee were sought after realising how rich and relevant the workshop data was for the health educationalists.

We converged the findings from our research and the Professional Identity Formation (PIF) workshop to construct the narrative presented here. Our research experiences and reflections may impact higher education broadly and the education of professionals specifically. The chapter concludes with an *ubuntu* framework that fosters representation and the development of context-sensitive curricula.

Literature review

The value-driven concept of professionalism is interlinked with social accountability through a contract with communities (Pearson et al., 2015).

The partnership between healthcare professionals and communities may thus be operationalised in a social contract. However, power imbalances exist between communities and healthcare professionals (Pearson et al., 2015). Public professionalism, which encompasses abiding by an ethical code, self-regulation, and accountability, is one of three key themes that characterise professionalism by medical educators. The other themes are the interpersonal, meeting patients' demands through self-sacrifice and service delivery, and the intrapersonal, where standards are maintained through a commitment to lifelong learning (Pearson et al., 2015).

The World Health Organization expanded 'social accountability' to include responsibility – an awareness of societies' priority health needs, and 'social responsiveness' – identifying societies' priority health needs (Pearson et al., 2015). Social accountability for healthcare professionals should be linked with higher-education institutions' goal of meeting societal health and other needs. The resulting combined responsibility will require higher-education institutions to produce graduates accountable to the societies they serve.

A phenomenological study with an autoethnographic component, where Mokhachane was both the researcher and a participant, identified two major contributions to professionalism and Professional Identity Formation (PIF). First, the study highlighted that professionalism lacks humaneness (*ubuntu*), resulting in patients being disrespected, disregarded, judged, and excluded from managing their health and well-being (Mokhachane et al., 2022; Mokhachane et al., 2023a; Mokhachane et al., 2023b). 'Too often, patients' needs and desires are secondary to the technical expertise of the physician, whose focus may be more on addressing a disease than on understanding the patient's experience' (Smith, 2016: 722). *Ubuntu/botho* is understood as 'morality, humanness and personhood' (Letseka, 2013: 337).

Second, Mokhachane's work highlighted the contribution of communities – that is, how one is raised and prior experiences of the healthcare system – to the development of professional identity. Childhood values shape individuals before they enter medical training (Mokhachane et al., 2022). Who we are and the values we bring into medical training determine how we deal with the negative experiences we may face in the clinical setting. African cultural expressions resonate with the experiences of those undergoing training to become medical professionals in a South African setting.

Concerns raised by Martimianakis et al. (2015) regarding the void of humanistic values in the hidden medical education curriculum were echoed in Mokhachane's work (Mokhachane et al., 2023a). To counteract the lack of humaneness/*botho/ubuntu* in contemporary and future graduates, Mokhachane developed an *ubuntu* perspective on professionalism using the five-finger collective theory (Mbigi & Maree, 2005). The five fingers represent: respect – knowing that everyone in front of you is a person who has a story that needs to be heard; dignity – making patients feel human and paying attention to their stories; compassion – being supportive, empathetic and caring; solidarity – fighting for justice with one voice; and survival – having a contextual response (Mokhachane et al., 2023a).

Professionalism is intricately connected to Professional Identity Formation (PIF) (Holden et al., 2012). For a medical student to connect and identify with the medical profession, professionals must embody *ubuntu/botho*. Metaphorically, the calabash, an important gourd used throughout Africa, embodies *ubuntu/botho*. The calabash has a soft centre that develops into a hardened exterior (Ellece, 2010; Mokhachane et al., 2022). The gourd feeds, quenches thirst, and symbolises community support and celebrations (Mokhachane et al., 2022). Medical students start being socialised as legitimate peripheral participants, having a 'soft centre' and emerging as professionals with a hardened exterior; their Professional Identity Formation (PIF) thus mirrors a calabash (Mokhachane et al., 2022). After training, a student becomes *ugqirha* – they resemble a calabash through the attributes of feeding, healing, and empowering communities. They emulate their mothers, who would balance the calabash full of water or food on their heads, leaving their hands free to carry more (Mokhachane et al., 2022).

Calabashes are used during *letsema*, celebratory occasions when communities work together for the benefit of others. For example, a community can assist someone in that community or another with ploughing during planting seasons or building a house. At the end of *letsema*, those who came to give a hand in making someone succeed are fed by the host. At the end of the meal, a calabash filled with traditional beer or water is passed around, creating oneness in the community (Mokhachane et al., 2022).In the case of professionalism and Professional Identity Formation (PIF), *letsema* (Letseka, 2013) could be viewed as the medical education community, namely clinicians, other healthcare workers, and patients working together to assist students in acquiring these attributes (Bosman, 2022; Mokhachane et al., 2022; Nkgudi et al., 2022; Setlhodi, 2023). The calabash is linked to various cultures throughout Africa, e.g. Southern Africa and Nigeria.

Mokhachane equated *lebollo* to trainees' socialisation for legitimate peripheral participation in communities of practice (Mokhachane et al., 2022). *Lebollo* is social indigenous education that predates Western civilisation and was intricately interwoven with 'social, cultural, artistic and recreation life of an ethnic group' (Letseka, 2013: 241). *Lebollo* is education or societal development that prepares young people for manhood and womanhood (Maharasoa & Maharaswa, 2004). Maharasoa and Maharaswa (2004: 107) 'compared fundamentals guiding lebollo with those of universities concentrating' on convergence and divergence. This comparison was sparked by the debate on contemporary higher-education graduates who are perceived to be unfit for the purpose of graduating; in other words, lacking graduateness (Maharasoa & Maharaswa, 2004).

In the traditional sense, *lebollo* is regarded as the pinnacle of socialisation in the community of practice. It is regarded as the key that opens the door or rite of passage into these communities of practice (Mokhachane et al., 2022). Education in *lebollo* includes *bohlweki* (purity), *thuto-kelello* (cognitive engagement), *makgabane* (virtues), *leruo* (economic development), *makunutu* (confidentiality), *bonatla* (warriorship), *boqapi le bokgeleke* (eloquence), *borapedi* (spirituality), *lenyora la tsebo* (appreciation of knowledge), and *tlhompho ya maemo* (respect for social structures) (Maharasoa & Maharaswa, 2004). These teachings and attributes are crucial not just for health professions education, but for all higher-education graduates.

Reflection: the components of *ubuntu* philosophy

Ubuntu and the accompanying aphorism of *umuntu ngunmuntu ngabantu* (a person is a person through other people) promote a philosophy that allows us to experience a deeper sense of African humanism within higher education and across society. Drawing from work in health professions education, we argue that graduates need appropriate Professional Identity Formation (PIF). This reflection explores the intersection of professionalism as a component of professional identity, and social accountability as a reflection of community participation and agency. The reflection is divided into three sections illustrating components essential to implementing an *ubuntu* philosophy within higher education: community, the social contract, and PIF.

Community – definition and agency

Bhagwan (2017) conceptualised community engagement within the higher education sector in two ways. He claimed that how one defines community is an essential feature of effective engagement: 'How do we interact with the communities, however we define the communities. And for us, it's mainly rural communities, mainly disadvantaged groups, mainly poor communities' (Bhagwan, 2017: 176). He further proposed that community engagement presupposes interaction with communities: 'My understanding of community engagement is it's about connecting the university with community, not just in a superficial way, but quite profoundly' (Bhagwan, 2017: 178). These conceptualisations inform the discussions which follow.

Community engagement in the education of health professionals is essential to ensure that communities can exercise agency, while also ensuring students learn the practice of cultural humility. Both aspects are required to fulfil the social contract in the interest of the common good. Walker et al. (2009) foregrounded the common good as an essential approach to professional education to explicitly alleviate poverty in a developing context, such as South Africa. The authors argue for an explicit focus on reducing poverty through professional education with two dynamic and connected components: the expanded capabilities of those being educated and their capacities to enhance the capabilities of poor and disadvantaged communities (Walker et al., 2009). Mpuangnan and Ntombela (2023) believed that this community empowerment manifests in shaping curricula through active engagement. These authors posited that this community engagement (promoting empowerment) fosters collaboration characterised by active participation, which, in return, may impact the community positively (Mpuangnan & Ntombela, 2023).

Community empowerment may be enhanced when professionals approach any engagement with diverse communities with a sense of cultural humility; this approach facilitates public engagement through active and empathic listening (Lokugamage et al., 2020). Cultural humility challenges implicit biases and fosters an open-minded professionalism capable of reordering the complex power imbalances in healthcare. However, it may restore the symmetry of the relationship (Lokugamage et al., 2020).

Health professionals' education and higher education, in general, are often imposed on communities for student learning or research without community involvement. If we apply the definition of community noted earlier and the nature of the engagement with communities is clear, we can expect that the current asymmetrical power relationships may be reconfigured.

It is essential that empowering communities becomes a focus of the education of professionals, especially health professionals. Empowerment requires curricula to be built around collaborative approaches to community engagement rather than acting upon a community because of asymmetrical relationships of knowledge and power (Walker et al., 2009). In the case of the delivery of health care and other services, the systems through which these are responded to may prevent empowerment because they operate from a model of deficit and need rather than recognising the capacity of communities (McKnight, 1997).

McKnight (1997) reasoned that substantial capacities already existent within communities should be harnessed. He proposed that communities be given the capacity to determine what they need. He described three levels of enhanced community engagement: system outreach (the system decides what needs to be done), volunteerism (co-opting the community without recognition), and citizen advisory groups (McKnight, 1997).

In the initial rungs of the citizen empowerment ladder proposed by Arnstein (1969), communities have little meaningful empowerment. He claimed that community involvement only becomes meaningful when citizens are empowered. McKnight (1997) argued that the lack of meaningful community empowerment results from the system's practice of creating a one-sided definition of needs, and then unilaterally deciding on the subsequent intervention. The consequence of this often leaves a community unaltered at the end of an intervention, still dependent and disempowered (McKnight, 1997; Arnstein, 1969). Laverack (2006) called for greater collaboration between professionals holding power and the people in communities. This collaboration requires the dispersal of power through accepting the community's pursuit of effective participation and the willingness of power blocs, such as professional communities, to cede some level of power (Laverack, 2006).

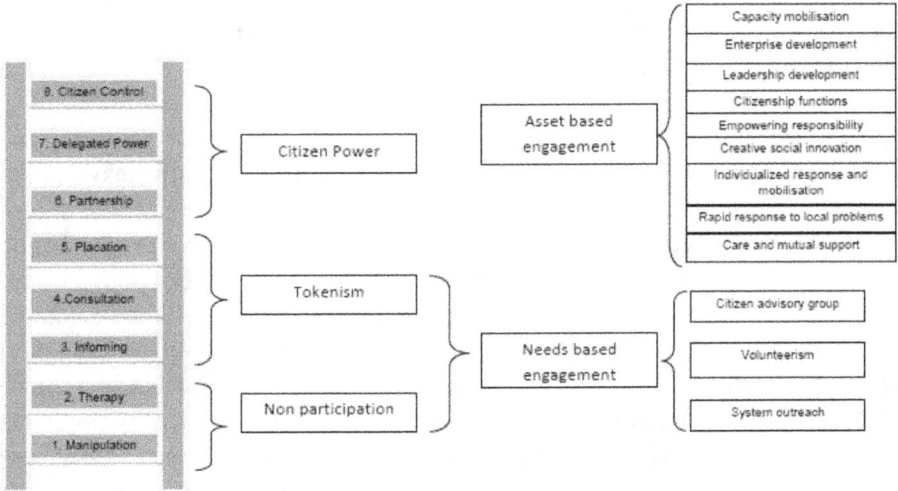

FIGURE 5.1: The relationship between Arnstein's ladder of citizen participation and McKnight's approach to community engagement

Adapted from Arnstein (1969) and Mcknight (1997) by Green-Thompson, 2014

Figure 5.1 synthesises ideas from both Arnstein (1969) and McKnight (1997). The ladder represents the progressive achievement of authentic empowerment. Arnstein (1969) suggested that when a system engages with a community, there is a danger of not progressing to full citizen empowerment unless the commitment to empowerment is explicit. In the healthcare environment, the earlier steps of engagement are nothing more than manipulation or therapy. Asymmetrical relationships of power determine the nature of the earlier rungs of Arnstein's ladder. For effective community engagement, the aim must be to reach the higher rungs of the ladder where citizens can demonstrate their capacity and share the authority to direct and contribute effectively to planning any required interventions (Arnstein, 1969; McKnight, 1997).

McKnight's contribution is a recognition that communities have a range of assets through which they can maintain a level of function and engagement. Bhagwan (2017), in his conceptualisation of dynamic and generative community engagement, allowed the co-creation of solutions in a space where there is a clear shift of power. Communities may bring a similar perspective to and relationship with higher education. Essentially, both the ladder of participation and the asset-based approach allow us to build community engagement premised on a community becoming empowered to be fully collaborative. Moving from a deficit-based to an asset-based approach unlocks possibilities that cannot be discovered in asymmetrical power plays. An asset-based approach resonates with social accountability by ensuring the community is an equal part of the conversation as others, like professional associations, policymakers, and practitioners.

Social accountability is the obligation that higher-education institutions (especially medical schools) have to train health professionals that meet the region or country's health priorities (Boelen et al., 2012). Boelen et al. (2019) proposed a partnership pentagram in which the partners share responsibility equally for building a health system that meets the needs of the community in which these institutions are located. The partners are the community, policymakers, health professionals, health managers, and academic institutions.

Green-Thompson (2014) explored the perceptions of communities (people not in need of care at the time of the group discussions) about their understanding of social accountability and the extent to which they may expect this from the doctors who treat them when they are unwell. The overwhelming reflection from the community was their inability to express how their doctors should be accountable. Instead, they reflected on their vulnerability within the consultation. The community constructed accountability as engaging with a good doctor. They expressed this as a need to be treated with 'love and respect' within the doctor-patient relationship, especially within the consultation. This 'love and respect' was represented as a shared space in which the professional allowed a collaborative approach to education and management of the disease presented to them in the consultation. In addition, communities speculated about what was being taught to their doctors. They questioned whether doctors were taught enough about people and their lived realities. Indeed, they asked why medical students were not being taught about *ubuntu* while they were at university (Green-Thompson, 2014). Green-Thompson framed these relationships within the context of *ubuntu* (Figure 5.2).

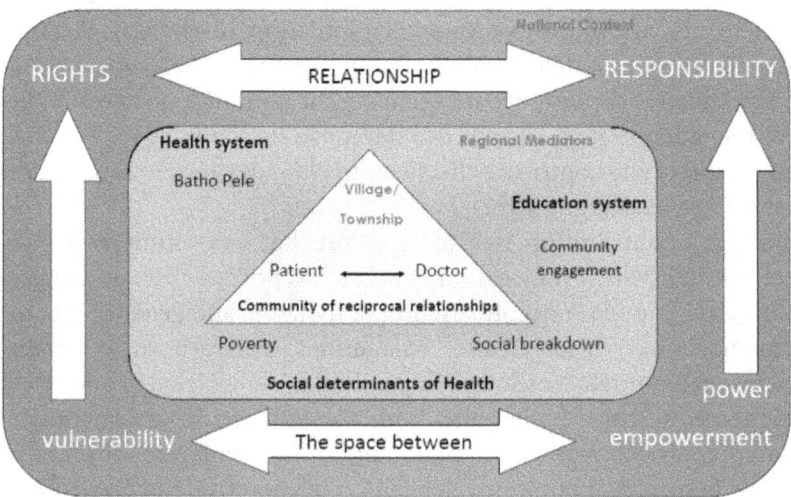

FIGURE 5.2: Social accountability – an *ubuntu* framework demonstrating the relationships between local and national contexts

Green-Thompson, 2014

The *ubuntu* framework recognises the all-embracing nature of African humanism (Figure 5.2). The outer layer (darker blue) emphasises that *ubuntu* governs our universal relationships, acknowledging the space between community vulnerability and the power held by professionals, such as doctors. Empowerment is positioned as the alternative to community vulnerability. In the central triangle (yellow), there is a recognition that the patient and the doctor are dynamic participants in 'a community of reciprocal relationships'.

In the intervening space (lighter blue), several systems are seen to potentially mediate the relationship between this community of reciprocal relationships and the embracing *ubuntu* framing of society. The social determinants of health highlighted by the community members included a deep understanding of the role of poverty and the consequences of social breakdown in their wellness (and disease). Communities also referred to the health system and the need to return to the civil service commitment of *batho pele* (people first) to enhance their experience of dignity within health care and their interactions with doctors. The intersection of the social determinants of health and the health system may be facilitated through health professions education that values community engagement. Community engagement brings to the fore the importance of *ubuntu* and the capacity for including diverse approaches to learning and teaching (Mpuangnan & Ntombela, 2023).

Ubuntu addresses the essence of being human, celebrating community while respecting individuality, as illustrated by some greetings. For example, *sawubona* in isiZulu translates to 'I see you', meaning 'I recognise you and I respect you'. Relatedness, sharing, forgiveness, community, dependability, and trust are all important principles in the *ubuntu* philosophy (Van Breda, 2019; Mayaka & Truell, 2021). Experiences as a collective are valued without negating the rights of individuals (Letseka, 2013). With *ubuntu*, identity is formed through relationships, stressing the importance of community (Lewis, 2010). Tutu and Biko, both philosophers in their own right, believed that Africa's contribution to the world is humanity (Biko, 1987; Hailey, 2008).

Ubuntu philosophy is a widely held philosophy in sub-Saharan Africa, with multiple perspectives and dimensions of expression. The post-1994 South African government employed *ubuntu* as a social theory in every aspect of governance, namely in healthcare through *batho pele* (people first), education, the legal system, and others (Muxe Nkondo, 2007; Metz, 2011). *Ubuntu* played a major role in smoothly transitioning from apartheid to the new South African government (Lewis, 2010). *Ubuntu* plays a crucial role in social work, marketing, leadership, theology, and ethics (Gathogo, 2008; Curle, 2015; Van Breda, 2019).

The practice of *ubuntu* echoes in the work of Paulo Freire (*Pedagogy of the Oppressed*) with potential consequences for the lives of those on the margins of society. Abdi believed Freire's philosophy has 'trans-spatial and transcultural connections with the humanist Ubuntu' (Abdi, 2022). *Ubuntu* and Freire's philosophies humanise everyday life, ontologies, education, and learning (Abdi, 2022). The transformative tenets of *ubuntu*, respect, dignity, solidarity, compassion, survival, and several other values are similar to Freire's reflective and reflexive transformative thoughts (Mbigi & Maree, 2005; Abdi, 2022). Our current medical education spaces are sometimes experienced as oppressive and dehumanising and need revolutionary measures to change the status quo (Mokhachane et al., 2022; Mokhachane et al., 2023a). These two philosophies bring us closer together while promoting respect for everyone, irrespective of their social standing, equalising communities with their healthcare professionals. The Freireian and *ubuntu* philosophies (counter-oppression and inclusive in theory) adopt a liberating stance that enhances humanisation (Abdi, 2022). The humanising nature of *ubuntu* philosophy renders it an anti-oppressive, socio-cultural philosophy, as seen during periods of transition from colonisation or apartheid to independence in South Africa and Zimbabwe (Swanson, 2007; Hailey, 2008; Abdi, 2022).

Cautions offered by scholars have balanced ongoing reflections on the generative nature of an *ubuntu* philosophy. A significant caution is that, in the singular pursuit of a single hegemonic form of *ubuntu*, there is a risk that the ideological approach may engender conformity and result in exclusion (Swanson, 2007). *Ubuntu* is also regarded as premodern and patriarchal, but *ubuntu* feminism can potentially stop the exigencies of patriarchy in society (Cornell & van Marle, 2015). *Ubuntu* is social rather than individualistic, meaning where one person experiences it, the community also experiences it. These expressions are found in the communal celebration of 'marriage, childbearing, divorce and death' (Curle, 2015: 5). As a consequence, there may be risks for how the community views women who do not marry or bear children (Curle, 2015).

The South African government employed principles of *ubuntu* in every aspect of society. Scholars raised concerns regarding the ramifications of potential negative impacts on South African communities and society as a whole (Nkondo, 2007; McDonald, 2010; Curle, 2015). Nkondo cautioned against *ubuntu* being used to enhance ethnic identities already prevalent in some parts of South Africa, a strategy similar to the apartheid 'divide and rule' ethos (Nkondo, 2007). The rigorous promotion of the black identity in post-apartheid corporate South Africa, under the umbrella of *ubuntu*, birthed a black middle-class elitist group which widened the gap between the rich and poor in South Africa; the rich (albeit of a changing demography) became wealthier and the poor poorer (Freund, 2007; McDonald, 2010).

Social contract – symmetry between professions and the people

Adams (2018) referred to the South African constitution as the quintessential social contract with a bold commitment to the mutual development of the whole of society. In a political reflection on the context of this social contract, the author proposes an understanding of social contract as 'an implicit agreement between the people to establish a new South African society, founded on the values of universal suffrage, equality, inclusivity, and democracy, designed to benefit all' (Adams, 2018: 103). This understanding presupposes, among others, the elements of agreement, equity, and common good as essential for the social contract.

Cruess and Cruess (2008) explored the nature of the social contract within the healthcare profession with particular reference to the relationship between medicine and society. The authors located the social contract within the relationship between medical professionals (with attendant knowledge, privilege, and rewards, including financial) and society (with expectations of self-regulated competence, morality, integrity, and social concern for the common good). The authors described the changing healthcare landscape in which the relationships have become more complex and involve more corporate interests. They argued that while the contract between medicine and society may change across communities and societies, there is an almost universal concept of the healer and their particular response to social needs. Their paper concludes with an emphasis on teaching professionalism in the social contract to facilitate appropriate interactions between medicine and society. They referred to the construction of the social contract and the implied interactions: 'the reciprocity inherent in the idea of a social contract underlines the importance of correctly interpreting the expectations of both medicine and society' (Cruess & Cruess, 2008: 592).

Acceptance of the reciprocal interaction between partners in the social contract suggests a level of equality discussed earlier in reference to the South African constitution. The Sustainable Development Goals (SDGs) (United Nations, 2024) continue to aim to achieve such equity in multiple domains, not least of which are the health of populations and the achievement of economic prosperity through education. The SDGs recognise that achieving equality requires intersectoral work. The ongoing pursuit of health equity through these SDGs reminds us of the social and power asymmetries prevalent between healthcare professionals and the communities they serve. The extent to which communities can hold their health professionals accountable is limited in a relationship which is characterised by the dichotomy between the vulnerability of the patient and the power held by the practitioner in the consultation (Green-Thompson, 2014).

The implicit authority afforded to professionals derives from the social contract. The social contract is an unspoken agreement because of professionals' educational attainment and the work entrusted to them. The challenge is how one can use professionalism as a tool for advocacy on behalf of the community instead of it being an instrument of embedding elitism and status.

Professional Identity Formation – building graduateness

Professionalism contributes to the Professional Identity Formation (PIF) of health professionals in a way that has largely been determined by colonial traditions and Western tropes of professionalism. Early constructions of the definition of professionalism referred to the privilege and independence granted by a society to a group of people due to their learning and capacity to self-regulate. The emergence of this independence is possible because of the presumed social contract between society and the professional.

Professionalism is essential in the mix of exit-level outcomes expected in the South African Quality Assurance framing of qualifications (South African Qualifications Authority, 2014). The SAQA framing of qualifications refers to a series of critical cross-field outcomes that form the basis for the graduate emerging from South African higher education (South African Qualifications Authority, 2014). The influence of both levels of outcome descriptions provides the context for considering professionalism as only one part of the holistic formation of a graduate (Ballim, 2022). Professionalism is a part of Professional Identity Formation (PIF), an organic and iterative process in the preparation and practice of professionals (Stack & Malsch, 2022). The process occurs in the culturally specific context applicable to any professional and disciplinary context (Stack & Malsch, 2022) and is influenced by several factors, including personal, social, cultural, professional, and political situations (Ivanova & Skara-MincLne, 2016). This process is similar for all professions, for example, teaching, health, engineering, and accounting. Professionals enter their professional training with inherent identities based on their axiological, ontological, and epistemological backgrounds (Choe et al., 2019). Professional identity is subsequently formed based on three components: awareness of one's personality in a certain profession, searching for personal meaning in that profession, and one's professional ambitions (Ivanova & Skara-MincLne, 2016; Choe et al., 2019). Classroom teachers believe that their professional identity is influenced by their previous professional and personal experiences (Ivanova & Skara-MincLne, 2016), while the convergence of multiple domains, such as identity formation and professionalism, play a major role in medical-identity formation (Holden et al., 2012). Professionalism is sometimes seen as a tool for social control in medical education that might hinder advocating for social justice (Frye et al., 2020).

In problematising professionalism, we argue that the social contract may have weakened over time as professionals have become increasingly elitist, with the definitions of professional conduct largely being predetermined by the group with a diminishing level of engagement of, or role for, the broader society. The definition of the professional proposed by the American Board of Medicine (Blank, 2002) refers to the competence represented by patient welfare (an attribute of the physician), autonomy (patient empowerment through information), and social justice (a professional commitment to the social location of the doctor-patient relationship) (Blank, 2002). In so doing, these concepts mark a call to return to the idea of the social contract. A commitment to a more global Professional Identity Formation (PIF) may enhance how these are inserted into curricula.

Professional Identity Formation (PIF) was recently examined for the exclusion of minority groups in North America (Wyatt et al., 2021). Mokhachane explored this idea among students and recent graduates from a medical programme who were involved in the #FeesMustFall protests of 2015/16. Mokhachane argued that what students imbue as their professional identity is often a product of their childhood and community-oriented upbringing coloured by *ubuntu* (Mokhachane et al., 2022).

Professionalism, and how it is taught, forces medical students to fit into the Western mould or construct of professionalism (Frost & Regehr, 2013). This 'right kind of doctor' approach limits critical thinking of what the situation requires or demands, for example, the need to protest for the benefit of others, that is, students, patients or society (Frost & Regehr, 2013). These issues are in stark contrast to Freire's education as the practice of freedom. When teaching professionalism, the problem of education and the conscientisation of Freire's pedagogy is often ignored. As it stands, professionalism follows standardisation rules that contradict and often inhibit freedom of expression and liberation. It often silences trainees (Mokhachane et al., 2023b).

Methodology

A conceptual framing of the relationship between society and the professional community was developed initially using work on social accountability and professional identity formation. This framing formed the basis for a voluntary national workshop attended by health professions educators and education managers from multiple health profession disciplines across Southern Africa. The 30 participants were invited to share their conceptualisation of Professional Identity Formation (PIF) in a word or phrase on a poster. The 24 vernacular posters were translated and grouped based on similar conceptualisations of Professional Identity Formation (PIF). The second part of the workshop was conducted using self-selected groups, and together the groups created images for the representation of professional identity formation. Ethical clearance was obtained from the University of Cape Town Human Research Ethics Committee (REF164/2024). The authors remain in contact with participants in order to translate that work into a national consensus statement on professional identity formation.

Findings

The opportunity to express Professional Identity Formation (PIF) in South African vernacular languages resulted in a rich fabric holding multiple images that give life to the ideas and process of forming the identity of health professionals (Figure 5.3). The analysis translating the vernacular contributions across the posters identified three major perspectives. The perspectives matched the different parts of Professional Identity Formation (PIF), namely professionalism, identity, and formation/development. Although derived from health profession educators, these perspectives are not exclusive to health professionals and may extend to other disciplines.

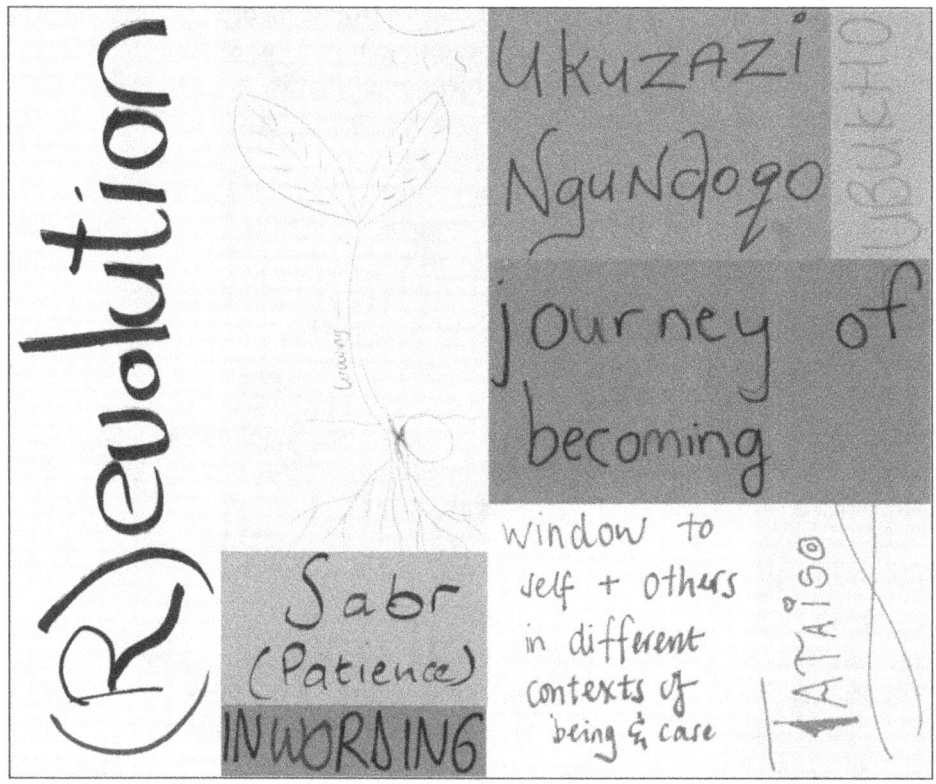

FIGURE 5.3: Selected expressions of Professional Identity Formation (PIF)

The perspective, 'Professional habitus – garments of a well-formed professional', is represented as a garment which clothes all aspects of the professional. Held within the embrace of this habitus are the professional attributes of self-knowledge expressed as '*Ukuzazi Ngundoqo*' and knowledge of one's craft reflected in the isiZulu word, '*Ingcweti*', which mirrors being a masterpiece or the achievement of master craftsmanship. A series of words capture the emotive side of the development of the professional: the Arabic word '*Sabr*' reflected a deep sense of patience and perseverance, the essential notions of care and compassion reflected as a 'window to self and others in different contexts of being and care'. Participants also highlighted that Professional Identity Formation (PIF) is a building of wisdom in the Setswana word, '*Moitsanape*', and formation as a progressive process of guidance, captured by the Setswana word, '*Tataiso*' (Figure 5.3). 'Identity' was described as 'The composite of what I am', involving active exploration and being fluid. Identity formation is a quest subject to the context of time and space.

'Becoming' was the theme which best characterised Professional Identity Formation (PIF) as a developmental process. This developmental nature is encapsulated in the participants' perspective using expressions like *'journey of becoming'*. This was echoed in the Afrikaans expression *'inwording'* (embryonic, blossoming, or emerging) (Figure 5.3). A sense of ongoing becoming was heard in terms like *'Konstante groei, sonder stagnering* #neverstoplearningorgrowing'. The personal growth involved in Professional Identity Formation (PIF) is portrayed in the sketch of the germinating seedling growing towards the sunlight (Figure 5.3) and the Irish or Scottish Gaelic term for growth *'a' fàs'*, while the perspicacious '(R) evolution' (Figure 5.3 conveys a sense that growth may be tinged with rebellion.

These ideas and expressions converge as an image of Professional Identity Formation (PIF) vivified using vernacular languages. Based on these outcomes, Professional Identity Formation (PIF) is a formative process that needs to be woven into the curricula that contain the required basic scientific knowledge. It manifests the humanistic ideas of professional habitus involving one's identity constantly evolving into the professional self, recognised as an ongoing becoming rather than a single moment of graduation.

The attributes of a medical professional emanate from two intersecting roles: healer and professional. The most universally accepted notion, the healer, requires one to be caring, compassionate, insightful, present, and to display respect for the healing function and patients. The professional role encompasses autonomy afforded by society, as well as self-regulating associations and institutions, and taking responsibility for society (Cruess & Cruess, 2008). These roles intersect regarding attributes such as competence, commitment, confidentiality, altruism, trustworthiness, integrity, and morality (Cruess & Cruess, 2008). The themes discovered in the national workshop appear to support these ideas and may offer a basis for further empirical work. The role of the teacher may be added to the intersection of the roles of healer and professional. Professionalism is, therefore, integral to all three roles, especially concerning students (or teaching) and society. In addition, more work is needed in South African higher education at the threshold between a university education and the encounter with the complex environment of work, whether this is in further study scenarios or professional workplaces. The teaching professional needs to respect the student and vice versa and demonstrate accountability to society. Society also has the right to demand respect and accountability and respect from the professional (Cruess & Cruess, 2008).

Framework for the future

Ballim's idea of graduateness demands that we develop South African graduates who are more than the sum of the knowledge they accumulate. Their Professional Identity Formation (PIF), which we must include in curriculum development, will prepare our graduates for a complex world. This chapter has discussed social accountability as a deepening relationship between communities and higher-education institutions, and *ubuntu* as the interconnectedness of people in a community that offers a vernacular framing of professionalism. The interface between social accountability (the emphasis on accounting for one's actions to society) and the reframing of the pursuit of Professional Identity Formation (PIF) (building the habitus of the complete professional) offers two dimensions for an *ubuntu*-based approach to curricular development and delivery.

The role of the community becomes essential to support the *ubuntu* framework. The contribution of social responsiveness in higher education is substantial and has been manifested in varying degrees of community engagement (Bhagwan, 2017). Boelen and Woollard (2011) developed a social obligation scale which describes the aspirational development of relationships with communities that enhance their interaction with curricula. The ultimate stage of responsiveness is accountability, in which communities are equal partners in the partnership which decides on the direction of curricula (Boelen & Woollard, 2011). The social obligation scale offers a heuristic to allow deeper explication of the role of communities within curricula.

TABLE 5.1: Social Obligation Scale
Adapted from Boelen & Woollard, 2011

	Responsiveness	**Responsibility**	**Accountability**
Social needs identified	Implicitly	Explicitly	Anticipatively
Institutional objectives	Defined by faculty	Inspired by data	Co-created with community
Educational programmes	Community-oriented	Community-based	Contextualised
Quality of graduates	Good practitioners	Meet criteria for professionalism	System change agents
Focus of evaluation	Process	Outcome	Impact
Assessors	Internal	External	Social system partners

Green-Thompson (2014), in his development of the understanding of social accountability in the education and practice of medicine, offered a ten-statement proposal for making an impact on health professionals' curricula. The first three statements highlight the importance of the social determinants of health (a move away from curative health to understanding the source of ill health), community empowerment (collaborative work that increases community agency), and aligning curricula with priorities in health (matching teaching with these). The following four statements speak to curricular delivery in which there is a renewal of relationships among the various stakeholders in healthcare: with the patient, understanding the relationships in community-based education, building a nurturing educating community of scholars and learners, and reframing professionalism for engaged citizenship. The final three statements may be seen as strategies for achieving this aim of a dynamic and interactive accountable curriculum. These emphasise a progressive, engaged student community and a faculty community that becomes a dynamic agent of change through intentional faculty development. The purpose of such development should be appropriate role modelling and defining the role of faculty to make a difference in a defined community (Green-Thompson, 2014). These statements are presented in Table 5.2 below.

TABLE 5.2: Unifying framework for the advancement of social accountability

See	Prioritise the social determinants of health
	Engage communities for empowerment
	Align curricula to priority health concerns
Focus	Revitalise the relationship of trust with the patient
	Promote relationship-centred community-based learning
	Nurture relationship-centred educating communities
	Reconstruct professionalism for engaged citizenship
Choose	Build a progressive and engaged student community
	Create faculty development for socially accountable role modelling
	Commit the faculty community to becoming change agents in defined communities

This unifying framework offers us a structure to adapt to an *ubuntu*-focused framework for the intersection of *ubuntu* and Professional Identity Formation (PIF). Following the constructivist development of this chapter, we propose the

following statements of intent to support this work in higher education:
- Recognise community knowledge and capacity for the advancement of collaborative learning.
- Prioritise the engagement of communities for empowerment.
- Rekindle trust as a key value in relationships with communities.
- Ensure that communities direct community-based education.
- Integrate Professional Identity Formation (PIF) as a central curriculum theme.
- Promote progressive and engaged students.
- Build faculty-development programmes which centralise role modelling for professional identity.

The explicit insertion of an *ubuntu*-based professional identity formation curriculum provides a backdrop for a general curriculum which facilitates the nurturing of 'graduateness' for our students and graduates emerging into a complex society. Recognising that professional identity formation may contribute positively to the transition to workplaces, it is essential to instil this approach into the teaching and learning activity in higher education.

References

Abdi, A.A. (2022). Freireian and Ubuntu philosophies of education: Onto-epistemological characteristics and pedagogical intersections. *Educational Philosophy and Theory*, 54(13): 2286–2296. https://doi.org/10.1080/00131857.2021.1975110.

Adams, R. (2018). South Africa's social contract: the Economic Freedom Fighters and the rise of a new constituent power? *Acta Academica*, 50(3): 102–121. https://doi.org/10.18820/24150479/aa50i3.5.

Arnstein, S.R. (1969). A Ladder Of Citizen Participation. *Journal of the American Institute of Planners*, 35(4): 216–224. https://doi.org/10.1080/01944366908977225.

Ballim, Y. (2022). The place of teaching, learning and student development in a framework of academic freedom: Attending to the negative freedoms of our students. *Journal of Education (University of KwaZulu-Natal)*, (89): 186–200. https://doi.org/10.17159/2520-9868/i89a10.

Bhagwan, R. (2017). Towards a conceptual understanding of community engagement in higher education in South Africa. *Perspectives in Education*, 35(1): 171–185. https://doi.org/10.18820/2519593X/pie.

Biko, S. (1987). *I Write What I Like*. Aelred Stubbs, C.R. (ed.). University of Chicago Press. https://doi.org/10.7208/chicago/9780226368535.001.0001.

Blank, L. (2002). Medical professionalism in the new millennium: a physicians' charter. *Clinical Medicine*, 2(2): 116–118.

Boelen, C. & Woollard, R. (2011). Social accountability: The extra leap to excellence for educational institutions. *Medical Teacher*, 33(8): 614–619. https://doi.org/10.3109/0142159X.2011.590248.

Boelen, C., Dharamsi, S. & Gibbs, T. (2012). The Social Accountability of Medical Schools and its Indicators. *Education for Health*, 25(3): 180–194. https://doi.org/10.4103/1357-6283.109785.

Boelen, C., Blouin, D., Gibbs, T. & Woollard, R. (2019). Accrediting Excellence for a Medical School's Impact on Population Health. *Education for Health: Change in Learning and Practice*, 32(1): 41–48. https://doi.org/10.4103/efh.EfH_204_19.

Bosman, G. (2022). Art and landscape: a rural letsema celebration. *South African Journal of Art History*, 37(1): 31–47.

Choe, N.H., Martins, L.L., Borrego, M. & Kendall, M.R. (2019). Professional Aspects of Engineering: Improving Prediction of Undergraduates' Engineering Identity. *Journal of Professional Issues in Engineering Education and Practice*, 145(3). https://doi.org/10.1061/(ASCE)EI.1943-5541.0000413.

Cornell, D. & van Marle, K. (2015). Ubuntu feminism: Tentative reflections. *Verbum et Ecclesia*, 36(2): 1–8. https://doi.org/10.4102/ve.v36i2.1444.

Cruess, R.L. & Cruess, S.R. (2008). Expectations and Obligations: Professionalism and Medicine's Social Contract with Society. *Perspectives in Biology and Medicine*, 51(4): 579–598. https://doi.org/10.1353/pbm.0.0045.

Curle, N. (2015). A Christian Theological Critique of uBuntu in Swaziland. *Conspectus*, 20(1): 96–120.

Ellece, S. (2010). Asking for a 'Water Calabash': Metaphor and Gender in 'Patlo' Marriage Ceremonies in Botswana. *Marang: Journal of Language and Literature*, 20(1): 63–77. https://doi.org/10.4314/marang.v20i1.56820.

Freire, P. (1970). *Pedagogy of the Oppressed*. Penguin Classics.

Freund, B. (2007). *The African city: A history* (Vol. 4). Cambridge University Press.

Frost, H.D. & Regehr, G. (2013). "I am a doctor": negotiating the discourses of standardization and diversity in professional identity construction. *Academic Medicine*, 88(10): 1570–1577.

Frye, V., Camacho-Rivera, M., Salas-Ramirez, K., Albritton, T., Deen, D., Sohler, N., Barrick, S. & Nunes, J. (2020). Professionalism: the wrong tool to solve the right problem? *Academic Medicine*, 95(6): 860–863.

Gathogo, J. (2008). African Philosophy as Expressed in the Concepts of Hospitality and Ubuntu. *Journal of Theology for Southern Africa*, 130: 39–53.

Green-Thompson, L. (2014). The Nature Of Social Accountability In South African Medical Practice And Education – A Qualitative Reflection. [Doctoral dissertation] University of the Witwatersrand. Available at: https://wiredspace.wits.ac.za/server/api/core/bitstreams/06e43d5b-5976-4064-ab33-99d2f7917ddc/content. Date accessed: 15 April 2024.

Hailey, J. (2008). Ubuntu: A literature review. Document. *London: Tutu Foundation*, 1–26.

Holden, M., Buck, E., Clark, M., Szauter, K. & Trumble, J. (2012). Professional Identity Formation in Medical Education: The Convergence of Multiple Domains. *HEC Forum*, 24(4): 245–255. https://doi.org/10.1007/s10730-012-9197-6.

Ivanova, I. & Skara-Mincēne, R. (2016). Development of professional identity during teacher's practice. *Procedia-Social and Behavioral Sciences*, 232: 529–536.

Laverack, G. (2006). Improving Health Outcomes through Community Empowerment: A Review of the Literature. *Journal of Health, Population and Nutrition*, 24(1): 113–120. Available at: https://www.jstor.org/stable/23499274.

Letseka, M. (2013). Educating for *Ubuntu/Botho*: Lessons from Basotho Indigenous Education. *Open Journal of Philosophy*, 3(2): 337–344. https://doi.org/10.4236/ojpp.2013.32051.

Lewis, B. (2010). Forging an understanding of black humanity through relationship: An Ubuntu perspective. Black Theology 8(1): 69–85.

Lokugamage, A.U., Ahillan, T. & Pathberiya, S.D.C. (2020). Decolonising ideas of healing in medical education. *Journal of medical ethics*, 46(4): 265–272.

Maharasoa, M.M. & Maharaswa, M.B. (2004). Men's initiation schools as a form of higher education within the Basotho indigenous knowledge systems. *South African Journal of Higher Education*, 18(3): 106–114.

Martimianakis, M.A., Michalec, B., Lam, J., Cartmill, C., Taylor, J.S. & Hafferty, F.W. (2015). Humanism, the Hidden Curriculum, and Educational Reform: A Scoping Review and Thematic Analysis. *Academic Medicine*, 90(11): S5–S13. https://doi.org/10.1097/ACM.0000000000000894.

Mayaka, B. & Truell, R. (2021). Ubuntu and its potential impact on the international social work profession. *International social work*, 64(5): 649–662.

Mbigi, L. & Maree, J. (2005). *Ubuntu: The Spirit of African Transformation Management*. Knowres Pub.: Randburg, South Africa.

McDonald, D.A. (2010). Ubuntu bashing: the marketisation of 'African values' in South Africa. *Review of African Political Economy*, 37(124): 139–152.

McKnight, J. (1997). A 21st-Century Map for Healthy Communities and Families. *Family in Society*, 78(2): 117–127.

Metz, T. (2011). Ubuntu as a moral theory and human rights in South Africa. *African human rights law journal*, 11(2): 532–559.

Mokhachane, M., George, A., Wyatt, T., Kuper, A. & Green-Thompson, L. (2022). Rethinking professional identity formation amidst protests and social upheaval: a journey in Africa. *Advances in Health Sciences Education*, 28: 1–22. https://doi.org/10.1007/s10459-022-10164-0.

Mokhachane, M., Green-Thompson, L., George, A., Wyatt, T. & Kuper, A. (2023a). Medical students' views on what professionalism means: an Ubuntu perspective. *Advances in Health Sciences Education*. (September, 15). https://doi.org/10.1007/s10459-023-10280-5.

Mokhachane, M., Wyatt, T., Kuper, A., Green-Thompson, L. & George, A. (2023b). Graduates' Reflections on Professionalism and Identity: Intersections of Race, Gender, and Activism. *Teaching and Learning in Medicine*, 36: 1–11. https://doi.org/10.1080/10401334.2023.2224306.

Mpuangnan, K.N. & Ntombela, S. (2023). Community voices in curriculum development. *Curriculum Perspectives*, 44: 49–60. https://doi.org/10.1007/s41297-023-00223-w.

Muxe Nkondo, G. (2007). Ubuntu as public policy in South Africa: A conceptual framework. *International Journal of African Renaissance Studies*, 2(1): 88–100.

Nkgudi, T.M., Maake, M.M.S. & Masekoameng, M.R. (2022). The Ilima-Letsema programme's contribution to poverty alleviation in Gauteng Province, South Africa. *Frontiers in Sustainable Food Systems*, 6. https://doi.org/10.3389/fsufs.2022.975127.

Pearson, D., Walpole, S. & Barna, S. (2015). Challenges to professionalism: Social accountability and global environmental change. *Medical Teacher*, 37(9): 825–830. https://doi.org/10.3109/0142159X.2015.1044955.

Setlhodi, I.I. (2023). Increasing Teaching Capacity for Supporting Students in an ODeL Institution: Employing Letsema. In *Promoting the Socio-Economic Wellbeing of Marginalised Individuals Through Adult Education*. IGI Global Scientific Publishing, 53–72. https://doi.org/10.4018/978-1-6684-6625-4.ch004.

Smith, M.K. (2016). Bringing Back Ubuntu. *Academic Psychiatry*, 40(4): 721–722. https://doi.org/10.1007/s40596-015-0451-5.

South African Qualifications Authority. (2014). National Policy for the Implementation of the Recognition of Prior Learning. Government Gazette.

Stack, R. & Malsch, B. (2022). Auditors' Professional Identities: Review and Future Directions. *Accounting Perspectives*, 21(2): 177–206. https://doi.org/10.1111/1911-3838.12289.

Swanson, D.M. (2007). Ubuntu: An African contribution to (re)search for/with a 'humble togetherness'. *Journal of Contemporary Issues in Education*, 2(2): 53–67. https://doi.org/10.20355/c5pp4x.

United Nations. (2024). The SDGS in Action. Accessed at: https://www.undp.org/south-africa/sustainable-development-goals. Date accessed: 1 May 2024.

Van Breda, A.D. (2019). Developing the notion of Ubuntu as an African theory for social work practice. *Social Work*, 55(4): 438–450. https://doi.org/10.15270/52-2-762.

Walker, M., McLean, M., Dison, A. & Peppin-Vaughan, R. (2009). South African universities and human development: Towards a theorisation and operationalisation of professional capabilities for poverty reduction. *International Journal of Educational Development*, 29(6): 565–572. https://doi.org/10.1016/j.ijedudev.2009.03.002.

Wyatt, T.R., et. al. (2021). "Changing the narrative": a study on professional identity formation among Black/African American physicians in the US. *Advances in Health Sciences Education*, 26(1): 183–198.

CHAPTER 6

Homo umoyanus, not homo neoliberalus: Socio-moral subjectivity for a transformed higher education

Shahieda Jansen

Abstract

In Higher Education, there might be frequent discourse on embracing disruptive change, yet institutions often remain bound to the norms and practices of universities as enclaves of neoliberal subjectivities. While it may be assumed that students are learning, high dropout rates suggest that transformative learning is difficult to achieve with 'natives from nowhere.' Without a deep understanding of learner personhood—meaning a recognition of their worldview, values, and existential presence—education risks being reduced to a hollow, mechanical transfer of information.

This chapter introduces a relational-ethical theory of self, grounded in an African multidimensional model of personhood that aligns with contemporary scientific perspectives on human beings as 'extensions of the universe.' The concept of the 'renewable energy' self is reflected in the ancient African notion of *Umoya*, meaning wind—a dynamic, life-sustaining force.

This chapter argues that reimagining the human resources of Higher Education as multivocal, *Umoya* selves is both urgent and essential. Instead of mimicking Descartes' machine model of humankind, personhood on two legs - belonging and governance- offers a more responsive framework for addressing critical challenges in Higher Education. This includes bridging the gap between learning and learners' onto-epistemologies, fostering unity that embraces diversity, and facilitating transformative teaching and learning.

Keywords: neoliberal subjectivity, personhood, relational-ethical selfhood, transformative learning, *Umoya*

Introduction

Higher education has sustained a lengthy and lingering fellowship with settler occupation, dispossession of indigenous people, racialisation, and slavery. While colonial education in Africa was a tool of empire building for the brutal consolidation of power over indigenous communities, American universities such as Harvard, Princeton, and Yale benefited from scientific racism, the violence of human bondage, and the genocides of indigenous people (Wilder, 2013).

Colonial education served as a means of occupying African minds (wa Thiong'o, 2009) in addition to being an effective method of land dispossession (Shizha & Kariwo, 2011). The goal of colonial education was the entrenched and lasting dehumanisation of indigenous people in South Africa and other parts of Africa (Shizha & Kariwo, 2011).

The segregationist educational order established during British rule was not only maintained but effectively systematised during the apartheid era, which was not dismantled with the onset of democracy in 1994 (Chirinda, Ndlovu, & Spangenberg, 2021; Muyambi & Ahiaku, 2025). Hence, pervasive and stark inequalities in the educational, economic, political, and technological spheres endure in present-day South Africa (Muyambi & Ahiaku, 2025).

Colonial education was organised to devalue the cultures and ways of living of the colonised, which induced a sense of inferiority among subjugated people (Shizha & Kariwo, 2011). This project to "disturb the minds" of the colonised continues into the 21st century, long after slaves have been freed and members of the "free world" have adopted human rights and democracy (Romm, 2024).

As one of the ways in which colonialism reproduces itself, this mental slavery is evident in present-day productions of identity, subjectivity, and modes of knowing or epistemology in postcolonial contexts (Romm, 2024). Ontology is concerned with the nature of reality, with ways of being, subjectivity, and context, whereas epistemology focuses on the nature of knowledge, with knowing (Romm, 2024). Onto-epistemology is a concept that combines ontology and epistemology because our ways of knowing (epistemology) are deeply connected to our ways of being (ontology) (Romm, 2024).

Over centuries, colonial systems of domination have extended their lifespan through several iterations of Western liberal humanisms of exclusion of 'inferior' others (Wynter, 2003). Its most recent form, neoliberal subjectivity, or homo neoliberalus (Teo, 2018), is set to continue higher education's founding crimes into the twenty-first century. Neoliberalism is a political and economic paradigm that rose to prominence in the late 20th century, and its defining characteristics are free-market capitalism, minimal government intervention, deregulation, and individualism with a focus on individual accountability (Naidoo, 2023).

According to Grosfoguel (2007), colonialism's victims are prone to take on the epistemic locations—that is, the modes of thought—of their colonisers, turning the colonised into colonial caricatures. Hence, the enduring neoliberal discourse in the local academy (Hlatshwayo, 2022) touches on what has been referred to as coloniality, the patterns of colonial power that continue to shape the reality, knowledge production, and practices of the colonised long after the end of colonial rule (Maldonado-Torres, 2007).

Many continue to grapple with the decolonisation of universities from numerous angles and with redressing the inequities of the past (Ammon, 2019; Badat, 2008; Heleta, 2018; Jansen & Walters, 2022; Zembylas, 2017).

Despite sustained attempts at decolonising South African universities, institutions of higher education seem to have adapted themselves to neoliberal principles of profit-making, competitiveness, and privatisation (Hlatshwayo, 2022). Universities operate like corporations, lecturers are viewed as knowledge suppliers, and students are viewed as consumers or clients (Hlatshwayo, 2022). It may even seem that the accumulation of capital has taken precedence over universities' primary goals (Rikap & Harari-Kermadec, 2020).

Neoliberal subjectivity's fit for purpose with empire is because it is both atomised and massified. When an individual gets atomised, they lose their communal identity and may end up joining collectives (masses) that are readily manipulated for the sake of massive power and control (Naidoo, 2023). This bounded, separate, private self is 'empty' according to Philip Cushman, referring to the atomistic individual in contemporary industrialised capitalistic cultures who is alienated from tradition and cut off from community (Cushman, 1990). Meaninglessness, therefore, results from Euro-American epistemic traditions' persistent incursions into both academic settings and individual potential (Naidoo, 2023).

Against popular opinion, Naidoo (2023) contends that neoliberalism does not support individualisation. On the contrary, it is enslaved by capitalist market forces. The neoliberal self is separated from itself and from others. Hence, this fragmenting neoliberal subjectivity is unable to participate in individual and collective forms of agency but is doomed to be terminally drafted into the enterprise of capitalism (Naidoo, 2023). Neoliberalism's exclusive goal is the accumulation of capital, thus everything, including individualism and collectivism—is subsumed in the pursuit of this singular goal (Naidoo, 2023).

Given the modern-day subjugation sustained through neoliberalist subjectivity, the concern of this chapter is the exploration of a perspective on subjectivity that is more resistant to enslavement to market forces. This chapter engages with a paradigm of personhood, meaning a shared understanding of what it means to be human (Mcintosh, 2018), as a site of resistance, potential, and self-invention (Naidoo, 2023).

Since human subjectivity is moulded by the times and places in which it takes place, culture can be broadly described as time and place (Keesing, 1974). Subjectivity includes the contextual and personal perspective of someone, their thoughts, feelings, and behaviours (Lundberg, Fraschini, & Aliani, 2023). This personal view is informed by the person's lived experience, which suggests that subjectivity incorporates personal views about reality as well as about the self (Lundberg, Fraschini, & Aliani, 2023). Personhood and subjectivity are thus closely related because personhood is about a contextually constructed understanding of what it means to be a person (Jecker & Atuire, 2024). Being a person, in turn, is about the subjective experience and interpretation of the world.

Furthermore, there is a connection between institutional cultures and subjectivities (Markus & Kitayama, 2010). People are shaped by the culture they interact with, and the culture they are a part of is shaped by them. Personhood and culture are therefore mutually constitutive; they constantly develop, disintegrate, and rebuild each other in addition to continuously altering and adapting to their surroundings (Markus & Kitayama, 2010).

One way, then, of potentially shifting the institutional culture could be through amendments to the subjectivity of the adherents of that culture. If it is true that the neoliberal subject is a fragmenting subjectivity that is unable to participate in individual and collective forms of agency, but doomed to be terminally drafted into the enterprise of capitalism (Naidoo, 2023), then it might be possible to disrupt the stranglehold of neoliberalism in the academy through the resuscitation of socially embedded subjectivity, the kind that survived centuries of colonial onslaught in the African context (Comaroff & Comaroff, 2001).

This chapter, therefore, encourages the revival of a culturally familiar, socially embedded personhood for the potential recentring of relational modes of knowing, doing, and learning that may run counter to the contemporary coloniality of being within university spaces (Maldonado-Torres, 2007). For this purpose, I articulate a personhood model of African (relational-ethical) identity that can do better at meeting the goals of transformation in higher education. The name of this model of personhood is African multidimensional personhood, an understanding of persons as complex combinations of material and immaterial (sociospiritual) forces (Jansen, 2022).

The African multidimensional personhood (AMP) was first known as the Afro-Eastern multidimensional personhood (AEMP), as my experiments with African personhood were influenced by my upbringing in Islamic (Eastern) sociospiritual self-understanding. However, the Eastern aspect of the AEMP was left out in this chapter, because a recently accepted manuscript on the AEMP was critiqued for not sufficiently theorising the Eastern part of the model of personhood (Jansen, 2025).

By identity, I mean social identity, understanding oneself as a member of social groups (Schulte, Bamberg, Rees, & Rollin, 2020). Let me further clarify what I mean by African identity. In his Vice Chancellor's address at Unisa's regional graduation ceremony in Cape Town, Professor Phaladi Sebate, a now retired professor of education, suggested that skin colour has no bearing on African identity. He said African identity is a values project, as he named the value of morality and relationship as integral to African identity (Sebate, 2019). Professor John Klaasen, in his writing on personhood, confirms that African identity is upheld by the pillars of relationship and morality (Klaasen, 2017).

The brief insertion of a culturally familiar model of personhood at the start of teaching or training sessions may serve as a bridge between education and the subjectivity of the student or scholar (Chitumba, 2013). This kind of personhood education can be integrated into the diverse disciplines within the university through 'basic orientation to socially embedded personhood' (Chitumba, 2013). More specifically, personhood education would involve interactive reflections on broader socio-cultural aspects of personal identity relevant to disciplines as diverse as mathematics and geography, although for practical purposes, I will be focusing on my own discipline of psychology (Chitumba, 2013).

In the remainder of this chapter, I start with a detailed description of the African multidimensional personhood (AMP), including an outline of its theory and implementation. The discussions that follow are about the practical application of the AMP in three educational settings, starting with an incident of connecting a learner with their onto-epistemologies. Because the AMP was used to bridge the gap between Western psychological paradigms and indigenous concepts of healing, a psychology student who found it challenging to interact meaningfully with the curriculum content because of the epistemic distance between herself and the Western-framed psychology curriculum narrowly escaped academic exclusion from the psychology master's programme of a university.

The next one discusses how the application of the AMP in multicultural university settings can be used to foster unity-within-diversity learning experiences that allow for the meaningful coexistence of multiple epistemologies.

The last setting involves the potential of the AMP as a creative cultural justice strategy in fostering transformative learning. Given that the AMP resonates with the most widespread self-understanding of South Africans, training educators in the AMP is likely to enhance the alignment of learner presence with the pedagogical transaction, which may support transformative learning. This will be followed by summarising and tying the main points together in the conclusion.

African multidimensional personhood

The African multidimensional personhood (AMP), also referred to as the *Umoya-self*, is a collection of integrating and balancing human capacities, including intelligence, personal power, emotion, spirituality, animal, and body. Foundational to the person is Moya – a socio-emotional-spiritual element (Baloyi & Ramose, 2016).

Umoya, a word which comes from the Nguni languages (Zulu, Xhosa, Swati, and Ndebele), literally means 'wind,' but is usually used in terms of its spiritual connotations (Baloyi & Ramose, 2016). Saying *Umoya* while pointing at someone highlights the status of the person as a socio-spiritual being. The *Umoya-self* is a dynamic, evolving self-through-others personhood, in other words, an *Ubuntu-self* (Mbiti, 1969). This relational self is characterised by connections at multiple levels, physical, psychological, spiritual, chronological, communal, and cultural (Nsamenang, 2006).

According to Letseka (2012), *Ubuntu* is a concept of African personhood that emphasises virtues like empathy, consideration for others, responsibility, and caring. A person who possesses the attributes of *Ubuntu* is called an *Umuntu* (Dladla, 2017). *Ubuntu*, then, is an African perspective on *Abantu*, humans. *Ubuntu* offers the viewpoint that we are humanised through contact with human others (Mbiti, 1969).

According to the AMP, the energy or socio-spirituality that drives integrating, balancing, and connecting processes is what makes up the self (Edwards, 2016). Moya, which is described as a life force or energy that is thought to be present in everything, highlights the idea that humans are social beings who derive their sense of identity and self-worth from their relationships and connections with other people (Baloyi & Ramose, 2016). *Umoya* is the cornerstone and ultimate nature of the AMP, characterising this personhood model as relational, socially embedded, and therefore unifying (Nobles & Mkhize, 2020). Unifying here suggests that all the dimensions of the self, intellect, emotions, spirituality, personal power, the shadow or 'lower self', and the body are separate parts of the self that act together (Frager, 1999). All these parts affect each other, and in turn are impacted by their centralising, pervasive human energy, referred to in different parts of the world as Umoya, Prana, or *Chi*, further elaborated on below.

Evidence of a pervasive human energy field known as *Prana* and *Qi* in the ancient spiritual traditions of India and China, respectively (Alvino, 1996), has been forthcoming from sciences like quantum physics and the biological sciences (Bhatnagar & Patra, 2023; Pearsall, 1999). Human consciousness, for instance, appears to be the result of unpredictable and even chaotic interactions between highly complex subcellular networks, among others, and environmental influences, including non-local fields (Haramein & Brown, 2019). Non-locality is a quantum dynamic where particles of the universe appear to be connected even across large distances. It is therefore suggested that human consciousness might play an overall role in the workings of the universe! (Haramein & Brown, 2019).

All energy particles of the universe are interrelated, according to the quantum physicist Brian Greene (Greene, 2000). Further justification for the reality of *Umoya* relates to the philosophical concept of confirmational holism, which holds that a belief's meaning and veracity are closely related to its coherence and consistency with similar beliefs of other spiritual traditions (Devitt, 2014).

Interrelated and integrated with *Umoya*, in other words, part-expressions of *Umoya*, are the dimensions, or layers of consciousness, which includes a body, meaning that personhood does not just exist in the abstract form, but that the self is regarded as inseparable from its physical, biological, and broader material contexts (Brown & Strawn, 2017). The tangible parts of the self are referred to as the material self. These can include locations and things that extend the self, for instance, 'objects of affection,' such as 'my chair,' 'my house,' 'my city,' and so on (Ahuvia, 2005). Additionally, the physicality of the self suggests the significance of materiality for social justice. For instance, personal belonging may include a sense of connection to the land and surroundings (Schein, 2009). A person's sense of self and community can be practically experienced in relation to a landscape; therefore, land confiscation may affect an individual's sense of self (Schein, 2009).

The intellectual dimension affirms that the very nature of African personhood is to be creative, growth-oriented, and perspective-taking. The spiritual aspect of human nature is foundational to this growth-oriented mindset (de Souza, 2012). According to de Souza (2004), spirituality can be defined as the internal, invisible dynamic impetus or movement outward from oneself to others or towards transcendence. Since spirituality has a biological foundation and is thus evolutionarily relevant, it is conceptualised as a unique form of universal human awareness (Hay & Nye, 2006). This dynamic spiritual orientation is what fuels intelligence, learning, and a growth mindset as a lifelong preoccupation (Pearce, 2002).

The emotional level of consciousness establishes that people are beings who feel and express emotions. This aligns with affective neuroscience, which suggests that the basis of the self is emotion, not cognition (Alcaro & Panksepp, 2017). Besides emotions being the seat of the self, human intelligence may turn out to be more a 'matter of the heart' than has previously been imagined. Neurocardiology, the discipline concerned with the interplay between the nervous and cardiac systems (Gurel & Ardell, 2022), suggests that emotions directly communicate with the brain (Pearce, 2002). Hence, the heart may hold part oversight of the brain and vice versa (Gurel & Ardell, 2022). Evidence from neurocardiology thus implies that human intelligence may be an expression of complex heart-brain interactions, perhaps wisdom, rather than mere intellectual brilliance (Pearce, 2002).

Personal power relates to that part of the *Umoya*-self that can assert itself, that can act, both in terms of showing courage and commitment, as well as in displaying the humility that enables growth and transformation (Frager, 1999). The involvement of courage and humility in the expression of personal power, in turn, suggests the connection between personal power and spirituality (Frager, 1999).

The animal or shadow side of human nature relates to the animalistic, instinctive, primal impulses such as self-preservation, reproduction, and the fight-or-flight response. These raw drives ground us in vitality, power, and creativity, as well as ensuring our survival, but if not contained, can unleash immense personal and collective suffering in the world (Frager, 1999). De Souza (2012) approaches the shadow as part of the negative side of spirituality. Her writings suggest that integrating the shadow aspects of the self is an integral aspect of maintaining positive spiritual and mental health.

On the other hand, the soul or personal spirituality is the centre of people's innate and personal spiritual nature. Within the context of a concept like *Umoya*, spirituality is about relatedness and the ethics that frame and protect relationships (Mkhize, 2021). The soul concerns human beings' connectedness to themselves and to others, including nature, animals, cultural and spiritual phenomena (Frager, 1999).

There are names for these intersecting dimensions of self in the Xhosa culture, like those of the ancient traditions of China and India (Alvino, 1996), as well as the historically more recent Islamic tradition (Frager, 1999). These are *umphefumlo* (soul or personal spirituality), *amandla omntu* (personal power), *isithunzi* (shadow or dark side), *ingqondo* (intellect), intliziyo (emotion), and *umzimba* (body) (Mnyandu, 1997).

Umoya represents the highest stage of consciousness development, or that the human essence is spirit (Nobles & Mkhize, 2020). Every part of this integrating and balancing intersectional self contributes to the relatedness, balance, and complexity that is continuous both internally, with itself, as well as externally, with animate and inanimate objects (Mnyandu, 1997).

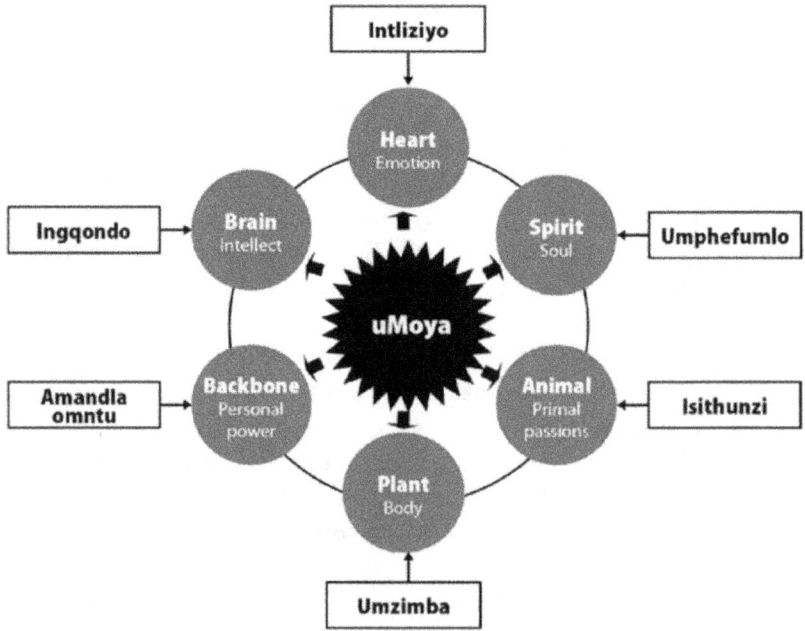

FIGURE 6.1: The African multidimensional personhood (Jansen, 2022, p 37)

The interconnected material, psychological and spiritual levels of African personhood is therefore functionally united with a non-material element, the sociospiritual human essence, *Umoya* (Baloyi & Ramose, 2016). Thus, the moniker African multidimensional personhood expresses the relational emphasis of African self-composition (Mkhize, 2021; Nsamenang, 2006).

The Afrocentric self-concept is relevant for South Africa as a cultural 'melting pot'. The model's emphasis on the relational basis of self can be applied to diverse racial/ethnic and religious groups in South Africa. The literature suggests that most South Africans conceive of themselves in relational terms (Laher & Dockrat, 2019), a social orientation to selfhood that may extend to the rest of the continent and beyond.

The intricacies and nuances of the AMP are too much for this chapter to cover, but some of it will continue in discussions of the theoretical frame of the practice of the AMP below.

Theorising the practice of the African multidimensional personhood

The AMP can be made sense of from within the epistemic underpinnings of pragmatism and complexity theory (Long, McDermott, & Meadows, 2018) as well as practical identity (Korsgaard, 2011). Complexity theory, also known as complex systems theory, is a multidisciplinary field that studies interacting components of open, dynamic, and adaptive systems that give rise to collective behaviour. Such a complex system may exhibit patterns and properties that cannot be easily predicted from the behaviour of individual components (Haramein & Brown, 2019).

Collective patterns may emerge from the interaction of the system's components. Besides emergence, some of the other principles of complex systems are adaptiveness, non-linearity, self-organisation, and dynamism (Schneider & Somers, 2006). This pragmatic philosophy of complexity theory places more emphasis on doing what makes sense in the context of a given situation than it does on theory or ideals. To put it another way, the goal is to act on what is practical and relevant in the given environment, not what is 'ideal' (Long, McDermott, & Meadows, 2018).

The AMP meets the criteria to be classified as a complex system not only because it is simultaneously physical, psychological, and spiritual, but also because it is composed of interconnecting masses of intricate sub-systems but also because human nature is arguably the most complicated of all complex systems (Brown & Strawn, 2017; Haramein & Brown, 2019). The AMP consists of countless emergent properties. Emergent properties or behaviours arise from interactions between components of the system, rather than due to pre-programming, which gives patterns of emergent behaviours that exhibit qualities of randomness, unpredictability, and unexpectedness (Haramein & Brown, 2019).

There are several assumptions and practices in the approach to the AMP that reflect the major principles of a pragmatic approach to complexity theory. Take the notion of self-organisation, the idea that, left to its own devices, systems will behave in ways to solve problems without outside interference (Long, McDermott, & Meadows, 2018). The AMP, as a human energy field with subcomponents of specialist human energy fields, carries out functions related to the expression of intellect, emotion, spirituality, and so forth. Human beings tend to self-organise in accordance with their nature as 'energy fields' (Alvino, 1996; Rogers, 1994).

This assumption of the self-organisational capacity of human nature, in turn, dovetails with the idea of practical identity. Practical identity is an approach to understanding self-constitutionality as a guide and motivation for behaviour. It covers how identity affects our agency and directs the decisions we make (Korsgaard, 2011). Our attitudes and behaviours may shift if we alter who we are and how we view ourselves (Korsgaard, 2011). For this reason, the concern of this chapter is with self-understanding as a path to transformation.

As human energy fields, human beings are constantly emergent, in non-linear ways, connecting, and cooperating in indeterminate and complex ways. Each part of the AMP works separately, as well as in tandem with all other parts. For instance, the body, or *umzimba* in Xhosa, and the intellect, or *ingqondo*, are not comprehended in isolation from one another.

As an example of the internal intersectionality of the AMP as a helpful framework of analysis in higher education, it is known that the high dropout rates from South African higher education institutions are linked to larger issues of poverty and inequality (Letseka & Breier, 2008), even though learning is typically regarded in a disembodied manner. It may go unnoticed, but scientific research has shown that food insecurity among students is a growing problem (Mabharwana, 2022; Munro & Msimango, 2023). Students who are preoccupied with money concerns or anxious about housing issues may find it difficult to concentrate on their studies (Letseka & Breier, 2008).

Even when material conditions are sufficient, intellectual potential can only be fully realised in relation to a person's values. Take harmony, for instance—another complex concept—which, at an individual level, can be understood as the alignment of one's experiences with what one values (Han, 2008). A highly intelligent person must still cultivate harmony between their values and their chosen career. This integration is achieved when there is coherence between the *intliziyo* (heart or emotions), the ingqondo (intellect), and actions (behaviour), reinforcing the interconnected nature of human existence.

To prevent educational policies from overemphasising academic excellence at the expense of considering the physically, emotionally, relationally, and existentially troubled realities of learners (Khumalo, 2019), the AMP promotes engagement with education as holistic, multifaceted, and grounded in diverse contexts. Additionally, the AMP can balance the ingqondo (intellect) and the intliziyo (heart). A simple listening project implemented in schools fostered greater empathy and connection in the classroom (Way & Nelson, 2018). Academic performance in an educational setting can only be improved by such efforts to bring intellect and the heart into harmony.

Implementation of the AMP is about paying careful attention to the process and remaining responsive to what emerges during the application of the AMP (Schneider & Somers, 2006). Pictures of the AMP usually operate as an 'evocative technique', evoking ideas about our status as interconnected beings, our social and cultural affiliations, values, beliefs, and so forth. But given the cultural diversity within South Africa, some may also experience the AMP in a less positive manner, as the association between personal transformation and ideas about communal human nature may be unfamiliar, or even threatening. The role of the facilitator is therefore to 'feed off the emergent process' as a guide to what to focus on or what to attend to next (Schneider & Somers, 2006).

Because participants, as human beings, are dynamic, they and the facilitator continuously adjust and co-evolve, reacting and altering in response to fresh inputs and contextual information (Schneider & Somers, 2006). As a result, the discussions develop and shift organically. The facilitator is aware that 'structure and content kill creativity' and is at ease with 'organised chaos' (Schneider & Somers, 2006). Instead of stifling the process with excessive structure and content, the facilitator prioritises the organic ebb and flow of participant engagement with the AMP.

Hence, the pragmatic application of this model of personhood is more akin to basic outlines, or 'bare bones' – it is intentionally vague and ambiguous, serving as a skeletal outline, a frame around which to weave naturally developing conversations about the AMP, arising from the diversity of the participants. Its goal is to provoke contemplation on the kind of culturally associated self-construction that has, for the most part, been abandoned in favour of the current global certainty of a constantly mutating, adaptable neoliberal subjectivity (Teo, 2018).

Introduction to the AMP is open-ended, processional, ritualistic, and a broad invitation to poke at it and try to find oneself reflected in it. After a brief description of the images, an interactive discussion usually follows (Jansen, 2022). The openness, flexibility, and adaptiveness of the AMP interactions are what make it appealing and advantageous. One can conveniently carry the collection of images around various contexts. It can be applied individually, as part of one-on-one teaching engagements with students, as I go into further detail below, or in training or therapeutic collectives. Additionally, it can be utilised in lecture halls, workshops, and small groups where screens can display the electronic representations of the images.

Most students recognise the self-representations of the AMP from their own culture. By briefly 'dipping into' shared self-understandings, the conversation moves towards the goal of the AMP – which is not to embark on an 'African cultural safari', but to channel into local onto-epistemologies (Laungani, 2005). This is partly a response to the call for curricular liberation and justice in higher education using indigenous philosophies like *Ubuntu* in the curriculum's epistemological reform (Hlatshwayo & Shawa, 2020).

I now shift to a discussion of the diffusion of the African multidimensional personhood within diverse educational settings.

The diffusion of the African multidimensional personhood within the university

Building bridges between learners and their onto-epistemologies

It is one thing to criticise other ways of being, like neoliberal subjectivity (Teo, 2018). But it is quite another to have one's own clear view of self (Pinker, 2002). Socialisation in *Umoya* personhood is more in line with the humanising pedagogies that Salazar (2013) describes, rather than being a cultural or political strategy, although it may have political ramifications.

Learning in a foreign culture in which one is unable to identify with oneself is stressful (Salazar, 2013). In more severe circumstances, learning outside of one's own cultural frameworks can lead to the development of self-hatred, which is also known as the anti-self-disorder (Akbar, 1984). The more of the person that the educational encounter permits, the less alienating, foreign, and distant the education (Salazar, 2013). According to Salazar's (2013) reflections on the American educational system's disjunction between humanity and education, the goal of humanised personhood is enhanced humanness, which is the process and ultimate purpose of African education (Letseka, 2000). Below, I offer a practical illustration of how the AMP can be used as a bridge to connect with personal and cultural worldviews and values, bringing the freedom to participate in education from unique points of view (Hlatshwayo & Shawa, 2020).

Several years ago, a Black Xhosa-speaking postgraduate psychology student from a rural background who spoke English as a third language was placed on the 'danger list' by her lecturers, like quite a few of the students I had contact with during this time. She was at risk of being excluded from her course of study. I responded to her request for assistance in my role as a clinical psychology internship trainer and supervisor.

On further exploration, the student appeared to be 'locked out' of her psychology studies on a cultural and language level. The gap between her cultural identity and the Western paradigm of psychology meant that she struggled to understand the concepts and assumptions that she was being schooled in. Many of the words she used turned out to be meaningless 'word salads' with little to no context.

We sat down with the AMP images arranged on the floor in front of us and started exploring her views not only on aspects of personhood per se, but also its guiding principles, values, and worldview. I 'translated' some of the indigenous healing concepts that she is familiar with, like *Ukuthwasa,* into Western psychological concepts. As part of becoming a traditional healer, *Ukuthwasa,* an indigenous healing process, involves 'becoming sick', which may entail physical symptoms and the experience of vivid dreams (Mlisa, 2019).

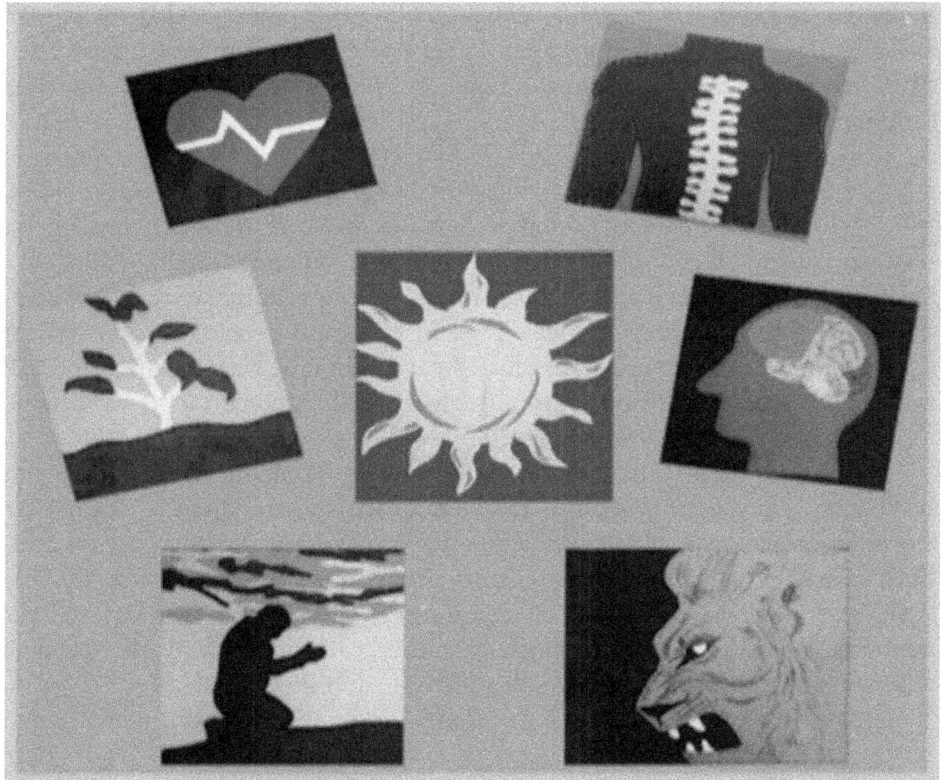

FIGURE 6.2: The African multidimensional personhood in relatable picture format (Jansen, 2022, p 40)

In one of our first meetings, I drew parallels between *Ukuthwasa* and the idea that the therapist's vulnerabilities can be a healing aspect of the therapeutic process, which reflects the importance of the therapist's person in psychotherapy (Aponte, 2022).

This understanding of the healer as 'wounded' suggests continuity between the personal and professional selves of the therapist (Kissil, Carneiro, & Aponte, 2018), a principle which may be broadly resonant with the *Ukuthwasa* process (Mlisa, 2019). The personal experiences of the therapist, including painful ones, can be judiciously applied with good therapeutic effect (Kissil, Carneiro, & Aponte, 2018). As we crossed Western and indigenous African psychological epistemologies over several meetings, the student actively contributed insights from within a Xhosa cultural frame of healing. Supported by the AMP framework, she increasingly gained epistemic access to Western psychological ideals through the prism of her own cultural worldview.

Fortunately, the story ended well, and she passed her examination. Which is of lesser relevance, the issue at stake is the epistemic violence that is committed (Mignolo, 2011), and the disservice to students when knowledge is not presented to them in a language, worldview, and values frame that they can relate to (Salazar, 2013). Students struggle to digest knowledge that is not organised in accordance with their own cultural frameworks, because the knowledge is unrelated to 'who they are' (Yazdi, 1992).

Senekal & Lenz (2020) had expressed concern about the lack of indigenous content to replace Eurocentric education in their exploration of academics' experiences with the decolonisation project. But the AMP is more than simply a concrete illustration of an alternative subjectivity; it's about reclaiming indigenous knowledge about oneself and repurposing it in a way that makes it accessible as knowledge that is still relevant today. The above example suggests that the student could access her own culturally informed system of healing via the AMP. The AMP is therefore a framework of onto-epistemology that can reflect the worldview, assumptions, and values that are consistent with local constructions of reality.

Once the student returned to her own ways of being in the world, her behaviour changed. She became 'free', 'emancipated', and open to engage the world from her own centre. The *Umoya*-self conferred dignity on herself as both an individual and as an extension of her sociocultural community. The AMP resonated with her sense of who she is in the world, which boosted her confidence. Because acting, developing, learning, and creating are all aspects of African personhood, her agentic side took over, and she succeeded.

Providing individuals with a sense of meaningfulness is another achievement of the AMP. This is because the AMP is a valuable tool for self-understanding in and of itself since it relates personhood to fundamental and universal human concerns such as belonging and morality (Molefe, 2020). Personhood is therefore logical and meaningful (Molefe, 2020). Furthermore, the meaning of words is the subject of philosophy (Letseka, 2000). Context as a determinant of what is real (Bhatnagar & Patra, 2023) shapes the meaning of words. Thus, if knowledge is estranged from the context of the learner, the learner may not have access to the meaning of those terms (Letseka, 2000).

Here, the AMP again associates with Salazar's (2013) frame of humanisation. The AMP became a tool of belonging, of inclusion, and of making the student feel part of a bigger whole, which was her own cultural framework. In this sense, the AMP becomes a framework of personhood that locates, rather than dislocates. A structure that can ignite inclusive and affirming ways of being with self and others. A self that is constructed through belonging and ethics is more able to live up to the promise of a higher education institution that is based on a shared reality, contextualised knowledge, and practices of inclusivity and justice. As said by Klaasen (2017), when we resolve the question of who we are, that is when development has taken place.

From the implementation of the AMP as a bridge to individual onto-epistemologies, I shift to its application as a tool that can foster unity among South African diversities of race, religion, and status.

The AMP as a tool of unity-in-diversity

Depending on the context, the application of the AMP may be modified to find common ground or shared values even with those who had not been culturally socialised to think of themselves in relational terms. Stated differently, the AMP can create unity in situations where it, unity, and common ground apparently do not exist. This occurred in the opening moments of a training event at a historically white university.

Right at the start of the training, with the pictures of the AMP on the floor in the circle of participants, I facilitated an icebreaker and team-building process by inviting interaction around the concept of *Umoya*. Most of the attendees who were from indigenous African traditions, in other words relational cultures, like Xhosa, Zulu, and Sotho-Tswana, not only recognised what was being shared with ease, but they identified with a view of the socially constructed self that was more culturally familiar to them than to myself, who experienced childhood exposure only to Abrahamic faith traditions, primarily Islam, with some immersion in the worship practices of Christianity.

I then translated *Umoya* into Afrikaans to culturally incorporate the White Afrikaans-speaking participants. As someone who was formally categorised as coloured by the former South African apartheid government, I share my mother tongue, Afrikaans, one of the official languages of South Africa, with white Afrikaners. In the spur of the moment, I described *Umoya* as '*so wyd soos die Heer se genade*' (as wide as God's mercy) to enhance insight into *Umoya* for the minority of White Christian attendees.

In this way, the idea of *Umoya* preserved the ideal of 'one humanity' across religious beliefs, encouraging all participants of this training to recognise themselves in it. This was accomplished by making a connection between a broader, more 'unfettered' non-theistic African spirituality of connectedness and Christian theistic spirituality (Mnyandu, 1997). Rather than concentrating on the accuracy of language translation, the main objective was risk-taking for the promotion of cross-cultural unity in a psychologically safe environment.

However, objections may be raised about equating the indigenous African concept *Umoya*, which captures the vital energy that permeates all existence, with a Western religious belief system that was once used to justify racial discrimination (Joebgen, 2016). In response, it is important to bear in mind that the concept *Umoya* (cautiously) complements views on quantum non-locality, with implications for perceptions of the unity of the universe, which can be extended to include the unity of all people (Haramein & Brown, 2019).

It instils a sense of hopefulness that the AMP, as a framework that facilitates engagement with diversity through an emphasis on the unity of all mankind, is generally well received by participants, even in settings beyond the educational context. Besides the lack of social cohesion in South Africa due to race and social class (Letseka, 2012; Ndinga-Kanga, Merwe, & Hartford, 2020), the history of colonialism and apartheid meant that South Africans have been overexposed to the extent of their differences, especially about race (Oelofsen, 2015). The AMP can be used in the service of unity-in-diversity, to promote social cohesion among South Africans of different races, religions, and statuses (Ndinga-Kanga, Van der Merwe, & Hartford, 2020). Many colonial subjects endured centuries of amplification of their difference (Shizha & Kariwo, 2011), but when diverse races come together in contemporary educational spaces, what compelling reasons do we provide for them to believe in their shared humanity?

The AMP promotes a reality built on human interaction and connectivity by reaffirming social individuality. Thus, in lecture halls, the *Umoya*-self serves as a tool to encourage cooperation and integration. The AMP places more emphasis on contextualised socio-cultural understandings of the self than it does on introducing individuals as unique individuals. Activities that promote cooperation, as well as the exploration of relevant cultural values and beliefs, may be incorporated as more social and unifying ways of starting relationships. Paying closer attention to human similarities gives one a fresh perspective on what makes each individual distinct. This may result in a balanced understanding of the self as simply different, but still a unique part of the same division of humanness.

After establishing some basis of unity, individuality and unique identities of race, ethnicity, gender, religion, sexual orientation, and a host of other diversities can be engaged with. *Umoya* personhood can therefore be applied as a powerful tool of building social cohesion, of helping people understand that they are connected in ways that may not be regularly considered (Haramein & Brown, 2019). This awareness of human unity has implications for peacebuilding and violence prevention (Ndinga-Kanga, Van der Merwe, & Hartford, 2020) in a country that is disproportionately plagued by violence (Long, 2019).

It may seem that decolonisation efforts in university spaces may remain challenging, not just due to the lack of indigenous knowledge content (Senekal & Lenz, 2020), or because of variables related to the subjectivities of university staff (Hlatshwayo & Alexander, 2021), but perhaps also due to decolonial competency deficits (Nyoni, 2019). The decolonial literacies and competencies required may range from self-awareness, critical groundedness in one's own cultural dynamics, to the ability to navigate and mediate complex socio-historical tensions in diverse academic spaces (Nyoni, 2019). Perhaps we underestimate the special skills required to guide complex identity negotiations, or to facilitate transformative, high-stakes, and deeply racialised and contested conversations. Which may include the productive integration of Western education with African values (Nyoni, 2019).

The discussion now shifts from issues of unity in a context of diversity to an examination of learner subjectivity in the pedagogical encounter between learner and educator. This discussion concerns aligning learner presence via the African multidimensional personhood (AMP) to the pedagogical transaction to achieve transformative learning.

Transformative learning theory suggests that learning is about the transformation of the person, it is meaningful, whole-person learning, not just the transfer of knowledge (Mezirow, 1997). Transformational learning theory, or transformative learning, is less about 'knowing more' but about undergoing a shift in perspective (Mezirow, 1997). Transformative learning disrupts the learner's usual way of viewing reality. This crisis of having one's long-held meaning frameworks challenged leads to a reassessment of assumptions, underlying beliefs, and long-held values (Mezirow, 1997).

However, in a post-conflict society like South Africa, most learners have not experienced education that is consistent with their 'usual view of reality' (Hlatshwayo & Shawa, 2020; Hlatshwayo, 2022; Heleta, 2018; Kumalo, 2018). Due to the ongoing Eurocentric nature of education, and the absence of local meaning frames in teaching and learning, learners are epistemically outcasted from the pedagogical transaction (Kumalo, 2018).

The concept of 'natives from nowhere', as used by Kumalo (2018), conveys the 'double jeopardy' of epistemic outcasts in untransformed learning institutions where education perpetuates their subjugation and intensifies the erosion of their humanity (Kumalo, 2018). To belong to such institutions, epistemic outcasts are forced to further betray already stretched and dwindling ties to their own worldview, values, and cultural grounding, exacerbating their sense of epistemic displacement (Kumalo, 2018).

However, curricula are embodied, and curricula transformation necessitates addressing the role of subjectivity in the ongoing coloniality of universities and attempts to arrest the alienation of current educational experiences in South Africa (Hlatshwayo & Alexander, 2021). Kwenda (2003) offers an embodied route to a transformative educational process by conceptualising epistemic injustice as cultural labour performed by individuals in postcolonial contexts like South Africa.

Kwenda names the invisible, frequently disregarded, but stressful cultural labour that occurs when people are compelled to live out their lives in languages, customs, and practices that are not their own as cultural injustice (Kwenda, 2003). He defines culture as social relations between people, their mores, norms, and taken-for-granted ways of doing things (Kwenda, 2003). Cultural injustice is not just being forced to live in accordance with the culture of someone else, but necessitates that one's own language, traditions, and taken-for-granted ways of being in the world are undermined and suppressed (Kwenda, 2003).

Transformative learning, as defined above, can therefore not proceed from the disruption of the learner's usual way of seeing the world, as the learner is epistemically absent from the learning encounter. There is nothing to disrupt as there is no presence, no perspective to transform (Kumalo, 2018). The achievement of transformative learning requires the presence of the learner, their lived experience, and cultural grounding, as transformative learning is about the transformation of a whole human being (Mezirow, 1997).

One response could be to incorporate the learner's cultural background into the educational process. However, the pedagogical transaction is defined by skewed power dynamics; hence, the learner cannot simply be culturally grounded in it. It is this power imbalance that is a primary obstacle to welcoming learners' worldviews and values into the pedagogical transaction. Thus, the focus must shift to the 'educator in the room' that needs to be addressed for any real change to occur (Kwenda, 2003).

As with the postgraduate psychology student discussed earlier, the insertion of the AMP in the pedagogical transaction may potentially form a bridge between learning and the subjectivity of the epistemic outcast. The AMP resembles the 'mother-tongue self', so named because it reflects a view of personhood consistent with the social and contextual self-reality of most South Africans (Eaton & Louw, 2002; Laher & Dockrat, 2019). The AMP can possibly socialise the educator in learner worldviews, meaning frames, and cultural principles relevant to the pedagogical transaction. The AMP may then be used as a practical strategy that aligns learner traditions and cultural grounding to the pedagogical transaction via identity education of the educator in the AMP.

A research proposal to train teachers, lecturers, and mental health practitioners in the AMP was submitted to the university where I work. In January 2025, Unisa's research ethics committee responded with ethics approval valid for the period February 2025 – February 2028, reference number 6637_2025_PRC_REC_001 for a 3-hour once-off workshop on the topic: Aligning learner presence via the Afro-Eastern multidimensional personhood (AEMP) to the pedagogical transaction to achieve transformative learning.

The discussions of this chapter have all been based on the reports of one person, the author's practice of the AMP. This mixed-methods study will provide an opportunity for some of the author's claims to be tested and to generate critical insights on the implementation and efficacy of the AMP.

In this workshop, educators will receive practical identity education in a culturally relevant model of personhood, the AMP, for integration in the pedagogical transaction. Educators will learn about local lived communal personhood, and the onto-epistemologies on which it is founded, as well as the skills required to practically integrate it in the pedagogical transaction.

Kwenda's concepts of cultural injustice and mutual vulnerability will be used to theorise the shift from cultural injustice to cultural justice with the AMP as a proxy for learner presence (Kwenda, 2003). Via the AMP, educators will engage with the context-bound personhood familiar to most South Africans, which will increase their awareness of the cultural injustice of learners (Kwenda, 2003).

As they grapple with the implications of such cultural awareness for their own identity and cultural grounding, as well as for the pedagogical transaction, they start to experience mutual vulnerability with the epistemically outcast learners (Kwenda, 2003). It is this experience of mutual vulnerability with the learners that increases the likelihood that they will share the stress of cultural injustice that holds the potential to 'level the playing fields' between learners and educators (Kwenda, 2003). Through socialisation with the AMP, educators become increasingly aware and accepting of the role of learner cultural dynamics in education. Such cultural awareness will assist in encouraging educators to create space for learners' worldviews and values within the pedagogical transaction, which may potentially increase the likelihood that transformative learning will take place.

In summary, the above examples of bridging the onto-epistemological divide within the pedagogical transaction, engendering of unity-within-diversity in educational spaces, and the 'shared suffering' and mutual empathy generated between educators and learners to promote transformative education, offer some practical insights into how the AMP may promote transformation in higher education settings. The AMP is an ongoing experiment, a work in progress of doing education differently. It can be seen as a form of epistemic disobedience, a breakaway from tedious cognitive injustice, an attempt to not just construct knowledge from the margins (Mignolo, 2011) but to stimulate structures and processes for the flow of relational-ethical discourses throughout the university.

There are many issues with colonial education, and with the historical and current injustices in education that we don't know how to overcome. Decolonisation is even more challenging in the absence of tools that can help to model learning as an expression of belonging.

Conclusion

The history of higher education has been characterised by some extreme and radical acts of violence, alienation, and othering. Thirty years after the end of apartheid, education still comes at a cost to identity; to succeed in society, one must be willing to adopt an identity that is at odds with one's own.

However, attempts to transform universities may fail because of disproportionate attention to factors outside of the individual and the neglect of the inner resources of people. One respondent made an important point in Hlatshwayo & Alexander's (2021) interviews with academics regarding the decolonisation of the university: they thought it would be better to concentrate on the subjectivity of academics rather than merely on curriculum adjustments.

This chapter carries a proposal to broaden decolonial efforts through the incorporation of a personhood instrument capable of disrupting the social reality of coloniality. Just as knowledge, identity, and subjectivity are used to extend coloniality, socially embedded personhood was introduced as a model of subjectivity that can promote institutional reform by offering a foundation of transformationally agile personhood from which to question the status quo and transform higher education.

To better synergise with the realities and meaning frames of South Africa's diverse relational cultures, the chapter explored the substitution of neoliberal subjectivity with sociospiritual humanness in the form of an African-centred theory of humanness. The AMP is a relational moral agent and a model of complex identity. It is a self that can act in line with its own values and convictions. As a result, it represents a self that interacts with education and information in ways that are grounded in its own worldviews and existential priorities. Through the infusion of socially embedded and locally accessible subjectivity within three different settings of the university, an incident of building bridges between individuals and their onto-epistemologies, facilitation of diversity and multiculturalism in South African educational spaces, and the humanisation of the pedagogical transaction to encourage transformative learning, the AMP sets about the possible destabilisation of the stranglehold of the violence of neoliberalism in the academy. Firstly, the AMP humanises learning through framing pedagogical encounters with the values and worldviews of students, linking the students' cultural knowledge base to the knowledge of the academy.

Secondly, the AMP approaches the discussion on personhood and transformation of higher education from the perspective of drawing attention to the common humanity among diverse people. This unity in humanity is mainly achieved through the immersion and exposure to activities that may enhance the direct experience of some of the principles of the AMP, like connecting, cooperating, and the intimacy that results from practicing being human with human others, similar and dissimilar to oneself. Furthermore, personhood based on relationality has a unifying effect on individuals that may spread out and impact the broader environment.

Thirdly, this model of relational personhood can support educators in effective engagement with learner onto-epistemologies. Through training in the AMP, the educator may begin to share some of the stress that students typically experience, as they, the educators, might be getting exposed to learning outside their own values and worldviews, like learners are usually forced to do. This mutual vulnerability between learner and educator may turn into a strategy for the design of a 'new epistemic horizon' in the pedagogical exchange. Unlike the unequal distribution of stress labour in the pedagogic transaction, where only one side's epistemology and humanity matter, and the other side suffers as a result, this 'new epistemic dispensation' may be accompanied by a tentative process of transformative education, positively impacting the pedagogical transaction.

The ritualisation of socio-moral personhood within the academy has the potential to challenge profit-worshipping academic discourses, even though it can be risky to disrupt the replication of modernity's imperialist projects in academic settings. Since development is a part of what it means to be human in African personhood, the AMP is a model that can enhance an African personhood approach to development, where people can be supported to self-transform and realise their human potential. Considering that people and institutional cultures are mutually constitutive, over time, the cultures of universities may be transformed one individual at a time.

References

Ahuvia, A. C. (2005). Beyond the extended Self: Loved Objects and Consumers' Identity Narratives. *Journal of Consumer Research*, 32(1), 171–184.

Akbar, N. (1984). Africentric social sciences for human liberation. *Journal of Black Studies*, 14(4), 395-414.

Alcaro, A. C., & Panksepp, J. (2017). The affective core of the self: A neuro-achetypical perspective on the foundations of human (and animal) subjectivity. *Frontiers in Psychology*, 8(1424).

Alvino, G. (1996). *The human energy field in relation to science, consciousness, and health*. Brookline, MA: Heart to Heart Associates (HTHA).

Ammon, L. (2019). Decolonising the University Curriculum in South Africa: A Case Study of the University of the Free State.

Aponte, H. J. (2022). The soul of therapy: The therapist's use of self in the therapeutic relationship. *Contemporary Family Therapy*, 44(2), 136-143.

Badat, S. (2008). Redressing the colonial/apartheid legacy: Social equity, redress and higher education admissions in democratic South Africa. *Conference on Affirmative Action in Higher Education in India, the United States, and South Africa*. New Delhi, India.

Baloyi, L., & Ramose, M. B. (2016). Psychology and psychotherapy redefined from the viewpoint of the African experience. *Alternation Special Edition*, 18, 12-35.

Bhatnagar, D., & Patra, S. (2023). A Holistic View to Approach Sustainable Development: Spiritual Roots and Evidence From Quantum Physics. In *Applied Spirituality and Sustainable Development Policy* (pp. 149-166). Emerald Publishing Limited.

Brown, W., & Strawn, B. D. (2017). Recognizing the complexity of personhood. In *Verbs, Bones, and Brains: Interdisciplinary Perspectives on Human Nature*.

Chirinda, B., Ndlovu, M., & Spangenberg, E. (2021). Teaching mathematics during the Covid-19 lockdown in a context of historical disadvantage. *Education Sciences*, 11, 177.

Chitumba, W. (2013). University education for personhood through Ubuntu philosophy. *International Journal of Asian Social Science*, 3(5):1268-1276.

Comaroff, J. L., & Comaroff, J. (2001). On personhood: An anthropological perspective from Africa. *Social Identities: Journal for the Study of Race, Nation and Culture*, 7(2), 267-283.

Cushman, P. (1990). Why the self is empty: Towards a historically situated psychology. *American Psychologist*, 45(5), 599.

de Souza, M. (2004). Teaching for empathy, compassion, meaning, and connectedness to create communities of greater social harmony and cohesion: Rediscovering the spiritual dimension in education. *Paper presented at the AARE International Education Research Conference in Melbourne.*

de Souza, M. (2012). Connectedness and connectedness: the dark side of spirituality –implications for education. *International Journal of Children's Spirituality*, 17(4), 291–303.

Devitt, S. (2014). *Defending conformational chorism against holism: Limited coherence and coordination as sources of epistemic justification.* In Conference of the Australasian Society for Cognitive Science (No. 50338, pp. 25-25).

Dladla, N. (2017). Towards an African critical philosophy of race: Ubuntu as a philopraxis of liberation. *Filosofia Theoretica: Journal of African Philosophy, Culture and Religions*, 6(1), 39-68.

Eaton, L., & Louw, J. (2002). Culture and self in South Africa: Individualism and collectivism. *Journal of Social Psychology*, 140, 210–217.

Edwards, S. D. (2016). HeartMath and Ubuntu integral healing approaches for social coherence and physical activity psychology. *African Journal for Physical Activity and Health Sciences*, 22(1:1), 49-64.

Frager, R. (1999). *Heart, self & soul: The Sufi psychology of growth, balance and harmony.* Quest Books.

Grosfoguel, R. (2007). The epistemic decolonial turn: Beyond political-economy paradigms. *Cultural studies*, 21(2-3), 211-223.

Gurel, N. Z., & Ardell, J. L. (2022). Stress-related dysautonomias and neurocardiology-based treatment approaches. *Autonomic Neuroscience.*

Han, A. G. (2008). Building a Harmonious Society and Achieving Individual Harmony. *Journal of Chinese Political Science*, 13(2), 143-164.

Haramein, N., & Brown, W. (2019). Unified Physics and the Entanglement Nexus of awareness. *NeuroQuantology*, 7(17), 40-52.

Hay, D., & Nye, R. (2006). *The spirit of the child Revised edition.* Jessica Kingsley Publishers.

Heleta, S. (2018). Decolonizing knowledge in South Africa: Dismantling the 'pedagogy of big lies'. *Ufahamu: A Journal of African Studies*, 40(2).

Hlatshwayo, M. N. (2022). The Rise of the Neoliberal University in South Africa: Some Implications for Curriculum Imagination(s). *Education as Change*, 26(1), 1-21. https://dx.doi.org/10.25159/1947-9417/11421.

Hlatshwayo, M. N., & Alexander, I. (2021). "We've been taught to understand that we don't have anything to contribute towards knowledge": Exploring academics' understanding of decolonising curricula in higher education. *Journal of Education*, http://dx.doi.org/10.17159/2520-9868/i82a03 .

Hlatshwayo, M. N., & Shawa, L. B. (2020). Ubuntu currere in the academy: a case study from the South African experience. *Third World Thematics: A TWQ Journal*, 5(1–2), 120–136 https://doi.org/10.1080/23802014.2020.1762509.

Jansen, J. D., & Walters, C. A. (2022). *The decolonization of knowledge: Radical ideas and the shaping of institutions in South Africa and beyond.* Cambridge University Press.

Jansen, S. (2022). *Masculinity meets humanity: An adapted model of masculinised psychotherapy.* Unisa Press.

Jansen, S. (2025). Inserting the African multidimensional personhood (AMP) model between the personhood of the mental health practitioner and psychological practice. Philosophical Psychology, Advance online publication. https://doi.org/10.1080/09515089.2025.2522321.

Jecker, N. S., & Atuire, C. A. (2024). Personhood: An emergent view from Africa and the West. *Developing World Bioethics*, 1-10.

Joebgen, M. L. (2016). "Learning From Mistakes of the Past: Christianity, Apartheid, and Social Movement Framing,". *Bridge/Work*, 2(1), Article 6.

Keesing, R. M. (1974). Theories of Culture. *Annual Review of Anthropology*, 73-97.

Khumalo, S. S. (2019). Implications of school violence in South Africa on socially just education. *Journal of Social Sciences and Humanities*, 16(8).

Kissil, K., Carneiro, R., & Aponte, H. J. (2018). Beyond duality: The relationship between the personal and the professional selves of the therapist in the Person of the Therapist Training. *Journal of Family Psychotherapy*, 29(1), 71-86.

Klaasen, J. (2017). The role of personhood in development: An African perspective on development in South Africa. *Missionalia*, 45(1), 29-44.

Korsgaard, C. M. (2011). Self-Constitution and Irony. In J. Lear, *A Case for Irony* (pp. 75-83). Harvard University Press.

Kumalo, S. H. (2018). Explicating Abjection – Historically White Universities creating Natives of Nowhere? *Critical Studies in Teaching and Learning*, 6(1), 1-17.

Kwenda, C. V. (2003). Cultural justice: the pathway to reconciliation and social cohesion. In D. Chidester, P. Dexter, & W. James, *Whatholdustogether: Social cohesion in South Africa* (pp. 67-80). Cape Town: HSRC Press.

Laher, S., & Dockrat, S. (2019). The five-factor model and individualism and collectivism in South Africa: Implications for personality assessment. *African Journal for Psychological Assessment*, 1(0), 1(1), 1-9.

Laungani, P. (2005). Building counselling bridges: The holy grail or a poisoned chalice? *Counselling Psychology Quarterly*, 18(4), 247-259.

Letseka, M. (2000). African philosophy and educational discourse. In P. Higgs, N. Vakalisa, T. Mda, & N. Assie-Lumumba, *African voices in education* (pp. 179-193). Juta and Company Ltd.

Letseka, M. (2012). In defence of Ubuntu. *Studies in philosophy and education*, 31(1), 47–60.

Letseka, M., & Breier, M. (2008). Student poverty in higher education: The impact of higher education dropout on poverty. *Edited by Simeon Maile, 83.*

Long, K. M., McDermott, F., & Meadows, G. N. (2018). Being pragmatic about healthcare complexity: our experiences applying complexity theory and pragmatism to health services research. *BMC Medicine,* https://doi.org/10.1186/s12916-018-1087-6.

Long, W. (2019). Shame, envy, impasse, and hope: On the psychopolitics of violence in SA. *WISER seminar, University of the Witwatersrand.* , https://wiser.wits.ac.za/system/files/seminar/Long2019. pdf.

Lundberg, A., Fraschini, N., & Aliani, R. (2023). What is subjectivity? Scholarly perspectives on the elephant in the room. *Quality & Quantity,* 4609-4529.

Mabharwana, N. (2022). Food security at the University of the Western Cape: An exploration of actions and programmes to address student hunger. *Master's in Development Studies,* University of the Western Cape.

Maldonado-Torres, N. (2007). On the coloniality of being. *Cultural Studies,* 21(2-3), 240-270, https://doi.org/10.1080/09502380601162548.

Markus, H. R., & Kitayama, S. (2010). Cultures and selves: A cycle of mutual constituion. *Perspectives on Psychological Science,* 5(4) 420–430.

Mbiti, J. S. (1969). *African Religions and Philosophy.* pp. 108-109: Nairobi: East African Educational Publishers Ltd.

Mcintosh, J. (2018). Personhood, self, and individual. *The International Encyclopedia of Anthropology,* 1-9.

Mezirow, J. (1997). "Transformative learning: theory to practice". *New Directions for Adult and Continuing Education,* 74, 5-12.

Mignolo, W. (2011). Epistemic disobedience and the decolonial option: A manifesto. *Transmodernity: Journal of peripheral cultural production of the Luso-Hispanic world,* 1(2).

Mkhize, N. (2021). African/Afrikan-centered psychology. *South African Journal of Psychology,* 51(3), 422-429.

Mlisa, L. R. (2019). I am an igqirha (healer): phenomenological and experiential spiritual journey towards healing identity construction. *Numen: revista de estudos e pesquisa da religião, Juiz de Fora,* 22(1), 220-239.

Mnyandu, M. (1997). Ubuntu as the basis of authentic humanity: An African Christian perspective. *Journal of Constructive Theology,* 3(1), 77-86.

Molefe, M. (2020). Personhood and a meaningful life in African philosophy. *South African Journal of Philosophy,* 39(2), 194-207.

Munro, N., & Msimango, L. (2023). Even hungrier for knowlege: A 10-year follow-up study on vulnerability to food insecurity among students at the University of KwaZulu Natal. *Perspectives in Education,* 41(4), 421-434.

Muyambi, G. C., & Ahiaku, P. K. (2025). Inequalities and education in South Africa: A scoping review. *International Journal of Educational Research Open.*

Naidoo, K. (2023). The simultaneous atomisation and massification of neoliberal reason. *Acta Academica,* 55(2), 170-186.

Ndinga-Kanga, M., Van der Merwe, H., & Hartford, D. (2020). Forging a resilient social contract in South Africa: States and societies sustaining peace in the post-apartheid era. *Journal of Intervention and Statebuilding*, 14(1), 22-41.

Nobles, W. W., & Mkhize, N. (2020). Charge and the challenge of illuminating the spirit (Skh Djr): The question of paradigm, episteme, and terminology for therapy and treatment. *Alternation*, 27(1), 6-39.

Nsamenang, A. B. (2006). Human ontogenesis: An indigenous African view on development and intelligence. *International Journal of Psychology*, 41(4), 293-297.

Nyoni, J. (2019). Decolonising the higher education curriculum: An analysis of African intellectual readiness to break the chains of a colonial caged mentality. *Transformation in Higher Education*, 4(0), a69.

Oelofsen, R. (2015). Decolinisation of the African mind and intellectual landscape. *Phronimon*, 16(2), 130-146.

Pearce, J. C. (2002). *The biology of transcendence: A blueprint of the human spirit.* Rochester: Park Street Press.

Pearsall, P. P. (1999). *The heart's code: Tapping the wisdom and power of our heart energy.* Harmony.

Pinker, S. (2002). The blank slate: The modern denial of human nature. *New York, NY, Viking. Popper, K.(1974). Unended Quest. Fontana, London*.

Rogers, M. E. (1994). The science of unitary beings: Current perspectives. *Nursing Science Quarterly*, 7(1), 33-35.

Romm, N. R. (2024). An indigenous relational approach to systemic thinking and being: Focus on participatory onto-epistemology. *Systemic Practice and Action Research*, 37, 811–842.

Salazar, M. d. (2013). A humanizing pedagogy: Reinventing the principles and practice of education as a journey towards liberation. *Review of Research in Education*, 37(1), 121-148.

Schein, R. H. (2009). Belonging through land/scape. *Environment and Planning A 2009*, 41, 811-826.

Schneider, M., & Somers, M. (2006). Organizations as complex adaptive systems: Implications of Complexity Theory for leadership research. *The Leadership Quarterly*, 17(4), 351-365.

Schulte, M., Bamberg, S., Rees, J., & Rollin, P. (2020). Social identity as a key concept for connecting transformative societal change with individual environmental activism. *Journal of Environmental Psychology*, 72.

Senekal, Q., & Lenz, R. (2020). Decolonising the South African Higher Education curriculum, investigation into the challenges. *International Journal of Social Sciences and Humanities Studies*, 12(1), ISSN: 1309-8063.

Shizha, E., & Kariwo, M. T. (2011). *Education and Development in Zimbabwe: A social, political and economic analysis.* Sense Publishers.

Teo, T. (2018). Homo neoliberalus: From personality to forms of subjectivity. *Theory & Psychology*, 28(5), 581–599.

wa Thiong'o, N. (2009). *Something torn and new: An African renaissance.* Basic Books.

Way, N., & Nelson, J. D. (2018). "The listening project: fostering connection and curiosity In middle school classrooms". *The crisis of connection: Roots, consequences, and solutions,* 274-298.

Wilder, C. S. (2013). *Ebony & Ivy: Race, slavery, and the troubled history of America's Universities.* New York: Bloomsbury Press.

Wynter, S. (2003). Unsettling the Coloniality of Being/Power/Truth/Freedom: Towards the Human, After Man, Its Overrepresentation – An Argument. *The New Centennial Review,* 3(3), 257-337.

Yazdi, M. H. (1992). *The Principles of Epistemology in Islamic Philosophy.* New York: State University of New York Press.

Zembylas, M. (2017). Re-contextualising human rights education: some decolonial strategies and pedagogical/curricular possibilities. *Pedagogy, Culture & Society,* 25(4).

SECTION 3

Conversations about Innovation and Technology

CHAPTER 7

Incorporating generative AI into academia: Implications for a disruptive pedagogy

Jerome D. Kiley

Key premise

GenAI automating cognitive tasks, including those critical to the academic endeavour, is pervasive, easily accessible, and widely adopted as following the path of least resistance is in human nature. If academia is to remain relevant in enhancing cognitive skills and employability, the existing knowledge acquisition paradigm must embrace GenAI pedagogies.

Abstract

The chapter explores the incorporation of generative artificial intelligence (GenAI) in higher education (HE) and the associated ethical and pragmatic implementation. The methodology used recognises the fast-paced development of GenAI theory, requiring a combination of formal and informal resources to understand its complex and evolving impact on HE. The essence of GenAI and ethical challenges, together with the purpose of HE, is first examined as a foundation for a model that aligns the functions of HE-related apps with related ethical challenges, academic skills they automate, and the impact on skills development. The argument is presented that HE ethically and responsibly embraces the evolving GenAI environment to remain relevant by adopting GenAI-driven pedagogies that counteract the risks of traditional assessments and drive higher-order skills development. The chapter promotes the strategic implementation of GenAI-driven teaching methods, the importance of digital literacy, and the open utilisation of GenAI tools. It concludes that future research focuses on developing assessment methods that actively involve students in ways that discourage using GenAI text generation.

Keywords: academia; artificial intelligence (AI); artificial intelligence agents; generative artificial intelligence (GenAI); disruptive pedagogy; knowledge generation.

Introduction

Generative artificial intelligence (GenAI) has been creeping stealthily into academia, the tipping point in the launch of ChatGPT-3.5 in March 2022, which propelled GenAI into the collective consciousness. GenAI applications (apps) can recognise patterns, identify and synthesise knowledge from data, analyse, summarise and interpret text, data and images, simulate reality, and make informed recommendations indistinguishable from human outputs (Kiley, 2024). There is a high adoption rate of GenAI technologies, given that humans are hard-wired to follow the path of least resistance (Hagura et al., 2017), with businesses embracing GenAI in their operations (Haan & Watts, 2023). GenAI poses unprecedented challenges and potential for the academic endeavour. GenAI can generate many of the outputs of 'traditional' pedagogies used in higher education (HE) to develop student skills and competencies. At the same time, GenAI also offers new and unique opportunities for skills development. The nature and purposes of HE are weighed against the potential benefits and threats of GenAI in teaching and learning using a pragmatic approach that considers the ethical risks and erosion of academic competencies.

The chapter starts by outlining the methodology used. It then provides a brief overview of GenAI, accompanying ethical issues, and the purposes of HE. A model aligning GenAI functions with its impact on HE and ethical risks are then presented.

Methodology

Traditional theoretical literature reviews comprise the analysis of the existing body of theory to identify shortcomings, focusing on peer-reviewed journals and the like (Saunders et al., 2023). However, the body of GenAI theory is evolving faster than recognised academic resources, with a lack of consensus in established viewpoints and theories, necessitating the incorporation of less formal resources and subjective observations. This appears counterintuitive, given hundreds of hits for ChatGPT and AI on academic search engines, including several systematic reviews on the impact of system ChatGPT in education (e.g. Ansari et al., 2023; Mai et al., 2024; Montenegro-Rueda et al., 2023). Rather than providing an exhaustive review, the chapter aims to provide broad practical guidelines regarding using GenAI in HE in the context of ethical principles and impact on competency development.

The point of departure is the author's subjective experience that while there is a general awareness of GenAI, with ChatGPT dominating the discourse, there is a limited understanding of GenAI's functioning, pervasiveness, and how it operates in the world.

CHAPTER 7

The nature of generative artificial intelligence (GenAI)

Artificial intelligence (AI) comprises tools designed to carry out tasks and solve problems that previously required human intelligence (Chubb et al., 2022). Traditional AI models trained with large quantities of labelled data to power recommendation systems have been used extensively in academia since the start of the 20th century with the introduction of web and academic search engines. Productivity apps such as Microsoft Office and Google Workspace utilise artificial intelligence (AI) in tasks such as spelling and grammar checking, referencing, design, and layout generation. AI is also utilised extensively in statistical and thematic analysis programmes to detect patterns, categorise data, test hypotheses, and provide visualisations (Kiley, 2024). Traditional AI performs routine tasks previously performed by humans, contributing to the user's productivity.

However, the advent of GenAI has advanced the field of AI, using large language models (LLMs) that apply machine learning algorithms to detect patterns and fundamental structures in massive unorganised training datasets. The resulting statistically weighted, algorithmic parameters are combined in neural networks to generate new, human-like text, music, images, and computer code operationalised in various apps (Kiley, 2024). The power, functionality, and accuracy of GenAI are evolving exponentially, e.g. ChatGPT-3.5 (released 15/3/22, 175 billion parameters) versus ChatGPT-4 (released 14/3/23, 1,76 trillion parameters) (Schreiner, 2023), and the number of apps available in the Google Play Store increasing from 16000 in 2009 to 3,72 million in 2023 (Turner, 2024).

Artificial intelligence has steadily improved its cognitive skills over decades and can now almost flawlessly detect faces and objects, transcribe speech-to-text, translate language, operate vehicles, create images, write detailed prose, develop realistic synthetic voices, and create beautiful music. Its capabilities for long-term planning, imagination, and the simulation of complex concepts are fast accelerating and it is expected to reach human-level performance of a wide range of cognitive tasks in the foreseeable future (Suleyman & Bhaskar, 2023).

The distinction between AI and GenAI is not as important as comprehending the capabilities of these technologies and recognising our limited comprehension of the underlying mechanisms. AI and GenAI are used interchangeably going forward in the chapter.

GenAI ethical and pragmatic concerns

GenAI (foundational models) are driven by algorithms, which are human-programmed, computerised decision-making systems that evolve through machine learning and are susceptible to inherent programmer and training data biases (Baker & Hawn, 2022). Mittelstadt et al. (2016) identify six criteria to evaluate the reliability and validity of algorithmic outputs, namely i) sufficient supporting evidence, ii) transparent and comprehensible correlation between data and conclusions, iii) the source data is of sufficient quality to support conclusions, iv) avoiding bias towards specific social categories, v) the absence of bias influencing reality perception, and vi) harmful effects can be tracked, source identified, and people held accountable. However, identifying biases is challenging as algorithms and training data are complex and opaque, use inferences, evolve, and are often kept secret (intellectual capital), confounded by the 'black box problem', namely the inability to understand GenAI's decision-making process and anticipate the outputs (Bathaee, 2017; Calderonio, 2023). Hallucinations and the occurrence of senseless or unfaithful outputs that do not match the input source are widely acknowledged shortcomings of LLMs (Alkaissi & McFarlane, 2023). The principle, where possible, is to identify an app's foundational model and the algorithms' limitations, and verify the generated outputs' authenticity. There is an evolving field of research on these issues, much of which is available in online open access journals. Nevertheless, considering the swift advancements in GenAI, non-scholarly resources, such as blogs, websites, and online articles, may also be useful (Kiley, 2024).

Malcolm Gladwell (2008) popularised the '10000-hour rule' as the necessary time of focused practise it takes to achieve mastery in a specific field. Performing activities requiring a particular set of cognitive skills aids in their development and refinement. GenAI offers many opportunities for efficiency, with proficiency in typing, reading, spelling, grammar, literature selection, organisation, analysis, critical evaluation, and synthesis no longer required by humans. However, using GenAI to perform tasks and make decisions humans previously made limits the users' opportunity to develop these. The question then arises as to what the purpose is of HE in the context of knowledge and skills development.

The purpose of higher education

The purpose of higher education is a contested space (Blackley et al., 2020), with aims varying from preparing students for the labour market to personal and societal growth, social mobility, and citizenship, while retaining and growing global knowledge (Brooks et al., 2020). Generally, students have utilitarian expectations in the form of quality employment and career advancement (Kiley, 2020).

University education aims to develop cognitive abilities, including knowledge acquisition, problem-solving, analytical thinking, reasoning, creativity, and critical thinking, outlined in level descriptors for the National Qualifications Framework (South African Qualifications Authority, 2012). Critical thinking involves mastering critical route analysis, logical reasoning, reflection, and evaluating intricate arguments. Elements of critical thinking include establishing the credibility of information, evaluating deductive conclusions, identifying underlying assumptions, planning processes, predicting probable consequences, making valid inferences from data, and interpreting semantics (Wannapiroon, 2008). Universities apply various pedagogical strategies to develop the desired skills and competencies, defined using classification such as Bloom's Revised Taxonomy (Krathwohl, 2002), the Structure of Observed Learning Outcomes (SOLO) (Brabrand & Dahl, 2009) and the 21st Century Personalised Learning Skills Taxonomy (Ward, et.al., 2021), all of which have the development of cognitive capacities at their core. Student development occurs within the context of the massification of HE with the significant growth in student enrolment and accompanying surge in class sizes and student-to-lecturer ratios (Hornsby & Osman, 2014).

HE assessments (e.g. tests, class discussions, quizzes, essays, portfolios, presentations, practical projects, reflective projects, research reports) vary along various dimensions. These dimensions include monitored versus independent, formal versus informal, immediate versus delayed feedback, spontaneous versus planned, individual versus group, oral versus written, graded versus ungraded, open-ended versus closed/constrained response, lecturer-controlled versus student-controlled, lecturer versus peer-assessed, process versus product-oriented, brief versus extended, scaffolded (lecturer/technology guided) versus independently performed (Trumbull & Lash, 2013).

GenAI tools relevant to HE, their functions, challenges, and ethical risks

LLMs such as ChatGPT, Bard, Turing Bletchley, Hunyuan, ERNIE, and xAI produce desired outputs based on natural language instructions (prompts). However, designing effective prompts (prompt engineering) that do not direct LLMs to biased outputs is complex and challenging, especially for non-AI experts (Zamfirescu-Pereira, 2023). GenAI apps are software codes performing specific functions, i.e., applying appropriate prompts. Apps are developed by human programmers using platforms such as Android and iOS, cross-platform app development tools, and low-code and no-code GenAI tools (Microsoft, undated).

The code used in app prompt engineering is generally not shared or understood when developed using low or no-code tools (Fui-Hoon Nah, 2023). While apps simplify GenAI functions, they add a layer of opaqueness to understanding the link between data and outputs.

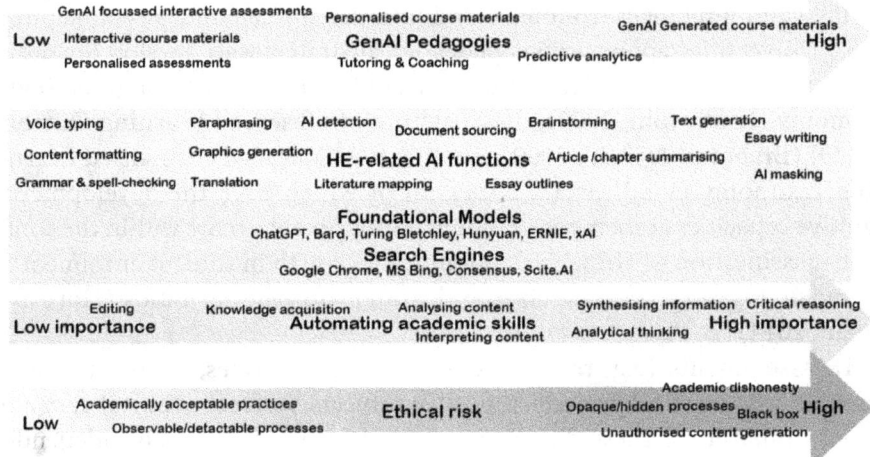

FIGURE 7.1: The HE GenAI landscape, ethical risks, and academic skills
Reproduced with permission from Kiley, 2024

Foundational models (large language models (LLMs)) are at the centre as they drive the applications and agents that perform various academic tasks on our behalf. Irrespective of the model, there is a lack of access to their algorithms and training data, inherent biases, and they can produce 'hallucinations', i.e. inaccurate or misleading outputs. LLMs are also self-learning and self-correcting, resulting in the 'black box effect', where the programmers who wrote the algorithms cannot predict the outputs reliably, which has the implication that there is no accountability for the outputs. At the same time LLMs and their accompanying apps and agents are evolving exponentially, becoming more reliable and increasing their functionality. GenAI is a reality in our world; however, the output should be continually evaluated and treated with a healthy level of scepticism.

The HE-related functions in the model are arranged from simpler ones, such as formatting and grammar checking, to more complex ones, such as literature mapping and text generation. In this context, complexity refers to the degree and ease with which the user can validate a particular functional output.

The automation of academic skills aligns closely with the complexity of the function performed by the app or agent; in-depth, the simpler academic skills, such as formatting and grammar checking, are relatively mundane and were often previously performed by human editors and assistants. However, when GenAI is used to perform advanced academic tasks, requiring advanced cognitive skills, the risk of negatively impacting the user's academic development becomes significantly greater.

The ethical risks related to using GenAI also become greater with the more complex functions, given that the outputs are more susceptible to the underlying weaknesses inherent in LLMs. The ethics of using LLMs to perform advanced academic functions, for example, in a literature review, is ethically suspect given that it takes over the advanced cognitive skills required to perform these tasks. There is also no accountability on the part of the LLM, and this is essentially equitable, as you get another human to perform your work for you.

Finally, and most notably in the context of this chapter, GenAI pedagogies incorporate artificial intelligence into higher education to immerse the student into the content and mitigate several of the risks that AI poses to traditional HE pedagogies. While not immune to the underlying weaknesses of LLMs, GenAI offers a huge range of potential for new pedagogies, especially when trained with reliable academic sources.

The discussion of GenAI apps is loosely arranged into six broad functional categories: writing support, data searching, text summarising, text generation, AI text detection, and delivering learning.

Supporting the writing process

Productivity tools (word processing, spreadsheets, slides, email, etc.), such as Google Workspace, Microsoft 365, and Adobe, incorporate GenAI to check spelling and grammar, format content, intelligent design, predict, translate, and transcribe text, optical character recognition, and collaboration. Function-specific GenAI apps assist with proofreading (e.g. Grammarly, Slick Write, Hemingway), readability (e.g. Readable, AotoCrit), paraphrasing (e.g. Quilbot, Jasper, WordAi, Wordtune), synonyms (OneLook Thesaurus), referencing (e.g. Zotero, Mendeley, Endnote), typesetting (typeset.io, SciSpace), managing notes and resources (e.g. Evernote), and collaboration (e.g. Trello).

These tools automate 'mechanistic' tasks, the previous mastery of which did not necessarily add value to academic development. While not discounting the advanced philosophical hermeneutics of grammar (Coeckelbergh, 2022), these tools contain limited biases (e.g. gender biases in AI translation (Prates et al., 2018)) and GenAI tools such as Fairslator and Bias Finder can detect these.

However, while GenAI makes the writing process more efficient, the danger exists that the author's authenticity is lost, particularly with paraphrasing and predictive text. In particular, junior students may not develop their own writing 'voice' and lose or distort the original text's intended meaning.

Search engines

Almost all data searches, scientific or otherwise, use AI-powered search engines (e.g. arXviv, Consensus, Google Chrome, Microsoft Bing, Sci-Hub) that rely on complex algorithms. Despite Google's 200 ranking parameters, the reliability of the data is not always perfect given that ranks can be manipulated and that the most frequently accessed data (clicks) is prioritised, rather than the most accurate information (Su et.al., 2010). How frequently do you navigate beyond the first page of search results on Google? Integrating GenAI into searches makes the results vulnerable to the biases inherent in their algorithms. Academic search engines, like Google Scholar and Semantic Scholar, have existed for a considerable time. These integrated tools are very effective in locating pertinent materials. Nevertheless, some difficulties need to be addressed, such as confirmation bias, the tendency to favour higher-rated researchers and journals, and the tendency of journals to overlook non-English publications. There is a possibility of reinforcing social prejudices against marginalised groups, who may either be excessively represented in published studies or, on the contrary, totally disregarded. The quality of the outputs is influenced by the inherent biases ingrained in search queries, meaning that the search engine provides results based on your specific request. It is important to note that auto-suggested searches are more likely to contain inherent biases in their provided outcomes.

Some apps (e.g. Scite.ai) aid in assessing the authenticity of research papers, while others map out how papers are connected and identify related studies and their ratings (e.g., Connected Papers, Litmaps, Inciteful, Research Rabbit). However, these apps are also susceptible to confirmation bias (Kacperski et al., 2023). A well-rounded literature review requires a critical perspective to identify inherent biases in search engines and reflect on personal biases influencing the formatting of search prompts.

Text summarising

GenAI article summariser apps (e.g., TLDR, Scholarcy, SciSummary) minimise reading time by compressing texts, journal articles, research reports, and book chapters into essential points, negating the need to read these. Apps like ChatPDF and Consensus Copilot take this further, generating answers to questions about texts, and producing integrated outputs from several sources, including statistics of which sources support a particular point of view. However, there is evidence that they exhibit bias against underrepresented groups and are influenced by the structure and style of documents (Brown & Shokri, 2023).

While these apps save time and effort, they provide interpretations that are not of the readers. Students using these applications do not gain critical reading experience, lose the opportunity to gain broader insights from the text, and do not develop the skills to analyse and synthesise information.

Text generating

GenAI's most prominent feature is its ability to generate reliable and high-quality text, often indistinguishable from human-generated text, using advanced foundational models (e.g., Alibaba, ChatGPT, Copilot, Bard, DeepSeek, ERNIE, Grok, Turing Bletchley). GenAI text generators can produce high-quality 'undetectable', customised, and adequately cited content, including academic essays, and are trained to mimic specific writing styles (e.g. Essai.pro, Hypotenuse AI, Cramly). Depending on the degree and extent to which GenAI is used to write content, the less the writers' accountability, objectivity, and rigour. While these tools are helpful for brainstorming and creating outlines, when used to write content it is the equivalent of using a ghost author. The student does not develop the intended cognitive skills, delivering work that is not their own.

There is still ambiguity and uncertainty regarding university AI ethical standards, policies, and guidelines. There is a case for academic misconduct, which comprises any act or attempted conduct that undermines the honesty and fairness of academic standards, potentially giving an unfair advantage (Tauginienė et al., 2018). A second ethical standard is that of unauthorised content generation (UCG), encompassing the act of creating academic work, either in its entirety or partially, to obtain academic credit, advance academically, or receive an award using unauthorised or undisclosed human or technological aid (Foltynek et al., 2023). Given the difficulty to detect GenAI text, Cotton et al. (2024) argue that a more feasible strategy is to educate students regarding the implications of using these tools and adopt automated and manual assessments that are less susceptible to the use of GenAI text. However, the efficacy of ethics classes in mitigating academic dishonesty remains contentious (Henning et al., 2013) and the massification of HE makes manual assessments less feasible.

GenAI's ability to generate accurate and reliable content, especially when trained with reliable academic sources, has great potential for HE pedagogies. For example, when used as a tutor, content and video generation in gamified learning, and the development of assessments that are closely aligned with reality and facilitate an engaged application of knowledge would be beneficial.

Detecting AI-generated content

Several apps (e.g. Turnitin, GenAI detection, Copyleaks, Originality.ai, AI Detector Pro, GPTZero) are available to detect AI-generated content by identifying textual indicators and patterns, unusual language usage, and GenAI watermarks. However, the effectiveness of these apps varies, with new applications constantly being developed to cloak AI-generated text (e.g. Undetectable AI, MachineMask). The most up-to-date guidelines for generating 'undetectable' AI text are on YouTube and Instagram, with influencers regularly introducing new apps or 'hacks'.

The implication is that traditional assessments conducted independently, such as essays and assignments, are becoming irrelevant given that they are no longer reliable measures of a student's competency.

GenAI as a disruptive pedagogy

Some scholars contend that reliance on GenAI may result in a deterioration of writing and critical thinking abilities, adversely impacting the quality of HE (Chan & Lee, 2023). However, GenAI, if used appropriately, can provide a disruptive pedagogy for the delivery of teaching and learning, which is especially valuable in the context of the massification of HE. GenAI can generate and personalise educational materials, including textbooks, lesson plans, and online courses, allowing for the involvement and adaptation of multiple learning methods. Chatbots can function as knowledgeable tutors, providing personalised support systems and customised coaching outside of class. GenAI can produce personalised, interactive assessments with personalised feedback and guidance, analyse performance, identify growth areas, and provide personalised interventions to achieve these. GenAI generates predictive analytics to accurately forecast student outcomes, identify at-risk students, and implement measures to improve their prospects (Romanov et al., 2020).

Some of the possibilities of GenAI as a disruptive pedagogy are outlined below.

Ringfenced and trained LLMs

Several open-source LLMs can be downloaded and then ring-fenced, i.e., they operate within a particular system and do not communicate with the host system or the internet. LLMs such as ChatGPT, Copilot, and Bard are privately owned, require a license, have restrictions, retain user information, and limit access to their algorithms and training data.

Open-source models offer an exciting and more ethical alternative. Hugging Face is the largest repository of open-source LLMs, with nearly 1,5 million models as of the beginning of 2025 (Hugging Face, 2025). By downloading open-source LLMs and placing them behind a firewall, data security and privacy are improved; they cost less and are more accessible, are transparent with code and their training data is accessible, they are more democratic as they allow community engagement, and they can be enhanced with additional training to mitigating biases (Luna, 2024). While open-source LLMs mitigate many of the ethical dilemmas outlined in Figure 7.1, it is important to consider copyright implications when using academic sources to train them.

Adaptive personalised learning materials

The advent of AI agents has significantly impacted the potential for autonomous personalised pedagogies. AI agents are programmes that autonomously respond to user inputs by interacting with external systems and tools, making decisions, and solving problems. An AI agent utilises accessible tools such as external data sets, web searches, computers, and other agents (Gutowska, 2024). AI agents can evaluate a student's educational past, discern strengths and shortcomings, and modify a curriculum based on previous interactions, assessments, and other available data. For example, an AI agent, based on using the outcomes of assessments and other student records, can personalise licensed learning materials, using information from academic platforms used by a university, and other activities, artforms, and materials for a student, and can modify these.

GenAI can transform personalised education by creating learning materials that adapt to students' learning paces, language, and interests, automatically updating content, generating exercises and case studies aligned with a student's performance, and providing the necessary challenges or foundational exercises. Personalised real-time interactive classes, assessments, and simulations can be generated to keep students engaged while providing targeted feedback, additional resources, and recommendations (Pataranutaporn et al., 2021). LLMs image and video generation models can generate visual aids and simulations to communicate complex topics (Mittal et al., 2024).

Intelligent tutoring

GenAI can develop sophisticated coaching systems that offer personalised feedback and help by formulating solutions, supplying hints, and explaining complex concepts (Mittal et.al., 2024). A GenAI social agent may serve as a guide, peer, expert, or any other learning collaborator or supportive guide throughout a course (Pratschke, 2024). Functions may include a possibility engine to generate alternative expressions of an idea, a Socratic opponent to engage in argument development, a collaboration coach to facilitate group research and problem-solving, a co-designer to aid in the design process, an exploratorium offering tools for data exploration and interpretation, and a storyteller to craft narratives encompassing diverse perspectives, abilities, and experiences (Sharples, 2023).

Learning gamification

There is a growing trend to reinvent learning to increase engagement and create processes effective in knowledge transfer (Deloitte, 2019). AI-powered gamification platforms have the potential to improve problem-solving and critical thinking skills by requiring students to address complex tasks that mimic real-world conditions in an immersive environment (Samala et al., 2023). Gamification has proven effective in improving teamwork, communication, increased enthusiasm, and engagement (Subhash & Cudney, 2018). Gamification can enhance pedagogical outcomes by boosting learning results and cultivating many forms of knowledge, including declarative, conceptual, and procedural knowledge, alongside soft skills and psychomotor proficiency (Castillo-Parra et al., 2022).

New insights: Digital transformation and technology

Academia must adapt to the realities of a world dominated by the proliferation of GenAI, or face becoming irrelevant. To this end, it must develop an in-depth understanding of how GenAI functions impact the HE endeavour.

The potential risks to skills development and ethical concerns must be acknowledged and addressed when traversing the evolving GenAI landscape. Text generation apps can undermine many traditional assessment pedagogies, making it essential to adopt GenAI-driven pedagogies to achieve critical HE outcomes strategically. Digital literacy must be prioritised, and students and academics must be educated about GenAI's fundamental mechanics, functionalities, and ethical constraints. GenAI apps' ethical and transparent use should be encouraged by implementing clearly defined user standards and guidelines that are updated regularly to stay abreast of the fast-paced and changing environment.

GenAI has the potential to revolutionise higher education pedagogies when employed effectively, GenAI may deliver interactive assessments with tailored feedback, individualised assistance and coaching, and generate individualised educational resources. GenAI can monitor student performance, identify improvement areas, and provide targeted interventions. Isolated and trained open-source language models contribute to the improvement of privacy and data security. GenAI fosters adaptable personalised learning, intelligent tutoring, and gamification of knowledge, resulting in improved student engagement, critical thinking, and problem-solving skills. Utilising GenAI will assist educators in creating more personalised, efficient, and effective learning environments.

Implications for future research and practice

Integrating GenAI into higher education has profound implications for both practice and research. In particular, when used for academic writing, a significant concern is the decline in students' writing and critical thinking abilities (Chan & Lee, 2023). However, when utilised appropriately, GenAI can facilitate a transformative and immersive pedagogy that enhances teaching and learning and offsets many of the risks of AI to the academic endeavour. Given the rapidly evolving nature of GenAI, action research is required to assess the implementation of AI agents, gamification platforms, intelligent tutoring systems, and GenAI-driven adaptive learning aids in HE. GenAI's impact on cognitive abilities development also needs to be researched, along with how these can be offset by incorporating GenAI pedagogies into the curriculum. Research also needs to examine the ethical implications of utilising GenAI pedagogies, in particular how issues related to data privacy, bias, and copyright infringement can be mitigated.

Reflecting on the use of AI in this chapter

Given the topic, it is prudent to reflect on the use of AI in the writing process. Google Scholar, Connected Papers, and Consensus were used to identify academic sources, and Google (improved by MaxAI) for general research and generating ideas. While these outputs stimulated my thoughts, I made a point of accessing the original sources. MS Word editing tools were supplemented using Grammarly for grammar checking, Quilbot for paraphrasing, and Mendeley for referencing. ChatPDF and Quilbot advised rephrasing and summarising; however, when used, the outputs were modified to reflect my 'voice' and ensure the original meaning was retained. I trust the academic integrity of the content, given that I spent over 100 hours writing the content and I am an experienced author who continually reflects on my writing process. I also value the power of GenAI in validating the writing process, and thus ran the chapter through Turnitin, generating 3% similarity and 0% AI scores. However, I doubt my literary, analytical, and critical skills would have been at the same level had I grown up with GenAI.

References

AIContentfy team. (2023). Unveiling the drawbacks: Exploring the disadvantages of AI in article writing. *AIContentfy*. Available at: https://aicontentfy.com/en/blog/unveiling-drawbacks-exploring-disadvantages-of-ai-in-article-writing.

Aitkins, M.J. (1995). *Assessment issues in higher education*. Report for Department of Employment: London.

Alkaissi, H. & McFarlane, S.I. (2023). Artificial hallucinations in ChatGPT: Implications in scientific writing. *Cureus*, 15(2): 1–4. https://doi.org/10.7759/cureus.35179.

Andreucci-Annunziata, P., Riedemann, A., Cortés, S., Mellado, A., del Río, M. T. & Vega-Muñoz, A. (2023). Conceptualizations and instructional strategies on critical thinking in higher education: A systematic review of systematic reviews. *Frontiers in Education*, 8. https://doi.org/10.3389/feduc.2023.1141686.

Ansari, A.N., Ahmad, S. & Bhutta, S.M. (2023).Mapping the global evidence around the use of ChatGPT in higher education: A systematic scoping review. *Education and Information Technologies*, 29: 11281–11321. https://doi.org/10.1007/s10639-023-12223-4.

Baker, R.S. & Hawn, A. (2022). Algorithmic Bias in Education. *International Journal oc Artificial Intelligence Education*, 32: 1052–1092. https://doi.org/10.1007/s40593-021-00285-9.

Balbay, S. (2019). Enhancing Critical Awareness through Socratic Pedagogy. *Eurasian Journal of Applied Linguistics*, 5(3): 515–536. https://doi.org/10.32601/ejal.651348.

Bathaee, Y. (2017). The Artificial Intelligence Black Box and the Failure of Intent and Causation. *Harvard Journal of Law & Technology*, 31: 889–934.

Blackley, S., Luzeckyj, A. & King, S. (2020). Re-valuing higher education: learning(s) and teaching(s) in contested spaces. *Higher Education Research & Development*, 39(1): 1–12.

Brabrand, C. & Dahl, B. (2009). Using the SOLO taxonomy to analyze competence progression of university science curricula. *Higher Education*, 58: 531–549.

Brooks, R., Gupta, A., Jayadeva, S. & Abrahams, J. (2020). Students' views about the purpose of higher education: a comparative analysis of six European countries. *Higher Education Research & Development*, 40(7): 1375–1388. https://doi.org/10.1080/07294360.2020.1830039.

Calderonio, V. (2023). The opaque law of artificial intelligence. *arXiv-Artificial Intelligence*.

Castillo-Parra, B., Hidalgo-Cajo, B., Vásconez-Barrera, M. & Oleas-López, J. (2022). Gamification in Higher Education: A Review of the Literature. *World Journal on Educational Technology: Current Issues*, 14(3): 797–816.

Chan, C.K.Y. & Lee, K.K. (2023). The AI generation gap: Are Gen Z students more interested in adopting generative AI such as ChatGPT in teaching and learning than their Gen X and millennial generation teachers? *Smart Learning Environments*, 10(1): 60.

Chan, R.Y., Brown, G., & Ludlow, L. H. (2014). *What is the purpose of higher education? A comparison of institutional and student perspectives on the goals and purposes of completing a bachelor's degree in the 21.* American Education Research Association(AERA) Annual Conference.

Chubb, J., Cowling, P. & Reed, D. (2022). Speeding up to keep up: exploring the use of AI in the research process. *AI & Society*, 37: 1439–1457. https://doi.org/10.1007/s00146-021-01259-0.

Coeckelbergh, M. (2022). The Grammars of AI: Towards a Structuralist and Transcendental Hermeneutics of Digital Technologies. *Technology and Language*, 3(2): 148–161.

Cotton, D.R.E., Cotton, P.A. & Shipway, J.R. (2024). Chatting and cheating: Ensuring academic integrity in the era of ChatGPT. *Innovations in Education and Teaching International*, 61(2). https://doi.org/10.1080/14703297.2023.2190148.

Deloitte. (2019). Deloitte Global Human Capital Trends. *Deloitte*.

Dobber, M., Zwart, R., Tanis, M. & van Oers, B. (2017). Literature review: The role of the teacher in inquiry-based education. *Educational Research Review*, 22: 194–214. https://doi.org/10.1016/J.EDUREV.2017.09.002.

Fui-Hoon Nah, F., Zheng, R., Cai, J., Siau, K. & Chen, L. (2023). Generative AI and ChatGPT: Applications, challenges, and AI-human collaboration. *Journal of Information Technology Case and Application Research*, 25(3): 277–304.

Gladwell, M. (2008). *Outliers: The Story of Success.* New York: Little, Brown and Company.

Gutowska, A. (2024). What are AI agents? *IBM.* Available at: https://www.ibm.com/think/topics/ai-agents. Date accessed: 2 March 2025.

Haan, K. & Watts, R. (2023). How Businesses Are Using Artificial Intelligence. Available at: https://www.forbes.com/advisor/business/software/ai-in-business/.

Hagura, N., Haggard, P. & Diedrichsen, J. (2017). Perceptual decisions are biased by the cost to act. *eLife.* https://doi.org/10.7554/eLife.18422.001.

Henning, M., Ram, S., Malpas, P., Shulruf, B., Kelly, F. & Hawken, S. (2013). Academic dishonesty and ethical reasoning: Pharmacy and medical school students in New Zealand. *Medical Teacher*, 35(6): e1211–e1217.

Hornsby, D.J. & Osman, R. (2014). Massification in higher education: Large classes and student learning. *Higher education*, 67: 711–719.

Hugging Face. (2025) Models. *Hugging Face.* Available at: https://huggingface.co/models. Date accessed: 2 March 2025.

Katz, L. (2014). Teachers' reflections on critical pedagogy in the classroom. *InterActions: UCLA Journal of Education and Information Systems*, 10(2). https://escholarship.org/uc/item/2c6968hc.

Kiley, J.D. (2020). Identity capital and graduate employment: an investigation into how access to various forms of identity capital relates to graduate employment. [Doctoral dissertation] University of Cape Town. Available at: https://open.uct.ac.za/items/1e78aa68-d510-43a1-b800-49ef91138ff2. Date accessed: 2 April 2024.

Kiley, J.D. (2024). Benefits, pitfalls, ethics, and realities of GenAI in research. In Towsend, K. & Saunders, M.N.K. (ed.) *How to Keep your Research Project on Track: Insights from When Things go Wrong* (second edition). Cheltenham: Edward Elgar (in progress).

Krathwohl, D.R. (2002). A Revision of Bloom's Taxonomy: An Overview. *Theory into practice*, 41(4): 212–218.

Luna, J.C. (2024). 9 Top Open-Source LLMs for 2024 and Their Uses. *Datacamp.*

Mai D.T.T., Da C.V. & Hanh, N.V. (2024). The use of ChatGPT in teaching and learning: a systematic review through SWOT analysis approach. *Frontiers in Educucation*, 9. https://doi.org/ 10.3389/feduc.2024.1328769.

Microsoft. (undated). A guide to app development. *Microsoft.* Available at: https://powerapps.microsoft.com/en-us/app-development/. Date accessed: 31 March 2024.

Mittal, U., Sai, S., Chamola, V. & Sangwan, D. (2024). A Comprehensive Review on Generative AI for Education. *IEEE Xplore*, 12, 142733–142759. https://doi.org/10.1109/ACCESS.2024.3468368.

Mittelstadt, B. D., Allo, P., Taddeo, M., Wachter, S. & Floridi, L. (2016). The ethics of algorithms: Mapping the debate. *Big Data & Society*, 3(2). https://doi.org/10.1177/2053951716679679.

Montenegro-Rueda, M., Fernández-Cerero, J., Fernández-Batanero, J.M. & López-Meneses, E. (2023). Impact of the implementation of ChatGPT in education: A systematic review. *Computers*, 12(8): 153.

Saunders, M., Lewis, P. & Thornhill, A. (2023). *Research Methods For Business Students* (ninth edition). Harlow: Pearson.

Pataranutaporn, P., Danry, V., Leong, J., Punpongsanon, P., Novy, D., Maes, P. & Sra, M. (2021). AI-generated characters for supporting personalized learning and well-being. *Nature Machine Intelligence*, 3(12): 1013–1022.

Prates, M., Avelar, P. & Lamb, L. (2018). Assessing gender bias in machine translation: a case study with Google Translate. *Neural Computing and Applications*, 32: 6363–6381. https://doi.org/10.1007/s00521-019-04144-6.

Pratschke, B.M. (2024). *Generative AI and education: Digital pedagogies, teaching innovation and learning design*. Cham: Springer.

Robinson, K. (2013). The interrelationship of emotion and cognition when students undertake collaborative group work online: An interdisciplinary approach. *Computers & Education,* 62: 298–307. http://dx.doi.org/10.1016/j.compedu.2012.11.003

Samala, A., Bojić, L., Vergara-Rodríguez, D., Klimova, B. & Ranuharja, F. (2023). Exploring the Impact of Gamification on 21st-Century Skills: Insights from DOTA 2. *International Journal of Interactive Mobile Technologies*, 17: 33–54.

South African Qualifications Authority. (2012). Level Descriptors for the South African National Qualifications Framework. Pretoria: Government Gazette.

Saunders, M., Lewis, P. & Thornhill, A. (2023). *Research Methods For Business Students* (ninth edition). Harlow: Pearson.

Schreiner, M. (2023). *GPT-4 architecture, datasets, costs and more leaked*. Available at: https://the-decoder.com/gpt-4-architecture-datasets-costs-and-more-leaked/. Date accessed: 29 March 2024.

Sharples, M. (2023). Towards social generative AI for education: theory, practices and ethics. *Learning: Research and Practice*, 9(2): 159–167.

Su, A.J., Hu, Y.C., Kuzmanovic, A. & Koh, C.K. (2010). August. How to improve your Google ranking: Myths and reality. In *2010 IEEE/WIC/ACM International Conference on Web Intelligence and Intelligent Agent Technology*, 1: 50–57. IEEE.

Subhash, S. & Cudney, E. (2018). Gamified learning in higher education: A systematic review of the literature. *Comput. Hum. Behav.*, 87: 192–206.

Suleyman, M. & Bhaskar, M. (2023). *The coming wave*. New York: Crown.

Trumbull, E. & Lash, A. (2013). *Understanding Formative Assessment: Insights from Learning Theory and Measurement Theory*. Available at: https://www.wested.org/online_pubs/resource1307.pdf.

Turner, A. (2024). *How Many Apps In Google Play Store?* Available at: https://www.bankmycell.com/blog/number-of-google-play-store-apps/ Date accessed: 29 March 2024.

Wannapiroon, P. (2008). Development of a problem-based learning model to develop undergraduate student's critical thinking skill. [Doctoral dissertation] Department of Curriculum, Instruction, and Educational Technology, Chulalongkorn University: Bangkok, Thailand.

Ward, R., Phillips, O., Bowers, D., Crick, T., Davenport, J., Hanna, P., Hayes, A., Irons, A. & Prickett, T. (2021). *Towards a 21st Century Personalised Learning Skills Taxonomy*. 2021 IEEE Global Engineering Education Conference (EDUCON): 344–354.

Zamfirescu-Pereira, J.D., Wong, R.Y., Hartmann, B. & Yang, Q. (2023). *Why Johnny can't prompt: how non-AI experts try (and fail) to design LLM prompts*. Proceedings of the 2023 CHI Conference on Human Factors in Computing Systems: 1–21.

CHAPTER 7

CHAPTER 8

Employability of graduates: Introducing dual higher education (DHE) as an innovative model in higher education in South Africa

Antoinette Smith-Crous

Abstract

The employability of graduates has become a critical issue in South African higher education. Our research shows that employers of graduates have exclaimed their reservations about graduates needing long periods of in-service training to close the gap between theoretical knowledge and standards of practice in the workplace. Graduates in general also do not have the higher-level cognitive competencies that is expected in the workplace such as personal efficacy, problem-solving, and application of knowledge to address innovation in the specific company or organisation where they are employed. This chapter introduces a new model for higher education that addresses the employability of graduates. The model, dual higher education (DHE), known as 'dual studies' in Germany, has been adapted to inculcate the differences in South African conditions, both in university curricula and needs of employers. Our research pointed at readiness of employers to become involved in higher education on their terms. University readiness transpired as including experiential learning in some programmes, but practitioners expressed a lack of institutional support for this mode of learning (Wickham, 2022). The chapter asks the critical questions: what is necessary to enhance the employability of graduates? What are the systemic changes that are necessary for universities and employers to collaborate on this very important issue? How can dual higher education contribute to these changes?

Alignment with book theme

This chapter aligns strongly to the theme of the engaged university, in the sense that it addresses the readiness of graduates to take up their role in society in the workplace. Practical experience in the workplace during studies is rare in academic programmes, unless it is a requirement in professional programmes where professional boards govern the requirements. In non-professional programmes this important component of workplace learning is excluded due to policy limitations on subsidies. An important role of universities to provide competent graduates for the workforce lacks in taking responsibility for employability of students. The critical question is: how will universities remain relevant if they do not fulfil this role? The second theme that the chapter aligns to is pedagogical innovation. DHE is a distinctive model of HE that combines learning in two places and shows how this learning model can lead to higher employability and readiness for the workplace after graduation.

Introduction

The concept of employability is a multifaceted and debated topic, as its interpretation varies widely among different stakeholders. Employers, policymakers, educators, and graduates themselves all view employability through different lenses, leading to discrepancies in understanding what it truly means. While some may define employability in terms of the ability to secure a job quickly after graduation, others may focus on a graduate's skills, adaptability, or their potential to contribute meaningfully to the workplace over time. Even when a more precise definition of employability is agreed upon, challenges arise in how to measure it effectively. Some measures focus on immediate employment statistics, while others emphasize long-term career progression or the development of transferable skills.

In recent years, the employability of graduates has become an increasingly urgent issue, particularly as high levels of unemployment and underemployment among recent graduates persist. This problem is not merely academic – long periods of in-service training and internship placements, often in lieu of permanent employment, result in frustrations for both graduates and employers. The mismatch between academic qualifications and labour market needs exacerbates this issue, as graduates often find themselves underprepared for the realities of the job market. As a result, the financial and personal investment made by graduates during their studies may not yield the returns they anticipate, despite their degrees.

The statistics are telling. For graduates aged 25–34 years, the unemployment rate rose by 6,9% to 22,4% in the first quarter of 2022. At the same time, unemployment among younger learners and graduates, aged 15–24 years, decreased from 40,3% to 32,6% (Statistics South Africa, 2022). While the drop in unemployment for the younger cohort may seem promising, it is important to consider whether this decrease is due to an increase in internships or if these graduates are finding stable, permanent positions. The increasing number of graduate internships, which often offer lower pay or temporary contracts, complicates the picture further. Even though graduate unemployment rates remain lower than the general unemployment rate in many countries, this is not necessarily a positive outcome. Given the financial and time investment required to earn a degree, the persistence of graduate unemployment or underemployment points to deeper structural issues within both the education system and the labour market.

Research conducted by the Human Sciences Research Council (HSRC) in 2023 further underscores the difficulty graduates face in finding employment that aligns with their qualifications. The mismatch between labour market demands and the skills or qualifications imparted by higher education institutions is a critical factor in this growing problem. This misalignment not only leads to underemployment but also wastes valuable human resources, which in turn negatively impacts economic growth and stability. Without addressing these gaps, the cycle of graduate unemployment may continue to persist, potentially causing long-term economic challenges (HSRC, 2023).

This chapter aims to explore potential solutions to this issue, focusing on improving graduates' readiness for the workforce. The goal is to present strategies that enhance employability without sacrificing the critical scientific knowledge, logical thinking, and academic competencies that form the core of higher education. By fostering a more balanced and holistic approach to employability, higher education institutions can better equip graduates to navigate the complexities of the job market while maintaining the integrity of their academic training.

This chapter provides context by explaining the historic development of universities in South Africa and the impact of colonialism in shaping 'African Higher Education' and specifically South African Higher Education (SAHE) which indirectly led to theory-based academic programmes with little exposure of students to real-world problems. The concept of employability, the lack of workplace learning and orientation in university programmes, and the questionable relationship between employers and universities that led to the dual higher education project (DHEP), are all interrogated. Dual higher education (DHE) is a South African (SA) construct derived from the dual studies system in European countries, in particular Germany and Austria. The chapter explains how the project came about, the results of the research done, the prototypes of the model, and how this model was applied to several existing academic programmes in Western Cape universities. As this model is different from any other models in SA, the policies that govern university programmes had to be reviewed to determine if the policy environment in SA is conducive to this model. The chapter asks the following critical questions:

1. What is necessary to enhance the employability of graduates?
2. What are the systemic changes that are necessary for universities and employers to collaborate on this very important issue?
3. How can dual higher education contribute to these changes?

Impact of SAHE historic development

A bird's-eye view of the history of South Africa (SA) shows that historically, universities in SA, (as in other African countries) were shaped by European colonialism, which established the idea of the elitism of knowledge and university education as privileged. Furthermore, the positivist tendency to generate knowledge for knowledge's sake rather than for its social value was strongly prevalent.

The SA HE system is closely linked to the African HE landscape. Since the turn of the century, a rhetoric connecting South African HE to its African heritage evolved (Waghid, 2004; Le Grange, 2006) and argued for 'Africanisation' of HE. In Africa, HE has been inevitably influenced by a colonial and postcolonial legacy that continues to define the nature of contemporary HE institutions on this continent (Teferra & Altbach, 2004). The role of HE in African society is evolving and contested, but the debate in Africa may be more closely interwoven with the development of an 'African identity' that, according to Nigerian novelist Chinua Achebe, 'is still in the making' (Le Grange, 2006: 1208). Generalising about an 'African identity' and the 'African university' is problematic, if the vastness and diversity (54 countries) of the continent is considered. However, Teferra and Altbach (2003: 3) argue that African universities share enough commonalities to allow reference to 'African higher education', while Waghid (2004) argues for an African philosophy of education based on the commonalities in the African orientation to learning. Despite this strong push towards an African HE, colonialism has left its legacy in Africa, including South Africa.

The most prominent factor among African HE institutions is the widespread impact of colonial education policies on all of them. Those policies significantly curbed access, made the language of the coloniser the language of instruction, limited what could be taught, and greatly restricted the autonomy of institutions of HE (Waghid, 2009). This leads Teferra and Altbach (2003) to conclude that, even though Africa can claim an ancient academic tradition, traditional centres of higher learning in Africa have all but disappeared or were destroyed by colonialism. The contemporary legacy on the continent is characterised by academic institutions that were shaped by colonialism and organised according to the European model, but most of which were subsequently nationalised to embody and champion the nationalist agendas of newly independent African states (Thomson et al., 2008; Waghid, 2009).

In South Africa HE did not escape the legacy of colonialism. It bore the markers of apartheid rule from 1948–1994 which divided public education institutions according to race. The consequences of this legacy have been extensive, but so were the imperatives launched to transform the HE system since 1994, when the first democratic elections took place, and the African National Congress (ANC) majority rule replaced the National Party minority rule. Policy imperatives and legislation led comprehensive nation (re)building and transformation of the inherited racially divided HE landscape (Government of National Unity, 1994; Gultig, 2000; Hall, 2006; Hay & Mapesela, 2009).

The higher education system was redesigned to desegregate and can currently be described as 'differentiated'. It comprises three institutional categories which culminates to 26 public universities in total:

- 11 traditional universities (including research-intensive universities), which offer theoretically oriented university degrees,
- six universities of technology offering vocational oriented diplomas and degrees, and
- nine comprehensive universities that offer a combination of both types of qualifications.

Many private universities have also been added to the system in the last 15 years. In 2019, there were 131 private higher learning institutions in SA (Council for Higher Education, 2022). Unfortunately, the importance of employability was not part of the redesigning of the system. Technical colleges, where work readiness was prioritised, became universities of technology and scaled down on workplace learning despite the intention of the National Plan for the Post-School System that recognised the importance of preparation for the world of work and requirements for a range of professional qualifications (Ministry of Education, 2001).

Factors contributing to the inception of DHE

Several practices evolved as part of the new SA HE system. The strong legislative messages to rebuild the country awakened practices that were focused on embedding social justice in university education and strengthening the focus on *ubuntu* to create graduates that would serve the country (DoE, 1997); the importance of the theory-practice nexus awakened in the forms of service-learning (even in traditional universities) and the expansion of the concept of work-integrated learning (WIL). Service-learning was characterised as favouring civil society partners to teach students the importance of using their knowledge and skills to the benefit of society and the upliftment of post-apartheid SA. Cooperative learning, then better known and practised by polytechnics, was transformed into WIL that comprised project-based, problem-based, and workplace learning, which emphasised the importance of experiential learning (Council for Higher Education, 2011). WIL mainly gave students workplace exposure while studying, but it was mostly based on teaching students practical skills in the workplace, but neglecting the integration of theory and practice in such a way as to prepare the student for the world of work.

Due to negative experiences of companies with students that are sent to their companies without properly structured learning outcomes, they developed the opinion that the education of students is regarded as a task of the state. Wickham (2022), in her research on the readiness of universities for DHE, posits that most of the practices still exist in universities, although varied, to provide students with hands-on experience, and experiential learning is still considered to be important (Wickham 2022).

When comparing this to the German model of dual studies, the combination of factual knowledge and personal skills alone are not sufficient for solution-oriented work in the world of work. In Germany, and especially in the dual study models, the focus is much more on method-based competencies and transfer of knowledge to company practice (Smith-Tolken & Behrens, 2021).

Universities do include graduate attributes in their vision statements to indicate what graduates should master during their university studies. For example, Stellenbosch University's vision for graduate attributes lists: 'An enquiring mind, an engaged citizen, a dynamic professional, [and] a well-rounded individual' (Leibowitz et al., 2012: 5). The University of the Western Cape has a long list of attributes with descriptions in their Graduate Attributes Charter, namely *ubuntu*, scholarship, critical citizenship, lifelong learning, creative and collaborative problem solving, technological agency, and entrepreneurship. The question arises whether these attributes can be achieved by campus-based learning only and whether future employers share the importance of these attributes.

One of the weak points of SA is the lack of collaboration between universities and prospective employers. The expectation is that universities are supposed to prepare graduates to be 'fit for the labour market', thus rendering employability an essential outcome of graduate studies. In a study done in the wine industry, employers indicated the following attributes they would want in their industry: academic knowledge, excellent communication and information management skills, leadership skills (excellent values and virtues; responsibility for one's own actions; loyalty to staff, clients, and workplace), personal development (emotional intelligence), ethics and accountability, and critical and analytical skills (Smith-Tolken & McKay, 2014). This clearly confirms that academic knowledge is not enough to be employable, but the development of the whole person with specific professional skills.

As for the state of workplace learning (WPL), specifically in universities of technology (UoTs), the South African Technology Network (2016) concludes that the data available in 2016, 'does not indicate a significant shift away from workplace-learning at UoTs' (South African Technology Network, 2016: 12) in the light of the Higher Education Qualifications Sub-Framework (HEQSF) re-curriculation process, but that the 'credit value assigned to workplace-learning has been reduced at most of the UoTs' (South African Technology Network, 2016: 13). Furthermore, the report points out that since the award of university status, 'less than a quarter of the total number of qualifications on the pre-HEQSF aligned PQM of UoTs includes a credit-bearing workplace learning component' (South African Technology Network, 2016: 9).

The South African Technology Network report also finds that since becoming UoT's, linkages with industries have been less formal, to the extent that some programmes (but by no means all) have removed work placements from their programmes. Comprehensive universities that have incorporated technikon programmes have similarly had close ties with industry partners in the past, but, as with the universities of technology, the diploma programmes in comprehensive universities are also less bound to industry requirements and the specific needs of related industries (South African Technology Network, 2016).

In this section, the motivation for introducing DHE in SA, is clarified. The misalignment between university graduate attributes and the attributes that employers require are clear. The gap between theory and practice, the decline of WPL, and the watering down of university-employer relations are some of the reasons why the dual higher education project came about.

Dual studies in European countries and beyond

The history of dual studies in Europe and specifically in Germany started over time and was mainly developed by one region Baden-Württemberg's government through legislation. Dual studies were mainly part of the vocational training in career academies and was gradually migrated to universities of applied sciences. Zhang and Schmidt-Herthab (2019) posits 'However, vocational school graduates are considered to lack sufficient theoretical knowledge'. Therefore, dual studies are now offered at many German universities, where students can acquire profound specialised knowledge and professional skills. Students are able to obtain both a Bachelor's degree (Bachelor of Arts, Bachelor of Science, or Bachelor of Engineering) and a professional qualification on graduation.

Research on what comprises dual studies, showed that the dual higher education model should involve two different 'learning places', namely the university and the work setting (companies, and other organizations such as hospitals, authorities, associations, and so forth). Students are taught the theoretical knowledge of the specific discipline at university, while during the practical phase in the work setting, they reflect on this theoretical knowledge by identifying and applying some of the learned knowledge in practice (Zhang & Schmidt-Herthab, 2019).

DHE uses teaching and learning methods that are directly related to its purpose – to enhance the employability of graduates and their 'ability to create and sustain work over time' (Bennett, 2018: 32) in a complex labour market. In this way, the substantial portion of time spent in the workplace setting exposes students not only to disciplinary knowledge, skills, and practices in their respective fields of study, but also provides them with the opportunity to conceptualise their future careers by prompting them to understand why they think the way they think, how to analyse and embrace the unfamiliar, and how their values, beliefs, and assumptions can inform (and be informed by) their learning, lives, and careers (Bennett, 2018).

Dual studies have not only migrated to Austria and Switzerland but has also been adapted for countries like the United States (US) (Powell & Fortwengel, 2014) and China (Zhang & Schmidt-Herthab, 2019). In the US, an export-driven economy such as Germany sees dual studies as a potential model to inculcate practical learning in college degrees to heighten employability. In China, potential success of a similar model to Germany is clear, but neither of these two countries have made progress to implement the model.

The economic environments in Germany and Austria for dual studies are very different from the SA economy. Companies contractually recruit students when they leave school and partner with universities to give the students the necessary theoretical knowledge to become employable while the students undergo their practical training in the company (Göhringer, 2002). These companies pay the student's tuition and pay them a small salary while they are studying. In Europe, dual academic programmes are 70% theoretical and 30% practical, although students spend 50% of their time at the university and the rest at the company. During the study tour, one of the most important observations was that this model would need to be adapted for SA.

Dual higher education in SA

The DHEP was conceptualised and proposed to the Department of Higher Education and Training (DHET) in 2019 by the Cape Higher Education Consortium (CHEC) after hosting a workshop on the topic in 2018. CHEC is a consortium formed by the four universities of the Western Cape (WC), namely Stellenbosch University (SUN), University of the Western Cape (UWC), University of Cape Town (UCT) and Cape Peninsula University of Technology (CPUT). The final proposal culminated in a collaborative University Capacity Building Programme (UCDP) where the CHEC universities would develop and pilot the dual model in SA, which was funded by DHET. The project comprised six main features namely:

- research on the European models and the readiness of universities and employers for DHE;
- developing a SA model of DHE;
- capacity development of the two main partners, namely universities and employers;
- exploring policy conduciveness for DHE;
- implementation of the pilots; and
- evaluation of the project.

The rest of this chapter describes the methods and results of a four-year project that is now in its final year of existence. The highlight of each feature culminates in a final terms of reference and an evaluative framework for future DHE programmes, which is still a work in progress.

Research

The SA universities and employer research done was mainly focused on gauging the readiness of universities and employers to participate in DHE. Although ethical clearance was obtained, the research was focused on prospectives for DHE and is mostly explorative, qualitative, and interpretative, where all the participants make sense of the phenomenon by describing their experience and make sense of it. Despite the difficulty of containing qualitative research within a single definition, it is often described as an interdisciplinary, trans-disciplinary, and sometimes counter-disciplinary field of enquiry that commits to a naturalistic perspective and the interpretive understanding of human experience that is shaped by ethical and political perspectives (Denzin & Lincoln, 2008). This description fits this research fairly accurately.

The names of universities and employers are confidential and are not disclosed. For this reason, the validation of findings was mainly meant to inform the DHEP, and no claim can be made that it is transferable or valid in other contexts. The study tour to Germany and Austria is considered the main form of enquiry, while the desktop, readiness, and curriculum comparison formed the backdrop of the study tour findings.

The research comprised the following methods of enquiry:

- Desktop research, including policy, previous studies, and website scans of public universities in SA to determine if WPL formed part of their practice. All 26 public universities were targeted.
- Questionnaires and interviews – programme convenors, WIL coordinators, and employers in the four CHEC universities as well as one other university were included in the enquiry.
- Comparative analysis: SA HE/German/Austrian curricula/accreditation structure. A curriculum analysis was done of two academic programmes from a German and SA university. This was used to compare the structure and learning methods used in the programmes.
- Study tour to Germany and Austria to observe and explore dual studies first-hand through conversations with teaching staff at universities, company representatives, and students studying in dual programmes.

The focus of the research done in SA is depicted in the Table 8.1 below.

TABLE 8.1: Focus and findings of the research

Focus of research	Findings of research
• Exploring the employment patterns and talent acquisition of employers of graduates. • The aim was to determine if they were ready to grow talent versus buying talent to their workforce. • The aim was further to determine their readiness to engage in DHE partnerships with universities.	• Employers welcomed the idea of DHE. • Future skills need to be recognized and both theoretical and practical knowledge is valued. • Students provide additional manpower and new ideas that broaden the workplace knowledge base. • Will grow talent provided their company have the necessary resources. • Training of supervisors in the workplace is non-negotiable. • Their involvement in curricula and assessment of students were found to be inconclusive.
• Exploring university structures and support systems that could enhance the implementation of DHE. • Interviews with practitioners of work integrated learning and service-learning explored how they experienced the support of their university. • Exploring the theoretical grounding of DHE based on existing practices in universities.	• Universities' mission and vision statements highlight the need for responsive institutions that prepare graduates for their roles in wider society and recognise that their graduates require both theoretical knowledge and practical experience. Some programmes include both components and show similarities to DHE institutional cultures where theory is valued over practice; where research is recognised and prioritised over teaching and learning. This impacts on the resource availability for champions who embrace similar models as DHE with both a practical and theoretical component.
• A comparative study of DHE programmes in a specific field and a similar programme in SA to determine if SA programme structures would lend itself to DHE. • Determine barriers that would prohibit DHE and catalysts that would support DHE in SA.	• The German curriculum structure is similar to that in SA. The difference is one credit equals 30 notional hours while in SA it is only ten. Degree programmes are hybrid (include different types of disciplinary content such as commerce and engineering in one programme). Content is coherently spread over years of study to achieve exit level competencies.
• A study tour to Germany and Austria to obtain first-hand experience of employers' motivation and benefits, experiences of faculty in practicing DHE, as well as students' experiences, both in the university and the workplace.	• See summary below.

The research done in Germany and Austria is briefly described below.

In order to better understand the dual system in Germany and Austria, South African project managers conducted a dual higher education fact finding tour in September 2021. In-depth discussions and interviews were held with representatives of the IDS in Lingen, the Baden-Württemberg Cooperative State University and the Joanneum University in Graz. Permission was granted to name these universities, while no persons interviewed are quoted. The sources of data collection are included in a confidential document. The findings generated were revised in a grid and mapped to the three main interest groups, universities, companies, and students, in a coherent way to the pilot project, and interpreted for its significance for higher education in South Africa. The main categories that were extrapolated from the data was dual studies model development, policy structure and requirements of support for dual studies, curriculum development, support structures in the university and company, financial considerations/structures, motivation for partnerships/relationship building, logistical considerations, and benefits (advantages) and challenges (disadvantages) of dual studies.

In the following section, the context, the curriculum structure, the triple-helix of engagement, the political and financial consequences, and finally, the implications for higher education in South Africa are briefly outlined (Smith-Tolken & Behrens, 2021).

The context describes the general regulations and the system in a particular country. In Germany and Austria, the dual study system is understood as a network partnership between universities and companies, including professional organisations and chambers of commerce. Companies play a much stronger role in Germany than in South Africa. In Austria, students only begin their enterprise component in their second year of study. Students must find their companies themselves, with the university supporting them in their search. Once the student is accepted into the company, they follow the same pattern as at German universities with some structural differences.

In Germany, it became clear that the link between theory and practice is pursued at a fundamental level from the first year of study and progresses with the learning of further procedural and applied work. Authentic learning experiences in the workplace provide students with further opportunities to integrate the theoretical-conceptual with theoretical-procedural knowledge gained in the classroom with the applied, practical-procedural, and practice competencies provided by employers. In this way, DHE requires 'a pedagogical shift towards process and relevance through reflection, engagement and experiential learning' (Bennett, 2018: 50). In addition to the traditional examinations, the modules are assessed through practical transfer projects (PTPs). These are transfer projects that combine and reflect on what has been learnt in the company with the academic content of each module. In principle, the structure of the curriculum is that the academic content remains stable, while the application takes place in the context of the company. In this model, practical and theoretical phases take place in regular alternation between workplace and university (Göhringer, 2002).

In the Austrian approach, workplace learning is represented by company placements, whereby learning is integrated at both locations. There is certain learning content that students must fulfil in the company for the curriculum. Nevertheless, the main goal is for students to contribute to the success of the company (Hochrinner 2021). Students are fully integrated into the work process. Reflection is an integral part of the learning process at both locations. Students must constantly use this process to link theory and practice by comparing an experience in practice with the theory learnt in class and vice versa.

The Austrian model was found to be more conducive for South Africa resulting in the aim to start the practical component in the second (three-year degree) or third year (four-year degree). Theory and practice could be split in a ratio of two thirds to one third. Valuable lessons were learnt from the Austrian as well as the German experience for the development of a SA model for DHE. What was very different in the two European countries was the flexible regulation in contrast with the SA highly state regulated HE system. The state universities in Germany and Austria are essentially financed by the state, including programmes with industrial components, as the company is considered an academic place of learning. Any tuition fees incurred in Germany are borne by the company (see Zhang & Schmidt-Herthab, 2019). One of the problems in South Africa is that students are not allowed to receive a salary if they receive a scholarship. This was seen as a challenge for the further implementation of dual higher education. The companies also have no guidelines for accepting students – each student is evaluated for the quality they can add to the company.

Conceptualising DHE in SA

Following the research, a description of DHE was developed from the research insights, the experiences abroad, as well as the interaction with faculty while analysing and restructuring curricula for DHE programmes. The conclusion was that DHE is the holistic integration of all forms of knowledge though workplace-learning, which can be described as follows:

- DHE has a substantial portion of WPL – representing a third of the total credits of the programme.
- DHE integrates different types of knowledge, namely theoretical, conceptual, and theoretical procedural with applied, practical procedural and practice (Muller, 2009).

- DHE focuses on exit level competencies that is aligned to standards of practice required in the societal sector relevant to the field of study.
- Reflection in both workplace and university bridges the theory-practice holistically, structured and assessed, which –
- demands a coherence between the levels of the programme as well as the Zone of Proximal Development (ZPD) (constructive alignment) of each subject in the programme across levels (Biggs, 1996).
- Finally, DHE builds competencies through careful scaffolding of learning experiences towards whole student development.

Developing prototypes of a SA model

The three prototypes developed for implementation in the SA context were as follows:

Undergraduate prototype

- Based on the knowledge gained from the German practice-integrated model and the Austrian model in particular, the undergraduate programmes are restructured to include a practical component from the end of the first or second year of study, depending on the length of the programme. These curricula include practical exercises, simulations, or institution-based case studies to prepare students for the work environment. These should be applicable skills that can be of use to the company in which the students complete their WPL.
- The transition to the company then begins in the year before the final year of study. In this phase, students should first learn everything about the company, its structures, goals, customers, products, services, management, etc. at a specific workplace. Here, students must be instructed on how to establish the theory-practice connection and write a reflective, assessable report.
- In the final year, they must complete either two three-month or one semester-long internship at the company as part of a final module, in which they apply all the knowledge they have gained from the degree programme in order to achieve the final objectives of their degree. Students are prepared to take on a management role in the company, at least at middle management level.

Postgraduate prototype

The postgraduate model applies to degree programmes in which an honours, postgraduate, or master's degree offers the opportunity to specialise in the same field as the undergraduate degree, whereby advanced knowledge and skills in the field are deepened in accordance with the respective level descriptions. This is in line with the German vocationally integrated model. In this model, working hours are reduced in consultation with the employer. In the time this frees up, dual students have the opportunity to complete their studies. Most of these students are already working but have the advantage that their programme is structured in such a way that it benefits their workplace in a structured and coherent way. Such programmes may already exist in South Africa, but the model will act as a catalyst for closer relationships between employers and a university.

Postgraduate reskilling prototype

In this model, graduates who already have a degree in a field in which they cannot find work are retrained and educated in a contextualised environment where some of their knowledge can be repurposed to mitigate skills shortages in the economy. This requires an internal university institute that can use the data from current graduates to match them with the skills and competencies required by companies and develop programmes that provide graduates with the knowledge, skills and competencies they need to fill existing gaps in the market. This programme can train students to become administrative and sales managers or trainers for the lower levels in a company. This prototype is also conducive to furthering the studies of dropouts from universities. These students may study further in a different direction or complete their studies through the dual model.

Policy challenges for DHE

After engaging with the current policies and directives for work-integrated learning (WIL) and discussions with employers and university practitioners, it was found that both employers and academic partners had concerns regarding national policy and the blockages this raises in the design, development, and delivery of programmes that involve two sites of learning. The consensus is that, while there are references to WIL in various policy documents, there is no clear policy on how academic programmes may include a practical component in the curriculum. In the South African Technology Network report this is articulated as follows: 'While many academic departments value workplace learning, it has not been regarded as an academic "subject" in the ex-technikon sector and has therefore not been funded – while "projects" are funded. It therefore makes financial sense to re-conceptualise WIL as project-based learning. It is also increasingly difficult to find appropriate placements for students as all programmes across all institutional types are expected to grow their student enrolments, and there is pressure from TVET colleges for placements' (South African Technology Network, 2016: 13). Quality assurance for academic programmes includes directives for WIL that regulate the interaction between universities and employers and concerns about the integrity of programmes, but at the same time subsidies do not include learning in the workplace unless it is regulated by a professional board (South African Technology Network, 2016). This issue will determine whether universities will embrace or reject DHE.

Triple-helix partnership for DHE

Partnerships and collaboration form a crucial part of the success of DHE. As in the German models, a reciprocal triad relationship is established between the employer, university, and student. The partnership that is built between the three parties is depicted in the Figure 8.1 below.

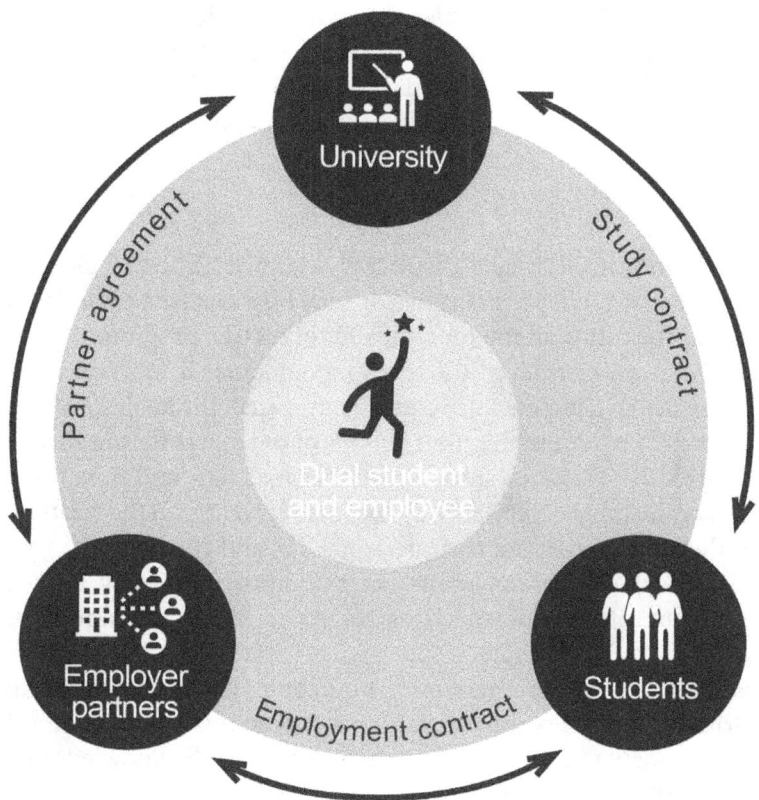

FIGURE 8.1: Triple-helix partnership for DHE

The university and the employer have a partner agreement that is based on the time that the student will be learning in the workplace. The university also has a study agreement with the student indicating how the learning will take place in both places of learning. The third part of the partnership is between the student and the employer. All three of these relationships work in sync to achieve the successful completion of the student's studies and ability to obtain the qualification. These relationships are unique in every university and the employer involved. Some employers would only have a contract with the student for the duration of their studies. In other cases, the student will be employed after the first year of study or in their final year or not at all. What is important is the clarification of roles and responsibilities in the triad partnership. There need to be clear benefits for all three parties across the years of study. The student functions as both student and employee during his/her studies. The two places of learning have their own activity system, namely the university system and the workplace system. Each have their own rules, community, and division of labour. In the university system, learning is the object and the student the subject, while in the workplace the object is production and the employee the subject. While fulfilling both roles, student learning becomes expanded to include student development and results in students attaining the necessary competencies that is needed for the world of work (Winburg & Nduna, 2021). In the DHEP, activity theory was accepted as a theoretical lens for partnerships as described above.

Importance of DHE in SA HE

In the evaluation of DHE as a distinct model of HE, it was clear that, after implementation of DHE programmes, it may be measured twofold; namely 1) if the programme fulfils all the prerequisites of a DHE programme and 2) if the intended programme achieved the learning outcomes it was meant to achieve. To determine which competencies could be expected, the analysis of the German curricula resulted in identifying four groups of outcomes for graduates, namely:

Personal skills: The skills students gain such as self- and time management, communication, and problem-solving, but also insight into the relation between processes they are exposed to, their personal life, and community.

Social-ethical skills: The ability of the student to view and reflect on knowledge from different perspectives, its impact on society, and in relation to a worldview.

Professional expertise: These are the outcomes pertaining to the knowledge content within the context of the industry. It contains the verb describing the ability of the student to understand, explain, and apply the knowledge in different contexts in a critical and synthesised way.

Comprehensive skills and abilities: The future-focused use of the knowledge gained through the module and industry exposure. The outcomes refer to how the student's ability to view their knowledge in the broader context of the body of knowledge and its relation to other industries.

It should be noted, however, that the skills and competencies for employability in the current context differ from those initially referred to as soft skills, which may have been provided in the co-developed curricula or from specific (often centralised) support structures in universities. The relevant competences and skills required can be described as those that allow individuals to solve complex problems in highly emergent contexts of action in a self-organised way, while enabling them to act successfully (Ehlers, 2020).

These skills categories were used as a basis to construe the expected outcomes of DHE in the SA context. The German categories were adapted into two categories of competencies, each consisting of five and four types of skills respectively (see Table 8.2 below). The competencies encompass all the generic skills that a graduate might need in the workplace, thus enhancing their employability. The importance of each skill can differ across programmes. This framework of outcomes differs from the so-called graduate attributes where universities aspire to produce graduates across the board with predetermined abilities and functionalities. This framework is programme and qualification specific, and assist programme coordinators to determine together with their employer partners which skills are needed for a specific job description in the specific sector. This will ensure that students are prepared for a specific sector's work opportunities.

TABLE 8.2: Framework of competencies for DHE in South Africa

Technical and business competencies	Social and people competencies
Academic knowledge Excellent subject knowledge, both expert and specialised; masterful application of knowledge in workplace	**Leadership skills** Excellent values and virtues; responsibility for own actions; loyalty to staff, clients, and workplace
People management skills Teamwork, managing and motivating employees and contractors; management of stakeholder interest and benefit	**Communication** Well-spoken and confident with different levels of business, including written, verbal and non-verbal
Information management skills Data analysis, interpretation of data, and efficient record keeping	**Personal development** EQ and respect for colleagues and clients; reliable, practical, willing, and keen; diligent and confident

Technical and business competencies	Social and people competencies
Critical and analytical skills Open-minded and dynamic; positive attitude; gather and analyse data in a new context and work environment	**Ethical aspects and accountability** High standards of behaviour, respect, and regard for others. Impact on their field and relevant sector in society.
Business organizational skills Planning, supply chain management, marketing, and costing	

Table 8.2 above has become a working document for universities to adapt and use to determine which of them are applicable in a wide variety of programmes as the project progresses with implementation.

Possible answers to pressing questions

In conclusion of this chapter, the questions that were posed in the introduction may be reconsidered.

1. **What is necessary to enhance the employability of graduates?**

In the DHEP journey, exploring the possibilities of DHE in SA, it was clear that bringing together universities and employers gives students an integrated understanding of the expectations and inner workings of places of work and, in addition, the opportunity to apply their knowledge gained through their studies. Furthermore, it sparks enthusiasm in educators when they experience first-hand how students thrive in their development and succeed in finding lucrative employment after their graduation. At the same time, educators are inspired by the innovation of this model which makes all the input expected from them worthwhile. The reason given by employers to lay out the fiscal investment in students is the loyalty that students develop for the specific company or organisation. When a placement leads to employment, the employer has a graduate that knows the business and is making a substantial contribution to innovation and advancement of the company. The conclusion is that DHE might not have all the answers but certainly proved to be a strong contender to enhance employability of graduates.

2. **What are the systemic changes that are necessary for universities and employers to collaborate on this very important issue?**

After the study tour to Germany and Austria, the most important conclusions concern the systemic changes that are necessary to implement DHE programmes in SA were anticipated and further explored. It was clear that universities need to take responsibility for the employability of students and ensure that students make the necessary links between theory and practice in the context of their future workplace. Universities are best placed to initiate this process and restructure their existing practices to facilitate more WPL in close collaboration with employers. To achieve this, the provision and building of capacity is required for both educators and employers. Students also need to change their expectation of having four breaks in their academic year and be willing to spend time in the workplace during the current holidays in SA. Furthermore, the government needs to maximise existing resources to build a new generation of graduates who start their studies with a career in mind and fill the necessary gaps in the economy, rather than flooding the labour market with graduates who are not purposefully trained and qualified. In addition, the reintroduction of WPL into programmes, where it is part of the learning process and credited, needs to be strengthened and subsidised. Three important hurdles have been identified to be addressed in this project. The first is the formulation of a WPL policy and the integration of DHE as a model for the implementation of WPL. The second hurdle is more flexibility in tweaking curricula without cumbersome processes to get approval for changes. The third hurdle is to incentivise employers with tax rebates when they participate in training students during their studies and simplify the access to SETA funding. On the other hand, employers need to change their talent acquisition from buying talent to developing talent and accept their role in developing more competent graduates.

2. **How can DHE contribute to these changes?**

The DHEP has developed valuable tools for the future of DHE. One project is, however, not enough to ensure the viability of such a model to be practiced widely in SA. More critical discussion and actioning of the above identified systemic changes is necessary to make DHE a successful and innovative model in SA.

References

Biggs, J. (1996). Enhancing Teaching through Constructive Alignment. *Higher Education*, 32(3): 347–364. Available at: http://www.jstor.org/stable/3448076.

Council for Higher Education. (2011). *Work-Integrated Learning: A Good-Practice Guide.* HE Monitor No 12, August 2011.

Council for Higher Education. (2022). *Briefly Speaking.* No 22, August 2022: Pretoria.

Department of Education (DoE). (1997). *Education White Paper 3. A Programme for Higher Education Transformation.* Government Gazette No 18207, 15 August 1997: Pretoria.

Statistics South Africa. (2022). *Census 2022.*

Ehlers, U-D. (2020). *Future Skills: The Future of Learning and Higher Education.* Wiesbaden: Springer.

Göhringer, A. (2002). University of Cooperative Education – Karlsruhe: The Dual System of Higher Education in Germany. *Asia-Pacific Journal of Cooperative Education,* 3(2): 53–58.

Government of National Unity. (1994). *White Paper on Reconstruction and Development: Government's strategy for fundamental transformation.* Pretoria: Government Printers.

Gultig, J. (2000). The university in post-apartheid South Africa: New ethos and new divisions. *South African Journal of Higher Education,* 14(1): 37–52.

Hall, M. (2006). Academic freedom and the university: Fifty years of debate. *South African Journal of Higher Education,* 20(3): 8–16.

Hay, D. & Mapesela, M. (2009). South African Higher Education before and after 1994. In Bitzer, E. (ed.) *Higher Education in South Africa: A scholarly look behind the scenes.* Stellenbosch: African Sun Media, 3–20.

Hochrinner, H. (2021). *Types of Dual Study Programs in Austria.* [Unpublished presentation].

Human Sciences Research Council. (2023). Graduate unemployment – closing the supply-demand gap. 31 March 2023. *Human Sciences Research Council (HSRC).* Available at: https://hsrc.ac.za/news/economic-development/graduate-unemployment-closing-the-demand-supply-gap/. Date accessed: 1 April 2024.

Le Grange, L. (2006). The changing landscape of the contemporary university. *South African Journal of Higher Education,* 20(4): 367–371.

Leibowitz, B. (convenor), Antonissen C., Carolissen R., Cilliers, F., Esler, K., Malan, J. & Müller A. (2012). *Draft strategy for teaching and learning for the Committee for Learning and Teaching.* Memorandum to the CLT: University of Stellenbosch, 29 August 2012.

Ministry of Education. (2001). *National Plan for Higher Education Transformation.* March 2001: Government Printer.

Muller, J. (2009). Forms of knowledge and curriculum coherence. *Journal of Education and Work,* 22(3): 205–226.

Powell, J.J.W. & Fortwengel, P. (2014). 'Made in Germany' – Produced in America? How Dual Vocational Training Programs Can Help Close the Skills Gap in the United States. *Issue Brief,* 47, June 2014. American Institute for Contemporary German Studies. Johns Hopkins University.

Smith-Crous, A. (2024). *Presentation at the third conference of the DHEP Annual Conference.* Stellenbosch: South Africa.

Smith-Tolken, A. & Behrens, E. (2021). *Study Tour Report. Dual Higher Education Project.* CHEC Cape Higher Education Consortium: Bellville, South Africa.

Smith-Tolken, A.R. & Gochermann, J. (2022). *Dual Education am Western Cape: Pilotprojekt zur Entwicklung Dualer Studiumgänge in Südafrika.* Duales Studium, 2022: 2, 25–37. DUZ Medienhaus, Deutschland.

Smith-Tolken, A.R., McKay, M., Alessandri, A. & Nell, M. (2015). The Impact of Service-Learning on Professionalism in Undergraduate Oenology Students. In Lin, P.L., Wiegand, M. & Smith-Tolken, A.R. (ed.) *Service-Learning in Higher Education: Building Community Across the Globe.* Indianapolis: University of Indianapolis Press.

Smith-Tolken, A.R. (2010). Community Engagement at a Higher Education Institution – Exploring a Theoretical Grounding for Scholarly-Based Service-Related Processes. [Unpublished Doctoral Dissertation] Stellenbosch University.

South African Technology Network. (2016). *Annual Report.*

Teferra, D.M. & Altbach, P.C. (ed.). (2003). *African Higher Education: An International Reference Handbook.* Bloomington: Indiana University Press, 3–14.

Teferra, D. & Altbach, P. (2004). African Higher Education: Challenges for the 21st Century. *Higher Education,* 47: 21–50.

Thomson, A.M., Smith-Tolken, A., Naidoo, A. & Bringle, R. (2008). *Service Learning and Community Engagement – A Cross-Cultural Perspective.* Working Paper Series, International Society for Third Sector Research: Eighth International Conference, Barcelona, Spain July 9–12.

Waghid, Y. (2004). African philosophy of education: Implications for teaching and learning. *South African Journal of Higher Education,* 18(3): 56–64.

Waghid, Y. (2009). Universities as public good. In Bitzer, E. (ed.) *Higher Education in South Africa: A scholarly look behind the scenes.* Stellenbosch: African Sun Media, 71–83.

Wickham, S. (2022). *Final UCDP report on Work Package 2.1.* Dual Higher Education Project. Cape Higher Education Consortium: Bellville, South Africa.

Winburg, C. & Nduna, J. (2021). *College-Industry partnerships: a critical review of the literature.* Professional Education Research Institute, Cape Peninsula University of Technology, Cape Town: 13 January 2021.

Zhang, Y. & Schmidt-Herthab, B. (2019). Dual studies in different cultural contexts: The work-study model in Germany and its applicability to China. *Innovations in Education and Teaching International,* 57(4).

SECTION 4

Conversations about Strategy and Policy

CHAPTER 9

Academic citizenship and effective governance: Nurturing a nation's future

Ayansola Olatunji Ayandibu

Abstract

This chapter explores the concept of academic citizenship and its critical role in fostering effective governance. It examines how academic institutions contribute to societal development by promoting education, research, and ethical leadership. The discussion highlights the responsibilities of academics beyond teaching and research, emphasising their role in public engagement, policy advocacy, and governance. Furthermore, the chapter delves into the principles of effective governance, including transparency, accountability, and ethical decision-making, and how these elements intersect with academic leadership. By encouraging collaboration, equity, and social responsibility, academic citizenship strengthens democratic governance and promotes sustainable societal growth. The chapter concludes by advocating for stronger integration of academic contributions into policymaking and governance frameworks to ensure national development.

Keywords: academic citizenship; democratic governance; ethical leadership; higher education; public engagement; research and innovation; social responsibility, transparency and accountability.

Introduction

Political and social engagement has both benefits and risks for the academic role. Sometimes it brings the aforementioned benefits directly through the effectiveness of what is done or through the application of knowledge to real-world problems (Vogel et al., 2012). But there are also indirect benefits that come to the academic profession, through the setting up of beneficial social policies or the promotion of intellectual values in wider society. The idea of alleviating social problems and inequality will resonate with the moral and intellectual concerns of many academics. On the other hand, there are risks that political involvement can distort or debase the knowledge that it seeks to apply, or that it can bring the academic into collusion with sectional interests at the expense of the wider social good (Herbert, 2023). In the worst case, state or military involvement can compromise academic autonomy and become a form of intellectual control

(Shook et al., 2020). Given these sometimes subtle and conflicting influences, it is safe to say that the impact of academic involvement on the wider society is variable and often contested. But in principle and on balance, it seems that an academically informed citizenship is a good thing for society, and there are voluminous instances in history where academics have brought intellectual values and constructive change to public life (Kranich, 2024).

The academic profession has a long and honorable tradition of service to society. This is enshrined in the practices of disseminating knowledge and of training future generations, which are themselves seen as contributions to the public good (Dwivedi et al., 2024). But there is also a more specific tradition of academics involving themselves in social and political issues, usually as a form of public service in addition to the work that they are employed to do. Academics have often spoken out on specific issues or on behalf of disadvantaged groups; they have sometimes taken on advisory or decision-making roles in governmental or voluntary organisations; and they have used their professional expertise in the context of work that is directly aimed at bringing improvements to society (Berkvens et al., 2023). Such activities can all be seen as forms of academic citizenship – using the knowledge, skills, and public status of the academic role to benefit wider society. In democratic societies, many of the features of academic citizenship are open to any individual who wishes to involve themselves in public issues. But because of their specialised knowledge and their educational role, academics have distinctive contributions to make, and they have sometimes been called a 'reserve army for social reconstruction'.

Importance of academic citizenship

Academic citizenship is defined as the moral and civil responsibilities that come with being a member of an educational community (Macfarlane, 2007). These responsibilities can be fulfilled through participation in an abundance of activities, from helping to maintain a clean and hospitable environment, to attending meetings, and to being supportive of the academic environment in general. Academic citizenship can be performed by anyone who has a stake in the quality of education, whether it be the students, the faculty, the staff, or even the administration (Pais & Costa, 2020). There are many types of academic citizenship that vary depending on the context in which the academic is involved and the values that the academic is trying to uphold. These can range from fulfilling minimal responsibilities to meeting expectations to going above and beyond the call of duty. As an example, Goodman (2009) describes the minimum responsibilities of a student to be the obligation to follow the rules of the university and to respect the student-teacher relationship. An above and beyond approach would be a more active role such as participating in student organisations, engaging in self-governance, or other various activities aimed at improving the quality of education as a whole. Although the level of involvement may vary, the common goal of all types of academic citizenship is to sustain and improve the academic community.

Role of effective governance

(Rinne et al., 2002; Carney & Beaupert, 2013; Rowlands et al., 2017).

Governance has been explained in six dimensions: steering, funding, assessment and decision-making processes, academic work, supportive resources, and (the output of the first five) the achievement of the institution's goals. These dimensions are too detailed for what we are attempting to do in this chapter but they highlight that governance is a complex process and should not be oversimplified. A simpler interpretation of governance is provided by Keep (2000), who writes that governance involves the setting of strategic directions and making sure that resources match the ends sought. Both interpretations are pointing out that governance is about ensuring that decisions are made that lead to the best possible outcomes for an organisation and putting these decisions into practice.

Governance is a term that is used very loosely and often there is little clarity about what it actually means. In many cases when people discuss governance what they are really talking about is the political processes of decision making and the implementation of decisions. In other words, they are focusing on who gets what, when, and how. This is indeed a critical aspect of governance but to only focus on this provides an incomplete picture.

Effective governance is fundamental for the success of higher education systems and their institutions (Ferlie et al., 2009). It is an issue that has received considerably little attention in comparison to its significance and the impact it has on an institution's capacity to function, and more importantly on the many stakeholders it serves. The main focus of this write-up is on governance and change in higher education, and thus, in this chapter, we attempt to sketch out a framework for understanding governance in higher education, clarify its importance to key stakeholders, and propose some reasons why it should receive greater attention by researchers.

Building a Strong Foundation

(Kahne et al., 2000; Schugurensky & Myers, 2003; Garba et al., 2012; Marej, 2020; Tagliaventi et al., 2020; Fremstad & Ewins, 2024).

This section will be discussing promoting education and research, encouraging collaboration and engagement, and fostering equity and inclusion.

Promoting education and research

Academic institutions play a vital role in developing the future of a nation through educating future leaders and generating new knowledge, which can lead to making societies both in poorer and richer nations more prosperous, equitable, and peaceful. Education is a powerful tool for changing the world. Promoting education and research for sustainable development is an area in which the leadership and expertise found in higher education institutions is critically important. This is true in today's rapidly changing and globalising knowledge-based societies and is even more the case for tomorrow's leaders, for whom the forces of globalisation and the complexity of sustainable development create a learning curve of steep gradients and high uncertainty. Yet education holds the key to transformation. At all levels, education informs students about the complexity of sustainable development, empowering them to make informed decisions. Education fosters critical thinking and leadership. Global challenges like climate change, loss of biodiversity, and poverty often require cooperation, and at times collective action that bridges national, social, and cultural boundaries. Educational exchange and increasing student and scholar mobility are preliminary, yet important steps in preparing the future workforce of sustainable development to be effective in international and cross-cultural settings. In order to educate the global citizenship that will be requisite for a transition to a more sustainable path, higher education will need to internationalise its curricula further, infusing global perspectives into all subjects and creating interdisciplinary programmes oriented towards addressing global issues. Nevertheless, the impact of higher education in promoting sustainable development is not limited to the students who will be the change agents of the future. Through its research, higher education generates the knowledge and innovation that provide the foundation for progress towards more sustainable societies. In the past few decades, human knowledge has advanced more rapidly than in all prior history, and much of this is driven by the rapid expansion of higher education and research. Yet the relevance of this knowledge for addressing the urgent issues of our times is open to question. Considering the global challenges that we face, the research capacity of higher education today, while an immense potential resource, remains an underdeveloped tool for sustainable development. An initiative to promote higher education and research for sustainable development would endeavor to realise this potential by producing a new generation of scholars and professionals equipped with the knowledge, skills, and motivation to improve the prospects of sustainable development around the world. This can be an investment in a brighter future that we cannot afford to forgo.

Encouraging collaboration and engagement

To achieve this, it is necessary to cultivate a dynamic, collaborative, and lifelong learning culture. Educators must be distinguished by their commitment to quality and student-centeredness. They should possess a range of effective teaching methods and technologies to meet the diverse needs of learners. Additionally, they should engage in shared leadership to create and enhance learning resources and experiences. By participating in professional learning communities, educators can continuously improve their skills and contribute to the field of education. This learning and teaching revolution will not only redefine the roles of educators and students, but also transform the entire learning environment.

Building a strong foundation, promoting education and research, fostering collaboration and engagement, ensuring equity and inclusion, and nurturing the nation's future by promoting a good society are all important goals. Research has shown that lifelong learners are disciplined, exhibit positive social behavior, and have a strong desire to learn. They also have a positive influence on their family, friends, and colleagues, ultimately contributing to the creation of a society that values learning. This proposition emphasises the importance of educators and students becoming seamless learners who mutually influence each other in order to create a learning-driven environment.

Ensuring equity and inclusion

Nurturing a nation's future requires say from the entire community, and the successful inclusion of all groups in society in the policy making and decision-making processes. Research shows that the experience of being actively listened to, and the opportunity to have a say in specifically political matters, has a direct impact on fostering the individual's sense of belonging and attachment to the nation. In creating and sustaining an inclusive and democratic public policy development process, the outcomes and decisions made will be better informed, more innovative and sustainable, and will have legitimacy and credibility with the wider community. It will also develop the knowledge, skills, and experience of the individuals involved in the process, generating a more active and informed citizenry. An actively informed citizenry goes hand in hand with effective governance and the leadership of the nation has the knock-on effect of developing leadership skills in younger generations, who when offered the chance, will effectively help to shape the future of the nation.

A socially healthy nation is characterised by the extent to which individuals in that society feel a sense of identity, belonging, attachment, and commitment to the nation as a whole. This attachment and commitment to the nation comes about through the experiences and situations individuals face in their day to day lives. It is thus 'the sum of the parts equals the whole'. In a climate where individuals are faced with social segregation, vilification, isolation, and marginalisation, social capital erodes, preventing society from achieving national productivity, national innovation, and overall social and economic development. Participation in the community and participation in wider society relies on the sense of inclusion an individual feels. It is the responsibility of government and various institutions to provide policies, structures, and activities which facilitate the inclusion of all groups in society and foster a sense of belonging and commitment to the nation.

Enhancing academic citizenship

Civic engagement and service learning provide a bridge between the academic community and the local/global communities in which institutions are situated. It is an opportunity to practice citizenship and develop leadership skills while addressing societal needs. Service learning has been promoted for the potential benefit it holds for students, communities, and as a means to reinforce an institution's public mission. However, it is important to consider the reciprocal nature of civic engagement and the potential to form mutually beneficial partnerships (Blackmore & Lund, 2022). This is an opportunity to demonstrate social responsibility and create social capital. For example, students can work in tandem with a local organisation to address a community issue and present their findings to the organisation and academic unit, facilitating and enriching the learning experience.

Active participation is a key component to academic citizenship. It enables individuals to develop an allegiance to their institution, assuming responsibility and ownership of their own educational experience. This can vary in nature from taking an active role in the classroom to becoming involved in decision-making processes at the department level (Peterson & Knowles, 2009). Research on student involvement suggests that the more time and energy students invest in various activities, the greater the growth and development in related outcomes such as values, skills, and competencies (Hollister et al., 2008). This includes informal activities such as contact with faculty and interaction with diverse peers, so it is important for institutions to provide environments conducive to such engagement. In terms of governance, involvement fosters a sense of community and shared purpose. It encourages the voices of all stakeholders to be heard and facilitates meaningful participation in shared decision-making. This is important for graduate students as well, who often become siloed in their studies and disconnected from departmental issues and policies. Encouragement and enabling of active participation should be viewed as an investment in human potential and an enhancement to the quality of the academic environment.

Academic citizenship includes participation in governance, in developing institutional policy, and in developing knowledge in one's discipline. In a sense, it applies to accountability and oversight in the academic and administrative sectors (Hollister et al., 2008). It also applies to a range of opportunities that enable students to engage in experiential learning and to practice leadership within an academic unit or student organisation.

Encouraging active participation

The benefits of active participation in the community are many. Through involvement in campus and community, students achieve a sense of belonging and gain social capital. They are more satisfied with their educational experience and learn more both in and out of the classroom. The civic responsibility of college students is an outcome associated with student 'involvement'. This civic responsibility is measured by students' attitudes, values, and behaviours and involves the three components of civic knowledge, civic skills, and civic mindedness, all of which are encouraged and gained through active participation. An additional benefit is that while in college, involved students have the opportunity to discuss important ethical, social, and political issues with informed professors and are more likely to achieve a higher level of personal growth in all of these areas (Hollister et al., 2008). Finally, and spanning into professional development, employers are increasingly seeking prospects who have a developed capacity to work with others. Such students are often more well-rounded and better prepared to enter the workforce post-graduation. With these many additional benefits to involvement, one would think that the activity of participation would be more prevalent on college campuses. Yet this is not the case. Many college students are apathetic or too busy with other matters, and feel that their involvement will not make a difference. It is at this time that educators must stress to these students the importance of their involvement and its connection to solving major social issues.

Developing ethical and responsible behaviour

In general, people are motivated to act unethically to achieve some end which they acknowledge to be inappropriate. They may be pressured – by competition for places, grades, or academic distinction; financial necessity or the need to achieve a higher standard of work than they feel capable of doing (Biswas, 2014). The most common area of doubtful behaviour is in the academic achievements of students who are otherwise ethical in their actions. A survey of student cheating in North American universities found over 80% of respondents admitting to having cheated at some time (Baldwin Jr et al., 1996). The motives were usually to overcome feelings of unpreparedness, to gain a higher grade, or because the task was felt to be of marginal relevance to the work they were engaged in. A further difficulty lies in the subjective nature of academics in defining what is and what is not ethical.

Implicit in the notion of good citizenship is a concern for others. It is to be hoped that those who have been encouraged to participate more actively will have a heightened sense of responsibility for the welfare of the academy and their fellow students. It has been recognised for some time that ethical behavior is not a fixed entity, but varies at different times and in different situations. It is a mistake, therefore, to assume that students who generally act ethically will not, when it suits them, misbehave.

Cultivating leadership skills

Undergraduates in many institutions do not see the need to cultivate leadership skills as important to their roles as students. This is due in part to an unclear understanding of leadership and a lack of awareness of its potential to affect the quality of student and institutional life. In an effort to foster a better understanding of leadership among students and improve the quality of their leadership development, the co-curricular programmes at some universities are using the Social Change Model of Leadership Development (Lyons, 2017). This model views leadership as a purposeful, collaborative, values-based process that results in positive social change. It is designed to enhance the student's ability to lead in civic and community matters. In connection with this, the Step into Social Change programme organised by the ICR will be an excellent platform for students to observe leadership in action within various communities in the Champaign-Urbana area. By working with community leaders and agencies on a myriad of social issues, students will gain a better understanding of the community's needs and assets and begin to apply leadership skills to create change and become active citizens. In addition, the Institute for Sustainability and the Environment (iSEE) ECBS ChangeMakers programme is another great opportunity for students to develop leadership skills as it offers a unique environment to work on sustainability projects, facilitated by leadership and coaching (Lyons, 2017). These projects are designed to implement applied sustainability initiatives developed by iSEE and partners, and students have the chance to work directly with clients and invest their time and resources in solving real-world problems in a complex social context. This experience will allow students to understand leadership in relation to project management and leading while taking into account the complexity of policies and systems. Given that the majority of students' past experiences with leadership involve elected positions entailing little formal training, these programmes are invaluable in providing students with structured developmental opportunities to apply and reflect on leadership theories in real-world situations.

Effective governance for a nation's future

The essence of the democratic process consists of a government that is accountable to its citizens, transparent in its decision making, open to criticism and new ideas, and that possesses the means to correct mistakes (Lee, 2012). The perfectibility of the democratic process underlies the essence of effective governance for a nation's future. It is the function of effective governance to improve the effectiveness of the democratic process and public institutions. Governance provides how we build and improve the mechanism and steer the course for change in the rules and decision-making processes that affect our lives (Sun, 2012). This is the platform upon which the quality of decision-making in government and its administration depends. An effective governance framework will seek to assure that decision-making is systematic, informed, and timely, with the best possible choice made and the desired outcome achieved (Elliott et al., 2019). Throughout the process there will be a clear allocation of responsibility. Co-decision (involving stakeholders) in the process and implementation of a decision enhances its quality and legitimacy. A commitment to the ongoing improvement of the decision-making process and its outcomes is the final requisite for effective decision-making in governance (Sun, 2012). High quality decision-making in government must build from a strong ethical basis. An effective governance framework will maintain an ethical focus that is aimed at serving the common good by doing what is right, rather than just doing what works (Robles & Mallinson, 2025). Such a focus will automatically build a strong level of accountability and transparency into the decision-making process, as decisions and their makers are held to account in terms of their commitment to their ethical standard and the decision's impact on stakeholders. Ethical decision-making is based on the habitual consideration of widely accepted moral values. The decision-maker will be critically aware of moral issues and have a good understanding of the relevant legislation and its intent (Lee, 2012). Finally, an ethical decision maker will always consider the implications of a decision on the dignity and autonomy of affected persons. In maintaining an ethical focus in decision-making, it is hoped that public trust in the integrity of public institutions will be upheld, an essential requirement for democratic governance.

Implementing transparent decision-making processes

The 'business' view of decision-making is characterised by the identification of a problem or opportunity, the search for a solution that will bring benefits exceeding the costs, and then the choosing of the best alternative from a range of options. Transparent decision-making, which can be defined as decisions where the process and the bases of the decisions are clearly communicated and open to scrutiny by stakeholders, is more or less a synonym for good decision making (Bosio, 2022).

In an environment of increased public accountability, detailed reporting, and transparency in decision-making, a fundamental challenge exists to balance this with the need for prompt and decisive action. Within the tertiary sector, this is frequently cited by administrative leaders as the major issue that prevents them from operating 'strategically' and results in an overly reactive, ad hoc management style (Chan & Chou, 2020). The pressure to meet the requirements of accountability and transparency is frequently manifested in administration in a call for more 'bottom line' thinking and 'business-like' approaches to management. While there are obvious limitations to using business as a model for a public sector institution, there are valuable lessons that can be learned in terms of improving efficiency, effectiveness, and transparency in management and decision-making. One critical element is to define clear decision-making processes and explain the rationale and criteria used in decision-making to all stakeholders in the institution.

Ensuring accountability and integrity

Integrity is adherence to a set of values and an ethical standard which is often self-imposed and based on shared norms in the absence of clear-cut rules and regulations. It implies an absence of corruption and debasing to vested interests, an openness to public scrutiny, and an alignment of espoused values and actual behavior (Frenkel, 2023). While corruption is an obvious antithesis of integrity and a concern in many societies, even in the absence of malfeasance, governance effectiveness can be undermined by ad hoc decision-making and frequent changes in direction; such a situation can be perceived negatively as a lack of governance.

Accountability is not a unitary concept. A basic distinction can be made between financial accountability, in relation to the spending of public funds and tuition fees, and accountability for the quality and effectiveness of educational programmes and services. These may sometimes conflict, for instance in the case of cost-cutting measures to reduce a deficit which may undermine a quality programme (Garcia-Gibson, 2023). More broadly, accountability is also answerability, blameworthiness, and the application of consequences for failure to live up to agreed-upon norms or mandates. In the context of governance, accountability means acknowledgment and assumption of responsibility for performance in terms of the agreed-upon role and mission and the effective use of resources – it is essentially a stewardship function.

Ensuring accountability and integrity of the governance process in higher education is an essential condition for its effectiveness and legitimacy. It represents a direct response to public concerns about the misuse of public funds and the violation of trust on the part of the government, the private sector, or the higher education institution. It also is an internal mechanism for self-assessment, and it serves to build trust with a key stakeholder – the academic staff (Gollagari et al., 2023).

Promoting innovation and adaptability

Globalisation's increases in complexity and the myriad of ways in which it impacts upon different sectors in society means that adaptive strategies are required to stay the course or to change direction. Simulation modelling can be a useful tool in understanding the impact of change and in identifying optimal strategies under complex and uncertain futures. Innovation and knowledge transfer are also essential to enable informed policy decisions and to produce desirable outcomes. Knowledge transfer is a two-way process involving the movement of knowledge between research and policy communities, and also learning by researchers on policy issues and by policy agents on research findings (Horlings et al., 2018).

High-quality research and production of skilled graduates are increasingly mobile internationally, therefore strategies to enhance domestic capabilities must result in comparative advantages. All is not successful change, and there are often uncertainties and unintended consequences resulting from both domestic and externally forced change. There is a clear role here for social science research to inform the understanding of change processes and to provide guidance on mitigation and adaptation strategies for detrimental outcomes. This, in essence, is a grand challenge for social science.

For the development of a balanced and knowledge-driven society in today's global context, the ability of a nation to adapt to the changing needs and demands of the environment is crucial. Innovation generally results in change, and change is frequently opposed or viewed with suspicion (Jessani et al., 2020). Thus, effective innovative activity is strongly dependent on the prevailing culture in an organisation or society. Innovation is a pragmatic process beginning with the generation of new ideas and leading through to selection of ideas which are implemented. The endpoint is the implementation of a new product, policy, or process, which produces a change from the original situation. Innovation is about creating and implementing change that results in enhanced effectiveness. Innovations can take many forms. Optimally, the process begins with identification of a problem or need, leading to targeted activity to develop new knowledge, and resulting in application of the new knowledge to produce change. Innovation results in increased productivity and productivity growth is vital for increased standards of living for the wider community. This is particularly pertinent for wealth generation in global economies. Innovation aimed at improved problem solving and efficiency is also intricately linked to improved effectiveness in public and third sector organisations (Kiss et al., 2022).

Conclusion

In recapitulating the essential aspects of academic citizenship and governance, it becomes evident that their interconnection forms a critical nexus vital for societal development and effective governance. Academic citizenship embodies the commitment of academia towards societal engagement, ethical conduct, and the pursuit of knowledge that transcends academic boundaries. Governance, on the other hand, involves the systems and processes through which societies are managed, emphasising accountability, transparency, and participatory decision-making.

References

Baldwin Jr, D.C., Daugherty, S.R., Rowley, B.D. & Schwarz, M.D. (1996). Cheating in medical school: a survey of second-year students at 31 schools. *Academic medicine* 71(3): 267–73.

Berkvens, L., Roets, A., Haesevoets, T. & Verschuere, B. (2023). Local civil society organisations' appreciation of different local policy decision-making instruments. *Local Government Studies*, 50(3): 1–28.

Biswas, A.E. (2014). Lessons in Citizenship: Using Collaboration in the Classroom to Build Community, Foster Academic Integrity, and Model Civic Responsibility. *Journal on Excellence in College Teaching*, 25(1): 9–25.

Blackmore, J. & Lund, R. (2022). Academic citizenship, collegiality and good university governance: a dedication to Associate Professor Julie Rowlands (1964–2021). *Critical Studies in Education*, 63(5).

Bosio, E. (2022). Embracing the Global South: Educators' understanding on the role of global citizenship education in Brazil, South Africa, and Ghana. In Öztürk, M. (ed.) *Engagement with Sustainable Development in Higher Education: Universities as Transformative Spaces for Sustainable Futures*. Cham: Springer International Publishing.

Carney, T. & Beaupert, F. (2013). Public and Private Bricolage: Challenges Balancing Law, Services and Civil Society in Advanced CRPD Supported Decision Making. *The University of New South Wales Law Journal*, 36(1): 175–201.

Chan, S.J. & Chou, C. (2020). Who influences higher education decision-making in Taiwan? An analysis of internal stakeholders. *Studies in Higher Education*, 45(10): 2101–2109.

Dwivedi, Y.K., Jeyaraj, A., Hughes, L., Davies, G. H., Ahuja, M., Albashrawi, M. A. & Walton, P. (2024). 'Real impact': Challenges and opportunities in bridging the gap between research and practice – Making a difference in industry, policy, and society. *International Journal of Information Management*, 78.

Elliott, C., Worker, J., Levin, K., & Ross, K.A.T.I.E. (2019). Good Governance for Long-Term Low-Emissions Development Strategies. *World Resources Institute*.

Fremstad, E. & Ewins, K. (2024). Academic citizenship through the bundle of academic roles. *Journal of Praxis in Higher Education*, 6(2), 42–54.

Ferlie, E., Musselin, C. & Andresani, G. (2009). The governance of higher education systems: A public management perspective. *University governance: Western European comparative perspectives*, 25: 1–19.

Frenkel, S.J. (2023). Embedded in two worlds: The university academic manager's work, identity and social relations. *Educational Management Administration & Leadership*, 51(5): 1087–1104.

Garba, S.A., Singh, T.K.R., Yusuf, N. B.M. & Saad, A.F. (2012). Toward Building a Solid Foundation for Social Science Education in Nigerian Educational System: A New Approach to Functional Citizenship Education. *International Journal of Social Science and Humanity*, 2(3): 196.

Garcia-Gibson, F. (2023). The ethics of climate activism. *Wiley Interdisciplinary Reviews: Climate Change*, e831.

Gollagari, R., Beyene, B.B. & Mishra, S.S. (2023). Ethical Leadership and Students' Satisfaction in Public Universities of Ethiopia: Mediating Role of Perceived Good Governance. *International Journal of Public Administration*, 46(13): 902–914.

Goodman, J.F. (2009). Respect-due and respect-earned: negotiating student-teacher relationships. *Ethics and Education*, 4(1): 3–17.

Herbert, J.M. (2023). Academic free speech or right-wing grievance? *Digital Discovery*, 2(2): 260–297.

Hollister, R.M., Wilson, N. & Levine, P. (2008). Educating students to foster active citizenship. *Peer Review*, 10(2–3): 18–22.

Horlings, L.G., Roep, D. & Wellbrock, W. (2018). The role of leadership in place-based development and building institutional arrangements. *Local Economy: The Journal of the Local Economy Policy Unit*, 33(3): 245–268.

Jessani, N.S., Valmeekanathan, A., Babcock, C.M. & Ling, B. (2020). Academic incentives for enhancing faculty engagement with decision-makers—considerations and recommendations from one School of Public Health. *Humanities and Social Sciences Communications*, 7(1): 1–13.

Kahne, J., Westheimer, J. & Rogers, B. (2000). Service learning and citizenship in higher education. *Michigan Journal of Community Service Learning*, 7(1): 42–51.

Keep, E. (2000). *Creating a knowledge driven economy: definitions, challenges and opportunities*. SKOPE.

Kiss, B., Sekulova, F., Hörschelmann, K., Salk, C.F., Takahashi, W. & Wamsler, C. (2022). Citizen participation in the governance of nature-based solutions. *Environmental Policy and Governance*, 32(3): 247–272.

Kranich, N. (2024). Civic Literacy: Reimagining a Role for Libraries. *The Library Quarterly*, 94(1): 4–34.

Lee, W.O. (2012). Education for future-oriented citizenship: implications for the education of twenty-first century competencies. *Asia Pacific Journal of Education*, 32(4): 498–517.

Macfarlane, B. (2007). Defining and Rewarding Academic Citizenship: The implications for university promotions policy. *Journal of Higher Education Policy and Management*, 29(3): 261–273.

Marej, K. (2020). Creating impact in citizenship education by transformative research: Indications for professionalisation. *JSSE-Journal of Social Science Education*, 19(2).

Lyons, L.M. (2017). 'Being Here Now' as a First-Year Student: Cultivating Global Citizenship and Mindfulness on the Move in a Co-Curricular Learning Adventure. In *International Forum of Teaching and Studies*, 13(2): 3.

Pais, A. & Costa, M. (2020). An ideology critique of global citizenship education. In Lapping, C. (ed.) *Freud, Lacan, Zizek and Education: Exploring Unconscious Investments in Policy and Practice* (72–87). Routledge.

Peterson, A. & Knowles, C. (2009). Active citizenship: A preliminary study into student teacher understandings. *Educational Research*, 51(1): 39–59.

Rinne, R., Kivirauma, J. & Simola, H. (2002). Shoots of revisionist 1 education policy or just slow readjustment? The Finnish case of educational reconstruction. *Journal of Education Policy*, 17(6): 643–658.

Robles, P. & Mallinson, D.J. (2025). Artificial intelligence technology, public trust, and effective governance. Available at: https://pure.psu.edu/en/publications/artificial-intelligence-technology-public-trust-and-effective-gov. Date accessed: 16 March 2025.

Rowlands, J., Rowlands, M. & Melchior. (2017). *Academic Governance in the Contemporary University*. Singapore: Springer.

Schugurensky, D. & Myers, J.P. (2003). Citizenship Education: Theory, Research and Practice. *Encounters in Theory and History of Education*, 4.

Shook, J.R., Rowlands, M. & Melchior. (2020). Ethical constraints and contexts of artificial intelligent systems in national security, intelligence, and defense/military operations. In Masakowski, Y.R. (ed.) *Artificial Intelligence and Global Security: Future Trends, Threats and Considerations* (137–152). Emerald Publishing Limited.

Sun, S.H.L. (2012). *Population Policy and Reproduction in Singapore: Making Future Citizens*. Routledge.

Tagliaventi, M.R., Carli, G. & Cutolo, D. (2020). Excellent researcher or good public servant? The interplay between research and academic citizenship. *Higher Education*, 79: 1057–1078.

Vogel, C., Susanne, C.M., Roger, E.K. & Geoffrey, D.D. (2012). Linking vulnerability, adaptation, and resilience science to practice: pathways, players and partnerships. In Kasperson, R.E. (ed.) *Integrating Science and Policy: Vulnerability and Resilience in Global Environmental Change* (pp. 97–127). Routledge.

CHAPTER 10

It's 2025: Are our higher education models still valid?

René Pellissier

Abstract

This chapter critically examines the validity of current higher education models in South Africa, particularly in light of global pressures to attain 'world-class' university status. The pursuit of this status has led to increased inequality, with elite institutions benefiting, while historically disadvantaged universities (HDUs) struggle. The rising costs of education, inadequate government subsidies, and the limited accessibility of higher education for marginalised communities have made it clear that the current model is unsustainable. The chapter draws on findings from the *Down with the World-Class University: How Our Business Models Damage Universal Higher Education* (2024) report, expanding on its methodology, authorship, and key insights relevant to South Africa. It also revisits the role of the #FeesMustFall and #RhodesMustFall movements with improved referencing.

A historical analysis of South Africa's higher education system, particularly the interaction between universities and technical and vocational education and training (TVET) colleges, as well as between HBUs and historically white universities (HWUs), is provided to offer greater context. Finally, this chapter proposes a new model of higher education that prioritises inclusivity, skills development, and financial stability.

Keywords: decolonise education; inclusivity; knowledge diversity; university models.

Introduction

The pursuit of 'world-class' status in higher education has become a dominant goal in many countries, including South Africa. Universities are under immense pressure to perform well in global rankings, attract international students, and secure prestigious research funding. However, these ambitions come at a cost. The *Down with the World-Class University: How Our Business Models Damage Universal Higher Education* (2024) report provides critical insights that are highly relevant to South Africa. This chapter reinterprets the findings of the report for the South African higher education landscape, arguing that the pursuit of world-class status perpetuates inequalities and undermines the goal of accessible, universal higher education (HEPI, 2024).

South Africa, with its stark socio-economic disparities and a growing youth population in need of education, must reconsider its higher education business models. Rather than striving for exclusivity and elite status, the system needs to prioritise inclusivity, affordability, and scalability. A broader, more collaborative approach to higher education is essential to address the challenges of access and equity while ensuring that universities remain financially sustainable and socially relevant (Badat, 2010; Cloete et al., 2015).

This chapter examines whether the current higher education models in South Africa remain valid, particularly in the context of the global drive for 'world-class' university status. While prestigious rankings and international competition have become benchmarks for excellence, these ambitions often exacerbate inequalities, particularly in countries with stark socio-economic disparities like South Africa. The pursuit of world-class status has led to a widening educational divide, favouring elite institutions and neglecting historically disadvantaged universities. High tuition fees and insufficient government subsidies compound the issue, as evidenced by the #FeesMustFall movement. The research follows a metacritical stance on literature and practice, critically analysing and evaluating existing scholarship, theoretical frameworks, and practical applications in a given field. This approach does not merely summarise prior work but actively interrogates underlying assumptions, biases, and the effectiveness of different models or methodologies.

Scholars in the field have long debated the role of universities in society and the unintended consequences of their commercialisation. Hence policy is critical towards sustainable and socially responsible higher education reforms. Governments and institutions must reconsider funding models, evaluation metrics, and academic priorities to ensure that higher education remains a tool for social mobility and innovation rather than a mechanism for reinforcing existing inequalities.

This chapter uses as theoretical framework the *Down with the World-Class University: How Our Business Models Damage Universal Higher Education* (2024) report. Higher education has undergone significant transformations in recent decades, largely influenced by the pursuit of world-class university status. The report *Down with the World-Class University: How Our Business Models Damage Universal Higher Education* (2024) provides a critical examination of this model and presents an alternative framework for more inclusive and equitable academic institutions. This paper serves as an important theoretical foundation for analysing the negative consequences of the world-class university paradigm, advocating for equitable access, and exploring alternative models that prioritise social impact over global prestige. Indeed, they challenge the prevailing 'world-class university' model, arguing that it prioritises elite status, research excellence, and global rankings over the broader mission of higher education, stating that current models often lead to the commercialisation of universities, where institutions function more like businesses than centres of learning and social transformation. The pursuit of world-class status frequently results in resource concentration among a few elite universities, creating systemic inequalities in global higher education. This critique aligns with discussions on the corporatisation of universities, as theorised by scholars such as Henry Giroux (2014), who argues that neoliberal policies have commodified education, making it inaccessible to many.

One of the most significant concerns raised in the report is the impact of the world-class university model on equity and inclusion. The emphasis on global rankings often leads institutions to prioritize international reputation over local educational needs. This practice disadvantages underprivileged students, particularly those from marginalised communities and developing regions, who may struggle to access the resources and opportunities concentrated in elite institutions. This perspective resonates with Paulo Freire's critical pedagogy (1970), which underscores the need for an education system that is participatory and inclusive rather than hierarchical and exclusionary. The report further presents alternative frameworks for structuring higher education institutions that prioritise collaboration, regional development, and community engagement over competition and ranking. This shift is essential for fostering a more just and equitable educational landscape. Rather focusing on societal impact than prestige, universities can contribute meaningfully to local economies, knowledge production, and workforce development. This approach aligns with global efforts to decolonise education and promote knowledge diversity, ensuring that institutions serve the public good rather than elite interests.

Existing higher education models

The global race toward 'world-class' status has shaped the priorities of many universities worldwide, including those in South Africa. Universities strive for high rankings, international recognition, and research prestige, often at the cost of accessibility and equity. The *Down with the World-Class University: How Our Business Models Damage Universal Higher Education* report (HEPI, 2024) highlights the detrimental effects of this model, particularly in countries with stark socio-economic disparities. The report, authored by leading education policy experts, draws from comparative case studies in Africa, Latin America, and Asia, analysing how business-driven models in higher education contribute to increasing inequality.

In South Africa, the emphasis on research output, internationalisation, and financial sustainability has deepened the divide between elite universities and under-resourced institutions. Historically disadvantaged universities continue to grapple with funding shortages, while the expansion of private and online education remains insufficient to meet the demands of the growing youth population. This chapter revisits the findings of HEPI's report and contextualises them within the South African higher education landscape, advocating for an inclusive, collaborative, and skills-driven system.

South Africa's higher education landscape is characterised by multiple models, each with distinct functions and shortcomings. The research-intensive university model prioritises research output, global rankings, and international partnerships (Le Grange, 2020). This model often diverts resources away from teaching and student support services to focus on high-impact research. It also reinforces elitism, favouring institutions with strong financial backing while marginalising HBUs (HEPI, 2024). The traditional public university model aims to provide broad-based academic education with a balance between research and teaching (Department of Higher Education and Training, 2013; Badat, 2010). However, many public universities suffer from chronic underfunding, outdated curricula, and bureaucratic inefficiencies. Additionally, limited student support services result in low retention and graduation rates, particularly among disadvantaged students (Ndofirepi & Cross, 2016). The technical and vocational education and training (TVET) model focuses on skill-based education aligned with industry needs, particularly in technical and artisanal fields (Cloete et al., 2015). However, TVET institutions remain underfunded and stigmatised as inferior to universities. There is a lack of articulation pathways between TVET colleges and universities, limiting upward mobility for students seeking advanced qualifications (Cloete et al., 2015). The private higher education model offers specialised or market-driven programmes, often with a strong vocational focus. While private institutions provide additional learning opportunities, they operate on a for-profit basis, making tuition fees prohibitive for many students. Additionally, quality assurance concerns persist, as not all private institutions maintain rigorous academic standards (UNESCO, 2020). Lastly, the open and distance learning (ODL) model expands access to higher education through online and blended learning platforms (Van Schalkwyk, 2020; UNESCO, 2020). Digital inequality presents a significant barrier, particularly in rural areas where students lack reliable internet access and technological infrastructure. Furthermore, high dropout rates are common due to limited student engagement and support structures (Van Schalkwyk, 2020).

The pitfalls of the world-class university model in South Africa

The 'world-class university' model has become synonymous with excellence in higher education, but it often fuels competition between institutions, driving them to prioritise prestige over public service. In South Africa, this model is not only financially unsustainable for most institutions but also exacerbates inequality in access to education. Elite institutions concentrate resources and attract funding while many historically disadvantaged universities struggle to keep up, further entrenching the educational divide (Cloete et al., 2015). However, South Africa's higher education sector faces numerous crises, for instance inadequate funding and insufficient access for most of its youth. High tuition fees and the rising cost of education make it difficult for many students, particularly from marginalised communities, to attend university. The 2015 #FeesMustFall movement was a clear signal that the current system, reliant on high tuition fees and shrinking state subsidies, is failing to meet the needs of South Africa's students (Habib, 2019; Department of Higher Education and Training, 2013). In addition, the quality of the school systems makes it difficult for students to be prepared for the higher education system.

Statistics underscore the pressing need to re-evaluate and reform South Africa's higher education models to enhance accessibility, retention, and employability outcomes. To put this into perspective, as of 2022, South Africa's gross tertiary enrolment ratio is approximately 27,17%, indicating that just over a quarter of the eligible population is enrolled in higher education institutions (Statista, 2025). In addition, student retention remains a significant challenge. A study analysing data from 2020 found that dropout rates increased notably among students in their third to fifth years of study, while first-year to second-year retention rates remained relatively stable. The unemployment rate among university graduates aged 15 to 34 was reported at 33,6% in the first quarter of 2023, highlighting the difficulties young graduates face in securing employment (www.statssa.gov.za).

The global competition for rankings and research prestige, as promoted by the world-class university model, often diverts resources away from teaching and student support services toward expensive infrastructure projects and international partnerships. While these investments may boost rankings, they do little to expand access to quality education for the majority of South Africans (Ndofirepi & Cross, 2016). At least, the Times Higher education ranking systems introduced a raking system based on impact focusing on stewardship, research, and sustainability. However, the result is a sector that prioritises select elite institutions, leaving others struggling to serve their local communities (HEPI, 2024).

Learning from emerging alternatives

As the *Down with the World-Class University: How Our Business Models Damage Universal Higher Education* (2024) report highlights, South Africa can learn valuable lessons from emerging non-university competitors and alternative education providers. These alternatives, which include online learning platforms, vocational training programmes, and industry partnerships, offer more affordable and flexible education options. In many cases, they are better positioned to meet the needs of today's workforce, providing students with the skills they need for immediate employment at a fraction of the cost of a traditional university education (HEPI, 2024). Adopting similar models, South African universities can expand their reach and reduce costs. Collaboration with industry, for example, can help universities align curricula with the needs of the job market while ensuring students gain practical, work-ready skills (Walker & McLean, 2020). Furthermore, online and blended learning platforms provide scalable solutions for expanding access to higher education, especially for students in rural or underserved areas (Van Schalkwyk, 2020).

In South Africa, where unemployment remains a significant challenge, universities must rethink their role in preparing students for the workforce. Rather than focusing solely on producing research or chasing global rankings, higher education institutions should prioritise employability, skills development, and partnerships with industries to create more pathways to meaningful employment (Marginson, 2011).

Reimagining South Africa's higher education system

South Africa's higher education system requires a fundamental reimagining. This means moving away from a one-size-fits-all approach based on world-class university aspirations and instead embracing a differentiated system that values diversity in providers, business models, and educational outcomes (Cloete et al., 2015). The *Down with the World-Class University: How Our Business Models Damage Universal Higher Education* (2024) report calls for the establishment of an independent commission to oversee this redesign. In South Africa, this could take the form of a multi-stakeholder body that includes government, industry, civil society, and educational institutions working together to craft a more inclusive and sustainable higher education system (HEPI, 2024).

This new system would move beyond traditional university education to include a variety of providers, such as technical and vocational education and training (TVET) colleges, online education platforms, and industry-led training programmes. By expanding the definition of higher education, South Africa can create more opportunities for its youth to gain valuable skills and qualifications without necessarily attending a traditional university (UNESCO, 2020). Furthermore, the new system must prioritise the development of credentials that reflect the demands of the modern workforce. These credentials should be more flexible and skills-oriented, focusing on conceptual and inquiry-based learning rather than purely technical qualifications (Department of Higher Education and Training, 2013). This shift would enable students to adapt to a rapidly changing job market and equip them with the critical thinking skills needed to solve complex problems (Le Grange, 2020).

Collaboration must replace competition in South Africa's higher education sector. Rather than relying on mergers or forcing struggling institutions to adopt unsustainable business models, universities should be encouraged to work together through group and federal structures. This approach would allow institutions to share resources, expertise, and infrastructure, ensuring that all universities, regardless of their historical or financial standing, can provide quality education (Ndofirepi & Cross, 2016).

The creation of collaborative networks between universities, TVET colleges, and industry partners would help to ensure that South Africa's education system is aligned with the needs of its economy. By pooling resources and knowledge, institutions can offer a broader range of programmes, improve student outcomes, and increase their financial sustainability (Cloete et al., 2015). Joint ventures, rather than hostile mergers, would allow universities to retain their unique identities while benefiting from collective strength (Walker & McLean, 2020).

In South Africa, the Department of Higher Education and Training (DHET) plays a crucial role in regulating and overseeing the higher education sector. However, as in the UK, there is a need to rebalance the regulatory focus to ensure that the financial and operational health of the entire sector is prioritised alongside student outcomes. The DHET should take a more proactive role in promoting innovation and collaboration, ensuring that regulations do not stifle creativity and the adoption of new business models (DHET, 2013). The DHET can also play a pivotal role in managing the transition toward a more diversified and sustainable higher education system by offering financial incentives and support for institutions willing to embrace new models. This would include offering loans or grants to institutions that want to develop innovative programmes, build partnerships with industry, or adopt group and federal structures (Badat, 2010).

Towards a redesign

South Africa's higher education system stands at a critical juncture, necessitating comprehensive reforms to address historical inequities and align with contemporary global standards. While existing recommendations provide a foundation, further strategies can be implemented to enhance the system.

A pivotal step in reforming higher education is the decolonisation of curricula. This involves revising academic programmes to reflect African contexts, knowledge systems, and languages, ensuring that education is both locally pertinent and globally competitive. Such an approach addresses historical biases and makes learning more accessible and meaningful to South Africa's diverse student body. By integrating indigenous knowledge and perspectives, institutions can foster a sense of identity and pride among students, while also promoting critical thinking and innovation. This transformation requires collaborative efforts among educators, scholars, and community leaders to redefine educational content and methodologies. The quality of education is intrinsically linked to the capabilities of its educators. Implementing comprehensive faculty development programmes focusing on active teaching methodologies, research skills, leadership, and the integration of technology can significantly enhance teaching quality and academic outcomes. Encouraging faculty to align their efforts with institutional goals ensures a cohesive approach to education. Moreover, continuous professional development opportunities can help educators stay abreast of evolving pedagogical trends and technological advancements, thereby enriching the learning experience for students. To improve student retention and success rates, robust support systems are essential. This includes academic advising, mental health services, and career counselling tailored to address the diverse needs of the student population, particularly those from historically disadvantaged backgrounds. By providing personalised guidance and resources, institutions can help students navigate academic challenges, manage personal issues, and plan for their future careers. Such support not only enhances individual student outcomes but also contributes to the overall success and reputation of the institution.

Bridging the gap between academia and industry is crucial for aligning educational programmes with labour market demands. Fostering collaborations between higher education institutions and various industries can ensure that academic curricula remain relevant and responsive to economic needs. These partnerships can facilitate internships, apprenticeships, and job placements, thereby enhancing graduate employability. Moreover, industry input can inform curriculum development, ensuring that graduates possess the skills and knowledge required in the workforce. Such synergies can also lead to joint research initiatives, innovation, and economic development.

In the digital age, investing in digital infrastructure and resources is imperative to support blended and online learning models. This approach can expand access to education, particularly for students in remote areas, and provide flexible learning opportunities that accommodate diverse life circumstances. By leveraging technology, institutions can offer a variety of learning modalities, from traditional in-person classes to fully online courses, catering to different learning preferences and needs. Additionally, digital platforms can facilitate continuous learning and professional development, essential in the rapidly changing world.

Higher education institutions have a responsibility to engage with and contribute to their local communities. Encouraging active involvement through service-learning programmes, research initiatives addressing societal challenges, and public outreach can strengthen the relationship between universities and communities. Such engagement ensures that education remains relevant and responsive to societal needs, fostering a sense of social responsibility among students. Moreover, community-based learning experiences can enrich academic learning, providing students with practical skills and a deeper understanding of societal issues.

There are no easy solutions as the situation is complex given the extent of stakeholders and regulations involved. In an ideal world, one could consider the following suggestions already in the public domain: 1) establish a South African independent commission, including stakeholders from government, education, industry, and civil society, to oversee the redesign of the higher education sector. This redesign should expand the definition of higher education to include non-university providers and alternative education pathways (HEPI, 2024). 2) Work with the Department of Higher Education and Training (DHET), the Council on Higher Education (CHE), and industry to develop new credentials that reflect both conceptual and skills-based learning. These credentials should equip students with the critical thinking and problem-solving skills needed for a dynamic workforce (DHET, 2013). 3) Create a transition fund to support institutions in adopting new business models, developing innovative programmes, and forming collaborative networks. This fund should prioritise scalability, affordability, and inclusivity in higher education offerings (Badat, 2010). 4) Encourage institutions to work together through group and federal structures, allowing them to share resources and expertise while maintaining their unique identities. Joint ventures and collaborations should be preferred over mergers to ensure the sustainability of the sector (Ndofirepi & Cross, 2016). 5) Adjust the role of the DHET to focus on the overall health of the higher education sector, promoting financial sustainability and innovation. This should include reducing regulatory burdens that inhibit creativity and supporting institutions in developing new, inclusive education models (Walker & McLean, 2020).

Conclusion

This chapter criticised the world-class university model's unsustainability and argued for a more inclusive, equitable, and scalable approach to higher education. Drawing on alternative educational models, such as online platforms, vocational training, and industry collaborations, the chapter suggests a shift toward diversified, flexible education systems. A reimagined higher education system must prioritise employability, skills development, and accessible learning opportunities for all South Africans. Collaboration, rather than competition, is essential in reshaping South Africa's higher education landscape to ensure financial sustainability and societal relevance. The world-class university model has proven to be financially unsustainable and socially exclusive in the South African context. It has diverted resources toward prestige and rankings while neglecting the broader goal of providing accessible, affordable, and relevant higher education for all. South Africa's higher education system must shift its focus toward inclusivity and collaboration, embracing new business models and partnerships that prioritise student needs over institutional prestige. South Africa can create a higher education system that is both financially sustainable and socially inclusive, ensuring that all citizens have access to the opportunities and skills they need to thrive in a rapidly changing world.

Following on the the *Down with the World-Class University: How Our Business Models Damage Universal Higher Education* (2024) report, this chapter provides a foundation for challenging the market-driven university model and advocating for a more inclusive, community-oriented approach to higher education. Its critique of the commercialisation of academia, emphasis on equity, and exploration of alternative university models provide valuable insights for policymakers, educators, and researchers seeking to reform higher education systems. As the global education landscape continues to evolve, it is crucial to reconsider the purpose and priorities of universities to ensure they serve society as a whole rather than a privileged few.

References

Badat, S. (2010). *The Challenges of Transformation in Higher Education and Training Institutions in South Africa.* Development Bank of Southern Africa.

Cloete, N. & Maassen, P. (2015). *Knowledge Production and Contradictory Functions in African Higher Education.* African Minds.

Department of Higher Education and Training. (2013). *White Paper for Post-School Education and Training: Building an Expanded, Effective and Integrated Post-School System.* Pretoria: Government Printer.

Freire, P. (1970). *Pedagogy of the Oppressed.* Bloomsbury Publishing.

Giroux, H.A. (2014). *Neoliberalism's War on Higher Education.* Haymarket Books.

Habib, A. (2019). *Rebels and Rage: Reflecting on #FeesMustFall.* Jonathan Ball Publishers.

HEPI Debate Paper 38. (2024). *Down with the World-Class University: How Our Business Models Damage Universal Higher Education.* Higher Education Policy Institute.

Le Grange, L. (2020). Decolonising the University Curriculum. *South African Journal of Higher Education*, 34(4): 1–16.

Marginson, S. (2011). Higher Education and Public Good. *Higher Education Quarterly*, 65(4): 411–433.

Ndofirepi, A.P. & Cross, M. (2016). *Knowledge and Change in African Higher Education.* Sense Publishers.

Statista. (2025). *Gross tertiary enrolment ratio in South Africa from 1970 to 2022.*

UNESCO. (2020). *The Role of Higher Education in Promoting Sustainable Development Goals.* United Nations Educational, Scientific and Cultural Organization.

Van Schalkwyk, F. (2020). Higher Education's Response to COVID-19 in South Africa: Managing Risks and Recovery. *University World News.*

Walker, M. & McLean, M. (2020). *Professional Education, Capabilities and the Public Good: The Role of Universities in Promoting Human Development.* Routledge.

CHAPTER 11

Unmasking neoliberalism: Exploring the dark side of leadership in a South African higher education institution

Lizl Steynberg and Jan P. Grundling

Abstract

The influence of neoliberalism in higher education has reshaped academic leadership, often fostering unchecked authority and self-serving agendas. This chapter examines toxic leadership behaviours such as coercion, manipulation, and abuse of power within a South African higher education institution (HEI), revealing their impact on institutional ethics. Using an idiographic and auto-ethnographic qualitative approach, the analysis is enriched through critical reflexivity, acknowledging the protagonist's positionality and biases. The chapter contextualises these leadership dynamics within national and international debates on university massification and neoliberalism, emphasising their systemic nature. Findings highlight the ethical dilemmas academic leaders face and stress the need for integrity, compassion, and equity in leadership. This chapter contributes to discussions on responsible academic governance by offering practical strategies for fostering ethical leadership and institutional accountability in higher education.

Keywords: academic justice; ethical challenges; higher education; leadership dynamics; neoliberalism.

Alignment with theme of book

This chapter, titled *Unmasking neoliberalism: Exploring the dark side of leadership in a South African higher education institution,* critically examines the pervasive influence of toxic leadership within higher education institutions (HEIs), mainly focusing on its darker manifestations influenced by neoliberal ideologies. Through personal accounts and scholarly insights, the authors delve into the coercion, manipulation, and abuse of power that characterise toxic leadership, highlighting their detrimental effects on organisational culture and employee well-being. Their exploration aligns closely with the book's overarching theme, as they contribute to meaningful dialogues about the future of academia by addressing pressing issues in ethical and responsible leadership. By shedding light on the impact of toxic leadership within South African HEIs, the authors aim to foster discussions on the importance of cultivating academic environments rooted in trust and integrity. Furthermore, they provide actionable strategies for navigating ethical dilemmas and advocating for positive change within HEIs, thereby contributing to the ongoing discourse on academic justice and the advancement of higher education.

Unmasking neoliberalism: Exploring the dark side of leadership in a South African higher education institution

Navigating the neoliberal university: A journey through the labyrinth of academia

Navigating the labyrinth of academia – facing challenges, overcoming obstacles, and searching for direction – reveals a complex and intricate world, where theoretical knowledge collides with personal experience within a South African higher education institution (HEI). This chapter embarks on a journey that transcends intellectual exploration; it becomes a pilgrimage of healing for the wounded soul, where scars may linger even after wounds have healed. It is written for those who have endured similar struggles and seek redemption, hoping to cultivate environments grounded in academic justice. By contextualising personal experiences within national and international debates on university massification and neoliberalism, the chapter exposes how neoliberal policies cultivate toxic leadership, emphasising the urgent need for ethical governance and systemic reform.

Beneath academia's pursuit of knowledge and enlightenment lies a corrosive force: toxic leadership. In South African HEIs, this leadership style profoundly affects institutional culture and employee well-being. As market-driven reforms push universities toward corporate management models, they create conditions where coercion, manipulation, and abuse of power flourish – undermining the very principles of academic justice.

As the protagonist (main character) navigates academic life, they confront toxic leadership embedded in educational institutions, experiencing first-hand coercion, manipulation, and abuse of authority. They examine their positionality and biases through critical reflexivity, uncovering the subtle yet pervasive ways toxic leadership distorts academic environments. These personal experiences are not isolated but reflect systemic inequalities deeply embedded within social, cultural, and political structures.

Moving beyond individual narratives, this chapter explores how toxic leadership fractures academic communities, erodes trust, and reinforces hierarchical control. By intertwining personal testimony with scholarly discourse, it illuminates the broader impact of neoliberalism on higher education

– highlighting the commodification of knowledge, the erosion of academic autonomy, and the transformation of students into consumers. This alarming shift underscores the need for collective resistance and institutional reform.

The chapter adopts an idiographic and autoethnographic methodology to critically examine these dynamics, utilising personal accounts and logbook reflections to document the protagonist's lived experiences. Critical reflexivity ensures the protagonist's positionality is acknowledged, aligning with Flick's (2018) view that autoethnographic research is inherently subjective yet capable of producing profound insights. Denzin and Lincoln (2011) similarly argue that while researchers cannot fully separate personal, moral, or political perspectives, rigorous thematic and content analysis can generate valuable understandings. By framing individual experiences within broader academic debates on neoliberalism and university massification, the chapter offers a comprehensive view of the systemic challenges confronting HEIs today.

Toxic leadership in academia is not merely an inconvenience but a direct threat to academic justice, integrity, and institutional well-being. Addressing this issue requires collective ethical leadership, and a commitment to transparency and fairness. By exploring the protagonist's encounters with these challenges, the chapter underscores the urgent need for transformative change. The following section delves deeper into how individual experiences intersect with systemic issues, revealing the far-reaching consequences of toxic and deceptive leadership in HEIs.

Embarking on the journey: The protagonist's lived experiences in the neoliberal university

As the narrative unfolds, the protagonist confronts the harsh realities of a neoliberal university, where market-driven metrics, efficiency imperatives, and deregulated structures erode traditional academic values. Neoliberalism's emphasis on competition, creativity, and measurable outcomes clashes with the intellectual rigour and stability that once defined higher education. Within this environment, relentless pressures threaten the protagonist's well-being, autonomy, and professional fulfilment.

Thrust into an academic environment shaped by economic principles and toxic leadership, the protagonist navigates a system where academic norms are subordinated to market forces. Giroux (2010) argues that neoliberalism promotes individuality and self-interest, realities that manifest in the protagonist's struggles with excessive workloads and rigid deadlines. This commercialisation of education aligns with Adorno's (1974) critique of neoliberalism, where individuals are valued primarily for their economic viability rather than intellectual merit. Critical theorists like Giroux (2010) and Brown (2015) further highlight how neoliberalism commodifies education, prioritising financial objectives over intellectual pursuits.

The overwhelming workload is a key source of distress, exemplified by managing over 350 fourth-year students with minimal institutional support. This strain, compounded by limited resources, leads to exhaustion, frustration, and diminished instructional quality. These challenges reflect systemic issues within South African higher education, where massification and performance-based funding have produced untenable student-to-lecturer ratios (Lo, 2016; ICEF, 2013; Ingleby, 2021).

Toxic leadership intensifies this burden. Characterised by coercion, micromanagement, and an obsession with institutional targets, this leadership style disregards faculty well-being. The protagonist's line manager exemplifies a 'compliant enforcer', prioritising numerical outputs over ethical considerations. Directives are imposed with little regard for human impact, fostering an environment of fear and moral disengagement (Sims, 2019; Thompson & Brown, 2022). Micromanagement further erodes faculty autonomy, as decisions – even assessment grading – are routinely undermined to satisfy consumerist student expectations. This practice reinforces neoliberalism's grip, reducing faculties to market value rather than recognising their intellectual contributions.

The transformation of students into consumers exacerbates these tensions (Barnes & Green, 2023). Faculties face mounting pressure to accommodate student demands, often at the expense of academic standards. The protagonist encounters this first-hand when students challenge grades without valid justification, only for managerial interference to force grade adjustments. This practice weakens academic justice, diminishing the credibility of assessment processes and eroding faculty authority.

The protagonist's psychological distress underscores the unsustainable demands placed on academic staff. Unethical governance practices – including lack of transparency, fraudulent assessment directives, and the systematic exclusion of faculty from decision-making structures – further reveal the contradictions within the neoliberal university (Smith & Jones, 2023; Klahn & Male, 2022). While institutional rhetoric may emphasise excellence, the faculty's lived reality is exploitative workloads and coercive management.

Breaking this cycle requires adopting ethical leadership practices and prioritising compassion, equity, and respect for academic staff. Performance-based funding models, which intensify pressure on academics to meet institutional targets at their own expense, directly conflict with academic justice – a principle that values integrity, fairness, and intellectual autonomy.

Despite these systemic challenges, the protagonist remains steadfast in upholding academic integrity. Their advocacy for compliance with university policies and efforts to correct moderation documentation errors demonstrate the resilience required to maintain ethical standards in an increasingly corporatised academic landscape. However, individual resistance alone is insufficient. Transformative change demands governance structures that prioritise transparency, inclusivity, and ethical leadership to counteract the harmful effects of neoliberalism and create a more just academic environment.

The protagonist's struggles with excessive workloads, managerial interference, and the erosion of academic integrity illustrate the broader forces within the neoliberal university. These personal experiences are not isolated but are symptoms of deeper structural issues that enable and sustain toxic leadership in academia. The following section delves into these systemic factors, examining how institutional policies and governance practices reinforce coercive management and hinder academic autonomy.

Unravelling toxic and deceptive leadership: Navigating challenges in higher education institutions

Toxic and deceptive leadership present significant challenges within HEIs and organisational culture, jeopardising employee well-being. Through the protagonist's journey within the institution, we gain insight into the profound implications of these leadership dynamics, exposing a landscape riddled with ethical dilemmas and systemic issues.

Toxic leadership, marked by manipulative and harmful behaviours, often manifests as workplace victimisation, mobbing, and psychological distress (Fahie, 2020 & 2022). These behaviours heighten workplace conflict, diminish job satisfaction, and drive higher turnover rates (Chen et al., 2021; Lee & Park, 2023; Wang et al., 2024). In the protagonist's experience, unethical practices such as falsified moderation reports and unauthorised grade changes further undermine institutional integrity, reinforcing the need for ethical leadership to preserve academic credibility (Wang et al., 2020; Zhang et al., 2022; Johnson et al., 2022).

The line manager's authoritarian leadership style exacerbates these issues, prioritising rigid compliance over empathy or collaboration. By enforcing directives without considering academic staff's well-being or professional needs, the manager cultivates a climate of fear and disillusionment, stifling creativity and trust. The protagonist's struggle with this coercive environment highlights the consequences of deceptive leadership styles within HEIs and their corrosive effect on faculty morale and institutional culture.

Deceptive leadership practices, such as delaying grievance procedures and manipulating assessment reports, perpetuate institutional dishonesty and breed mistrust (Teo, 2019; Taylor & Clark, 2023; Rodriguez & Garcia, 2022). The promotion of faculty members implicated in plagiarism and report falsification to managerial roles illustrates how deceptive leaders exploit systemic weaknesses for personal gain, disregarding ethical principles and institutional values (Wang et al., 2020).

The protagonist's encounters with deceptive leadership underscore the systemic nature of these issues. The appointment of ethically compromised individuals to leadership positions undermines faculty trust, perpetuates a culture of dishonesty, and signals institutional tolerance for unethical conduct (Johnson et al., 2022; Lee & Park, 2022). Research emphasises the destructive effects of such leadership on organisational culture, reinforcing the urgency of addressing these practices to safeguard employee well-being and institutional integrity.

Addressing toxic and deceptive leadership requires systemic reforms and proactive interventions (Park et al., 2024) and implementing safe, anonymous feedback mechanisms for faculty to evaluate managers, incorporating ethical screening tools in hiring processes, and fostering accountability through transparent governance structures are essential (Smith & Johnson, 2023). The protagonist's experiences highlight how environmental factors, such as institutional dysfunction and the absence of accountability, create conditions where unethical behaviour flourishes (Martinez & Johnson, 2022).

Weak governance structures and misaligned cultural values, evident in routine policy violations and the silencing of dissenting voices, further illustrate the need for leadership models that prioritise integrity, compassion, and fairness (Gomez & Rodriguez, 2021; Ramirez & Nguyen, 2023). Proactively addressing these systemic issues can help HEIs rebuild trust, support faculty well-being, and foster academic environments where excellence and ethical conduct are valued equally.

A critical analysis of the protagonist's journey reveals the far-reaching consequences of toxic and deceptive leadership on organisational culture, productivity, and employee resilience. Understanding these systemic issues is crucial for cultivating healthier, more equitable academic environments. By implementing structural reforms, prioritising ethical leadership, and reinforcing mechanisms for faculty support, HEIs can protect their integrity, nurture a positive organisational culture, and ensure a sustainable, supportive environment for all stakeholders.

Exposing toxic leadership: Impact on institutions and employees

In academic settings, toxic leadership erodes trust and respect, fostering stressful, anxious, and disengaged workplaces (Nguyen & Nguyen, 2023). Asha and Snigdha (2019) identify psychological distress as a common consequence, while Lipman-Blumen (2009) defines toxic leadership as a process where leaders inflict enduring harm through destructive behaviours. Williams (2005) describes a spectrum of toxicity, from unintentional harm to deliberate malice. Some leaders may be incompetent and unaware, but others intentionally cause psychological or physical harm. In academia, micromanagement, favouritism, and a lack of transparency heighten faculty stress and disengagement, leading to declining research productivity, increased turnover, and deteriorating institutional culture.

Understanding destructive leadership requires exploring leadership dynamics.

Ryan et al. (2021) describe leadership as an interactive influence process shaped by leader-follower relationships. McCallum and Price (2022) highlight the role of institutional culture in either curbing or reinforcing toxic behaviours (Smith & Jones, 2023). Garcia et al. (2022) further suggest that the organisational climate can mitigate or amplify toxic leadership's impact, offering insights into potential.

Toxic leadership often creates a cycle where short-term operational gains come at the expense of long-term employee well-being (Craig & Kaiser, 2021). Common traits include coercion, manipulation, and abusive compliance, which lower morale, self-esteem, and performance (Smith & Williams, 2023). Nguyen and Tran (2024) link toxic leadership to increased turnover, while Garcia and Patel (2023) connect it to heightened stress, anxiety, and depression. Jones et al. (2023) underscore broader consequences: reduced productivity, creativity, and engagement. However, Kim and Lee (2023) suggest that the relationship between toxic leadership and work engagement is complex, calling for further research into its effects on academic environments.

These findings are mirrored in the protagonist's experiences within a HEI, highlighting the real-life impact of destructive leadership. Each instance of micromanagement, lack of empathy, favouritism, bullying, and manipulation mirrors the literature, emphasising the need for structural reforms to foster healthier academic environments. The line manager's behaviours reflect key elements of toxic leadership, exacerbating workplace dysfunction and harming employee well-being:

Dictatorial micromanagement: The line manager imposes rigid controls, stifling creativity and autonomy, leading to diminished job satisfaction and a toxic work atmosphere.

Lack of empathy and poor communication: The manager's absence of empathy and ineffective communication skills exacerbate feelings of isolation and disillusionment, fostering an environment of disappointment, mistrust, confusion, fear, and resentment.

Favouritism and divisive behaviour: The manager shows a bias toward select faculty members, undermining fairness, fracturing team dynamics, and amplifying feelings of loneliness and exclusion.

Bullying and intimidation: public humiliation and belittlement heighten stress and anxiety, shifting the protagonist's focus from contributing to the institution to self-preservation, fostering self-doubt and disgust.

Lack of transparency and accountability: Unilateral decision-making and evasion of responsibility damage trust and professional reputations, leading to disengagement, anger, and betrayal towards the manager and the institution.

Manipulative conduct: flattery and false promises are used to control faculty, breeding disillusionment and further straining professional relationships.

These experiences highlight toxic leadership's profound impact on individual well-being and institutional effectiveness. The protagonist's story underscores the urgent need for transformation within HEIs to address destructive leadership and foster environments conducive to growth, collaboration, and innovation.

The toxic leadership style of the line manager exerts profound effects on the protagonist and the institution. Decreased job satisfaction stems from micromanagement and favouritism, leaving the protagonist feeling undervalued despite their dedication. Heightened stress and burnout emerge as constant pressures; unrealistic deadlines and lack of support take their toll. Restricted autonomy and limited professional growth stifle creativity, while favouritism strains collegial relationships, fostering resentment and undermining trust. Consequently, collaboration and teamwork – essential for academic success – deteriorate, further intensifying the toxic environment.

Ultimately, the line manager's toxic leadership significantly diminishes job satisfaction, well-being, and professional development, emphasising the urgent need for change and reform within the HEI. Shifting focus from the institutional and employee-level impacts of toxic leadership, the discussion will now explore the personal and psychological consequences of these harmful behaviours. By analysing the protagonist's experiences, the objective is to reveal the psychological effects of toxic leadership within the academic setting. The goal is to comprehend toxic leadership's psychological effects thoroughly. As we navigate the protagonist's journey through the complex and harmful leadership environment, it lays the foundation for a deeper exploration of this critical issue's impact on workplace challenges and psychological well-being.

The psychological effects of toxic leadership: A personal journey

The protagonist's journey illustrates the multifaceted impact of toxic leadership within academic settings, revealing profound psychological consequences beyond workplace challenges. The pervasive toxicity encountered undermines professional progress and poses a persistent threat to psychological health and overall well-being. Research by Rasool et al. (2021) aligns with these lived experiences, showing that toxic work environments significantly increase stress and anxiety.

In what should be a supportive intellectual environment, the protagonist faces severe mistreatment and instability, which hinder their career growth and erode their mental health. These personal struggles are mirrored in empirical findings: Jones et al. (2023) emphasise the detrimental effects of such environments on employees' psychological well-being, reinforcing the protagonist's heightened stress and anxiety. Similarly, Garcia and Patel (2023) highlight the compounding effects of chronic workplace toxicity on mental health, which resonate with the protagonist's persistent distress.

This growing body of evidence underscores the urgent need for organisations, especially HEIs, to address toxic workplace cultures. Neglecting employee well-being damages morale, decreases productivity, and perpetuates distress and dysfunction in academic settings. HEIs must foster psychological safety and implement robust support systems to cultivate healthier, more productive work environments.

Furthermore, research highlights the severe long-term effects of toxic leadership. Berg et al. (2016) document extreme outcomes such as heart attacks and suicides, emphasising the critical impact of leadership toxicity. More recently, Thompson et al. (2023) revealed a rise in depression and anxiety cases among faculty exposed to sustained toxic leadership, while Nguyen and Tran (2024) demonstrated the physiological effects of chronic workplace toxicity, including elevated cortisol levels and increased cardiovascular risk. These findings echo the protagonist's escalating health issues, reinforcing the tangible harm caused by toxic leadership.

Toxic leadership erodes trust and professionalism, fostering social isolation and fractured relationships (Shore & Chung, 2021). The protagonist's experience of social withdrawal and stigma is reflected in Kim and Lee's (2022) research, which shows how favouritism and lack of transparency reduce collaboration and intensify feelings of exclusion. The resulting 'social incarceration' amplifies psychological distress, further entrenching the cycle of harm.

Moreover, toxic environments stifle professional growth through harassment, intimidation, and biased practices, limiting opportunities for career development (George, 2023; Johnson et al., 2024). Employees resisting toxicity may face retaliation, disengagement, and communication breakdowns with colleagues (Botez & Cotet, 2021). Lee and Park (2023) illustrate how micromanagement and secrecy suppress employees' potential, leading to compounded feelings of incompetence and self-doubt – experiences that deeply mirror the protagonist's struggles.

Enduring relentless mistreatment, the protagonist experiences depression, panic attacks, and sleep disturbances, which is reflected in broader research findings. Studies by Asha and Snigdha (2019) and Hansen et al. (2014) show that emotional exhaustion diminishes coping abilities, leaving employees more vulnerable to distress. Professional advancement becomes tangled in a web of favouritism and intimidation, deepening feelings of isolation and hopelessness (George, 2023).

The protagonist's experience, mirrored in research, reveals how toxic leadership erodes moral integrity and decision-making (Johnson et al., 2022). Emotional exhaustion mediates the relationship between toxic leadership and turnover intentions, reinforcing the severe psychological toll of toxicity in academic settings (Smith & Jones, 2024). These findings strengthen the call for urgent organisational reform and underscore the urgent need for HEIs to reform leadership practices and prioritise employee well-being. The protagonist's journey underscores the importance of proactively addressing toxic leadership behaviours and fostering environments of support and integrity within academic institutions. Through this synthesis of individual experiences and empirical evidence, it becomes clear that there is a pressing need for organisational change. This necessitates stakeholders to take decisive action towards creating environments conducive to academic excellence and employee well-being.

Addressing toxic leadership requires HEIs to promote psychological well-being through leadership development programmes, supportive workplace policies, and stress management interventions (Kim & Lee, 2023; Lee & Park, 2024). Providing psychological support services can further mitigate long-term harm (Nguyen & Tran, 2023), reducing the risk of lasting trauma.

Ultimately, the protagonist's journey is a stark reminder of the urgent need for reform within HEIs. By recognising and addressing the toxic culture perpetuated by ineffective leadership, institutions can protect employee well-being and foster environments conducive to academic excellence and personal fulfilment. This synthesis of personal narrative and empirical evidence illustrates the profound psychological effects of toxic leadership and underscores the pressing need for systemic change to create healthier academic landscapes.

As this exploration of psychological effects concludes the broader organisational implications of toxic leadership come into focus. Building on the protagonist's narrative, the following section explores how toxic leadership ripples through institutional culture, affecting effectiveness and morale and illuminating pathways toward healthier academic environments where leadership practices support individual and collective success.

Organisational implications of toxic leadership: Navigating the shadows of academia

Toxic leadership casts a long shadow over HEIs, distorting organisational culture and eroding employee well-being. The profound impact of toxic leadership on academic environments comes to light through the protagonist's narrative, intertwined with scholarly perspectives.

As the protagonist navigates the complex landscape of academia, their personal experiences reveal how toxic leadership permeates institutional structures, distorting academic integrity and governance. By blending personal reflections with scholarly insights, the narrative exposes the far-reaching effects of toxic leadership on organisational dynamics.

The detrimental impact of toxic leadership in academia is well-documented, with research highlighting environments of hostility, fear, and disengagement (Tepper & Duffy, 2023). These findings mirror the protagonist's encounters, where workplace bullying and coercion led to feelings of isolation and withdrawal (Einarsen & Einarsen, 2021). Toxic leadership is also associated with heightened anxiety and depression, underscoring the psychological toll on employees and its cascading effect on institutional well-being (Lee & Park, 2024). Consequently, the HEI struggles with declining work performance, strained staff relationships, and reputational harm.

In academia, leadership shapes not only administrative processes but also organisational culture. Toxic leaders, often employing coercive tactics and lacking transparency, create environments reminiscent of organisational prisonisation, perpetuating cycles of fear and mistrust (Lee & Park, 2024). This atmosphere stifles innovation and erodes collegiality, impeding intellectual progress.

The intersection of scientific research with the protagonist's narrative further illustrates the multifaceted nature of toxic work environments. Discrimination, bullying, and aggression contribute to increased stress and anxiety levels (Rasool et al., 2021). These dynamics weaken employee morale, increase staff turnover, and heighten the risk of legal disputes, ultimately threatening the institution's stability (Shapiro & Stefkovich, 2016).

Beyond individual experiences, toxic leadership permeates institutional structures, distorting academic integrity and governance. For instance, the protagonist's coercion by a faculty member to inflate grades, coupled with a line manager's enforcement of these revised grades, exemplifies how toxic practices undermine educational standards and institutional credibility (Lee & Park, 2024). Such incidents highlight the corrosive influence of unethical leadership on academic values.

Moreover, the protagonist's experiences reveal how neoliberal ideologies exacerbate these challenges. In neoliberal academia, profit-driven metrics often overshadow ethical considerations and scholarly values, perpetuating leadership behaviours prioritising institutional optics over integrity (Hughes & Scott, 2023; Lee & Park, 2022). Budget cuts and resource allocation decisions disproportionately favour economically profitable disciplines, neglecting fields essential for social progress.

In a neoliberal university, toxic leadership intensifies workplace tensions and impacts employee psychological well-being. As recounted by the protagonist, instances of verbal abuse, intimidation, and public beratement illustrate how toxic behaviours corrode trust and hinder intellectual inquiry (Griffin et al., 2023). These actions foster professional ostracisation, amplifying the negative impact on employee well-being and departmental cohesion.

Ethical dilemmas further complicate the landscape of academic leadership. Delayed grievance procedures and deceptive assessment practices undermine institutional governance and public trust (Shapiro & Stefkovich, 2016; Lee & Park, 2022). Addressing these ethical lapses and promoting transparency and accountability within HEIs are crucial to upholding academic standards and rebuilding public trust (Hughes & Scott, 2023; Lee & Park, 2022). Proactive steps are essential to address unethical leadership behaviours and foster a culture of integrity and accountability in academic leadership.

Consider, for instance, the protagonist's discovery of a systematic concealment of assessment irregularities orchestrated by senior faculty members to uphold the appearance of academic excellence. Despite the protagonist's attempts to raise concerns through official channels, institutional leaders turned a blind eye to ethical violations. This failure of institutional leadership to address ethical breaches effectively perpetuates a culture of impunity and organisational toxicity.

Having explored the pervasive effects of toxicity, it is evident that transformative change is imperative within HEIs. The following section will delve into cultivating ethical leadership and initiating systemic change. By dismantling toxic practices and fostering integrity, compassion, and equity, HEIs can reclaim their foundational purpose – cultivating environments where academic freedom, collaboration, and intellectual inquiry can thrive.

Navigating the path forward: Cultivating ethical leadership and transformative change in higher education institutions

This chapter explores the landscape of toxic leadership within South African HEIs, blending personal narratives, scholarly research, and theoretical frameworks to illuminate the harmful effects of neoliberalism and managerial agendas on academic communities. It highlights the pervasive impact of toxic leadership on organisational culture, employee well-being, and core academic values.

A central theme is the urgent need to foster environments characterised by integrity, compassion, and equity. Ethical leadership is essential for building trust, transparency, and accountability, creating conditions where employees can thrive. The chapter calls for transformative change, encouraging HEIs to break free from toxic leadership structures and embrace authenticity and solidarity as guiding principles.

The chapter emphasises the importance of adopting holistic strategies to address toxic leadership, including proactive measures and responsive interventions. Ongoing research is vital to deepen understanding of leadership dynamics and develop nuanced solutions considering the complex interplay between leaders, followers, and the broader organisational context.

The protagonist's experiences offer valuable insights into leadership dynamics within South African HEIs, illuminating the hidden complexities of neoliberal leadership marked by authoritarianism and self-interest. These narratives enrich the discussion by revealing the darker aspects of academic leadership, adding depth to the scholarly discourse on leadership and institutional culture.

Additionally, the chapter confronts ethical dilemmas in leadership, addressing toxic behaviours such as coercion, manipulation, and abuse of power. It provides practical guidance for navigating moral challenges and fostering HEI cultures grounded in integrity, compassion, and fairness.

Contributing to ongoing discussions on ethical leadership, the chapter outlines actionable strategies for academic leaders, including integrating screening mechanisms in recruitment processes, establishing feedback channels to assess faculty leaders' performance, and promoting whistleblowing for transparency and accountability. These steps provide practical pathways to combat toxic leadership and nurture supportive academic environments.

Ultimately, this chapter serves as a resource for understanding and addressing leadership complexities within South African HEIs. Incorporating critical reflexivity and autoethnography contextualises the protagonist's experiences within national and international literature, illustrating how neoliberal policies can foster toxic leadership. It underscores the need for ethical leadership that prioritises scholarly excellence alongside enduring values of integrity, compassion, and equity.

As we move forward, inspired by the protagonist's resilience, let us answer the call to action. By collectively cultivating ethical leadership, we can ensure that transformative change, positive organisational climates, and a steadfast commitment to academic integrity shape the future of higher education.

Disclaimer

The views and opinions expressed in this chapter are solely those of the authors and do not necessarily represent the official policy or position of any affiliated agency, institution, or organisation associated with the authors. The authors bear sole responsibility for the content presented herein, and any discrepancies or concerns should be directed to them directly. This chapter is intended for academic and scholarly purposes only and should not be construed as representing the views or endorsements of any specific entity or institution. Readers are encouraged to exercise critical judgment and discretion when interpreting the information presented in this chapter.

References

Adorno, T. (1974). *Minima Moralia: Reflections from damaged life.* London: Verso (1994).

Asha, B. & Snigdha, R. (2019). Toxic leadership: Emotional distress and coping strategy. *International Journal of Organization Theory & Behavior,* 22(1): 65–78. https://doi.org/10.1108/IJOTB-02-2019-0026.

Barnes, L. & Green, J. (2023). Reconceptualizing student-academic relationships in neoliberal higher education: A critical analysis. *Studies in Higher Education,* 48(3): 421–438. https://doi.org/10.1080/03075079.2023.12345678.

Berg, H., Huijbens, E. & Gutzon, A. (2016). Toxic leadership in academia: A cautionary tale. *Journal of Academic Ethics,* 14(3): 183–200. https://doi.org/s10805-016-9273-x.

Botez, R. & Cotet, A. (2021). Consequences of toxic leadership: Employee disengagement and communication breakdown. *Journal of Leadership Studies,* 38(4): 489–504. https://doi.org/10.1177/0149206319877456.

Brown, W. (2015). *Undoing the Demos: Neoliberalism's Stealth Revolution.* New York: Zone Books.

Chen, Y., Zhang, X. & Qian, Y. (2021). Toxic leadership, psychological capital, and employee voice behavior: A moderated mediation model. *Frontiers in Psychology,* 12. https://doi.org/10.3389/fpsyg.2021.723564.

Craig, A. & Kaiser, R.B. (2021). *Toxic leadership: Why it occurs and how to address it.* Boston, Massachusetts: Harvard Business Review Press.

Denzin, N.K. & Lincoln, Y.S. (2011). *The SAGE Handbook of Qualitative Research.* California: Sage.

Einarsen, K. & Einarsen, S.V. (2021). Combating workplace bullying: Interventions and the role of the organization's ethical infrastructure. In Smith, P.K. & Norman, J.O. (ed.) *The Wiley Blackwell Handbook of Bullying: A Comprehensive and International Review of Research and Intervention* (538–557). New Jersey: Wiley Blackwell. https://doi.org/10.1002/9781118482650.ch30.

Fahie, D. (2020). The lived experience of toxic leadership in Irish higher education. *International Journal of Workplace Health Management,* 13(3): 341–355. https://doi.org/10.1108/IJWHM-07-2019-0112.

Fahie, D. (2022). Toxic leadership in higher education: A comprehensive review and future research agenda. *Educational Management Administration & Leadership,* 50(1): 47–66. https://doi.org/10.1177/1741143220937891.

Flick, U. (2018). *An Introduction to Qualitative Research.* Los Angeles: Sage.

Garcia, A. & Patel, S. (2023). The impact of toxic work environments on employee well-being: A systematic review. *Journal of Organizational Behavior,* 45(2): 211–225. https://doi.org/10.1002/job.2334.

Garcia, M., Patel, R. & Thompson, J. (2022). The impact of toxic leadership on organizational culture and employee well-being: A case study of higher education institutions. *Journal of Higher Education Management,* 18(3): 87–102. https://doi.org/10.1016/j.jhem.2022.03.005.

George, S. (2023). Toxic leadership and workplace environment: A comprehensive analysis. *Journal of Organizational Psychology,* 45(3): 301–315. https://doi.org/10.1002/job.2345.

Giroux, H. (2010). Public values, higher education and the scourge of neoliberalism: Politics and the limits of the social. *Culture Machine,* November 2010. Available at: http://www.culturemachine.net/index.php/cm/issue/view/12. Date accessed: 10 March 2004.

Gomez, M. & Rodriguez, L. (2021). Pressure, silence, and ethical collapse: Examining organizational factors in higher education. *Journal of Academic Ethics,* 39(3): 345–362. https://doi.org/10.1007/s10805-021-09425-6

Griffin, B., Liao, Y., Luthans, F. & Liu, Y. (2023). The role of authentic leadership in mitigating the negative effects of toxic leadership on employee attitudes and performance. *Journal of Leadership & Organizational Studies,* 30(1): 15–30. https://doi.org/10.1177/1548051821992433.

Hansen, A.M., Hogh, A., Garde, A.H. & Persson, R. (2014). Workplace bullying and sleep difficulties: A 2-year follow-up study. *International Archives of Occupational and Environmental Health,* 87(3): 285–294. https://doi.org/10.1007/s00420-013-0860-2.

Hughes, R.L. & Scott, R.W. (2023). *Leadership, ethics, and neoliberalism in higher education: Navigating the new normal.* Oxfordshire: Routledge. https://doi.org/10.4324/9781003123674.

Ingleby, E. (2021). *Neoliberalism Across Education: Policy and Practice from Early Childhood through Adult Learning.* Cham.: Palgrave Pivot.

International Consultants for Education and Fairs (ICEF). (2013). South Africa: An important regional hub for international students. Available at: http://monitor.icef.com/2013/11/south-africa-an-importantregional-hub-for-international-students. Date accessed: 14 February 2025.

Johnson, A., Smith, B. & Martinez, C. (2022). Deceptive leadership and its impact on organizational culture: A comprehensive study. *Journal of Organizational Behavior,* 47(3): 321–335. https://doi.org/10.1002/job.12345.

Johnson, R., Smith, K. & Brown, M. 2024. The impact of toxic organizational cultures on career development: A longitudinal study. *Journal of Applied Psychology,* 110(2): 201–218. https://doi.org/10.1037/apl0000678.

Jones, M., Smith, R. & Brown, K. (2023). Toxicity in the workplace: Understanding its impact on employee mental health. *Journal of Occupational Health Psychology,* 18(3): 334–349. https://doi.org/10.1037/ocp0000261.

Shapiro, J.P. & Stefkovich, J.A. (2016). *Ethical leadership and decision making in education: Applying theoretical perspectives to complex dilemmas.* New York: Springer. https://doi.org/10.1007/978-3-030-18632-1.

Kim, S. & Lee, J. (2022). The role of toxic leadership in undermining trust and collaboration among academic staff: A longitudinal study. *Journal of Interpersonal Relations,* 28(2): 345–360. https://doi.org/10.1080/0092653X.2021.1992847.

Kim, S. & Lee, J. (2023). The relationship between toxic leadership and employee work engagement: A longitudinal study. *Journal of Occupational Health Psychology,* 28(4): 567–580. https://doi.org/10.1080/08959285.2023.04567.

Klahn, A.B. & Male, T. (2022). Toxic leadership and academics' work engagement in higher education: A cross-sectional study from Chile. *Educational Management Administration & Leadership,* 50(2): 262–280. https://doi.org/10.1177/17411432211030888.

Lee, J. & Park, S. (2024). Understanding the psychological effects of toxic leadership: A longitudinal study in the academic setting. *Journal of Applied Psychology,* 109(4): 577–589. https://doi.org/10.1037/apl0000563.

Lee, S. & Park, H. (2022). Leadership ethics in higher education: A systematic review of the literature. *Studies in Higher Education,* 47(3): 457-476. https://doi.org/10.1080/03075079.2021.1976750

Lee, S. & Park, J. (2023). Toxic leadership and employee well-being: The mediating role of job stress and job satisfaction. *Journal of Applied Psychology,* 108(3): 432–448. https://doi.org/10.1037/apl0000567.

Lipman-Blumen, J. (2009). Toxic Leadership: A Conceptual Framework. In Bournois, F. (ed.) *Handbook of Top Management Teams* (214–220). Claremont, California.

Lo, W.Y.W. (2016). The recalibration of neoliberalisation: Repoliticising higher education policy in Hong Kong. *Higher Education,* 73: 759–773.

Martinez, R. & Johnson, K. (2022). Fostering a culture of accountability: The role of ethical leadership in academic institutions. *Higher Education Research and Development,* 41(2): 210–225. https://doi.org/10.1080/07294360.2021.1956547.

McCallum, F. & Price, M. (2022). Academic leadership for changing times: A systematic literature review. *Educational Management Administration & Leadership,* 50(1): 7–27. https://doi.org/10.1177/17411432211017550.

Nguyen, H. & Tran, H. 2024. Physiological responses to toxic leadership in academia: A prospective study. *Journal of Applied Physiology,* 42(3): 301–315. https://doi.org/10.1037/app0000123.

Nguyen, T. & Tran, L. (2023). Stress management interventions and psychological support services for employees affected by toxic leadership: A systematic review. *Journal of Business Ethics,* 39(4): 489–504. https://doi.org/10.1007/s10551-023-04957-8.

Nguyen, T.T. & Nguyen, H. (2023). The impact of toxic leadership on employee well-being in higher education institutions: A meta-analysis. *Journal of Organizational Behavior,* 45(2): 215–230. https://doi.org/10.1002/job.2556.

Park, S.H., Krishnan, R. & Kim, J. (2024). The role of ethical leadership in mitigating the negative impact of toxic leadership on employee outcomes. *Journal of Business Ethics,* 183(4): 685–700. https://doi.org/10.1007/s10551-023-04820-x.

Ramirez, L. & Nguyen, T. (2023). Understanding ethical climate and governance structures in higher education institutions. *Journal of Higher Education Governance,* 17(2): 210–225. https://doi.org/10.1080/21520704.2023.1890274

Rasool, S., Ahmad, M. & Khan, M. (2021). Toxic leadership and its impact on employee well-being: A case study of the education sector. *International Journal of Management,* 28(3): 301–315. https://doi.org/10.1177/09713557211001111

Rodriguez, M. & Garcia, A. (2022). Managerial deficiencies and organizational culture: A case study of higher education institutions. *Journal of Educational Leadership,* 38(3): 210–225. https://doi.org/10.1177/08959048211002345.

Ryan, P., Odhiambo, G. & Wilson, R. (2021). Destructive leadership in education: A transdisciplinary critical analysis of contemporary literature. *International Journal of Leadership in Education,* 24(4): 1–27. https://doi.org/10.1080/13603124.2019.1640892.

Shore, L.M. & Chung, K.W. (2021). Toxic leadership in academic institutions: A qualitative study. *Journal of Applied Psychology,* 106(4): 569–587. https://doi.org/10.1037/apl0000514.

Sims, M. (2019). Neoliberalism and new public management in an Australian university: The invisibility of our take-over. *The Australian Universities' Review,* 61(1): 22–30. https://doi.org/10.3316/ielapa.240166071363526.

Smith, A.R. & Johnson, M.K. (2023). Strategies for enhancing ethical leadership in higher education: A comparative analysis. *Higher Education Policy,* 25(3): 321–336. https://doi.org/10.1007/s10734-021-09876-5.

Smith, J. & Williams, L. (2023). Understanding coercive tactics and manipulative behaviors in toxic leadership. *Leadership Quarterly,* 30(2): 201–215. https://doi.org/10.1016/j.leaqua.2023.01234.

Smith, T. & Jones, L. (2023). Toxic leadership in higher education: Implications for organizational culture and employee well-being. *Educational Leadership Review,* 22(2): 45–62. https://doi.org/10.1080/13632434.2023.1956789.

Smith, T. & Jones, L. (2024). Emotional exhaustion mediates the relationship between toxic leadership and employee well-being: A longitudinal analysis. *Journal of Occupational Health Psychology,* 39(4): 489–504. https://doi.org/10.1037/ocp0000478.

Taylor, E. & Clark, L. (2023). The impact of ethical leadership on organizational culture: A study of higher education institutions. *Journal of Educational Administration,* 41(2): 210–225. https://doi.org/10.1080/09515518.2022.2050506.

Teo, P. (2019). Teaching for the 21st century: A case for dialogic pedagogy. *Learning, Culture and Social Interaction,* 20: 170–178. https://doi.org/10.1016/j.lcsi.2019.03.009.

Tepper, B.J. & Duffy, M.K. (2023). Toxic leadership: A conceptual framework. *The Leadership Quarterly,* 34(1): 101556. https://doi.org/10.1016/j.leaqua.2022.101556

Thompson, L., Baker, A. & Smith, D. (2023). Mental health impacts of toxic leadership in academia: A longitudinal analysis. *Journal of Occupational Health,* 35(2): 201–215. https://doi.org/10.1097/JOH.0000000000000478

Thompson, R. & Brown, K. (2022). Governance challenges in neoliberal higher education: Balancing autonomy and accountability. *Studies in Higher Education,* 47(4): 689–706. https://doi.org/10.1080/03075079.2022.2034521.

Wang, L., Zhang, Y. & Chen, H. (2024). The impact of toxic leadership on organizational effectiveness: A meta-analysis. *Journal of Organizational Behavior,* 45(2): 234–251. https://doi.org/10.1002/job.2654.

Wang, Q., Li, Y. & Zhang, L. (2020). Unethical leadership and employee misbehavior: A moderated mediation model of justice sensitivity and ethical climate. *Frontiers in Psychology,* 11: 1895. https://doi.org/10.3389/fpsyg.2020.01895.

Williams, D.F. (2005). *Toxic Leadership in the U.S. Army.* Carlisle Barracks, PA: Army War College.

Zhang, Y., Li, X. & Zhu, F. (2022). The impact of ethical leadership on employees' work–family conflict: The role of leader–member exchange and ethical climate. *Frontiers in Psychology,* 13: 720926. https://doi.org/10.3389/fpsyg.2022.720926.

CHAPTER 12

Beyond tokenistic civically engaged curriculum design and delivery

Rika Swanzen

Know all the theories, master all the techniques,
but as you touch a human soul be just another human soul
– Carl Jung

Abstract

Since the Council of Higher Education promoted their service-learning (SL) framework in 2006, numerous changes occurred in the higher education (HE) sector to accommodate the inclusion of academic community engagement (CE). If these initiatives are not addressing societal ills, subsidised resources are being wasted. Against the backdrop of critical SL criteria, participatory theory, and performance within sustainable development goals and engaged curriculum outcomes, a protocol was designed for HE institutions. This scoping review provides the triggers for a critical conversation on identified areas where practices need to move from tokenistic to truly inclusive and impactful endeavours that are sensitive to the developmental and social justice needs of a country.

Keywords: critical service learning; impactful curriculum; review protocol for civically engaged participation.

Introduction and background

The third principle of the Earth Charter calls for the building of 'democratic societies that are just, participatory, sustainable, and peaceful' (Earth Charter International, 2023). During a recent Global Sustainable Development Congress the resolution was that universities need to act more radically and at a larger scale and pace than before if they wish to progress on their impact towards the United Nations (UN) Sustainable Development Goals (SDGs) (Sowula et al., 2022). They need to accelerate leveraging of their status, economic reach, research, and teaching capacity 'to act in partnership with civil society, governments, NGOs, media and industry' (Sowula, et al., 2022: 4). Their recommendation includes the development of diverse and interdisciplinary curricula, demonstrating stewardship for their engagements with the public, and to consider how universities' impact is communicated (Sowula, et al., 2022). 'The Civic Mission of Schools… forcefully argue that civic learning not only promotes civic equality and participation, but produces better educational and life outcomes' (Glover et al., 2021: 602). Davis (2021: 25) urged: 'Those who support higher learning will not persuade through talk of economic impact. We need practical demonstrations of how teaching and research bring prosperity to community, opportunities for the young, a richer and more engaged life for all'.

A regard for a 'scholarship of engagement' is required, consisting of '1) research, teaching, integration, and application scholarship that 2) incorporate reciprocal practices of civic engagement into the production of knowledge' (Barker, 2004 in Keet & Muthwa, 2021: 222). Boyer (1996 in Andrews & Leonard, 2018: 148) described community-engaged scholarship as reflective practitioners who prioritise the '1) discovery and increase of knowledge [in the search for answers to our most pressing social, civic, economic, and moral problems]; 2) integration of diverse disciplines; 3) sharing knowledge through communications with peers and future scholars; [and] 4) application of knowledge to ensure relevance of their scholarship'. Although not necessary occurring in silos, four types of civic engagement can be identified as political, social, economic, and ethical or moral civic engagement (Dolan, 2022). McCartney (2013 in Glover et al., 2021: 602) 'makes a helpful distinction between "civic" engagement, referring to involvement in the life of the community, and "political" engagement, activities which aim to impact or alter public policy or political structures as a whole', while Haward and Shea spoke of the latter being the more challenging 'vertical' engagement as opposed to the horizontal engagement on community level. Significant to the focus of this chapter is the coining of the term 'service learning advocacy' by Mooney and Edwards (2001 in Glover et al., 2021: 605) referring to courses that 'encourages students to become actors in the drama of producing a more just society', which for the researcher encapsulates the concept of CSL.

Through a scoping review of interrelated concepts, triggers were identified for a critical conversation on moving practice from tokenistic engagement to truly inclusive and impactful endeavours that are sensitive to the developmental, social justice needs of society. To derive at a review protocol of intersecting theoretical concepts (or criteria) linked to authentically engaged higher education (HE) practices, the ethically approved study will focus on synthesising various core theoretical approaches. The rationale for linking participatory theory elements that increase social capital, social justice, sustainable development and civically engaged impact, to the critical conversations needed in HE is to promote developmentally focused and inclusive projects. The starting point is service-learning (SL), which for the purpose of this chapter means the evidence-based, credit-bearing educational experience, meeting identified community goals within an organised service activity that enhance civic responsibility, and focusing on the four Rs: respect, reciprocity, relevance, and reflection (Bowie & Cassim, 2016; Hunter, 2019). SL differs from volunteer work through its stronger emphasis on the academic and personal growth of the participants of the activity (Choi et al., 2023). While a link is made to sustainability, it is only done within the realm of health and welfare, supported by the notion that civic activities 'focus on voluntary associations that promote the health and wellbeing of a community' (Hylton, 2018: 88).

Through the study, a protocol is designed to inform the critical conversation needed to ensure that universities' engagement endeavours meet the criteria for inclusive and impactful societal change. The core of the critical conversation raised with this study involves the depth of authentic, reciprocal partnerships, students developing as active citizens, and participation of stakeholders within initiatives heralded as SL.

Civically engaged curriculum

The purpose of this section is to relay the accepted context from earlier writings within which most HEIs have been practicing SL, and to then provide a deeper exploration of discussions around its place in civic engagement from sources published in the last ten years. Early categorisation of the types of university engagement and community partnership were academic knowledge transfer, university continuing education, and community-based research and service learning (Mastuti et al., 2014). From a programmatic perspective, the two prominent means through which HEIs promote community partnerships have always been either extracurricular or curricular (Bringle & Hatcher, 1996). The CE partnership of HEI knowledge and resources with the public and private sectors is the process, while its purpose is to enrich scholarship research, enhance curriculum, prepare engaged citizens, and address critical societal issues, contributing to public good (Saltmarsh et al., 2015). The '[d]epth of impact can be demonstrated by the extent to which service-learning is integral to degree programmes and majors, faculty work and rewards, student learning outcomes, institutional mission, and long-term reciprocal partnerships with community organizations that address community needs' (Bringle & Hatcher, 2009: 38). While the needs for different communities will vary, one earlier approach to SL activity in HE interestingly made use of quality-of-life indicators as topics for students to focus on – these included demographic profile, economic prosperity, environmental quality, transportation, educational excellence, human services, public safety, health, housing, recreation, tourism, arts, and governance (Lowery, 2007). 'Critical citizenship is an existing concept related to critical thinking that leads to individual transformation and the development of responsible and accommodating individuals in multicultural societies'. Beyond the notion of driving public good focused on improving quality of life, a critical focus on transformation and multi-cultural responsiveness is required for civic engagement (Costandius & Odiboh, 2016: 1).

Fletcher (2008: 36) aptly stated: 'One obstacle to realizing the core value of community participation is the absence of training for community-based partners. In its absence, we 1) reinforce inequitable distributions of power, 2) compromise the comfort and confidence of community partners to fulfil their roles as researchers and health promoters, and 3) jeopardize the validity and relevance of the work being done'. To ensure authentic partnerships the HEI needs to reach out to communities as far as needed, ensuring that marginalised communities are not excluded regardless of their remoteness geographically. Indigenous communities that mostly have different cultures, values, and beliefs than mainstream society, may often have greater potential to shape and lead social change, and at the very least should not be under-represented in these partnerships (Fletcher, 2008). Regarding the development of partnerships with communities there are constraints to the helping framework. True reciprocity as an element of sustaining partnerships is enabled through the organising model as an alternative to the one-directional service model (Kari & Skelton, 2007). The two models operate on a continuum as follows (Kari & Skelton, 2007): where the service model aims to fix problems, the organising model builds power through networks; the former partners through short-term, need-based programmes or projects, while the latter develops leaders and capacity over a longer period; with service, individuals or clients are included, while an organising approach involves institutions, communities and groups; and the one results in time-bound activities such as projects, reports, and studies, while the organising model results in action that leads to change and transformation. Sustaining partnership requires the negotiation of power and collaboration towards mutual learning and continuity (Kari & Skelton, 2007).

Russel Edgerton's (Saltmarsh et al., 2015: 122) call for engaged universities is to 'realize that all of the critical tasks we do – teaching, research, and professional outreach – need to change if we are truly to connect with the larger community'. Critics of traditional SL highlight that it can produce a saviour mentality in students, instead of exercising consciousness of the root causes to social problems (Andrews & Leonard, 2018). Transformational change on campus should not just look like the fixing of discrete problems but should intentionally alter the culture of the institution in a pervasive way, by changing select underlying assumptions behind institutional behaviours and making a fundamental paradigm shift from normative technocratic framing of CE toward a democratic orientation, where institutions share power and view themselves as part of communities (Saltmarsh et al., 2015). The objective and experimental mode of knowing that dominates higher education is however more inclined to lead to a depersonalised view of society (Zlotkowski, 2007).

Earlier studies on challenges with the integration of SL in South Africa (SA) indicated concerns with unequal power relations; the lack of multisectoral approaches, one set of disciplinary engagement activities dominating; the sustainability of projects; limited environmental awareness; needing more attention paid to indigenous knowledge to create African solutions to African problems; coordinated multidisciplinary responses to community-identified concerns; ongoing conceptual confusion in engagement discourses; and the need for a wider range of African partners (Preece, 2013). Indigenous refers to '[g]roups of people whose social, cultural and economic conditions distinguish them from other sections of the national communities, and whose status is regulated wholly or partially by their own customs or traditions or by special laws or regulations' (The World Bank, 1998: 4), and indigenous knowledge (IK) includes 'the expressions, practices, beliefs, understandings, insights, and experiences of Indigenous groups, generated over centuries of profound interaction with a particular territory' (Grey, 2014: 3230). QoL is influenced through ecological and sociocultural IK (Grey, 2014).

In the 1970s the call to universities on the African continent already urged African HEIs to 'be committed to active participation in social transformation, economic modernization, and the training and upgrading of the total human resources of the nation, not just of a small elite'(Preece, 2013: 118). The extent to which CE can be Africanised depends partly on its relationship to knowledge production and specifically model 2 knowledge that is socially produced and context specific, rather than disciplinary focused (Preece, 2013). Conscious subaltern thinkers and activists share the rejection of the Eurocentric notion that one can think from nowhere, as a type of empty objective space (Zondi, 2021). Four driving imperatives for CE by HEIs are: to provide students with the opportunity to engage and link their learning with the needs of society; improving the institution's social consciousness; student or academic activist layers in the institution arising from ideological imperatives to engage; and types of projects that emerge through the intervention of local governments or communities who challenge the HEI to respond to development issues (Bawa, 2007). Institutionalising SL requires a relationship between the institutional mission and purposes and goals of SL; community participation and partnerships; academic role of and acceptance by faculty, departments, and students; and structural and programmatic support necessary to advance and sustain SL (Furco, 2007).

CSL expands SL to include social justice principles, compelling an interrogation of authenticity in relationships, systems, and structures of inequality, hidden biases, power imbalances, and oppression within service activities and social and economic systems (Johnson et al., 2018). Civil society as the third sector of non-profit groups, as opposed to the state and market sectors, is part of society that is formed to facilitate collective action (Taylor, 2007). Where SL has an altruistic aim, CSL aims to create opportunity for social change, community connections for equity building, with students as change agents (Johnson et al., 2018). Students as youth representing their communities have a voice that should be the cornerstone of CSL. 'Instead of their input remaining at the discussion level, youth conceptualize, research, and develop action plans to make recommendations to policymakers. This places youth in a unique position to advocate for their communities, which provides a real-world opportunity for them to learn components of the change process' (Johnson et al., 2018: 12). A warning is sounded, however, that CSL can lead to self-censorship, where politically polarising discussions can cause students to withhold their true opinion if it is perceived that the audience will disagree (Lewing, 2020). The South African government regards public participation synonymous with democracy, service delivery, and constitutional rights, and is seen as the process whereby individuals obtain the opportunity to influence public decisions (Maphazi et al., 2013). '[P]articipation serves three particularly important democratic values: legitimacy, justice, and the effectiveness of public action' (Fung, 2006: 74). 'Poor public participation provides a recipe for lack of legitimacy of decisions and actions, civic disobedience and riots' (Maphazi et al., 2013: 65).

Participatory citizenship implies citizens that are active and well informed of their community and larger society including knowledge about social, economic, and political systems, available services, and their rights and responsibilities to these (Sutton, 2008). An active and informed citizen will continually upskill and participate in life-long learning, willingly perform expected duties, and hold representatives in government accountable for their decisions (Sutton, 2008). Structures and approaches to enhance community consultation and participation in SA involve ward committees facilitated by municipalities, community development work programmes, an integrated development plan that enables community-based planning and ownership of services, traditional tribal authorities, advisory panels, focus groups, forums, and sector outreach programmes used to identify community needs (Maphazi et al., 2013).

Students participating in community-based learning report that their understanding of social issues and root causes expand (Guo-Brennan et al., 2020). Eight specific skills required for students to be engaged citizens were enumerated as: political knowledge and critical thinking skills; communication skills; public problem-solving; civic judgment; civic imagination and creativity; collective action; coalition building; and organisational analysis (Welch, 2007). While key concepts will emerge from the designed protocol, it will be worthwhile to mention an earlier proposed public participation continuum by Cogan and Sharpe (Parker, 2003). This continuum provides direction to strategies for each level from passive to active, moving from publicity and public education techniques aimed at influencing passive citizens towards obtaining input on planning and interacting with the public, leading to actual partnerships where there can be participation in decision-making (Parker, 2003).

Fung (2006) indicates eight mechanisms for selecting the actors of participation, ranging from the more exclusive state (government) towards the more inclusive public, and these are: expert administrators; elected representatives; professional stakeholders; lay stakeholders; random selection; open or targeted recruiting; open or self-selection; and diffuse public sphere. Together with consideration of modes of communication and decision-making and the extent of power and authority, Fung (2006) suggests a democratic cube instead of a ladder of participation. For this author, the participant mechanisms lie across the cube (shaping the inside), while the authority levels (direct authority, co-govern, advise/consult, influence, individual education) run from the centre of the cube upwards and communication and decision modes (technical expertise, deliberate/negotiate, aggregate/bargain, develop preferences, express preferences, listen as spectator) from the middle out to form the breadth of the cube. An even later metaphor involves a wheel of participation as a more comprehensive way 'to explain why what happens works or not' and 'to envisage types of engagement that may lie in between each of the idealized types' (Reed et al., 2018: S11). The four types of stakeholder and public engagement that forms part of this wheel representation rotatable cogs are: top-down one-way communication and/or consultation; top-down deliberation and/or co-production; bottom-up one-way communication and/or consultation; and bottom-up deliberation and/or co-production (Reed et al., 2018).

A full discussion of the intricacies of curriculum design that is sensitive to civic participation falls outside of the protocol designed as part of this study, but some mention of assessment practices for SL activities is important. Lowery (2007) captures the four questions that should be asked and answered for such engaged projects: does the service component meet a public need; does the course provide a mechanism that enables students to link their service experience to course contents and reflect on why it is important; are all stakeholders involved in a reciprocal partnership; and is the final work product presented to the community, with an opportunity for the community to engage in dialogue?

Methodology

The research question is to determine the various integrating concepts that should be considered to implement civically engaged curricula in HE. The aim of the study is to establish the level of HE CE/SL engagement needed to address societal needs, especially within courses which should be contributing to the targets and indicators of SDG3. Seeing that it is not possible to reflect on all the SDGs, the general one of 'ensure healthy lives and promote well-being for all at all ages' should target concerns for a variety of vulnerable populations and should therefore link to SL projects aiming to meet the needs of communities. By default, SDG17 are touched on with the discussion of partnerships as key to authentic CE. A systematic review is used as a method to critically appraise, summarise, and synthesise available evidence, according to a pre-specified protocol to minimise bias (Hanley et al., 2013). A scoping review does not aim to produce critically appraised results from the synthesis as is the case with a systematic review, but rather aim to offer an overview or map of the available evidence (Munn et al., 2018). A scoping review was therefore sufficient for the purpose of this study.

The search procedures and search terms were conducted on literature sources informing the design of the protocol of criteria for authentic civic engagement by HEIs. This involved the searching of relevant sources on these databases ERIC, SAGE Open Journals, E-books on EBSCOhost, Taylor & Francis Online, ResearchGate, Academia, and relevant hard copy books from a university library. Eligibility criteria for deciding on the relevance of the citation for the study focused on sources of the last ten years (from 2014). Sources speaking to the theoretical frameworks mentioned were screened for their relevance to guiding HE towards authentic, civically engaged institutions, and specifically in operationally identifiable terms – leading to exclusion of sources that did not contribute to this. To note is that Academia searches could not be done with the ten-year period filter as this requires premium membership. This platform was mainly used for specific citation searches. EBSCOhost produced significantly more sources with the keyword searches, even with the use of less Boolean operators and more keyword combinations, but seemed to have produced less significant matches to the concepts searched for. Since the best matches are listed first, on average the first ten to 20 pages only were screened. The ERIC database produced more focused results, although this is understandable with the delineation of education-based content inherent in this database of journals. An observation by the researcher was that the majority of the matches found on SDGs and in university focused on leadership, and did not deliver significantly to the insights used in this chapter. Even though there were only a few books published on the keywords in the past ten years, foundational and visionary concepts were captured in these. Starting with them as the core to unpack the concepts, articles were added for concepts not covered through the chapters or were acknowledged in the protocol for confirming descriptions of the concepts. What was excluded in the conceptual framework of the study is corporate social responsibility. While it focuses on a company's civic duty, the study focuses within the range of academic community engagement activities that influences the curriculum only. Articles containing book reviews were also excluded. Although it may be insightful to include key legislative and policy documents to evaluate proposed interventions to vulnerable populations, especially considering principles that apply to CE in HE, such scope falls outside the results discussed in this chapter.

The capturing of the various sources was guided by a visual mapping (or data charting) through the 'Framing conceptual synthesis Excel dump' (Pacheco-Vega, 2016). A large number of publications on SL were evident in the first decade of the 2000s. While these sources were used to contextualise the theoretical framework of the study, they were excluded from the data used for the design of the review protocol. The mentioned excel document allowed for various tabs to be created to represent the key concepts, and to then capture the citation of the sources linked to each concept it represents. This not only shaped the creation of the protocol, but also assisted with identifying duplicates and repetition of concepts. Displaying of the total number of sources, screening, and final selection is done through the 'PRISMA flow diagram' (Page et al., 2021), noting again that a full systematic review was not done, and registration of the review was not a requirement.

Data extraction considered the use of these keywords in the database search: 'civic engagement and university; critical service-learning and university; engagement and sustainable development goal three; participatory theory and social capital'. Considering that the scoping review conducted did not intend to provide the more formal evaluation typical to systematic reviews, a review team was not considered for the analysis of the sources and emerging themes. Instead, the researcher considered screening features to assess the validity of the citations which included the exclusion of discipline specific content in order to obtain generically applicable concepts from the literature. While the results related to CSL were included, the papers' discussion of the application of the principles to various disciplines like design, social work, etc, were excluded. This was done to allow a usable and concise protocol of the core CSL concepts to allow for a general evaluation of meeting the criteria. Writing for a SA context also prompted the researcher to intentionally seek out relevant sources from non-Western countries as well, or those publications that showed some sensitivity to indigenous considerations. Pieces specifically discussing application in Western countries only were excluded if they did not add new theory or did not focus on immigrants, for example. The scoping review considered sources available through an academic library and included both subscription-based, hard copy texts, and open-source databases or institutional websites that did not require member login, for the design of the protocol. With the use of the previously mentioned Excel tool, sources related to emerging key topics were renamed to be more identifiable and where duplicate files could be more easily identified. Where data saturation was reached with extracted concepts repeating themselves within the literature sources, stricter screening was done, to not only add the source as a support to another.

Protocol of criteria for civically engaged HE

Because a protocol accompanied by descriptions of all its parts would require a type of manual, this chapter aims to only focus on the final set and overview of criteria used. Extended definitions are therefore not included but could be studied through the extensive list of references obtained through the scoping review. The key concepts forming the basis of the protocol are, however, discussed next in the next section, in order to provide the context for the protocol. Figure 12.1 is the PRISMA diagram showing the results of the number of sources that were used to design the protocol.

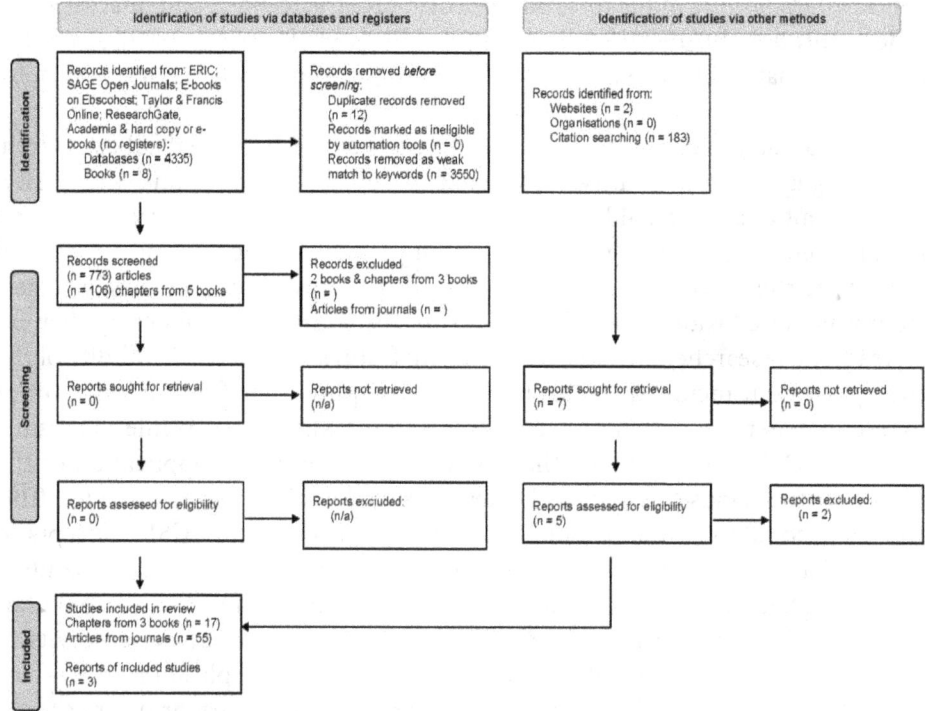

FIGURE 12.1: PRISMA diagram showing results of the number of sources used to design the protocol

Authentic partnerships: The idea of engagement is to create meaningful links between the university and its many constituencies, to effect local forces to defend the worth of universities (Davis, 2021). While it can be argued that universities are responsive, the questions raised are who they are responsive to and whether the driving force of engagement is societal need (Hollister, 2021). Reflecting on the UN's claim that partnerships had fallen short of what was needed towards the 2030 Agenda, Stanberry and Bragan (2024) speak of moving partnerships from 'pedantic to panacea'. The following nine enhancements to partnerships to achieve global goals are (Stanberry & Bragan, 2024: 116): an optimal partner mix; effective leadership; stringent goal-setting; sustained funding; professional process management; regular monitoring, reporting, and evaluation; active meta-governance; favourable political and social context; and fit to problem-structure. 'It is important to recognize that if the community partner does not feel as though they are part of the planning and implementing of the project, it will not offer lasting change. Having students and faculty develop authentic relationships builds trust and offers students the opportunity to unpack biases that they may have of others' (Warren-Gordon et al., 2020: 22). University-community boundary spanning roles were depicted on a matrix by Weerts and Sandmann (2010 in Preece, 2017), having the institution versus community focus on the vertical axis and technical, practical versus socio-emotional, with leadership tasks on the horizontal axis. From these, quadrant roles were identified as the community-based problem solver (technical-community) and engagement champion (socio-emotional-community) on the top half, and technical expert (technical-institutional) and internal engagement advocate (socio-emotional-institution) at the bottom (Preece, 2017). This matrix serves as a model for contextualising equal ownership and active participation.

Public participation and social capital: The 'Ladder of Citizen Participation', created by Sherry Arnstein in 1969, is one of the most widely referenced and influential models in the field of democratic public participation, and also motivated later models, including Elizabeth Rocha's Ladder of Empowerment and Roger Hart's Ladder of Children's Participation (Abbott & Holley, 2024). The ladder features eight 'rungs' or levels describing three general forms of citizen power in democratic decision-making: nonparticipation, which indicates no power at the bottom of the ladder (levels: manipulation and therapy or a focus on curing a problem); degrees of tokenism, which is counterfeit power (levels: informing, consultation and placation); and degrees of citizen power, which is actual power (levels: partnerships, delegated power, and citizen control) (Abbott & Holley, 2024). For Arnstein's higher rungs to work better, technology can be utilised for more direct involvement, since new and user-friendly technologies and open data will allow engagement by the community without the need to necessarily involve a technician at a cost (Falco, 2019). Three stages of citizen engagement in a democracy include: information provisioning (access, but one-way relationship); consultation (two-way relationship with opportunity to provide feedback); and active participation (engaged in defining the process and content of policy-making) (Oni et al., 2019). Oni et al. (2019) also highlight the benefits of E-consultation and E-petitions to broaden inclusivity. The purpose of this chapter is to challenge the notion that a level of consultation where there is no assurance that citizens' opinions will be taken into account or placating them with their inclusion only to demonstrate that there was involvement from the public, while they can still easily be outvoted, is sufficient for effective CSL in HE. Considering the effect citizen unsatisfaction, evidenced in public demonstrations, can have on HE and its link with government and civil society, as shown through the helix discussed next, public participation is an important consideration for HE curriculum. Since low amounts of trust will trigger attention to political decisions, it is advisable for local governments to be proactive by establishing efficient participation processes to avert negative effects on local government satisfaction (Weber et al., 2019). 'A rise in participation rates as a result of both supply and advertising public participation projects will lead to a higher participation quality, and as a result, bias will be reduced' (Weber et al., 2019: 492). The concept of 'emergent participatory citizenship' shapes the development of immigrant youths' development of civic competencies through their daily routines, proximal social contexts, and historically rooted beliefs and cultural practices (Barber et al., 2015). Social capital exists in an individual's social ecology and is non static, defined as 'the ability of people to secure advantages by virtue of membership in social networks or other social structures' (Dolan, 2022: 259). Its benefits are tangible, for example living in safe neighbourhoods, a sense of health and happiness, engagement in democratic systems, and access to economic prosperity (Dolan, 2022), but social capital also comprises engagement in civil society organisations and the promotion of reciprocity and interpersonal trust (Rasmussen & Reher, 2019). Social trust in a society does, however, impact on the level of association by its members, leading to the conclusion that social trust determines the exclusiveness of inclusiveness of civic engagement (Liu & Shen, 2021). 'The competing natures of particularised [connects "in-groups" such as families, extended kinship and face-to-face communities in which people know each other and interact closely, and where social sanctions are strong] and generalised [imbedded in interactions with unfamiliar people, or the "out-group", from which a sense of engagement, tolerance, prosperity and democratic relationships are developed] trust have been the central focus of research on the relationships between trust and civic engagement' (Liu & Shen, 2021: 422).

The stakeholder helix: 'Knowledge, as a resource, is created through creative processes, combinations, and productions in so-called "Knowledge models" or "Innovation models" and thus becomes available for society' (Carayannis et al., 2012: 3). The quintuple helix innovation model calls for socioecological transition by incorporating university-industry-government relations (the original triple helix), media-based and cultural influence, public and civil society (quadruple helix), and the perspective of the natural environments of society – highlighting the importance of socio-ecological sustainability and an even greater need for inter-disciplinarity (Carayannis et al., 2012). With the previous inclusion of the fourth (quadruple) helix, a bottom-up approach was incorporated where innovation is informed by societal demands (Neary & Osborne, 2018). The 'Talloires Declaration on the Civic Roles and Social Responsibilities of Higher Education' signed in 2005 by university heads from 23 countries, now grown to a membership of 388 from 77 countries, (Hollister, 2021) shows parallel points to the need for stakeholder integration. From the declaration: 'The university should use the processes of education and research to respond to, serve and strengthen its communities for local and global citizenship. The university has a responsibility to participate actively in the democratic process and to empower those who are less privileged' (Tufts University, 2005: 1). From the now-Tisch College of Civic Life, the Centre for Information and Research on Civic Learning

(CIRCLE), became a data source on young people's civic behaviour, informing the media and public policy (Hollister, 2021). As a guide to the engagement of other entities, an emerging concept captures the ideological aim of doing good into practical terms. The 'Convivialist Manifesto' calls for a turn from self-centred and undesirable developments towards a vision of a harmonious life where there is a positive focus on the quality of social relationships and our relations to nature (Adloff, 2019). Conviviality links to the overall aims of public good and sustainable development through its various dimensions (Adloff, 2020): requiring, at minimum civil standards, nonviolence and tolerance of difference; striving for interactions where people's encounters are not exhibited as mutual stereotyping or defamatory assumptions of others; stressing 'equality and self-organisation and calls for non-hierarchical and democratic forms of organisation' (Adloff, 2020: 118); not living at the expense of others, to not realise present needs at the expense of future generations, and attempting to avoid negative consequences. Synergy also exists with the concept of 'Grimpact' discussed later in this section.

Community-based research: is a collaborative approach including both academic researchers and the community, working together to enhance the ability of the community to meet their needs, with students playing an important role in the collaborative process (Dials-Corujo, 2019). 'All partners share ownership, control, influence, and decision making and contribute their expertise according to each individual's knowledge and skills' (Israel et al., 1998 in Fletcher, 2008: 35). Within this research space, citizen science that is not limited to scientific science has numerous classifications that describe the various typologies involved. It is defined as 'work undertaken by civic educators together with citizen communities to advance science, foster a broad scientific mentality, and/or encourage democratic engagement, which allows society to deal rationally with complex modern problems. This definition shifts the focus from the action-oriented, data-centered point of view of collect, participate, and contribute (e.g., the instrumentalist point of view) towards a re-framing, based on civic education, of how science and society should respond to a call for openness, inclusiveness, responsiveness, democratic engagement, consultation, dialogue, and commons, e.g., the capacity-building point of view' (Ceccaroni et al., 2019: 10). Engebretsen et al. (2021) believe that the SDGs confront universities with a dual research commitment to firstly contribute to development that will optimise the use of resources around the world (innovation), and secondly to continuously scrutinise developments to counteract the overuse of natural and human resources (counter innovation). Building from the asset based community development (ABCD) framework that promotes the use of asset mapping to explore the resources that exist in a community, the extended framework of asset based community engagement (ABCE) actions the exploration of community assets (in terms of accessibility, affordability, connectedness, and social networks) utilised by its members through recognising potential barriers to engagement, with a particular focus on the inclusion of marginalised groups through 'assertive linking' (Collinson & Best, 2019).

Building an engaged curriculum: Two dimensions of curriculum need to be interrogated: the academic curriculum consisting of the knowledge, behaviour, and identity difference in disciplinary and professional contexts being taught in the classroom, and the institutional curriculum that is not visibly structured and not subjected to assessment – the knowledge encoded in dominant beliefs and embedded in institutional behaviour (Lange, 2021). Faculty members will be more likely to incorporate SL into the curriculum if administrative assistance exists and if the academic has freedom to develop a course to include civic engagement (Bobick, 2019). To develop a self-directed learner, faculties need to assist students to formulate their own learning goals while also attaining awareness on how they learn (Swanzen, 2015). Integrated with the development of an intuitive approach towards CE, the student needs to know how to identify community needs. During the planning phase, community profiling and Swanepoel and De Beer's Participatory Rapid Appraisal and Planning (PRAP) can be used that provide various techniques for the types of information needed (Swanzen, 2015). At the termination stage of the SL project, the End-of-Programme Survey for community partners can be used, which allows the partner to provide feedback on their view of the impact the activity had on the student, their motivation for participating, their satisfaction with the roles and responsibilities in the process, the level of the community's involvement, and the influence the partnership had (Swanzen, 2015). Core to the development of socio-emotional skills is the use of reflection and critical thinking.

Deepening critical thinking and reflection: Hunter (2019: 31) stated: 'Currently, many in academia promote service learning as the primary pedagogy for the development of civic competencies such as critical thinking... Faculty members need to know how to effectively use the civic engagement investigation cycle of planning, participation/action, reflection and demonstration... [Critical thinking] is viewed as an active process where one generates questions, explores relevant information, and develops solutions, as opposed to passively acquiring information from others'. Reflection acts as a bridge that supports the scrutiny of the community service experience in terms of the mastery of the course content, which can take the form of the experiential research paper, journalling, oral or presentations (Hunter, 2019). Garrison et al. (2000 in Chadha, 2022) built from John Dewey's early concept of learning problem-solving through first-hand experience, intended for face-to-face classes to integrate the need for critical reflection to an online platform called the 'community of inquiry model' (COL). Not only will the consideration of the latter mitigate the risk pandemics can hold for the interruption of CE, but the integration of the reflection and critical thinking capabilities into the learning outcomes for students contribute to a civically engaged curriculum.

Civic responsibility and transversal skills: In terms of planning activities within a citizen participation context, the types are community or advocacy planning (ensuring community voice and interests are considered towards course of action), equity planning (carried out by planning officials within government agencies towards a single plan), and communicative or collaborative planning (interpretive and argumentative, centred around dialogue and focused on inclusive transactions and consensus-building) (Falco, 2019). These skills are increasingly in high demand for learners to successfully adapt to changes and to lead meaningful and productive lives. Civic values incapsulated through the SL experience comprise of justice, tolerance, mutual assistance, self-restraint, self-respect, freedom, equality, diversity, authority, privacy, truth and patriotism (Huda et al., 2019). Civic responsibility refers to attitudes and actions associated with democratic governance and social contributions (Dials-Corujo, 2019). Students who participate in service activities report higher levels of civic responsibility characteristics (Kim, Carter and Armstrong, 2019). 'Adaptability, openness, and confidence are important attributes for citizens living in a globally interconnected world and society' (Guo-Brennan et al., 2020: 52). The development of social empathy with an understanding of contextual factors, increases a student's sense of social responsibility, although the absence of experiencing life situations first-hand, requires the ability for macro-perspective-taking (Hylton, 2018). 'Transversal skills are those typically considered as not specifically related to a particular job, task, academic discipline or area of knowledge but as skills that can be used in a wide variety of situations and work settings' (UNESCO, 2014: 2). Different to foundational and specialised competencies, transversal competencies entail critical and innovate skills; inter-personal skills (e.g. teamwork and communication); intra-personal skills (e.g. perseverance and self-discipline); global citizenship (tolerance, cultural intelligence); and media and information literacy (locate, access and scrutinize information) (UNESCO, 2014).

Development for impact is used here as an encapsulating term to point to engagement aimed at purposeful societal development. With 193 nations who signed up to it (Muff et al., 2017), the most evident and internationally endorsed way to evaluate such development for impact is the UN's SDGs. The SDGs focus on targets for prosperity, people, planet, peace, and partnership (five Ps) that are time-bound (Sachs et al., 2019). The goals follow a 'triple bottom line' approach to well-being, 'with a focus on economic development, environmental sustainability and social inclusion' (Neary & Osborne, 2018: 339). Stanberry and Bragan (2024: 110) argue that 'ecological reflexivity, as developed and advanced by deliberative democracy and the Earth System Governance Project, belongs at the apex of those capacities needed for implementing the Agenda for Transformation. Ecological reflexivity conceptually grounds inclusive, open, critical, and consequential engagement of discourses situated among capable representatives, advocates, and citizens'. Signifying the role business plays in the space of sustainability and impact (as framed by the UN Global Compact of 2021), shareholder reports and investment strategies are also dictated by environmental, social and governance (ESG) considerations (Stanberry & Bragan, 2024). A sustainable society is one that 'meets the need of the present without compromising the ability of future generations to meet their own needs' (Gordon & Dixon, 2021). Sowula et al. (2022) captures the recommendations from congress delegates to shortly be: the need to ask the right questions from an equitable partnership where decisions are made collectively; embed the SDGs within all partnerships; know your baseline indicators that will depict impact success; strengthen coordination function and define the purpose of the partnership with a public schedule of activity; have consistent key performance indicators and interoperability of metrics across schools or departments with a single database and scorecard that everyone in the institution can access and understand; meaningfully integrate SDGs interdisciplinary to secure it against disruption; embrace criticism and risk; and incentivise all partners to have a clear and transparent return on their investment, whether reputational or financial. The detailed recommendations were incorporated into the designed protocol as key requirements for authentic partnerships, especially in consideration of meeting the SDGs. Sustainable development takes place on both the local and global level and therefore must be understood in the context of 'gloCal knowledge economy and society' (Carayannis et al., 2012). Apart from the Times Higher Education's Impact Rankings that internationally assess universities against the SDGs (Times Higher Education, 2024), a global database of civic societies exists that group them by association to the SDGs (Union of International Associations, 2022). It is believed that a concerted effort should be made to register HEIs or their affiliated centers to international bodies like these, to ensure increased visibility that not only stimulate accountable reporting of activities, but can also accelerate opportunities for the funding of projects. The Sustainability Tracking, Assessment & Rating System (STARS) also exists to assist universities to track their sustainability progress through a self-reporting framework (Association for the Advancement of Sustainability in Higher Education, 2024). This framework scores the institution on its contribution towards the SDGs through the sections of academics (percentage of academic departments with courses and outcomes on sustainability), engagement (involved in co-curricular sustainable activities), operations (improve ecological management of buildings and grounds), and planning and administration (establish a vision of a sustainable future with measurable objectives) (Association for the Advancement of Sustainability in Higher Education, 2024). SDG3 constitutes nine overlapping targets: 'to reduce maternal and child mortality rates, communicable and non-communicable diseases, substance abuse, road traffic accidents, and death and illness from hazardous chemicals and pollution, as well as to ensure universal health coverage and access to sexual and reproductive healthcare services' (Engebretsen et al., 2021: 113). These authors highlight the difference between being accountable as an external accounting for one's actions versus having a sense of responsibility that depends on inner motivation. Pursuing the SDGs are driven in terms of accountability for quality indicators, while responsibility relies on interest and an active and inclusive political space – making indifference the biggest risk for the effective implementation of the SDGs (Engebretsen et al., 2021). The GAP Frame translates the SDGs into relevant national grand challenges within the four sustainability domains of the planet or environment, society, economy, and governance (Muff et al., 2017). Initiatives mentioned in this section enable HEIs to align their endeavours in a clear and operationalised way.

Quality of life (QoL) indicators: Considering the WHO's description of QoL as 'an individual's perception of one's position in life in the context of culture and value systems in relation to goals, expectations, standards, and concerns' Wilson and Newmark (2015: 258) believed that an integrated framework of CE with rural ecological QoL platforms can promote social transformation. According to the UN, intergenerational and global justice are main aspects of sustainability and for this reason Wiesli et al. (2021) sees sustainable QoL (SQoL) as connecting 'the local with the global and the present with the future', expanding on the more individual perspective of QoL indicators. SQoL components from various sources were combined through a Swiss study as the following nine indicators: social relations and equality; participation, identification, and collective emotions; nature and landscape; education and knowledge; health and safety; leisure and recreation; income and employment; living; and mobility and access (Wiesli et al., 2021). Specific to the African continent, the African Union expresses the intention to attain 20 goals over a 50-year plan, to bring the continent closer to 'The Africa we want' (African Union Development Agency – NEPAD, 2022). While the goals are specific to the progress needing to be made by its 54 member states, there are some similarities with the SDGs, especially for the purpose of this chapter, namely Agenda 2063 Goal 3 which strives for healthy and well-nourished citizens, and Goal 18 that focuses on engaged and empowered youth and children (African Union Development Agency – NEPAD, 2022). One of the five related operational priorities, termed the African Development Bank Group's 'High 5s', involves improving the QoL for the people of Africa (African Union Development Agency – NEPAD, 2022). According to the second continental report, Africa performed satisfactorily on the achievement of Goal 3, specifically women's access to reproductive health services, reduction of tuberculosis infections, and positive impacts resulting from the attention given to curbing the COVID-19 pandemic, but did not drop neo-natal mortality rates to the expected 15,5 deaths per 1000 births, as well as registering an increase in malaria infections (African Union Development Agency – NEPAD, 2022). Considering how much development is still needed, it is not implausible to expect SA HEIs to be concerned with outcomes related to the improvement of the quality of life of its people, as a general and cross-disciplinary aim.

An opposing concept to positive impact from academic research or engagement has been identified. Where public valuation of academic impact is viewed as negative, it is referred to as 'Grimpact' (Wouters et al., 2018). The authors describe that the identification of grimpact instead considers normal versus extraordinary impact, where the former follows the expected social contract, while the latter deviates from the intended impact for the expected outcomes of research or effect in a particular sector of society. 'Our analysis allows us to distinguish grimpact into four overarching headings, namely the violation of normal impact, the diffusion of attribution, academic transgressions and its contagion effects' (Wouters et al., 2018: 1203). Because of the potential risk to society, research ethics processes should consider the impact of the study as well and not be a mere checklist or compliance exercise.

Transformation Agenda: Concerned that SL may only present ameliorative change, CSL pedagogy is concerned with promoting social justice through the education of students to deconstruct the 'power structures that underlie many traditional views of the world (Campus Compact, 2020 in Harkins et al., 2020: 22). Critical consciousness, seen as the ability to recognise oppressive social conditions and how to counteract them, influences critical action which results in intentional acts of social justice (Andrews & Leonard, 2018). 'A transformed higher education system was one which would actively focus on addressing the developmental needs of the new democracy in terms of knowledge, skills and citizenship' (Lange, 2021: 277). Attempting a definitional framework for transformation in HE, the following elements were identified (Keet & Muthwa, 2021): inclusion in the social structure of the academy and its governance processes evident in redress of inequity; Africanisation of curriculum, research, language, aesthetics and governance; configuration of power relations with fair distribution of authority within the knowledge generation process; the advancement of critical and post-conflict pedagogies; and the promotion of equalising relationships between HE, the state, the private sector, interest groups, pressure formations, and broader society. These elements can be addressed within the three-tier conception of large-scale configuration of the system; response to global and local processes and influences; or social justice and human rights programming, including cultural tolerance (Keet & Muthwa, 2021). From The World in 2050 initiative, modular building blocks for SDG transformation were introduced: 1) education, gender, and inequality; 2) health, well-being, and demography; 3) energy decarbonisation and sustainable industry; 4) sustainable food, land, water, and oceans; 5) sustainable cities and communities; and 6) digital revolution for sustainable development (Sachs et al., 2019: 805). These authors offered a highly useable table that links the transformation areas to the ministries responsible for them, SDG interventions, and how the intermediate outputs will speak to the various scaled SDGs. Preece (2017 in Keet & Muthwa, 2021) challenged the notion of engagement being equated with addressing issues of disadvantage and only focusing on developing students as responsible citizens. Such a discursion traps it pragmatically within an orientation of charitability and philanthropy, instead of viewing it from a transformation perspective of increasing opportunities as an equity imperative (Keet & Muthwa, 2021).

If the transformation agenda is not embedded into all HE activities, civic engagement will also fall short and merge into mere charity projects. Placemaking is the process by which 'human beings transform the places in which we find ourselves into places we live' and scholars ask what is done in a place, how it is done, and the value underlying the activities, to obtain important background information (Moore, 2014: 19). Extending representativeness through placemaking practices democracy and examples of this include community tourism, continuing education, and university extension (Moore, 2014). While barriers to the civic university involve the limitation of external projects, partnerships not being part of core business, or internal policies not being understood by external stakeholders, drivers are government policy changes, changes in institutional vision, and the creation of high-level structures to drive research, innovation, and engagement (Johnson, 2020).

The protocol (Table 12.1) was designed with the aim to have a referenceable matrix type set of criteria representing the multitude of concepts behind the chosen key words. It is therefore acknowledged that it is challenging to capture all the nuances of the represented literature. For each main category of criteria, up to the top seven descriptors or concepts were included for each to create a usable tool for wide-ranging evaluation. These representative keywords aim to offer the operationalised or task-oriented indicator of the concept in practice. The keywords are roughly positioned as most important to less important in order of appearance, but this is only based on the perception gained from the reviewed literature and not tested for standardisation.

TABLE 12.1: Criteria protocol: Components of authentic civic engagement in higher education

Engagement category	Representative key word or identifying concept						
	a	b	c	d	e	f	g
	Designing curriculum for civic engagement						
Knowledge creation (mode 2)	knowledge produced in context of application	transdisciplinarity	heterogeneity and organisational diversity	social accountability and reflexivity	quality control	coevolution of innovation (mode 3)	
Critical service-learning	providing a social change orientation	working to redistribute power	developing authentic relationships	interdependence and reciprocity	analyses of social change	self-directed learning	responsive university
Deepening critical thinking	use of civic engage investigation cycle:	planning and participation / action,	reflection and demonstration; and	use high impact educational strategies	use of critical thinking prompts	seek big picture information	connect to previous knowledge
Strengthen reflection	real/genuine needs and reciprocal	move beyond conditioning	critical enquiry into three presences:	cognitive presence – construct meaning	social presence – seek connection	teaching presence – regular monitoring	

Engagement category	Representative key word or identifying concept						
	a	b	c	d	e	f	g
Social justice orientation	develop social empathy	recognise social injustice contextually	exercise macro-level perspective taking	critical consciousness of social responsibility	tacit knowledge of know-how and experience	development of knowledge for public good	social ecology
Civic engagement skills	relationship-based versus task-centered engagement	intellectual stimulation instead of performance	professional development instead of student learning	incorporate transversal skills	co-created problem-solving	open expression instead of self-censorship	
Global citizenship	tolerance	openness	respect for diversity	intercultural understanding	information literacy (access and analyse)	emerging participatory citizenship	

Engagement category	Representative key word or identifying concept						
	a	b	c	d	e	f	g
			Building authentic partnerships				
Citizen science/'wheel' of participation	Instrumental – discrete actors	capacity building	top-down consultation	top-down co-production	bottom-up consultation	bottom-up co-production	
Placemaking – ask:	what is done	how it is done	values that underlie the activity in the place		community tourism	continuing education	university extension
Embed quadrant roles	community-based problem solver		engagement champion		technical expert	internal engagement advocate	
Asset mapping of community	accessibility	affordability	connectedness/linking	social networks	inclusion of marginalised groups		
Participation planning	advocacy planning (community voice)	equity planning (government officials)	collaborative planning (interpretive dialogue)	use of participatory commons (e.g. Zooniverse)			
Enhancements to partnership to meet goals	an optimal partner and effective leadership	stringent goal-setting and sustained funding	professional process management	regular monitoring	reporting and evaluation	active meta-governance	favourable political and social context, and fit to problem-structure

CHAPTER 12

Engagement category	Representative key word or identifying concept						
	a	b	c	d	e	f	g
Quintuple helix (stakeholder relations)	education system (human capital)	economic system (industry/ commerce)	natural environment (natural capital)	media-based and culture (social and info capital)	political system (nation-state)		
Infusing cultural sensitivity							
Interculturalism & social capital	Search for common human needs across cultures	examine religious, ideological and cultural facets of society	understanding one's own traditions, habits and conventions	particularised social trust	generalised social trust	indigenous knowledge systems	
Conviviality	basic tendency toward human cooperation	convivialist test asks four questions, is:	common humanity and equal human dignity respected	greatest good lies in the quality of social relations	principle of individuation respected	are conflicts allowed but controlled	
Focus on developmental impact							
Sustainable QoL indicators	social relations and equality	participation and identification	nature and landscape	education and knowledge	health and safety, and leisure and recreation	income and employment	living and mobility

251

Engagement category	Representative key word or identifying concept						
	a	b	c	d	e	f	g
SDG trans-formations	education, gender, and inequality	health, well-being, and demography	Energy decarbonisation, and sustainable industry	sustainable food, land, water, and oceans	sustainable cities and communities	digital revolution for sustainable development	
GAP Framework (grand challenges in four sustainability domains)	planet (eight challenges)	society (six challenges)	economy (five challenges)	governance (five challenges)	total of 64 indicators against the 24 challenges	participate in High 5s of the African Union Agenda (SA context)	
Address inequality contexts	vital inequality (life expectancy)	existential inequality (dignity and rights)	resource inequality (realise capacity)	distantiation (confidence)	exploitation (domination)	exclusion (barring access)	Hierarchisation (ranking/power)
Institutionalising critical service-learning							
Criteria for SL in HE	relevant and meaningful service with the community	enhanced academic learning	purposeful civic learning	structured opportunities for reflection	academic leadership, faculty roles and rewards	democratic rather than technocratic management	
Advocacy courses	knowledge on active legislative processes	mapping of issues' organisational fields	media campaigns & issue framing	real-time lobbying efforts	driving vertical (political level) engagement	driving horizontal (community level) engagement	

Engagement category	Representative key word or identifying concept						
	a	b	c	d	e	f	g
Civic engagement strategies for students	coordinate candidate forums on campus and in the community	coordinate and host mock elections and mock debates	organise debate-watching parties	engage in voter registration drives	organise lobbying training on campus and in the community	engage in service-learning in community advocacy organisations	advance or defeat active bills
Critical SL student experiences	understanding and providing benefits that recipients really need	designing and planning a project by themselves	solving a real-world problem	collaborating with diverse people	undertaking a specific role of responsibility	recognising and managing uncomfortable feelings	reflecting on their interests and abilities
Responsive university	social responsiveness	market responsiveness	managerial responsiveness	regional responsiveness	epistemic responsiveness		
Tracking SL activities (existing examples):	Participatory Rapid Appraisal and Planning (PRAP)		Sustainability Tracking, Assessment and Rating System (STARS)		End-of-Programme Survey for community partners		
Celebration	share findings with community	award civic honours at graduation	offer active citizen internships	end of field placement seminars			
	Mitigating barriers to critical service-learning and/or civic engagement						
Pre-emptive strategies to minimise	supporter-fatigue	counter 'grimpact'	training of all role-players	enable administrative and resource processes	legal considerations	correct positioning of CE unit	identify champions, advocates and experts

Applicability of the protocol and implications for higher education

While it fitted well with the concept of public participation and even QoL, social capital did not emerge from the literature as much as the research initially indicated it could. Navigating the various frameworks extended the protocol with more nuances to consider when academic community engagement is intentional and within a SA context. 'Africa is committed to deepening the culture of good governance, strengthening democratic values, gender equality, respect for human rights, justice, and upholding the rule of law' (African Union Development Agency – NEPAD, 2022). A core theme throughout the content that made up the protocol is respect for humanity and opposing inequalities that supresses human well-being. While this may likely not be made overt, the remaining presence of disparities, like gender inequality in academia, detracts from the claims of a civic university, as it is not concerning itself with social justice principles within.

The designed protocol can be adapted with criteria from the other SDGs' indicators to enable a broader review. A similar focus on a longer-term can offer a deeper evaluation of the true state of authentic civic engagement, and this chapter does not claim to fully represent all current projects and planned endeavours in this space. A critical conversation on the current findings may very likely point to a return to more specific elements of authentic partnerships towards civically engaged societal development, needing a more in-depth discussion of the protocol designed for the purposes of this study. One concern was the perceived decline in publications, where the early 2000s showed a spike in publications on service learning and civic engagement within HE but seemed to have tapered off in the last decade. This concern seems partially confirmed by the American Political Science Association (APSA) handbook that speaks of 'warnings about a decline in civic engagement education have been sounded by organizations' (Glover et al., 2021: 599).

When engagement is authentic communities will experience its impact, and consequences of social ills can be buffered. The more implemented best practices are evident, the more likely it will contribute to the required changes. Without an integrated set of principles to broadly evaluate the implementation of the broad CE principle, a scanning of universities' activities will not fairly provide a comprehensive picture of the true range and impact of activities. Results from such a review indicating success in a couple of areas only will be likely, as projects were shaped by only one or two of the set of concepts depicted in the protocol. While HE is pressed on their 'third mission' (among teaching and research), little guidance is given to the urging to connect with civic society (Neary & Osborne, 2018). Moreso, 'there is no real linkage between economic development and higher education planning at the ministerial level, and higher education issues are limited to only one ministry' (Neary & Osborne, 2018: 348), a similar situation in which HE in SA finds itself. The CE space has evolved enough to adopt a classification of the complex concepts involved in CE in HE. Only then can a guiding framework for authentic and civically involved engagement be offered as the yardstick for measurement. The need for a more standard set of criteria cannot be underestimated at the emergent time of natural disasters and unrest the world finds itself in, major elements that increase inequality, especially in the Global South.

To expand on the protocol towards a standardised classification system, a similar exercise can be done with the other 16 SDGs and the related policy frameworks from core disciplines that should address the targets of each SDG. The observation shared under the methodology section of this chapter leads the researcher to deduct that a small number of publications looking at the link between SDGs and CSL in HE have been produced in the last decade. On a wider platform, this observation was supported by Neary and Osborne (2018) who indicated that the one partner that is rarely discussed in SDGs is that of the university. A worthwhile initiative that deserves mention in this aspect is the partnership that was evident between the International Symposium of Service-Learning (ISSL) and conservation organisations such as the ACTION platform and AGROS project, where the former provided a platform to the latter at their 2021 conference held in Cyprus to link the matter of environmental adaptation with civic engagement. Other interesting concepts were discovered through the review process but were movements in themselves, and minimally overlap with the core concepts in this study, and could therefore not be included in the protocol. Some of these, for interest's sake, are autoethnography being used as a form of participant research, the use of participatory archives and mediated projects, and the anthropocene (the earth's new geological epoch).

Social justice focused legislation can be used to determine if HE is responsive to the key drives of society – for instance, having a noticeable voice in HE on policies on integrated service delivery, intermediary services and paediatric palliative care. A practical example in which this can be approached is provided by the Educational Network for Active Civic Transformation (ENACT), where students are guided to select a bill currently under review and then develop advocacy efforts to advance or counter the proposed piece of legislation (Glover et al., 2021). In the wake of the #RhodesMustFall (initiated from the University of Cape Town) and #FeesMustFall (initiated from the University of the Witwatersrand) movements of 2015, new challenges for South African universities remain a reality (Bawa, 2021). These 'hashtag' movements organised themselves around decolonised and fee-free education (Zondi, 2021). The previous CEO of Universities South Africa (USaf), Professor Ahmed Bawa (2021: 207), fittingly stated that 'South Africa's social, political and economic travails, the galloping evolution of the new technological movement, a deepening set of crises around global warming, new epidemics of infectious and life-style diseases, a fracturing of the multilateral global governance system, a slide towards anti-intellectualism, and a growing distrust of science and experts, all present a powerful impetus for the emergence of a new social compact'. He also claimed that should engagement be the way for HEIs to understand their public, this has remained in the periphery of universities (Bawa, 2021). While coordinating bodies like the South Africa Higher Education Community Forum (SAHECEF) provide meaningful explorations of the knowledge project, they leave the core of finding donor funding, relationships with society, and involvement of students up to the individual institutions (Bawa, 2021). A basis for a new social compact would involve a reconsideration of the socioeconomic project of HE and whether a decisive shift towards a social justice rubric is needed, but the evolving of this compact will require a process that includes a wide diversity of voices, both local and global (Bawa, 2021). A significant number of recent publications link SDGs to civic engagement, which in the next decade will likely not be separated. The researcher wishes to echo that 'knowledge on sustainability – including a wide range of topics from green technologies to human rights – seems essential' (Wiesli et al., 2021: 15). The need for a HE response through academic civic engagement is becoming inexorable and arguably already became dire.

References

Abbott, S. & Holley, K. (2024). Ladder of Citizen Participation. *Organizing Engagement*. Available at: https://organizingengagement.org/models/ladder-of-citizen-participation/. Date accessed: 7 March 2024.

Adloff, F. (2019). Practices of Conviviality and the Social and Political Theory of Convivialism. *Novos Estudos CEBRAP*, 38(1): 35–47. https://doi.org/10.25091/S01013300201900010002.

Adloff, F. (2020). Experimental Conviviality: Exploring Convivial and Sustainable Practices. *Open Cultural Studies*, 4(1): 112–121. https://doi.org/10.1515/culture-2020-0011.

African Union Development Agency – NEPAD. (2022). *Second Continental Report on the Implementation of the Agenda 2063*. Midrand. Available at: www.nepad.org.

Andrews, G.P. & Leonard, S.Y. (2018). Reflect, Analyze, Act, Repeat: Creating Critical Consciousness through Critical Service-Learning at a Professional Development School. *Education Sciences*, 8(3): 148. https://doi.org/10.3390/educsci8030148.

Association for the Advancement of Sustainability in Higher Education. (2024). *STARS Technical Manual*. Boston. Available at: https://stars.aashe.org/resources-support/technical-manual/. Date accessed: 15 March 2024.

Barber, C., Torney-Purta, J., Wilkenfeld, B. & Jessica Ross. (2015). Immigrant and native-born adolescents' civic knowledge and attitudes in Sweden and the United States: Emergent citizenship within developmental niches. *Research in Comparative and International Education*, 10(1): 23–47. https://doi.org/10.1177/1745499914567818.

Bawa, A. (2007). Rethinking the Place of Community-Based Engagement at Universities. In McIlrath, L. and Mac Labhrainn, I. (ed.) *Higher Education and Civic Engagement: International Perspectives*. England: Ashgate, 56–63.

Bawa, A. (2021). Reimagining South Africa's universities as social institutions. In Brink, C. (ed.) *The Responsive University and the Crisis in South Africa*. Leiden: Brill, 179–215.

Bobick, B. (2019). Promoting Civic Engagement Through University Curricula. In Information Resources Management (ed.) *Civic Engagement and Politics: Concepts, Methodologies, Tools, and Applications*. Hershey, PA: IGI Global, 776–793. https://doi.org/10.4018/978-1-5225-7669-3.ch038.

Bowie, A. & Cassim, F. (2016). Linking classroom and community: A theoretical alignment of service learning and a human-centered design methodology in contemporary communication design education. *Education as Change*, 20(1): 126–148.

Bringle, R.G. & Hatcher, J.A. (1996). Implementing Service Learning in Higher Education. *Journal of Higher Education*, 67(2).

Bringle, R.G. & Hatcher, J.A. (2009). Innovative practices in service-learning and curricular engagement. *New Directions for Higher Education*, (147): 37–46. https://doi.org/10.1002/he.356.

Carayannis, E.G., Barth, T.D. & Campbell, D.F. (2012). The Quintuple Helix innovation model: global warming as a challenge and driver for innovation. *Journal of Innovation and Entrepreneurship*, 1(1): 2. https://doi.org/10.1186/2192-5372-1-2.

Ceccaroni, L., Bowser, A. & Brenton, P. (2019). Civic Education and Citizen Science: Definitions, Categories, Knowledge Representation. In Information Resources Management Association (ed.) *Civic Engagement and Politics: Concepts, Methodologies, Tools, and Applications*. Hershey, PA: IGI Global, 1–23. https://doi.org/10.4018/978-1-5225-7669-3.ch001.

Chadha, A. (2022). Civic Engagement: Modeling an Online Deliberative Collaboration. *International Journal of Web-Based Learning and Teaching Technologies*, 17(1): 1–13. https://doi.org/10.4018/ijwltt.316158.

Choi, Y., Han, J. & Kim, H. (2023). Exploring key service-learning experiences that promote students' learning in higher education. *Asia Pacific Education Review*. https://doi.org/10.1007/s12564-023-09833-5.

Collinson, B. & Best, D. (2019). Promoting Recovery from Substance Misuse through Engagement with Community Assets: Asset Based Community Engagement. *Substance Abuse: Research and Treatment*, 13. https://doi.org/10.1177/1178221819876575.

Costandius, E. & Odiboh, F. (2016). Introduction. In Costandius. E. & Odiboh, F. (ed.) *The Relevance of Critical Citizenship Education in an African Context*. Stellenbosch: African Sun Media, 1–18.

Davis, G. (2021). An irredeemable time? The rising tide of hostility towards universities. In Brink, C. (ed.) *The responsive university and the crisis in South Africa*. Brill, 15–26.

Dials-Corujo, S. (2019). Connecting Concepts of Self-Efficacy, Engaged Scholarship, and Civic Responsibility Among Student-Veterans. In Information Resources Management Association (ed.) *Civic Engagement and Politics: Concepts, Methodologies, Tools, and Applications.* Hershey, PA: IGI Global, 320–333. https://doi.org/10.4018/978-1-5225-7669-3.ch016.

Dolan, P. (2022). Social support, empathy, social capital and civic engagement: Intersecting theories for youth development. *Education, Citizenship and Social Justice*, 17(3): 255–267. https://doi.org/10.1177/17461979221136368.

Earth Charter International. (2023). *The Earth Charter – Preamble*. Available at: https://earthcharter.org/read-the-earth-charter/download-the-charter/. Date accessed: 15 March 2024.

Engebretsen, E., Wahlberg, A. & Ottersen, O.P. (2021). Counter Innovations: The responsibility of universities to act on the SDGs. In Brink , C. (ed.) *The responsive university and the crisis in South Africa*. Leiden: Brill, 106–119.

Falco, E. (2019). Digital Community Planning : The Open Source Way to the Top of Arnstein's Ladder. In Information Resources Management Association (ed.) *Civic Engagement and Politics: Concepts, Methodologies, Tools, and Applications*. Hershey, PA: IGI Global, 152–176. https://doi.org/10.4018/978-1-5225-7669-3.ch008.

Fletcher, F. (2008). Community-University Partnerships: Community Engagement for Transformative Learning. *Canadian Journal of University Continuing Education*, 34(2): 31–45.

Fung, A. (2006). Varieties of Participation in Complex Governance. *Public Administration Review*, 66: 66–75.

Furco, A. (2007). Institutionalising Service-Learning in Higher Education. In McIlrath, L. & Mac Labhrainn, I. (ed.) *Higher Education and Civic Engagement: International Perspectives*. England: Ashgate, 65–81.

Glover, R.W., Lewis, D.C., Meagher, R. & Owens, K.A. (2021). Advocating for Engagement: Do Experiential Learning Courses Boost Civic Engagement? *Journal of Political Science Education*, 17(S1): 599–615. https://doi.org/10.1080/15512169.2020.1831932.

Gordon, N.A. & Dixon, J. (2021). The United Nations Sustainable Development Goals: a setting for Professional and Research skills. *New Directions in the Teaching of Physical Sciences*, (16). https://doi.org/10.29311/ndtps.v0i16.3660.

Grey, S. (2014). Indigenous Knowledge. In Michalos, A.C. (ed.) *Encyclopaedia of Quality of Life and Well-Being Research*. Springer, 3229–3233.

Guo-Brennan, L., Vanleeuwen, C. & Guo-Brennan, M. (2020). Community-Based Learning For International Graduate Students: Impact and Implications. *Michigan Journal Of Community Service Learning*, 26(2): 39–71.

Hanley, T., Winter, L.A. & Cutts, L. (2013). What is a systematic review? *Counselling Psychology Review*, 28(4): 3. Available at: https://www.researchgate.net/publication/259592128.

Harkins, D.A., Grenier, L.I., Irizarry, C., Robinson, E., Ray, S. & Shea, L.M. (2020). Building Relationships For Critical Service-Learning. *Michigan Journal Of Community Service Learning*, 26(2): 21–38.

Hollister, R.M. (2021). Mobilising the full resources of universities for civic engagement and responsiveness: The comprehensive infusion strategy of Tufts University. In Brink, C. (ed.) *The Responsive University and the Crisis in South Africa*. Leiden: Brill, 27–46.

Huda, M. Qodriah, S., Jasmi, K.A. & Alas, Y. (2019). Empowering Civic Responsibility: Insights From Service Learning. In Information Resources Management Association (ed.) *Civic Engagement and Politics: Concepts, Methodologies, Tools, and Applications*. Hershey, PA: IGI Global, 1325–1341. https://doi.org/10.4018/978-1-5225-7669-3.ch066.

Hunter, M.F. (2019). Deepening of Critical Thinking Skills Through the Use of Civic Engagement. In Information Resources Management Association (ed.) *Civic Engagement and Politics: Concepts, Methodologies, Tools, and Applications*. Hershey, PA: IGI Global, 24–39. https://doi.org/10.4018/978-1-5225-7669-3.ch002.

Hylton, M.E. (2018). The Role of Civic Literacy and Social Empathy on Rates of Civic Engagement Among University Students. *Journal of Higher Education Outreach and Engagement*, 22(1): 87–106.

Johnson, A., McKay-Jackson, C. & Grumbach, G. (2018) *Critical Service Learning Toolkit: Social Work Strategies for Promoting Healthy Youth Development* (first edition). USA: Oxford University Press.

Johnson, B.J. (2020). Community engagement: Barriers and drivers in South African higher education. *South African Journal of Higher Education*, 34(6): 87–105. https://doi.org/10.20853/34-6-4116.

Kari, N. & Skelton, N. (2007). Place Matters: Partnerships for Civic Learning. In McIlrath, L. & Mac Labhrainn, I. (ed.) *Higher Education and Civic Engagement: International Perspectives*. England: Ashgate, 171–184.

Keet, A. & Muthwa, S. (2021). The transformative, responsive university in South Africa. In Brink, C. (ed.) *The responsive university and the crisis in South Africa*. Leiden: Brill, 216–242.

Kim, Y.K., Carter, J.L. & Armstrong, C.L. (2019). Civic Responsibility Development Among College Students: How Is It Different by Student Race? In Information Resources Management Association (ed.) *Civic Engagement and Politics: Concepts, Methodologies, Tools, and Applications*. Hershey, PA: IGI Global, 1068–1086. https://doi.org/10.4018/978-1-5225-7669-3.ch053.

Lange, L. (2021). South African universities between Decolonisation and the fourth industrial revolution. In Brink, C. (ed.) *The Responsive University and the Crisis in South Africa*. Leiden: Brill, 272–299.

Lewing, J.M. (2020). Finding Common (Moral) Ground in Critical Service Learning: Promoting Balance and Civil Discourse Through Moral Foundations Theory. *Journal of Community Engagement and Higher Education*, 12(1): 82–88.

Liu, Y. & Shen, W. (2021). Perching birds or scattered streams: a study of how trust affects civic engagement among university students in contemporary China. *Higher Education*, 81(3): 421–436. https://doi.org/10.1007/s10734-020-00548-9.

Lowery, D. (2007). Community-based Quality of Life Indicators: A Service-Learning Exercise in a Graduate Statistics Class. *Journal of Public Affairs Education*, 13(2): 425–438.

Maphazi, N., Raga, K., Taylor, J.D. & Mayekiso, T. (2013). Public participation: A South African local government perspective. *African Journal of Public Affairs*, 6(2): 56–67.

Mastuti, S., Masse, A. & Tasruddin, R. (2014). University and Community Partnerships in South Sulawesi, Indonesia: Enhancing community capacity and promoting democratic governance. *Gateways: International Journal of Community Research and Engagement*, 7: 164–173.

Moore, T. (2014). Community – University Engagement: A Process for Building Democratic Communities. *ASHE Higher Education Report*, 40(2): 1–129. https://doi.org/10.1002/aehe.20014.

Muff, K., Kapalka, A. & Dyllick, T. (2017). The Gap Frame – Translating the SDGs into relevant national grand challenges for strategic business opportunities. *International Journal of Management Education*, 15(2): 363–383. https://doi.org/10.1016/j.ijme.2017.03.004.

Munn, Z. Peters, M.D.J., Stern, C., Tufanaru, C., McArthur, A. & Aromataris, E. (2018). Systematic review or scoping review? Guidance for authors when choosing between a systematic or scoping review approach. *BMC Medical Research Methodology*, 18(1). https://doi.org/10.1186/s12874-018-0611-x.

Neary, J. & Osborne, M. (2018). University engagement in achieving sustainable development goals: A synthesis of case studies from the SUEUAA study. *Australian Journal of Adult Learning*, 58(3): 336–364.

Oni, A.A., Ayo, C.K. & Azeta, A.A. (2019). Development of an Inclusive Participatory Democracy System. In Information Resources Management Association (ed.) *Civic Engagement and Politics: Concepts, Methodologies, Tools, and Applications*. Hershey, PA: IGI Global, 217–236. https://doi.org/10.4018/978-1-5225-7669-3.ch011.

Pacheco-Vega, R. (2016). Synthesizing different bodies of work in your literature review: The Conceptual Synthesis Excel Dump (CSED) technique. *Raul Pacheco-Vega, PhD: Understanding and solving intractable resource governance problems*. Available at: http://www.raulpacheco.org/2016/06/synthesizing-different-bodies-of-work-in-your-literature-review-the-conceptual-synthesis-excel-dump-technique/. Date accessed: 5 March 2024.

Page, M.J., McKenzie, J.E., Bossuyt, P.M., Boutron, I., Hoffmann, T.C., Mulrow, C.D., Shamseer, L., Tetzlaff, J.M., Akl, E.A., Brennan, S.E., Chou, R., Glanville, J., Grimshaw, J.M., Hróbjartsson, A., Lalu, M.M., Li, T., Loder, E.W., Mayo-Wilson, E., McDonald, S., McGuinness, L.A., Stewart, L.A., Thomas, J., Tricco, A.C., Welch, V.A., Whiting, P. & Moher, D. (2021). The PRISMA 2020 statement: an updated guideline for reporting systematic reviews. *Systematic Reviews*, 10(1). https://doi.org/10.1186/s13643-021-01626-4.

Parker, B. (2003). *Planning Analysis: The Theory of Citizen Participation*. Available at: https://pages.uoregon.edu/rgp/PPPM613/class10theory.htm. Date accessed: 7 March 2024.

Preece, J. (2013). Towards an Africanisation of community engagement and service learning: The global context for universities and engagement. *Perspectives in Education*, 31(2): 114–122.

Preece, J. (2017). *University Community Engagement And Lifelong Learning: The Porous University*. Palgrave Macmillan. https://doi.org/10.1007/978-3-319-56163-9.

Rasmussen, A. & Reher, S. (2019). Civil Society Engagement and Policy Representation in Europe. *Comparative Political Studies*, 52(11): 1648–1676. https://doi.org/10.1177/0010414019830724.

Reed, M.S., Vella, S., de Vente, J. & Challies, E. (2018). A theory of participation: what makes stakeholder and public engagement in environmental management work? *Restoration Ecology*. Blackwell Publishing Inc., S7–S17. https://doi.org/10.1111/rec.12541.

Sachs, J.D., Schmidt-Traub, G., Mazzucato, M., Messner, D., Nakicenovic, N. & Rockström, J. (2019). Six Transformations to achieve the Sustainable Development Goals. *Nature Sustainability*, 2(9): 805–814. https://doi.org/10.1038/s41893-019-0352-9.

Saltmarsh, J., Janke, E.M. & Clayton, P.H. (2015). Transforming Higher Education Through and For Democratic Civic Engagement: A Model for Change. *Michigan Journal of Community Service Learning: The SLCE Future Directions Project*, Fall 122–127.

Sowula, T., Boland, M. & Cader, I. (2022) *How universities can achieve equitable, accountable and measurable change for sustainability: A Global Sustainable Development report*. University of Glasgow. Available at: https://s3.amazonaws.com/bizzabo.users.files/149250/388152/8742165/Global%20Sustainable%20Development%20Congress%202022%20event%20report.pdf. Date accessed: 15 March 2024.

Stanberry, J. & Bragan, B.J. (2024). A conceptual review of Sustainable Development Goal 17: Picturing politics, proximity and progress. *Journal of Tropical Futures: Sustainable Business, Governance & Development*, 1(1): 110–139. https://doi.org/10.1177/27538931231170509.

Sutton, M. (2008). Knowledge citizenship for active informed citizenship. *South African Journal of Information Management*, 10(4). https://doi.org/https://doi.org/10.4102/sajim.v10i4.335.

Swanzen, R. (2015). Enabling the adoption of service-learning in the higher education curriculum. In Lin, P.L. et al (ed.) *Service-learning in Higher Education: Building community across the globe*. Indianapolis: University of Indianapolis Press, 179–194.

Taylor, R. (2007). Concepts of Citizenship in the Context of Political Education. In McIlrath, L. & Mac Labhrainn, I. (ed.) *Higher Education and Civic Engagement: International Perspectives*. England: Ashgate, 3–12.

The World Bank. (1998). *Indigenous Knowledge Definitions, Concepts and Applications.* Available at: https://chm.cbd.int/api/v2013/documents/4A27922D-31BC-EEFF-7940-DB40D6DB706B/attachments/209070/Hoda%20Yacoub%20-%20IK%20Report%20(1).pdf.

Times Higher Education. (2024). *University Impact Rankings 2025.* Available at: https://www.timeshighereducation.com/impactrankings. Date accessed: 25 March 2024.

Tufts University. (2005). *The Talloires Declaration: On the Civic Roles and Social Responsibilities of Higher Education.* Available at: https://talloiresnetwork.tufts.edu/wp-content/uploads/TalloiresDeclaration2005.pdf. Date accessed: 25 March 2024.

UNESCO. (2014). *Policy Brief: Skills for Holistic Human Development.* 2. Available at: https://unesdoc.unesco.org/ark:/48223/pf0000245064/PDF/245064eng.pdf.multi. Date accessed: 30 March 2024.

Union of International Associations. (2022.) *UIA Global Civil Society Database.* Available at: https://uia.org/s/sdg/en/. Date accessed: 25 March 2024.

Warren-Gordon, K., Hudson, K. & Scott, F. (2020). Voices of Partnerships Within the Critical Service-Learning Framework. *Journal of Community Engagement and Higher Education,* 12(2): 17–25.

Weber, P., Wagner, S.A. & Kabst, R (2019). Public Participation Distribution and Marketing: An Inseparable Duality. In Information Resources Management Association (ed.) *Civic Engagement and Politics: Concepts, Methodologies, Tools, and Applications.* Hershey, PA: IGI Global, 483–495. https://doi.org/10.4018/978-1-5225-7669-3.ch024.

Welch, M. (2007). Identifying and Teaching Civic Engagement Skills through Service Learning. In McIlrath, L. & Mac Labhrainn, I. (ed.) *Higher Education and Civic Engagement: International Perspectives.* England: Ashgate, 103–120.

Wiesli, T.X., Liebe, U., Hammer, T. & Bär, R. (2021). Sustainable Quality of Life: A Conceptualization that Integrates the Views of Inhabitants of Swiss Rural Regions. *Sustainability (Switzerland),* 13(16). https://doi.org/10.3390/su13169187.

Wilson, L. & Newmark, R. (2015). The university of the future: Quality-of-life platforms integrated with effective practice in community engagement. In Phylis, L. et al (ed.) *Service-learning in Higher Education: Building community across the globe.* Indianapolis: University of Indianapolis Press, 255–271.

Wouters, P., Derrick, G.E., Faria, R., Benneworth, P., Budtz-Petersen, D. & Sivertsen, G. (2018). *Towards characterising negative impact: Introducing Grimpact.* Proceedings of the 23rd International Conference on Science and Technology Indicators.

Zlotkowski, E. (2007). The Case for Service Learning. In McIlrath, L. & Mac Labhrainn, I. (ed.) *Higher Education and Civic Engagement: International Perspectives.* England: Ashgate, 25–36.

Zondi, S. (2021). Protests and Pursuits: The South African University in turmoil and the search for a decolonial turn. In Brink, C. (ed.) *The responsive university and the crisis in South Africa.* Leiden: Brill, 243–271.

CHAPTER 13

Transformative dynamics in South African higher education: An economic lens on student and staff transformation

Leigh Neethling

Abstract

This chapter offers a comprehensive descriptive analysis of students and staff in the South African higher education sector. Drawing on extensive data from the Department of Higher Education, Council on Higher Education, and Statistics South Africa spanning the years 2004 to 2021, this chapter delves into the shifting landscape of student enrolment by race and gender, as well as the evolving staff profiles in terms of race, gender, and qualification.

This chapter provides an insightful exploration of the complex challenges and opportunities embedded within the South African higher education system and endeavours to present a nuanced and holistic view of the ongoing transformation in South African higher education through the presentation of data. It underscores the intricate relationship between socioeconomic factors and the educational journey, offering fresh perspectives on how South African higher education has attempted to address disparities and become a driver of equitable economic development. This chapter is an important contribution to the ongoing discourse on the pivotal role of education in fostering inclusivity and driving economic transformation in South Africa.

Keywords: enrolment; progression; transformation; trend analysis; higher education.

Critical issue: diversity and inclusion: overview of the higher education landscape 2004–2020

Introduction

South Africa remains one of the most unequal countries in the world on two key metrics often used to interrogate the status of an economy – income and wealth (Hundenborn et al., 2018; Leibbrandt & Pabón, 2021; Orthofer, 2016). Income in a broad sense is what individuals earn through the supply of their labour, and the resulting distribution of income is often used as a measure of the health of an economy. On the other hand, wealth is the accumulation of economic assets over time. While income is typically considered to be a flow variable, changing from year to year, wealth is considered a stock variable as it usually measures the value of accumulated economic assets at a particular date. Quite clearly the two concepts are closely related – one cannot hope for wealth accumulation without excesses of income to build the pool of accumulated economic assets that grow into wealth.

The level of income that individuals earn is largely dependent on their educational attainment (Branson et al., 2009), and this is especially true in a country like South Africa which has one of the highest levels of income and wealth inequality in the world. Studies on the distribution of income in South Africa stretch quite far back, peaking during the 1990s and 2000s. Research based on South Africa's labour market shows that we have the highest returns to education in the world and that the return or premium to completed education remains high. In fact, Keswell and Poswell (2004) show that the returns to education rise with the level of education completed, and that completed tertiary education demands the highest marginal returns in the South African labour market. This finding is insensitive to the methodology and time period of analysis.

The economic benefits of post-secondary schooling at an individual and societal level are well established (McMahon, 2009). Research for South Africa shows that individuals with tertiary qualifications are significantly less likely to be unemployed, more likely to be formally employed (Branson & Leibbrandt, 2013), face shorter periods of unemployment (Nonyana & Njuho, 2018), are twice as likely to obtain employment than individuals who only completed grade 12, and are significantly more likely to be self-employed than unemployed (Branson et al., 2009). In addition to the labour market participation effects noted above, individuals with tertiary education qualifications are expected to earn significantly higher lifetime earnings compared to individuals with incomplete high school or matric qualifications. Relative to individuals with incomplete high school qualifications, individuals with a degree or certificate earn between 170% and 220% more, and individuals who completed a degree earn between 250% and 400% more than individuals who had incomplete matric qualifications between 2000 and 2007 (Branson et al., 2009).

Numerous socio-economic issues confront South Africa, such as excessive income and wealth inequality, high unemployment rates, and underwhelming basic and secondary education systems. Given these difficulties and the improved labour market outcomes noted earlier, the HE system can play a significant role in eliminating social disparities by enhancing access and outcomes by producing graduates with the necessary skills to ensure the nation's economic success. Along with encouraging access to opportunities that increase labour market participation, this also increases social mobility by increasing income and wealth mobility (Statistics South Africa, 2019).

When we enter discussions on the role of the HE sector in promoting improved distribution of income and wealth, the discussion tends to focus on access to higher education (HE). Studies investigating the impact of HE on labour market opportunities and returns are predicated on educational attainment and not access or participation. For an economy to grapple with educational attainment, it remains crucial to understand how students progress through HE by focusing first on access and participation. This naturally leads to an evaluation of student success within HE.

The *White Paper for post-school education and training: Building and expanded, effective and integrated post-school system* (2013) sets out South Africa's post-school transformation imperatives and documents the vision for the type of system the government hopes to achieve by 2030. This aligns with the National Development Plan (NDP) (National Planning Commission, 2011) which details many 2030 economic development goal targets. A key imperative is to create a transformed HE sector with respect to educational access and attainment, as this will empower previously excluded groups to access better paying jobs and, in turn, stimulate wealth creation. One specific target is to achieve headcount enrolment of 1,6 million in public universities within a system that is cognizant of the demographics of the country. In addition to improving equity of access, there should be a focus on improving equity in student outcomes. On the staffing side, there is a need to change the profile of academic staff to become more representative, especially from a demographic point of view.

This chapter traces student and staff transformation at an aggregate level, discussing in detail some of the specific issues facing South African HE today, from who qualifies for entry to student success rates for the period 2004–2021. The chapter draws on extensive data from the Department of Higher Education and Training (DHET), the Council on Higher Education (CHE) and Statistics South Africa. While the first part of this chapter focuses on student outcomes within the sector, the second part focuses on academic staff within the system. It is important to place this discussion in context – while South Africa has improved access to HE, the same level of gains have not been noted in success or throughput rates for each identified population racial group. Each of the three issues mentioned above – access, enrolment, and progression – are discussed in further detail in each sub-section.

Before applying the economic lens to HE data, it is useful to describe and discuss the national South African HE landscape. This is relevant because it provides the background and context for the subsequent chapters and findings, and shows the entrenched disparities in educational and economic outcomes that permeate the South African economy.

The primary objective of this chapter is to present an exploratory and descriptive analysis of the South African HE sector over the period 2004–2021. This chapter focuses on a descriptive analysis of key South African HE indicators and outcomes to emphasise the differentiated set of academic outcomes that are observed across the student body and the heterogeneity of students' experiences. The first objective is to evaluate access to HE: the pool of potential entrants is identified by examining the school-leaving cohort of each year. The second objective is to identify racial enrolment, progression, and completion patterns and observe whether significant changes have occurred over the period. This should be viewed relative to the goals of the DHET and NDP.

Since the end of Apartheid, higher education institutions (HEIs) have been open to all South Africans. The South African government broke down and removed structural blockages that prevented students from attending HEIs of their choice and implemented policies to expand the HE sector to encourage participation. This included creating special units within universities that focused on increased affirmative action admissions into dedicated programmes designed exclusively for previously disadvantaged students only. It also entailed updating admission criteria to take into account the possible under-preparedness of students from government or public sector high schools; and setting targets or benchmarks in the admission profile of new entering first-year students. Despite these interventions, the HE sector is still categorised by low participation and high dropout rates (Fisher & Scott, 2011). This chapter presents a detailed discussion on the South African landscape of access and enrolment to present a background on the current state of HE and to draw attention to the differences that may exist between different groups.

It is widely acknowledged that challenges in the basic education system hamper access to and participation in HE.[5] Branson et al. (2014) conducted one of the most thorough reviews of progress through school (primary and high school) using data from South Africa's only longitudinal survey, the National Income Dynamics Study, and they found that only about 50% of students who start grade 1 reach grade 12. They tracked individuals over time and followed young people through their schooling careers and found that most dropout occurs in high school after grade 7, the largest numbers being between grades 9 and 11. Their findings support those of the Department of Basic Education that almost 40% of students have dropped out by the time they reach Grade 11, leaving a smaller pool of students to write the school exit examinations and even fewer who qualify for access to HE.

South Africa has one of the lowest rates of HE relative to adult population in the world. Despite some improvements in participation in the HE sector, only 2,2% of South Africans between the ages of 25 and 64 have completed a HE qualification (Statistics South Africa, 2019). This compares unfavourably with

---

[5] Basic education refers to the 12 years of primary (seven years) and high (five years) school in South Africa.

other middle-income or developing countries and leaves South Africa trailing developed economies significantly. In Brazil, at least 5% of the adult population have a bachelor's degree, and the proportion is much higher in the US at almost 30% (OECD, 2021).

Completion rates in the universities are also problematic. Only 45% of those who register for university degrees in South Africa ever complete their degrees (Fisher & Scott, 2011; DHET, 2018). In addition, there are considerable differences in graduation rates by race, gender, and qualification type (Fisher & Scott, 2011). Not only do race and gender affect HE entry and graduation rates, they also affect the grades obtained by students and hence their prospects for entry to higher levels of tertiary study. This is an issue that has received little attention to date. In addition, little attention has been given to staff transformation in HE. This is especially true for academic staff, who are typically engaging with students on a daily basis.

Before proceeding to the detailed discussion in the following sections, it is prudent to briefly define key concepts that recur within the discussion. The first concept that requires a specific definition is 'success'. The term success, as used in this chapter, refers to individuals who have completed the requirements for the award of the qualification.

The racial classifications commonly applied in South Africa may be problematic for those unfamiliar with the country. The apartheid government divided the population into four primary population groups or classifications, namely white, black (African), coloured, and Indian (including individuals of Asian descent), and these classifications were enforced via identity numbers and identity documents. The coloured group represents individuals of mixed-race and served as a catch-all for those who were not included in the other three groups. For the purposes of this chapter, the terms 'black' and 'African' are used interchangeably, with African being the preferred term for black South Africans.

Data and methods

This chapter draws on extensive data from DHET, CHE, and StatsSA, covering the period 2004 to 2021. The data includes detailed information on student enrolment, progression, graduation, and dropout rates, as well as staff demographics in South African higher education institutions. The analysis focuses on public universities, which enrol the majority of students in the higher education sector, as data on private institutions is limited and less consistently reported. The time period was selected to capture the transformative dynamics in South African higher education following the end of Apartheid, and to highlight changes that may be uncovered through simple data exploration.

The study employs a descriptive and exploratory data approach to analyse trends in student and staff transformation. Key indicators such as gross enrolment ratios (GER), course success rates, graduation rates, and dropout rates are examined to assess progress in achieving the goals outlined in the National Development Plan (NDP) and the *White Paper for post-school education and training: Building and expanded, effective and integrated post-school system* (2013). The analysis is disaggregated by race and gender to highlight disparities and progress among different demographic groups. Additionally, the study tracks changes in the racial and gender composition of academic staff to evaluate progress in staff transformation. Data on student outcomes is analysed at both the aggregate level and by cohort, with students tracked over a ten-year period to account for extended study durations and delayed graduations.

While the data provides valuable insights into the state of HE in South Africa, there are several limitations to note. First, the analysis is constrained by the availability of publicly reported data, which may not capture all dimensions of student and staff experiences. Second, the study relies on aggregate data, which limits the ability to conduct institution-specific analyses or explore the impact of individual-level factors on student outcomes. Finally, the data does not always account for contextual factors such as socioeconomic background, school quality, or geographic location, which may influence access to and success in HE. Despite these limitations, the study offers a comprehensive overview of the transformative dynamics in South African higher education and provides a foundation for future research and policy interventions.

Students

Access

Access to HE in South Africa is determined almost entirely based on student performance in the grade 12 school-leaving final examinations[6]. These standardised examinations are written by approximately 400000 – 550000 scholars[7] per year and overseen by the Department of Basic Education in conjunction with provincial departments of basic education, running over an eight-week period from October to early December each year[8]. Students' final results determine if they receive firm offers for a place of study in HE in the next academic year. Approximately 70% of grade 12 students who achieve bachelor passes go on to enter HE, and only 45% of these students will ever graduate with an undergraduate degree (DHET, 2018).

The South African education system has experienced notable growth in recent years, especially in higher education. While there has been an increase

---

[6] In recent years universities have required students to write the National Benchmark Tests (NBTs). The results from the NBTs and the student's grade 12 examination results would determine if an offer for a place of study is made. However, for the period covered by this thesis, the NBTs are not relevant.

[7] Use of the term 'scholar' is indicative of an individual in the basic education system. Student refers to an individual in the higher education sector.

[8] In South Africa, the academic and calendar years coincide.

in the absolute number of youth enrolling in higher education, the observed increases have been in line with the increases in South Africa's youth population (Branson et al., 2009). Compared to a decade ago, a larger proportion of young people enter higher education today. Growth in this sector has resulted from three major sources. First, there has been a substantial increase in the number of scholars completing basic education each year. Many more South Africans are completing high school with a bachelor pass[9] and thereby qualifying for entry to HE today compared to ten years ago. Second, there have been modest increases in the number of places available. Between 2011 and 2015 the number of study places available increased by 47011. This translates into an annual average growth rate of 1,2% over the same period, significantly down from an average rate of 4% over the previous five-year period. Lastly, the graduation rate is higher than the enrolment rate, averaging 4,5% higher over the 2011–2015 period. This counter-intuitive outcome is likely due to the fact that students who enrolled in earlier years are graduating in later years, or taking longer to complete qualifications, leading to higher graduation rates relative to enrolment in a given year (DHET, 2018). We observe a much higher demand for higher education today while the supply of places has plateaued in recent years.

Figure 13.1 shows a summary of the school exit examinations between 2004 and 2021. The number of students writing the school exit examinations has fluctuated over the period under consideration but has shown a general upward trend. The proportion of students passing and meeting some minimum criteria for entry to HE, shown by the proportion of bachelor passes, has consistently increased. This is one indicator of rising demand for HE due to increased eligibility.

---

[9] Grade 12 students writing their final examinations must achieve a government-mandated pass criteria called a bachelor pass that grants students entry to HE. Many universities set entrance requirements much higher than the minimum criteria for a bachelor pass.

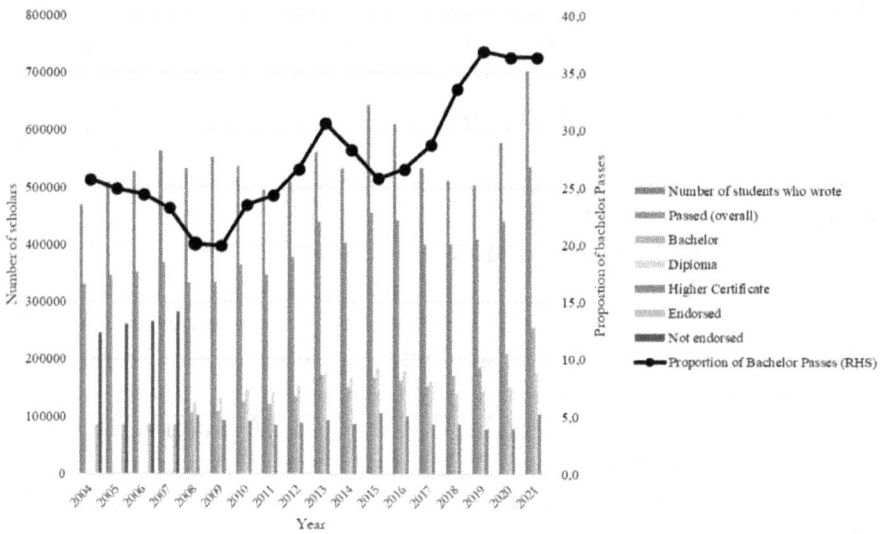

FIGURE 13.1: Summary of high school exit examinations: 2004–2021
Data: Department of Basic Education (2004–2021) and Statistics South Africa (2018)

Prior to 2008, scholars wrote the old senior certificate (SC) curriculum examinations where students were required to achieve an endorsed pass on their final school-leaving examinations to be eligible to enroll at a HEI. In an effort to improve the quality of schooling and cognitive outcomes for school-leavers, the new senior certificate (NSC) was introduced, with the first cohort writing these school exit-level exams at the end of 2008. The NSC ranked eligibility to HE on a three-tiered system: bachelor (university) entry, diploma and higher certificates (at the college level) from highest to lowest respectively. To be eligible for degree-level (bachelor) studies on the new senior certificate (NSC) students must achieve a minimum of a 2 or 30% for their chosen home language subject and at least a 4 or 50% in four chosen subjects.

The two school-leaving exit systems are not directly comparable as the government did not set strict matching criteria between the old and new systems. Research conducted in 2010 reveals that NSC results map to SC about 20% higher depending on the students' location in the distribution, meaning that a student who would have achieved 60% on the old SC exams could expect to achieve 80% on the NSC exams (Schoer et al., 2010). Further research in this area, and across cohorts of students exiting with the NSC, have shown similar results.

This grade inflation is one reason for the significant jump in university qualifiers between 2007 and 2008. Figure 13.1 shows the number of students who are eligible for entry to bachelor's study between 2007 and 2008 increased by 9% points from 23,2% in 2007 to 32,2% in 2008, or roughly an increase of 21820 students.

Between 2008 and 2021, there was a 138% increase in the number of scholars who passed their school-leaving examinations with a bachelor's pass. During this period there were no additional universities opened in South Africa nor a significant expansion in the availability of study places, placing undue pressure on the already limited places available.

An important caveat to highlight at this juncture is that access to HE is multi-faceted and cannot be reduced to a single-factor barrier. The difficulty in accessing information around the availability of opportunities including programme offerings, entry requirements, and how to apply remain significant barriers to improved access. These barriers are exacerbated by differences in location or geography, with rural students at a distinct informational disadvantage, as well as students from poorer schools who have significantly poorer trajectories through school and in school leaving examinations (Branson et al., 2014; Schoer et al., 2010).

The next section examines enrolment patterns and trends by racial composition to trace any changes from qualifiers to enrolments.

Enrolment

The South African HE landscape is a deeply fragmented one. Prior to 1994, universities were not freely open to all students. Instead, access was based on race. Once the democratic government took over in 1994, the process began to de-racialise HEIs. Historical legacy issues meant that enrolments at the different HEIs were still skewed based on race and income, creating a highly divided HE sector.

The HE sector has undergone a significant transformation over the past few years. To create a more efficient HE sector, the government consolidated the number of institutions while re-purposing others. Until 2014, South Africa had 23 public universities. Between 2003 and 2005 the HE sector underwent significant transformation and the number of HEIs were consolidated from 36 to 23 (DHET, 2023). Two new universities opened in 2014, namely the University of Mpumalanga and Sol Plaatje University. The Sefako Makagatho Health Sciences University commenced operation in 2015, enrolling its first students for the 2015 academic year. This takes the present-day number of public universities to 26 that enroll the majority of students in the HE sector. About 15% of university students enroll in private universities but very little is known about students' performance in private HEs, so this analysis focuses on the public universities where information is available more freely.

Identifying the absorptive capacity constraints in public universities has been rather difficult as many universities do not disclose their enrolment capacity constraints. The reason many universities face capacity constraints is largely due to space constraints, with campus and building size constraints being binding in terms of national health and safety regulations.

Initial investigations reveal that the number of places for new first years has remained static over the period under consideration. Universities such as the

University of Cape Town (UCT), University of Johannesburg (UJ), University of the Witwatersrand (Wits), and Stellenbosch University (SU) have not significantly increased their enrolment capacity over the period of investigation. As universities are not obliged to publicly report an annual admissions or enrolment (absorptive) capacity, the next best option is to evaluate the limited enrolment statistics over the period.

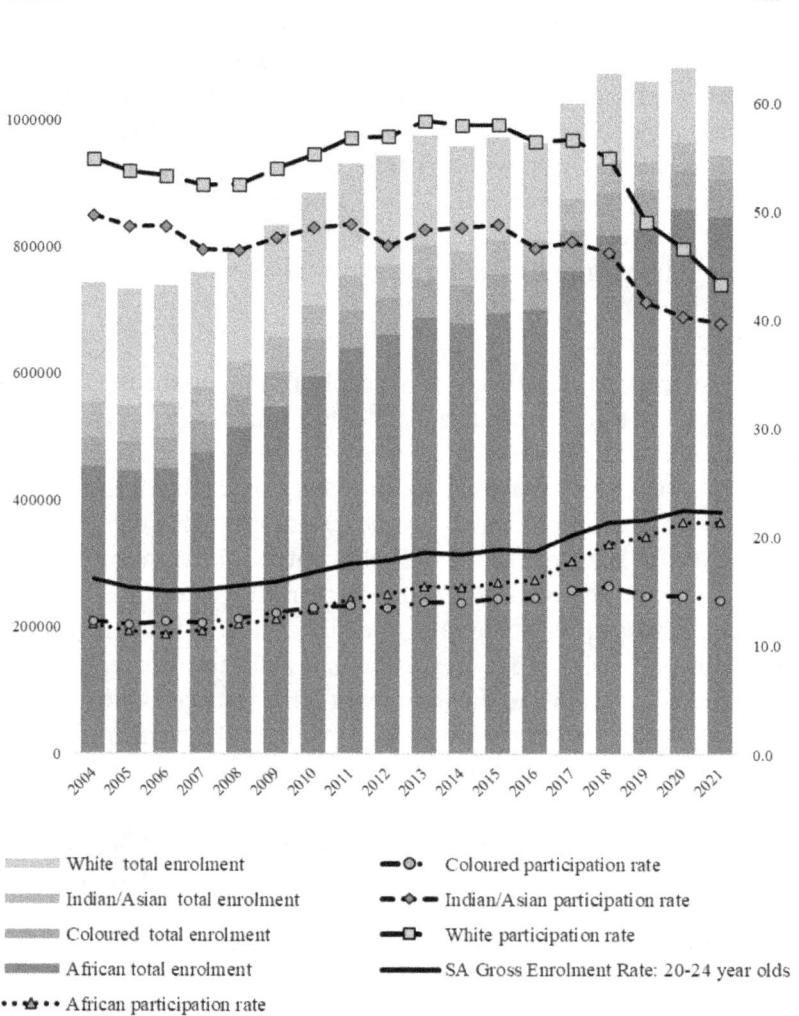

Figure 13.2: South African higher education enrolment: 2004–2021

The figure shows headcount enrolments and participation rates (RHS) in South African higher education from 2004 to 2021. Participation rates are calculated as the proportion of 20–24 year-olds in a particular group who are enrolled in HE.

Data: Council on Higher Education (2023) and Statistics South Africa (2022)

The first indicator of significance is the gross enrolment ratio or GER. The National Plan for Higher Education (2001) sets out a post-secondary participation target of 20%, as defined by the gross enrolment ratio (GER) (Ministry of Education, 2001). The GER is a participation rate measuring the number of 20–24 years olds in the general population who are enrolled in HE. Figure 13.2 shows enrolment and participation rates in HE by race, highlighting the disparities between different racial groups. While white students have the highest participation rates, African students show steady growth over the period, reflecting ongoing efforts to improve access for historically disadvantaged groups. For context, in 2014, North America had a gross enrolment ratio in excess of 84% compared to Sub-Saharan Africa at approximately 8% (Roser & Ortiz-Ospina, 2013). The long-term GER for South Africa is 15%, which is above Sub-Saharan averages but compares poorly to other middle-income countries. This new target was set to promote and achieve equity in access and success, improve transformation in the HE sector, and to increase the number of graduates in South Africa. Importantly, from the transformational perspective, the DHET has set out to transform the sector to replicate the demographic profile of the country within HE. This is to ensure that the country has a steady supply of graduates that will also transform the labour market in the future and create equity and equality amongst labour market participants.

At an aggregate level an improvement in HE participation is noted. Figure 13.2 shows that by 2015, South Africa had not yet reached one million students participating in HE. It is evident from Figure 13.2 that the HE system shows continuous increases in enrolment over the period with significant gains between 2008 and 2012.

The GER target was first exceeded in 2017, and this has been maintained since. Between 2008 and 2013 the South African participation rate increased by 2,6% points from 16,6% to 19,2% (StatsSA, 2013). The aggregate percentages mask significant racial differences observed in the data. Figure 13.2 shows the actual headcount for South African HE and the participation rates by race. It is evident from Figure 13.2 that the participation rate for whites has increased quite strongly from 2008 to 2017, while the coloured participation rates has remained largely flat. African individuals display slow but steady growth over the whole period. Indian/Asian students show an average decline in the participation rate over the period, with a trend that mirrors that of white individuals. Note that the coloured participation rate does not exceed the benchmark 20% at all during the period, while African participation rates exceed the GER benchmark for a first time in 2019. This pattern has persisted in the presence of favourable affirmative action policies at historically white institutions.

Another indicator of significance is a measure of the ratio of the number of first-time entering (FU) students to the number of bachelor passes in the previous academic year. Figure 13.3 graphically presents this absorptive indicator. This ratio is a measure of the absorptive capacity of HEIs. The ratio shows that not all students who qualify enter HE in the year immediately following their grade 12 year due to various factors. It also shows that some sort of HE capacity constraint was reached by 2010. After 2010 the ratio exhibits a downward trend. The ratio may fall for two reasons. As Figure 13.1 shows consistent increases in the number of students writing exit examinations and achieving bachelor-level passes, neither the numerator nor the denominator in this ratio remains constant, implying relative changes in each variable may be driving the pattern observed in Figure 13.3. In this instance, a faster rise in the number of students achieving bachelor passes relative to the number of students entering HE is indicative of the absorptive capacity of institutions reaching a ceiling. Furthermore, without additional absorptive capacity being created by HEIs either through the creation of new HEIs or existing HEIs enrolling more students, matriculants are left with fewer post-school choices. This observation is consistent with trends observed in labour market statistics where more young people are filtering into the labour market each year. The lack of work opportunities means that many youths do not enter employment instead of education, causing a rise in the number of young people not in education, employment, or training (NEET) category.

Despite African participation rates increasing by 31% over the period, the increase comes off a relatively small base. The increase in nominal terms amounts to almost a quarter of a million students. Even in the face of such large nominal increases, it is still not enough to meet the targeted participation rate of 20% or to create equitable participation in HE as desired by the government.

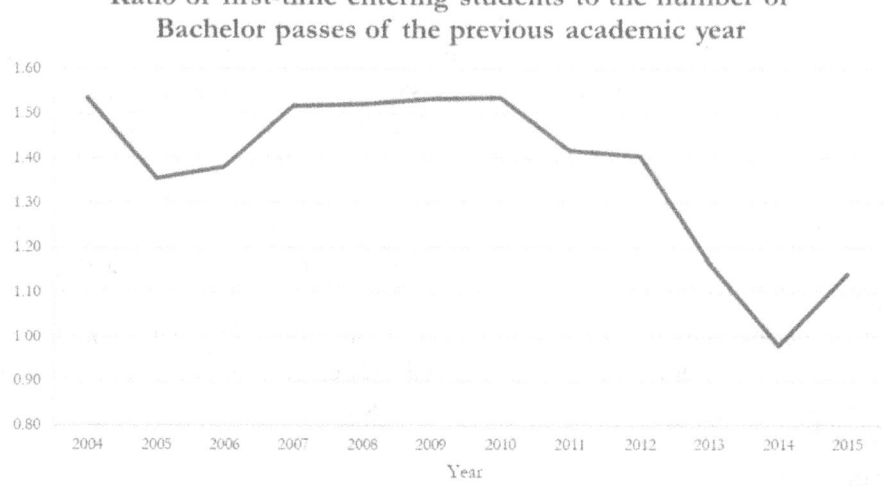

FIGURE 13.3: Ratio of first-time entering students to the number of bachelor passes of the previous academic year

Data: DHET, 2023

Despite this growth from the demand side in the HE sector, only 2,2% of South Africans between 25 and 64 have completed a higher education qualification (StatsSA, 2016). When broken into narrower age categories, higher education acquisition shows significantly more variation. For individuals between the ages of 25 to 34 years, South Africa has a share of 5,6% in 2018, compared to Brazil with 21%, and the US 51,8% over the same age range. Russia, Canada, and South Korea exceed the 60% share of individuals aged 25–34 years with completed higher education. This does not compare favourably with other middle income or developing countries, and leaves South Africa trailing developed economies quite significantly.

Progression and dropout

There are notable gains in terms of success in the HE sector, even though the sector remains highly fragmented. The previous section highlighted the increasing headcount enrolments in HE over the period under investigation, which were largely driven by a sharp increase in the number of African students, which increased by over 30% for the period under consideration. The next subsection breaks down the throughput and success categories and examines outcomes by race and gender to gain greater insight into the differences between groups. The breakdown by race largely aligns with the commonly held belief that race is a strong proxy for income levels in South Africa, where income levels are also often a proxy for the quality of school education obtainable as South African state schools are not all free. The gender breakdown aligns with commonly reported statistics on performance and correlates with an appreciation of the gender gap in education.

Progression

Success in HE may be viewed from a number of perspectives as there is no common definition or universally accepted measure of student success. Universities use a variety of measures as indicators of success as the institutional level allows for the interrogation of data at the individual student level. The use of multiple measures is meant to cut across a static representation of the data to show a more detailed and nuanced picture of the student experience over time.

The most common indicator used worldwide is that of the number of students who graduate. As mentioned above, with the low historical completion rate in South Africa, this indicator is important because it allows for South Africa to be compared to other countries. While this is significant, it remains critical to know how students move through the system, leading to the next measure, that of success rates.

Course success rates

South African universities are required by law to measure and release indicators of success rates. Course or student success rates are one such measure of success and is an established primary indicator of student progression. Course or student success rates measure the percentage of courses that as student has successfully completed in any given year. Nationally, a benchmark of 80% was set by the DHET, indicating that students are required to pass a minimum of 80% of all enrolled courses in any given year of study to maintain the highest chances of meeting the minimum requirements for award of the qualification within the n+2 period. Figure 13.4 shows a breakdown of course success rates by race to illustrate how students have fared relative to the benchmark.

There are three important points raised by the data in Figure 13.4. First, at the national level, no race group exceeded the 80% benchmark prior to 2008. Since 2008, only one group has exceeded the national benchmark – white students. While other race groups show upward trends in course success rates over time, the other three main groups have not exceeded the benchmark. Importantly, the graph does not allow for analytical breakdown of success rates by race across institutions, an analysis that is very important in the context of highly unequal post-secondary institutions in South Africa.

The second important observation from Figure 13.4 is that African students show the largest improvements over the period when compared to all students. White students show the second-highest improvement over the period, but start from a much higher base. There was an almost 12% improvement in course success rates for African students between 2005 and 2017. Coloured students had the lowest improvement over time at approximately 8%. There was also a marginal narrowing of the differential between white and African students over the period. From a course success perspective, this narrowing in progression performance is small and amounts to approximately 2% points. Of the three observations noted in Figure 13.4, this is the least encouraging.

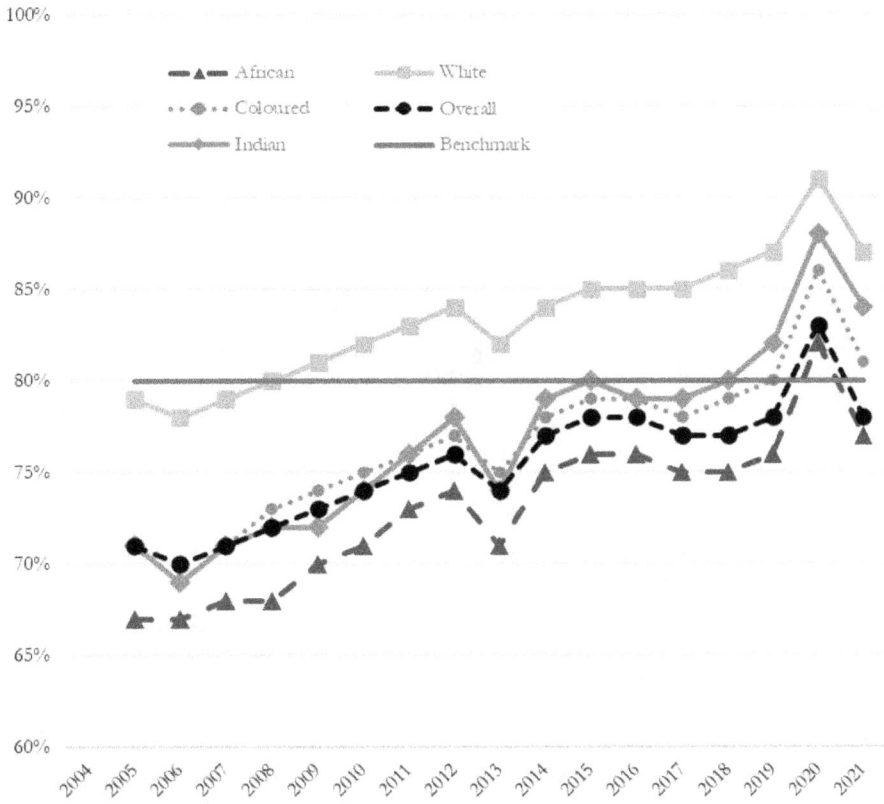

FIGURE 13.4: Student/course success rates by race: 2005–2021

Data: Council on Higher Education (2012, 2015, 2018 & 2023); data for 2004 was unavailable

The third observation from Figure 13.4 that is worth noting is that all race groups showed an upward trend over time. At first glance, this improvement in course success is indicative of an improvement in performance. On the other hand, it could be that standards have dropped at course level, translating into higher pass rates and better apparent performance. More cannot be said about the drivers of this improvement without further information.

Aggregate completions

A general measure of success is that of the aggregate number of qualifications awarded over time. Figure 13.5 shows the aggregate number of diplomas and degrees awarded between 2004 and 2018, with the later years extending beyond 2015 to account for the delay in reporting data when following a specific cohort of students.

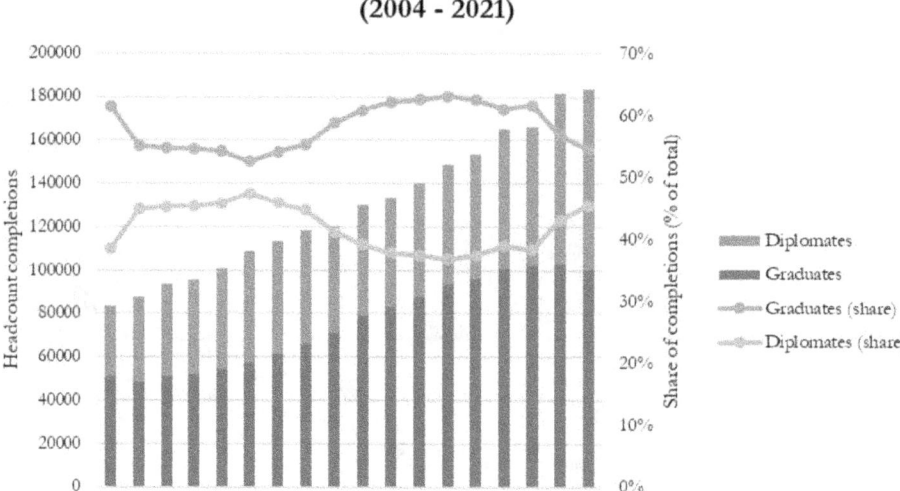

FIGURE 13.5: Degree and diploma level undergraduate completions (2004–2021)

Data: Council on Higher Education (2023)

It is evident from Figure 13.5 that most qualifications awarded in South Africa remain university degrees as opposed to technikon-based diplomas.

While the previous section emphasised first-time enrolling students in the HE sector, this section focuses on students completing undergraduate degree or diploma qualifications. Figure 13.5 shows the number and share of degree and diploma graduates in South Africa between 2004 and 2021. Over this period, the number of students successfully exiting HE with a first qualification almost doubled, increasing from 83665 total completions in 2004 to 183662 completions in 2021, representing an annual growth rate of 6%. Throughout the period, the number of graduates from universities exceed the number of diplomates[10] from technikons or universities of technology. Graduates include students completing three-year undergraduate degrees, four-year undergraduate degrees, or four-year professional degrees. Diplomates include students completing diploma-level one, two, or three-year qualifications at either a university or technikon. As most students do not complete qualifications in minimum time in South Africa, the above graph shows an extended time period relative to other graphs in this chapter to capture the extra time students spend in the HE-sector.

Between 2004 and 2009, the share of degree graduations steadily declined while the share of diploma graduations increased. From 2010 to 2016 this trend reversed with a rising share of degree graduations and a falling share of

---

[10] While graduates tend to come from universities only, diplomates may come from either a university or technikon.

diplomates. Figure 13.5 also confirms that the completion or graduation rate increased faster than the enrolment rate over the period.

While aggregate information like Figure 13.5 is illuminating, it is much more informative to dig deeper into the data to evaluate other measures of success. One of the most revealing measures is completion rates by race group.

Completions by race

Student completion or graduation rates in South Africa remain extremely low, especially when broken down by race. The numbers also do not fare well when compared to similar middle-income countries (Roser & Ortiz-Ospina, 2013).

Figure 13.6 shows cumulative graduation rates by cohort, broken down by race. The information was adapted from key 2019 and 2023 reports by the DHET. The graphs show the cumulative graduation rates for each cohort between 2004 and 2021. Each graph has the same y-axis to facilitate ease of reading and interpretation. Students are tracked for up to ten years when calculating completion rates. This is the DHET's preferred time frame for following students, especially when it can be shown that many students do not enter HE in the year immediately after completing high school.

Figure 13.6 clearly shows that completion rates increase at relatively rapid rates until years four or five and that this may differ by race group. Thereafter, the rate of increase in completion rates slows down, indicating that the n+2 rule has some impact from year six onward. This is true across all race groups. It is also evident that white students experience higher graduation rates from year three relative to the other three race groups.

The most fascinating observations in this data lie within race groups rather than between. On average, African students experience the lowest completion rates in undergraduate studies, and white students experience the highest. This has been attributed to many things, the predominant amongst these being a lack of academic preparedness that hampers performance from the beginning of African students' academic careers. For each subsequent cohort in the data, the completion rate rises steadily. This is clear when looking at later cohorts' data, for example, when comparing the 2011 cohort to the 2004 cohort.

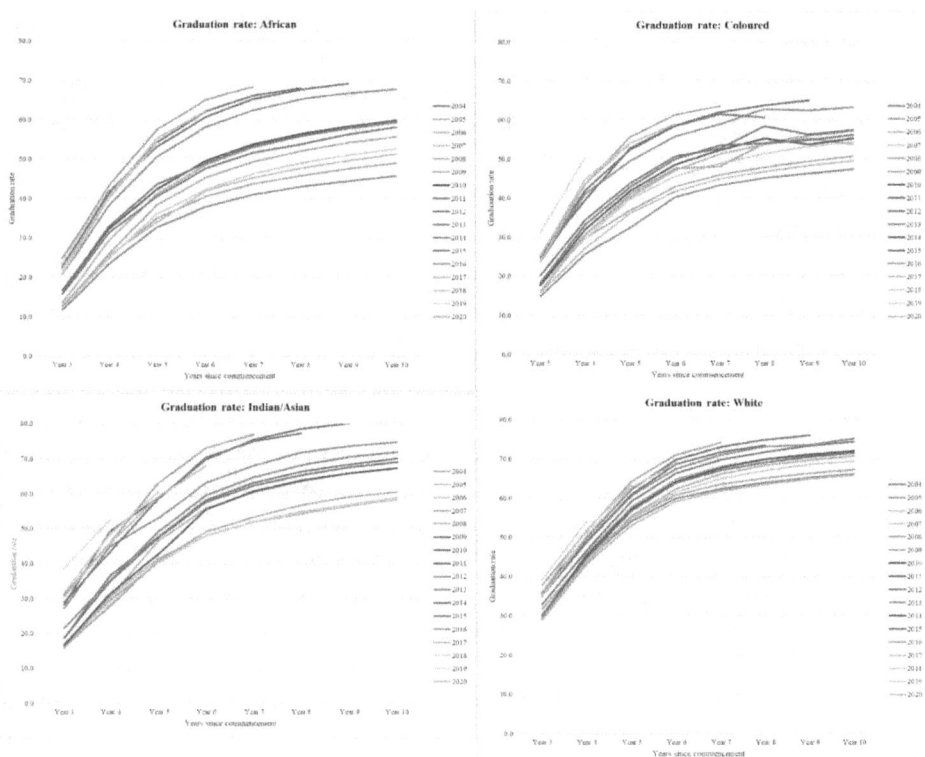

FIGURE 13.6: Cumulative graduation rates by race group

Each line per chart represents a cohort from 2004 to 2015. Data: Adapted from (DHET) 2023

Most South African students register for a three-year undergraduate qualification (DHET 2019 & 2023). This makes year five the first important point at which to analyse the data in Figure 13.6. Many, if not all, institutions impose an n+2 rule on student progression. Students are required to ensure that they complete any qualification in no longer than the minimum formal time or duration of the qualification plus two additional years. Since four-year qualifications comprise a much smaller percentage of all qualifications, the most useful metric remains year five. An analysis of intra-group performance in year five shows that African students experienced the highest increase in success rates, at approximately 54%, compared to white students, who experienced a 12% increase over the same period. The improvement for coloured students is similar to that of African students at 51%. However, when the success rates are broken down further, the impressive improvement in graduation rates is not sufficient to raise the ten-year graduation rates for coloured and African students above the year five graduation rate for white students.

Importantly, white students start out with the best performance in every category, leaving little to no room for improvement as these students tend to be the top performers.

Without additional information, it is difficult to pinpoint the reasons for the observed convergence of success rates. A few potential reasons have been suggested, such as increased extension of student funding (including financial aid), grade inflation across all institutions, and institutions admitting significantly stronger students compared to earlier cohorts.

The key finding from the data in Figure 13.6 is the convergence of graduation rates between African and white students over time. By 2013, the African five-year graduation rate is 50,6%, compared to 54,1% for white students in 2004 and 60,6% in 2013. The substantial catch-up exhibited by African students is indicative of a decline in another, arguably more important academic outcome; that of dropout.

Dropout

In line with the general patterns displayed in the previous section, Figure 13.7 shows that there has been a steady decline in the number of dropouts over the period. This is shown by the dropout curve for each cohort successively shifting upward over time. This is also partly mirrored by steady increases in the number of students graduating each year. Evidence for this is shown in Figures 13.6 and 13.7 via the different outcome measures that are tracked by the DHET. We suggest that Figures 13.6 and 13.7 are viewed in parallel as they tend to tell the same story from a data perspective.

An interesting standout from Figure 13.7 is that African students do not necessarily experience the worst dropout rates from HE in South Africa over an extended period of tracking. At an aggregate level, the data suggests that coloured students experience the highest dropout rates when the same cohort is tracked over time or the general trend evaluated for each subsequent cohort. However, many HEIs monitor the six-year dropout rate as this is correlated with the six-year graduation rate. On this measure, African students have the lowest graduation rate and the highest dropout rate after six years. In the period 2004 to 2015, there was a noticeable 4,6% decline in the differential between the dropout rates of white and African students.

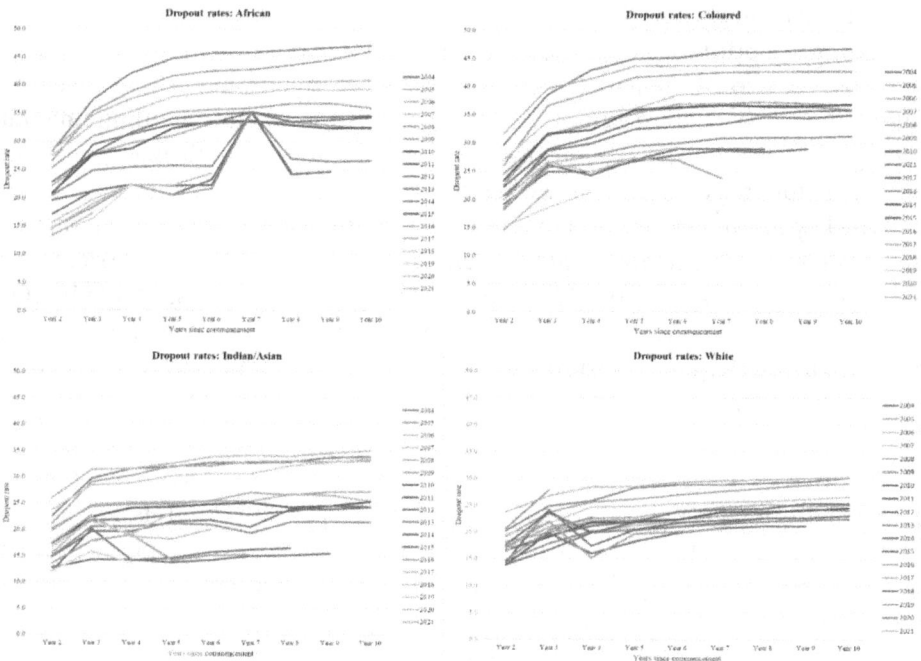

FIGURE 13.7: Cumulative dropout rates by race group

Each line per chart represents a cohort from 2004 to 2021. Data: Adapted from DHET (2023)

Importantly, the six-year dropout rate of African students fell by 13,9% points while the ten-year dropout rate fell by 20% points. This is an impressive outcome for a system that continues to display inequities in admission and performance. Coloured students displayed a similar trend for the six-year dropout rate but had slightly higher ten-year dropout rates than African students.

An important distinction, absent from the aggregate dropout data, is the separation of dropout statuses into voluntary and involuntary dropout. HEIs have set rules against which student progression is measured each year. When students fail to meet these minimum progression requirements, they are involuntarily excluded from that institution. Detailed figures concerning students refused re-entry to South African universities on academic grounds is not publicly available but could shed considerable light on the South African HE dropout problem, where years three and four dropout may be driven by involuntary dropout but subsequent years are predominantly voluntary dropout.

Staff

There are significantly more factors to investigate with respect to student academic performance and outcomes. Fewer metrics are available to evaluate staff transformation in HE. However, we attempt to evaluate changes in the demographic profile of academic staff to establish a first attempt at understanding the trends within this space.

This next section focuses on academic staff who are the primary teaching and research staff at HEIs across the country. Figure 13.8 shows the changing racial profile over the period. In 2004, when data first became available, African staff accounted for slightly more than 20% of all academic staff in the country, compared to white staff at more than 60%. However, over time the racial profile of academic staff has changed quite significantly where there appears to be an even split between African and white staff. This represents a significant change relative to the starting point of our data series. It is also notable that over the period there are no significant changes in the profile of Indian/Asian and coloured academic staff in the HE sector. The largest changes are therefore concentrated between the white and African groups.

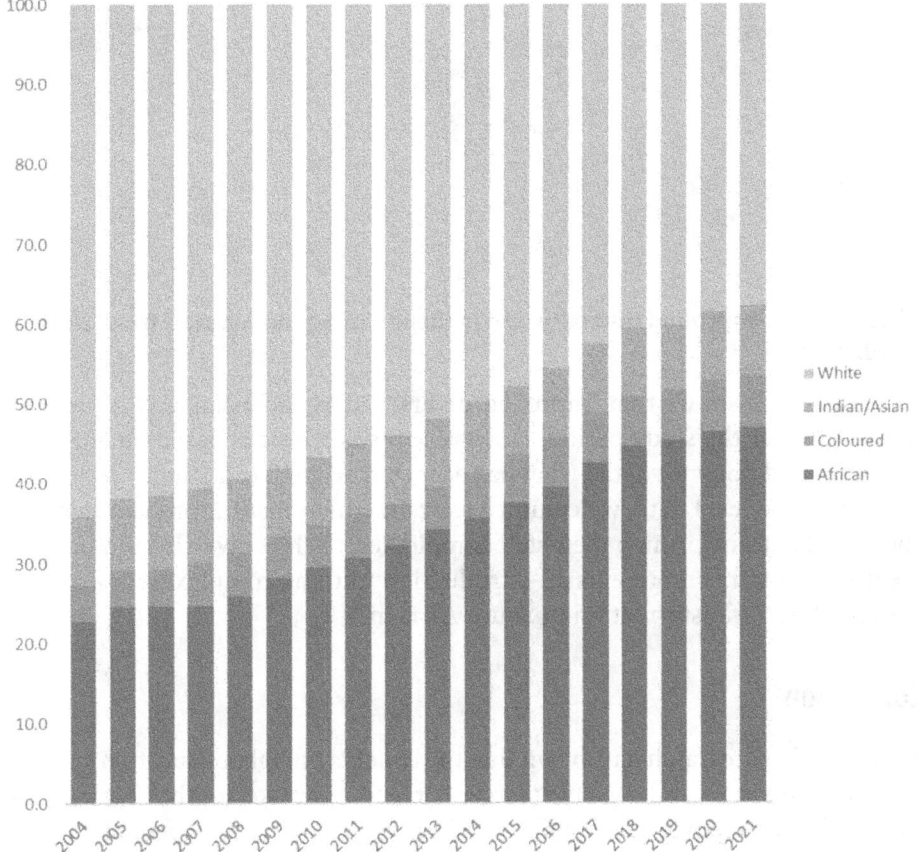

FIGURE 13.8: The changing racial profile of academic staff from 2004 to 2021

To make further sense of the changing staff profile shown in Figure 13.8, we impose the idea of an index to track changes over time. This allows us to see when the largest changes occurred and how groups compare to each other relative to the starting point in 2004. Note that the trend information contained in Figure 13.9 should be interpreted with caution, as it is relative to the 2004 starting point. Should the starting point in the series be changed, it may result in a dramatically different pattern of hiring for all racial groups.

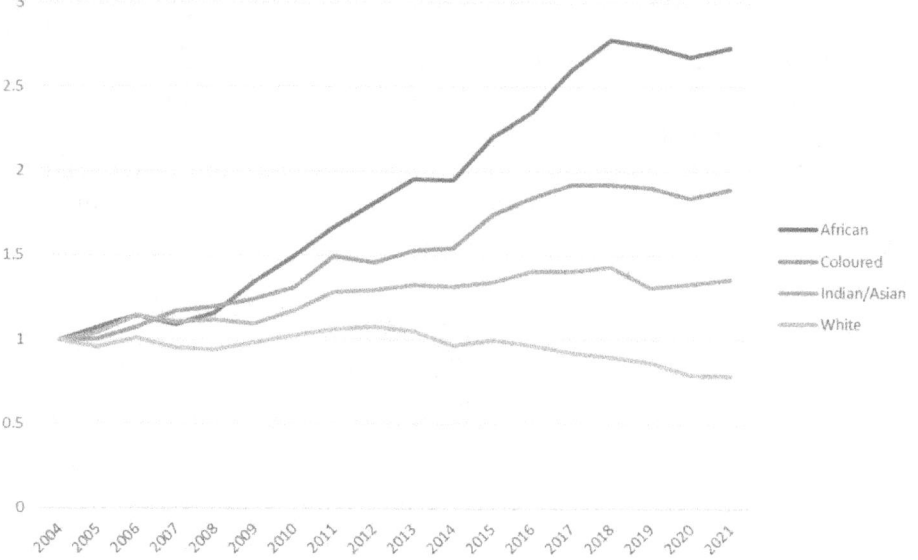

FIGURE 13.9: Improved diversity and inclusion of academic staff from 2004 to 2021

Figure 13.9 shows that improved diversity and inclusion was achieved in the sector over the study period. However, this outcome is based on aggregate-level data and does not detail what has occurred at specific institutions. Without the individual level data, we cannot ascertain which institution has been most successful in transforming their staff complement. While diversity and inclusion are important, this represents an introduction into the complexities of true and sustained staff transformation in South African HE.

Conclusion

A large body of research has shown that the benefits of higher education accrue to both the individual and society at large. For a country like South Africa, defined by high levels of poverty, inequality, and unemployment, the unequal nature of access to and participation in HE ensures that unequal access to more lucrative jobs, income opportunities, and wealth accrual persist until greater equity is achieved in both access and success in HE.

The South African HE landscape is characterised by low participation and high dropout. The Department of Higher Education and Training has shown that approximately 45% of all students who enroll in HE exit the system with a qualification. This is below regional and international standards and ensures that South Africa continues to lag behind its peers.

This discussion has highlighted that the limited absorptive capacity of the HE sector has been prohibitive of the required expansion to widen access for significantly more students to HE. In addition, the negligent increases in enrolment over the period, despite the addition of three new universities, shows a sector that is struggling to expand and afford opportunities to more individuals, likely to reflect as a stagnating GER in the near future. This is cause for concern as full equity in outcomes have not yet been achieved and are likely to be more challenging to reach as the sector stagnates.

Once students are in the HE system, the differentials in performance between sub-groups have narrowed over time. White students have the highest student success rates exceeding 80% over the period. Other groups do not catch up to these rates but do show some improvement. When graduation rates are evaluated, white students again display the highest rates but other groups, especially African students, show improvements in performance over time. Lastly, the decline in dropout rates is discernible in the data, with a trend analysis showing a fall in the dropout rate for all students.

Taken together, this chapter provides evidence for persistence but slower progression through HE. Successively higher course success rates lead to improved graduation and dropout outcomes for all students. The rate at which the identified sub-groups progress through the system is different, but evidence is suggestive of a decrease in the African-white differential at the aggregate level.

At the staff level, we note that there have been improvements in the demographic distribution over time. Importantly, the data shows that institutions have placed greater emphasis on hiring under-represented staff, and these efforts appear to have gained momentum since 2008. While full representation has not yet been achieved, greater emphasis on policies that promote equity and diversity in HE will continue to bode well for the health of the sector moving forward.

South Africa has been making gains in this sector, albeit at a rather slow but sustained pace.

References

Branson, N., Hofmeyr, C. & Lam, D. (2014). Progress through school and the determinants of school dropout in South Africa. *Development Southern Africa*, 31(1): 106–126.

Branson, N. & Leibbrandt, M. (2013). *Educational Attainment and Labour Market Outcomes in South Africa, 1994–2010* (Working paper 1022). OECD Economics Department: OECD Publishing. http://dx.doi.org/10.1787/5k4c0vvbvv0q-en.

Branson, N., Leibbrandt, M. & Zuze, T.L. (2009). *The demand for tertiary education in South Africa*. South African Labour and Development Research Unit.

Council on Higher Education. (2012). *Vital stats. Public higher education 2010*. Pretoria: CHE.

Council on Higher Education. (2015). *Vital stats. Public higher education 2013*. Pretoria: CHE

Council on Higher Education. (2018). *Vital stats. Public higher education 2016*. Pretoria: CHE.

Council on Higher Education. (2023). *Vital stats. Public higher education 2021*. Pretoria: CHE.

Department of Basic Education. (2015). Annual Reports. *Department of Basic Education of the Republic of South Africa*. Accessed at: https://www.education.gov.za/Resources/Reports.aspx.

Department of Higher Education and Training. (2013). *White Paper for post-school education and training: Building and expanded, effective and integrated post-school system* (As approved by Cabinet on 20 November 2013). Pretoria: DHET.

Department of Higher Education and Training. (2018). *Statistics on post-school education and training in South Africa: 2016*. Pretoria: DHET.

Department of Higher Education and Training. (2023). *2000 to 2021 first time entering undergraduate cohort studies for public higher education institutions*. Pretoria: DHET.

Fisher, G. & Scott, I. (2011). *Background paper 3: the role of higher education in closing the skills gap in South Africa* (Closing the skills and technology gap in South Africa). The World Bank.

Hundenborn, J., Leibbrandt, M.V. & Woolard, I. (2018). *Drivers of inequality in South Africa* (No. 2018/162). WIDER Working Paper.

Keswell, M. & Poswell, L. (2004). Returns to Education in South Africa: A retrospective sensitivity analysis of the available evidence. *South African Journal of Economics*, 834–860.

Leibbrandt, M. & Pabón, F.A.D. (2021). Inequality in South Africa. *The Oxford Handbook of the South African Economy*, 175–194.

McMahon, W.W. (2009). *Higher learning, greater good: The private and social benefits of higher education*. JHS Press.

Ministry of Education. (2001). *National Plan on Higher education in South Africa*. Pretoria: Government Printer.

National Planning Commission. (2011). *National Development Plan: Vision for 2030*. Pretoria, South Africa: The Presidency of the Republic of South Africa.

Nonyana, J.Z. & Njuho, P.M. (2018). Modelling the length of time spent in an unemployment state in South Africa. *South African Journal of Science*, 114(11-12): 1–7.

OECD. (2021). Population with tertiary education (indicator). *OECD Publishing*. http://dx.doi.org/10.1787/0b8f90e9-en.

Orthofer, A. (2016). Wealth inequality in South Africa: Evidence from survey and tax data. *Research Project on Employment, Income Distribution & Inclusive Growth*, 15.

Roser, M. & Ortiz-Ospina, E. (2013). *Tertiary education.* Available at: https://ourworldindata.org/tertiary-education

Schoer, V., Ntuli, M., Rankin, N., Sebastiao, C. & Hunt, K. (2010). A blurred signal? The usefulness of National Senior Certificate (NSC) Mathematics marks as predictors of academic performance at university level. *Perspectives in Education*. 28(2): 9–18.

Statistics South Africa. (2019). *Education series volume V: higher education and skills in South Africa* (Report 92-01-05).

Statistics South Africa. (2022). *Mid-year population estimates, South Africa.* Pretoria: Government of the Republic of South Africa.

CRITICAL CONVERSATIONS IN HIGHER EDUCATION

CHAPTER 14

Universities as economic drivers

Eugene Cloete

Abstract

Universities are increasingly recognised as key drivers of economic growth, attracting the attention of policymakers, investors, and funding agencies (Power & Malmberg, 2008; Roessner et al., 2013).

Their economic impact is multifaceted. Students and staff contribute directly to local economies through their consumption of goods, services, and real estate. Many alumni go on to establish successful businesses, generating employment opportunities for thousands.

Universities also enhance productivity and innovation across industries. Their research, innovation, and educational programmes lead to the development of new technologies, products, and services (including analytical services) while producing highly skilled professionals through formal degree programmes. Additionally, professional development programmes offer continuous learning opportunities.

Beyond academics, universities stimulate regional economies through events such as conferences, cultural festivals, and music competitions, which boost tourism and its associated benefits. Infrastructure investments and campus renewal projects further contribute to economic growth.

As Junaidah et al. (2020) state, 'Universities are recognized as critical assets for urban and regional economies, providing the physical and functional infrastructure to support innovation and socio-economic development.'

This chapter will review and give examples of how universities contribute to economic development.

Keywords: economic impact; research impact.

Introduction

The economic impact of universities can be direct when considering the buying power of students and staff. They are important consumers of goods and services that stimulates the local economy. However, the impact on the economy goes beyond purchasing of goods and services and includes purchasing of real estate and development of infrastructure.

However, the economic impact of universities goes well beyond staff and student spending. Universities play a vital role in driving economic growth by fostering innovation and producing skilled graduates necessary for the advancement of the economy (Kuranchie et al., 2021). They also serve as incubators of innovation that stimulate economic growth through new products and technologies contributing to job creation and societal impact. Commercialisation of intellectual property is a focus area for most universities. Spin-off companies that are created and incubated can add significantly to the economy and job creation.

Capacity development, innovation, entrepreneurship, and alumni contributions create a powerful and multifaceted economic impact. Many alumni have gone on to become world class entrepreneurs creating billion Rand companies employing thousands of people.

Conferencing and professional development leads to a direct economic benefit in a region. So does social innovation projects like the Woordfees in Stellenbosch. The hosting of sports events like the Varsity Cup equally impacts on local economies. Music competitions like the UNISA International Piano Competition is a highly influential event in the world of classical and jazz piano. It enhances South Africa's reputation in the international music community while fostering local talent and cultural exchange, and impacting on the economy of Pretoria where UNISA is located.

As regions and nations grapple with economic challenges, the strategic importance of universities as engines of growth and development has become increasingly recognised (Power & Malmberg, 2008; Roessner et al., 2013).

Direct economic impact of students and staff

The presence of a university has an impact on the local economy through student spending. Students contribute to the local housing, food, transportation, and entertainment sectors (Dyason & Kleynhans, 2017). This supports local businesses, driving real estate development, and attracting businesses to university towns including high-tech and other innovative companies (Bramwell & Wolfe, 2008; Audretsch et al., 2013; Borhani et al., 2020).

Universities furthermore contribute to the economy through the employment of faculty staff, administrative personnel, and support staff. As the student and faculty population grows, so does the need for housing, which results in investment in residential and commercial real estate projects (Dyason & Kleynhans, 2017). This creates new jobs in the construction and real estate sectors, as well as generate additional tax revenue for local governments (Clauß et al., 2018).

The economic impact of universities extends well beyond their immediate sphere of influence. Successful alumni, who have honed their skills and expertise within the university environment, often go on to become leaders in their respective fields, contributing to the local and global economy through their entrepreneurial ventures, high-skilled employment, and philanthropic endeavours (Roessner et al., 2013). Good examples of this were the creation of Capitec Bank, Naspers, Rand Merchant Bank, Shoprite Checkers, PSG Consult, and Pepcor, amongst others.

Human capacity development and contract research

Universities have a mandate to produce highly qualified people that contribute to the economy by producing skilled graduates for a wide range of industries (Klofsten et al., 2019). These highly educated individuals form the backbone of the workforce, bringing specialised knowledge and expertise that fuel the growth and competitiveness of businesses (Junaidah et al., 2020). At the postgraduate level, human capacity development happens through sponsored research projects. Sponsored postdoctoral fellows form an integral part of this cohort of researchers.

From a critical perspective, neoliberal policies have marketised higher education, encouraging mass enrolment without necessarily ensuring job opportunities for graduates. Universities, driven by financial sustainability, may continue to produce graduates without aligning their programmes with national employment needs, exacerbating the problem.

Hence, the issue of unemployed graduates is a growing concern in many countries, reflecting a disconnect between higher education systems and labour market demands (Brown et al., 2011). Despite increased access to university education, many graduates struggle to find employment due to skills mismatches, economic conditions, and structural weaknesses in labour markets (Tomlinson, 2017). Many universities continue to produce graduates in fields with low job absorption rates, while industries demand skills in emerging fields such as digital technology, artificial intelligence, and green energy. This skills mismatch leaves graduates with qualifications that may not align with current job opportunities, leading to underemployment or unemployment. High unemployment rates among graduates are also linked to slow economic growth, limited job creation, and saturated job markets. From a critical perspective, neoliberal policies have marketised higher education, encouraging mass enrolment without necessarily ensuring job opportunities for graduates (Marginson, 2016). Universities, driven by financial sustainability, may continue to produce graduates without aligning their programmes with national employment needs, exacerbating the problem (Archer & Davison, 2008). Addressing graduate unemployment requires a multifaceted approach that includes education reform, economic development, industry collaboration, and policy interventions. Without strategic efforts to align higher education with labour market demands, the issue of unemployed graduates will persist, affecting economic growth and social stability (York, 2006).

Contract research is key to the success of a research-intensive university. Contract research serves as a significant economic driver by fostering collaboration between academic institutions, private companies, and government agencies. It allows businesses to outsource research and development to universities or reducing costs and speeding up innovation. Through contract research, universities and research organisations generate revenue, create jobs for scientists and technical staff, and advance knowledge in key industries, for example healthcare, technology, and engineering (Etzkowitz & Zhou, 2017).

Moreover, contract research leads to new products, processes, and technologies, contributing to economic growth by increasing industrial competitiveness. It also promotes knowledge transfer, helping businesses stay at the cutting edge of innovation, which in turn drives productivity and market expansion.

Contract research in South African universities is sponsored by a variety of stakeholders, including government bodies, private sector companies, and international organisations. Some of the key sponsors include:

1. **Government agencies:**

- Department of Science and Innovation (DSI): DSI funds research initiatives that align with national priorities, such as innovation in agriculture, technology, health, and environmental sustainability.
- National Research Foundation (NRF): The NRF provides funding for academic research, often in partnership with industry, and supports university research programmes through its various grants and research chairs (SARChI).
- Technology Innovation Agency (TIA): TIA sponsors research and development projects at universities that focus on technology commercialisation, supporting innovations with market potential.

2. **Private sector:**

- Mining and energy companies: Companies like Anglo American, Sasol, and Eskom fund contract research in fields such as mining safety, energy solutions, and environmental management, often partnering with universities for specialised expertise.
- Pharmaceutical companies: Firms such as Aspen Pharmacare and GlaxoSmithKline (GSK) sponsor research in drug development and healthcare solutions through partnerships with institutions like the University of Cape Town's Drug Discovery and Development Centre (H3D).
- Financial and technology companies: Companies like Standard Bank, Naspers, and Vodacom fund contract research related to fintech, data science, and telecommunication innovations through collaborations with universities like the University of Pretoria, Stellenbosch University, and the University of the Witwatersrand.

3. **International organisations:**

   - World Health Organization (WHO): The WHO sponsors medical and healthcare research at South African universities, particularly in areas like infectious diseases, HIV/AIDS, and tuberculosis.
   - Bill & Melinda Gates Foundation: The foundation funds research in public health and agriculture, partnering with South African institutions on projects that target disease prevention and food security.
   - European Union (EU) and USAID: Both sponsor university research focused on development challenges, from renewable energy to urban infrastructure and education reforms.

4. **Non-Profit and philanthropic organisations:**

   - Wellcome Trust: This global health charity supports biomedical research, including collaborations with South African universities on issues such as malaria, HIV, and public health infrastructure.
   - Alan Gray Philanthropies: Through initiatives like the Jasisri Entrepreneurship Project, Alan Gray Philanthropies funds research and development to support entrepreneurship and economic development in South Africa, often partnering with universities.

These diverse sponsors collaborate with universities to drive innovation and address societal and economic challenges through research.

Innovation and commercialisation

The transformation of the traditional role of universities has been a key driver in their emergence as prominent innovation stakeholders. As universities have adapted to the changing needs of the knowledge economy, they have become increasingly engaged in activities that go beyond their traditional teaching and research functions (Viale & Bathelt, 2014). This transition has enabled universities to play a more active role in regional economic development and social change, contributing to the creation of new jobs, the growth of innovative industries, and the overall competitiveness of their surrounding communities.

Universities have been increasingly embracing an 'entrepreneurial' mindset, focusing on commercialising research and fostering economic development (Clarysse et al., 2011). They have become increasingly active in technology transfer and commercialisation. Through the establishment of technology transfer offices and the implementation of robust intellectual property management strategies, universities can facilitate the transition of research findings from the laboratory to the marketplace. This process can involve the patenting of innovative technologies, the licensing of these patents to external parties, and the creation of spin-off companies that commercialise university-developed technologies (Roessner et al., 2013; Clauß et al., 2018; Klofsten et al., 2019; Pasha, 2019). This has led to the development of so-called techno-parks at leading research-intensive universities as they can benefit from the pool of skilled graduates, collaborative research opportunities, and the overall intellectual and cultural vibrancy of the university environment (Bramwell & Wolfe, 2008; Borhani et al., 2020).

Entrepreneurial universities therefore play an important role in regional and national economic development, not only through the commercialisation of intellectual property but also by facilitating knowledge transfer, supporting new venture creation, and maintaining the competitiveness of established firms (Roessner et al., 2013; Clauß et al., 2018; Klofsten et al., 2019; Borhani et al., 2020).

Several successful South African university spin-off companies have emerged from academic research and innovation, contributing to both the economy and industry. Here are some notable examples:

- **CapeRay Medical** (University of Cape Town and Cape Peninsula University of Technology): CapeRay is a medical technology company that developed the Aceso system, which combines X-ray and ultrasound imaging to detect breast cancer more effectively. This spin-off has received international recognition and investment, contributing to advancements in cancer detection technology.
- **CSense Systems** (University of Pretoria): CSense Systems developed advanced industrial process control and optimisation software. The company was acquired by General Electric (GE) in 2011, a testament to its innovative approach to industrial automation, and has since integrated its technology into GE's global operations.
- **SenTech** (University of Stellenbosch): SenTech specialises in advanced sensor technology used in various industries, including aerospace and defense. This company leverages research in sensor systems to develop innovative products that are used in local and international markets.
- **Recom Technologies** (University of Johannesburg): Recom Technologies focuses on renewable energy and sustainable technologies. It originated from university research on improving the efficiency of solar energy systems and has contributed to the growing renewable energy sector in South Africa.
- **BioCODE** (Stellenbosch University): BioCODE developed a technology for rapid diagnostic testing and monitoring of diseases, particularly in low-resource settings. This spin-off focuses on creating affordable and accessible healthcare solutions, addressing critical public health needs in Africa and beyond.

These spin-offs highlight the role of South African universities in promoting innovation and entrepreneurship, with many of them addressing key societal challenges and gaining traction in global markets.

It could be argued that universities focusing on entrepreneurial endeavours is a neoliberal approach that focusses on economic growth rather that public good. Neoliberalism, while credited with promoting economic efficiency and entrepreneurship, has been widely criticised for its negative social and economic consequences. One major concern is increased inequality, as neoliberal policies often favour the wealthy, while reducing public spending on essential services like education and healthcare, making them less accessible to lower-income groups. The undermining of public institutions is another key issue, as funding cuts to social programmes weaken education, healthcare, and welfare systems, while corporate influence shifts research priorities toward profit-driven interests rather than public benefit. Additionally, neoliberalism contributes to precarious employment and labour exploitation, with deregulated labour markets leading to temporary, low-paying jobs with few benefits, particularly in the gig economy and academia. The framework also prioritises profit over social welfare, often at the expense of environmental sustainability and worker safety, as seen in the 2008 financial crisis, which was fuelled by deregulated financial markets. Lastly, critics argue that neoliberalism leads to the erosion of democratic values, as corporations and wealthy individuals gain outsized influence over policymaking, often shaping public policies to serve market interests rather than the broader public good. While neoliberalism fosters competition and innovation, its emphasis on market efficiency often comes at the cost of social equity, public welfare, and long-term economic stability, highlighting the need for a more balanced economic approach (Klein, 2007; Giroux, 2014; Brown, 2015).

Infrastructure projects

Infrastructure projects have a direct impact on the local economy. Universities often embark on campus renewal projects and expansion of existing infrastructure to accommodate expansion of student housing and new facilities for research and development. Well-developed infrastructure attracts foreign and domestic investments, as funding agencies seek state of the art facilities.

University infrastructure projects can range from large-scale construction to technological upgrades and sustainability initiatives, all contributing to both academic development and regional economic growth. Here are a few examples:

- **Research facilities**: Universities often build specialised research centres, such as the Biomedical Research Institute (BMRI) at Stellenbosch University, which promotes innovation in medicine and health research including pandemic preparedness and prevention by providing state-of-the-art laboratories and collaboration spaces. The University of Pretoria recently completed the Future Africa Campus promoting collaboration

across Africa.
- **Innovation hubs**: Stellenbosch University has built the Launchlab that is an accelerator and incubator space that supports student and faculty startups, fostering entrepreneurship and contributing to the local economy.
- **Student housing and campus expansions**: Projects include residential facilities and academic buildings, improving student access to resources while creating construction jobs and driving local economic activity.
- **Green initiatives**: Many South African universities have invested in sustainable infrastructure projects, and green buildings that reduce energy costs and optimise water usage to promote environmentally conscious innovation.
- **Digital infrastructure**: Following the COVID-19 pandemic, most South African universities have created online platforms that represent significant investments in digital infrastructure, expanding access to higher education and creating a global platform for learning and collaboration.

These projects not only improve the academic environment but also contribute to local development, job creation, and technological progress.

Universities and industry partnerships

In today's globalised, knowledge-driven economy, universities have become central players in driving innovation ecosystems. By connecting academia, industry, and government, universities facilitate the flow of knowledge, encourage technological commercialisation, and contribute to economic and social development. Their unique position enables them to act as catalysts for innovation, creating a synergy that benefits not just the academic world but also broader society and the economy (Etzkowitz, & Zhou, (2017).

Universities leverage their research capabilities to tackle complex problems, often in collaboration with external partners, translating these into practical applications (Junaidah et al., 2020). It is therefore not uncommon for universities to work closely with industry, non-governmental organisations, local government, and non-profit organisations to identify the needs of society and to address them in a fact-based collaborative manner (Sengupta et al., 2020). Their unique position at the intersection of academia, industry, and government has enabled universities to play a pivotal role in fostering innovation ecosystems.

This industry engagement enables universities to move beyond the confines of the classroom and laboratory to play a leading role in achieving social and economic growth (Sengupta et al., 2020). This facilitates the exchange of knowledge, resources, and expertise, leading to the development of cutting-edge research and groundbreaking discoveries. Often, this collaboration results in the sponsorship of endowed research chairs adding to the long-term sustainability of the relationship.

Universities have been recognised as important engines of economic growth and development. From attracting top talent and investment to catalysing innovation and cultural enrichment, these institutions can play a pivotal role in revitalising local economies. Case studies have demonstrated how universities can drive the revitalisation of towns and cities, attracting skilled professionals, entrepreneurs, and investors (Power & Malmberg, 2008).

Furthermore, universities often collaborate with industry partners to tailor educational programmes, ensuring that graduates are equipped with the skills and competencies demanded by the job market (Borhani et al., 2020). Upskilling and reskilling have become crucial strategies for organisations to address the skills gap, as they aim to equip their employees with the necessary competencies to thrive in the digital age.

The increasing engagement of universities in economic and social activities can be understood through a neoliberal framework (Brown, 2015). As state funding declines, universities have sought alternative revenue streams, leading to the marketisation of higher education. Institutions now compete for external funding, corporate partnerships, and tuition-paying students, often prioritising commercially viable research and applied knowledge over purely academic pursuits. This shift has sparked debates about the commodification of knowledge and the tension between academic freedom and market demands.

At their core, universities remain institutions of academic learning and research. They generate new knowledge, explore theoretical frameworks, and contribute to the development of fundamental research that drives innovation. University research has long been central to advancements in fields like medicine, engineering, and the sciences. However, the role of universities has expanded in response to the demands of industry and government.

While basic research is still critical, universities are increasingly engaged in applied research – work that can be directly translated into tangible technologies, products, or services. This shift reflects the broader market-driven nature of the knowledge economy, where universities are expected to generate not just theoretical insights but also practical solutions that can be commercialised or applied to societal challenges.

Conferences, workshops, and short courses

The economic impact of conferences, workshops, and short courses is a topic of significant interest to academic institutions, businesses, and policymakers alike. These events can have a substantial influence on local and regional economies, affecting various sectors such as hospitality, transportation, and retail (Brown & McNamara, 1994).

Conferences bring immediate financial benefits through attendee spending and create long-term advantages by fostering business growth, innovation, and regional development. The overall impact can be substantial, particularly for cities and regions that position themselves as premier destinations for business and academic events.

Many conference attendees extend their stay for leisure, leading to increased tourism activities. This generates revenue for local attractions, tour operators, and cultural institutions. Conferences often bring together professionals, investors, and business leaders. These gatherings create opportunities for networking and partnerships that may lead to future business investments in the region.

Many South African universities offer short courses aimed at professional development across various fields. Here are some prominent institutions providing such programmes:

1. **University of Cape Town (UCT)**

- UCT Graduate School of Business (GSB): Offers short courses in leadership, management, and finance. The UCT Professional Development Project also provides courses in law, education, and health.
- UCT online short courses: Through partnerships with platforms like GetSmarter, UCT offers online courses in project management, data analysis, digital marketing, and business strategy.

2. **University of Pretoria (UP)**

- Gordon Institute of Business Science (GIBS): GIBS offers various executive education programmes in leadership, entrepreneurship, and business management.
- Continuing Education at UP (CE at UP): Offers a wide range of short courses in fields like engineering, health sciences, law, education, and public administration.

3. **University of the Witwatersrand (Wits)**

- Wits Business School (WBS): Provides professional development programmes in business management, leadership, finance, and entrepreneurship.
- Wits Plus: Offers part-time and short courses in areas like digital marketing, HR management, and financial planning for professionals looking to upskill.

4. **Stellenbosch University**

   - Stellenbosch University Business School (USB): Offers executive short courses in leadership, strategy, and business innovation, with a strong focus on sustainability and ethics.
   - Stellenbosch University Enterprises: Provides a wide range of professional development courses, including in agriculture, health sciences, and data science.

5. **University of South Africa (UNISA)**

   - Centre for Lifelong Learning: Offers numerous professional development short courses, including in supply chain management, business leadership, and public administration.
   - UNISA Online Courses: UNISA offers a flexible range of online short courses in fields such as education, IT, project management, and communication.

6. **North-West University (NWU)**

   - NWU Continuing Education: Provides professional development courses in engineering, law, education, and health, among other areas.
   - NWU Business School: Offers leadership and management short courses tailored to the needs of professionals in various industries.

7. **University of Johannesburg (UJ)**

   - UJ Centre for Professional Development: Offers short courses in areas like business, IT, health sciences, engineering, and education.
   - UJ Online Short Courses: Provides professional development programmes in project management, public sector management, and digital transformation.

8. **Durban University of Technology (DUT)**

   - DUT offers a variety of short courses through its faculties, including in fields like engineering, health sciences, management, and IT.

9. **Cape Peninsula University of Technology (CPUT)**

   - CPUT provides industry-relevant short courses in fields such as engineering, business, information technology, and health sciences, focusing on skills development for professionals.

10. **Nelson Mandela University (NMU)**

- NMU offers professional development courses in business management, environmental management, law, and education through its Extended Learning division.

11. **Rhodes University**

- Rhodes University provides specialised short courses through its institutes, focusing on fields like journalism, education, environmental science, and business leadership.

These universities offer flexible options for professionals seeking to upgrade their skills, pursue career advancement, or gain expertise in new fields. Courses are available both online and in-person, catering to various industries and disciplines.

Sporting events

University sporting events can significantly boost the local economy through direct spending, job creation, and long-term regional development. They also strengthen the connection between universities and their surrounding communities, promoting regional development and tourism. A good example of this is the Varsity Cup tournament. The Varsity Cup is one of South Africa's premier university rugby tournaments, launched in 2008, and has subsequently been expanded to include a few other sport codes like netball. It features top university rugby and netball teams competing in an exciting and highly competitive format, and it has grown to become a major event on the South African sporting calendar. It not only provides a platform for young sport talent but also strengthens the identity of participating universities, stimulates local economies, and enriches the university experience for students. The Varsity Cup significantly boosts the local economies of the cities hosting the matches, particularly smaller university towns. Large crowds of students, alumni, and rugby fans attend the games, benefiting local businesses such as restaurants, bars, and hotels.

Social innovation projects

Universities do not only focus on technological innovations to impact the economy, but also offer the possibility of social innovation. A prime example of this is the Woordfees. The Woordfees (Stellenbosch University's Festival of the Word) is a major cultural event in Stellenbosch, Western Cape, with significant economic impact on the local economy. As one of South Africa's premier arts festivals, it attracts thousands of visitors each year, offering a platform for literature, music, theatre, visual arts, and film.

The Woordfees showcases the work of hundreds of local and international artists, authors, musicians, and performers, providing them with a platform to reach new audiences. This can lead to future opportunities, collaborations, and long-term economic benefits for creatives.

Music festivals

Universities are often hosts of music festivals. One such festival is the UNISA International Piano Competition that is one of the most prestigious piano competitions in South Africa and globally, hosted by the University of South Africa (UNISA) in Pretoria. It attracts talented pianists from around the world, providing a platform for young musicians to showcase their skills and advance their careers. The competition draws participants from across the world, with past contestants from countries like the USA, Russia, South Korea, China, and various European nations. The competition boosts the local economy in Pretoria, attracting visitors, musicians, and judges who spend on accommodation, dining, and tourism.

Analytical services

University analytical services, such as laboratory testing, consulting, and research facilities, can have a significant economic impact on local, regional, and national economies. These services are often provided by university departments or specialised research centres that support industries and public sectors through various technical and scientific services. University labs provide critical services such as product testing, materials analysis, and quality assurance for local industries, including agriculture, manufacturing, pharmaceuticals, and food production. This helps businesses ensure compliance with national and international standards, improve product quality, and reduce costs.

Universities offer Small and Medium Enterprises (SMEs) access to advanced technologies, scientific equipment, and skilled researchers that they might not otherwise afford. These analytical services provide SMEs with tools for product testing, environmental analysis, and process improvement, helping them remain competitive.

University analytical services significantly impact the economy by supporting industries with testing, consulting, and research capabilities. These services foster innovation, create jobs, support SMEs, and attract investment, while enhancing the competitiveness of sectors like agriculture, healthcare, and manufacturing. The resulting partnerships between academia and industry contribute to sustained economic growth, technological advancement, and the development of skilled labour.

Discussion and conclusion

Universities play a crucial role in driving economic growth and development. However, they also face complex challenges in balancing their educational missions with economic goals. While the economic impact of universities is well-documented, striking the right balance between economic goals and educational missions remains a key challenge. Universities must carefully navigate the tensions between their roles as hubs of innovation and economic growth, and their core responsibilities as institutions of higher learning and providers of public good.

Rather than viewing universities as simple 'knowledge factories' that can directly drive innovation and economic development, a more nuanced understanding of their evolving role within broader innovation ecosystems is required (Bramwell & Wolfe, 2008). Universities are better conceptualised as 'catalysts' that can stimulate and support regional economic growth, rather than the sole drivers of that growth.

To harness the economic potential of universities, policy makers should focus on supporting university-industry partnerships that facilitate the transfer of knowledge and technology from academia to the private sector. This may involve providing funding and incentives for collaborative R&D projects, as well as creating platforms and intermediaries to bridge the gap between university researchers and industry (Steen & Enders, 2008).

Governments should continue to invest in building high-quality higher education infrastructure, including state-of-the-art research facilities and technology transfer offices. These physical and functional assets are crucial in enabling universities to fulfil their economic development role (Junaidah et al., 2020).

Policies should be designed to promote a more entrepreneurial culture within universities, encouraging faculty, staff, and students to commercialise their ideas and start new businesses.

While the expanded role of universities brings opportunities for innovation and societal impact, it also raises challenges related to academic integrity, research independence, and equitable access to education. Understanding this transformation requires a critical analysis of the economic, political, and social forces shaping contemporary higher education. By theorising and contextualising these shifts, scholars can better assess whether universities are fulfilling their core mission or being reshaped by external pressures.

References

Archer, W. & Davison, J. (2008). *Graduate Employability: What Employers Think and Want*. The Council for Industry and Higher Education (CIHE).

Audretsch, D.B., Link, A.N. & Legazkue, I.P. (2013). Academic Entrepreneurship and Regional Economic Development. *Economic Development Quarterley*, 27(1): 3–5. https://doi.org/10.1177/0891242412473191.

Borhani, M., Amiran, H. & Shahriari, J.E. (2020). Quantitative Indicators of Local Economic Readiness for Entrepreneurial Universities. *International Journal of Engineering Research & Technology (IJERT)*, 9(3). https://doi.org/10.17577/ijertv9is030379.

Bramwell, A. & Wolfe, D A. (2008). Universities and regional economic development: The entrepreneurial University of Waterloo. *Research Policy*, 37(8): 1175–1187. https://doi.org/10.1016/j.respol.2008.04.016.

Brown, P., Lauder, H. & Ashton, D. (2011). *The Global Auction: The Broken Promises of Education, Jobs, and Incomes*. Oxford University Press.

Brown, S.M. & McNamara, K.T. (1994). Impacts of a University's Instructional Programs on the Local and State Economies. *Journal of the Community Development Society*, 25(2),: 202–212. https://doi.org/10.1080/15575339409489881.

Brown, W. (2015). *Undoing the Demos: Neoliberalism's Stealth Revolution*. Zone Books.

Chaparro, X.A.F., Takahashi, C K. & Figueiredo, J.C.B.D. (2022). The triple helix and the quality of the startup ecosystem: a global view. *Revista de Gestao*, 30(3): 238–252. https://doi.org/10.1108/rege-04-2021-0077.

Clarysse, B., Wright, M. & Van Hove, J. (2011). **A look at the university spin-off process: A triple helix perspective**. *Industrial and Corporate Change*, **20**(3): 747–777.

Clauß, T., Moussa, A. & Kesting, T.. (2018). Entrepreneurial university: a stakeholder-based conceptualisation of the current state and an agenda for future research. *International Journal of Technology Management (IJTM)*, 77(1/2/3): 109–109. https://doi.org/10.1504/ijtm.2018.091726.

Dyason, D. & Kleynhans, E.P. (2017). A university in a small city: Discovering which sectors benefit. *Acta Comercii: Independent Research Journal in the Management Sciences*, 17(1). https://doi.org/10.4102/ac.v17i1.513.

Etzkowitz, H. & Zhou, C. (2017). **The Triple Helix Innovation Model: From Academia to Industry to Government.** In *The Triple Helix Innovation Model* (1–21). Springer, Cham.

Eðvarðsson, I.R. & Durst, S. (2017). Universities and knowledge-based development: a literature review. *International Journal of Knowledge-Based Development (IJKBD)*, 8(2): 105–105. https://doi.org/10.1504/ijkbd.2017.085155.

Giroux, H.A. (2014). *Neoliberalism's War on Higher Education*. Haymarket Books.

Heaton, S., Siegel, D.S. & Teece, D.J. (2019). Universities and innovation ecosystems: a dynamic capabilities perspective. *Industrial and Corporate Change*, 28(4): 921–939. https://doi.org/10.1093/icc/dtz038.

Junaidah, J., Basyar, S., Pahrudin, A. & Fauzan, A. (2020). Strategic Management Roadmap: Formulation, Implementation, and Evaluation to Develop Islamic Higher Education Institution. *Tadris: Jurnal Keguruan dan Ilmu Tarbiyah*, 5(2) : 335–347. https://doi.org/10.24042/tadris.v5i2.7301.

Klein, N. (2007). *The Shock Doctrine: The Rise of Disaster Capitalism.* Metropolitan Books.

Klofsten, M., Fayolle, A., Guerrero, M., Mian, S.A., Urbano, D. & Wright, M. (2019). The entrepreneurial university as driver for economic growth and social change – Key strategic challenges. *Technological Forecasting and Social Change,* 141: 149–158. https://doi.org/10.1016/j.techfore.2018.12.004.

Kuranchie, A., Okyere, M. & Larbi, E.. (2021). A Non-state University's Contribution to the Tertiary Education Landscape in Ghana. *International Journal of Academic Research in Progressive Education and Development,* 10(1). https://doi.org/10.6007/ijarped/v10-i1/8327.

Marginson, S. (2016). **The worldwide trend to high participation higher education: Dynamics of social stratification in inclusive systems.** *Higher Education,* **72**(4), 413–434.

Pasha, A. (2019). Role of Entrepreneurial Universities, Research Centres and Economic Zones in Driving Entrepreneurship and Innovation in Cluster Ecosystems. *RELX Group* (Netherlands). https://doi.org/10.2139/ssrn.3352301.

Postle, G. & Sturman, A. (2003). Widening Access to Higher Education – An Australian Case Study. *Journal of Adult and Continuing Education,* 8(2): 195–212. https://doi.org/10.7227/jace.8.2.6.

Power, D. & Malmberg, A. (2008). The contribution of universities to innovation and economic development: in what sense a regional problem? *Cambridge Journal of Regions, Economy and Society,* 1(2): 233–245. https://doi.org/10.1093/cjres/rsn006.

Roessner, D., Bond, J., Okubo, S. & Planting, M.A. (2013). The economic impact of licensed commercialized inventions originating in university research. *Research Policy,* 42(1): 23–34. https://doi.org/10.1016/j.respol.2012.04.015.

Sengupta, E., Blessinger, P. & Yamin, T.S. (2020). Introduction to University Partnerships for Sustainable Development. Emerald Publishing Limited. In Sengupta, E., Blessinger, P. & Yamin, T.S. (ed.) *University Partnerships for Sustainable Development,* 3–13. https://doi.org/10.1108/s2055-364120200000020004.

Steen, M.V.D. & Enders, J. (2008). Universities in Evolutionary Systems of Innovation. *Creativity and Innovation Management,* 17(4): 281–292. https://doi.org/10.1111/j.1467-8691.2008.00496.x.

Tomlinson, M. (2017). Forms of graduate capital and their relationship to graduate employability. *Education & Training,* 59(4): 338–352.

Viale, R. & Bathelt, H. (2014). University spin-offs in a knowledge-based economy: A systematic review of the literature. *Technological Forecasting and Social Change,* 89: 1–14.

Yorke, M. (2006). *Employability in Higher Education: What It Is – What It Is Not.* Higher Education Academy.

CONTRIBUTING AUTHORS

Dr Hanelie Adendorff is a senior advisor in the Centre for Teaching and Learning at Stellenbosch University. She has a PhD in chemistry but has been working in professional development since 2002. Her career and professional development started with an interest in blended learning, but she has since included work in the areas of assessment, facilitation of collaborative learning, science education, and, more recently, the decolonisation of the science curriculum and generative AI in teaching, learning, and assessment. [https://orcid.org/0000-0002-6405-1507] Email: hja@sun.ac.za

Dr Sharon Margaretta Auld is a postgraduate academic leader, supervisor, and senior lecturer in the School of Psychology at The IIE's Varsity College, Durban North. She has lectured in the discipline of psychology at the University of KwaZulu-Natal where she was also a Postdoctoral Fellow with the National Institute for The Humanities and Social Sciences. Sharon is a clinical psychologist with an interest in long-term psychodynamic psychotherapy. Her PhD involved work with policemen who suffered post-traumatic stress disorder in the line of duty. Her research interests include the social construction of psychopathology, critical identity studies, and the transformation of higher education. [https://orcid.org/0000-0002-3057-3921] Email: sauld@varsitycollege.co.za

Prof Ayansola Olatunji Ayandibu is an Associate Professor and Head of the Department of Business Management at the University of Zululand, South Africa. He holds a BSc Hons in Accounting, an MBA, and a PhD in Leadership Studies (strategy, innovation, and entrepreneurship). With 12 years in academia and eight years in the corporate sector, he has published over 44 accredited articles and book chapters, and one edited book. He has presented at local and international conferences in the UK, USA, Mauritius, Canada, France, Nigeria, and South Africa. His research interests include entrepreneurship, innovation, and strategic leadership. [https://orcid.org/0000-0001-5870-2388] Email: AyandibuA@unizulu.ac.za or ayansola.ayandibu@gmail.com

Prof Eugene Cloete has been the Chief Executive Officer at Cape Higher Education Consortium (CHEC) since 1 September 2022. A microbiologist and water expert, Prof Cloete was the Deputy Vice Chancellor: Research, Innovation, and Postgraduate Studies at Stellenbosch University for ten years. During his tenure as DvC, Stellenbosch University became internationally recognised as a leading research-intensive university. He recently received the Chancellor award from Stellenbosch University for his contribution during his ten-year term. Before taking up this position in September 2012, Prof Cloete served as the Dean of the Faculty of Science at Stellenbosch University. He has promoted more than 110 MSc and PhD students, authored five books, holds ten patents, and has more than 165 scientific publications to his credit. He also leads Entrepreneurship Development in Higher Education (EDHE) and is a Board member of ASSAf. [https://orcid.org/0000-0001-6207-1371] Email: eugene.cloete@chec.ac.za

Dr Ann George, BSc (cum laude), BSc Hons, PhD, is a senior lecturer in the Centre for Health Science Education at the University of the Witwatersrand, Johannesburg. Her broader research interest is improving health professions education; her specific focus is designing meaningful learning interactions. She has received several National Research Foundation grants, a Female Academic Leaders Fellowship (2021), institutional and faculty teaching awards, and the Southern African Association of Health Educationalists (SAAHE) Best Publication Award (2023). Ann is a deputy editor for Human Resources for Health, and associate editor for the Journal of Patient-Centered Research and Reviews. [https://orcid.org/0000-0002-9042-2279] Email: ann.george@wits.ac.za

Prof Lionel Green-Thompson (MBBCh, MMed, PhD) serves as the Dean: Faculty of Health Sciences at the University of Cape Town. His PhD explored social accountability in medicine. He co-leads a national innovation, applying workplace-based assessment for competent and trustworthy medical specialist practice. Prof Green-Thompson chaired the South African Committee of Medical Deans (2022–2023). He serves on the research committee of AMEE and leads the network which manages the grant for Medical Education in Resource-Constrained Settings (MERCS). Prof Green-Thompson serves on the board of The Network – Towards Unity for Health as Vice Secretary General (2023-2027). Prof Green-Thompson currently represents USAf on the HPCSA Council. [https://orcid.org/0000-0002-2950-9527] Email: lionel.green-thompson@uct.ac.za

Dr Jan P. Grundling brings rich experience from academia. Holding degrees from Stellenbosch University and the University of South Africa, he served as a Senior Officer in the South African Defence Force before transitioning to academia. At Tshwane University of Technology, he directed the Centre of Entrepreneurship and contributed extensively to research, supervising over 50 postgraduate students. With over 42 journal articles, 80 conference papers, and 22 academic book chapters, his research interests include linear programming, local economic development, and entrepreneurship. Dr Grundling has received 11 industry and academic awards, is a senior research associate at the University of Johannesburg, and a Visiting Professor at Chang'an University, China. [https://orcid.org/0000-0002-0106-4597] Email: jangrundling@gmail.com

Dr Nicoline Herman is the Director of the Centre for Teaching and Learning at Stellenbosch University. She has 25 years of experience as an academic developer at various higher education (HE) institutions and holds a PhD in HE. Her research interests are educational leadership, aspects of teaching-learning-assessment (TLA) in HE, and the professional learning of academics for their teaching role with a focus on an ethics of care. She has co-supervised Master's and PhD students, has authored and co-authored a number of publications, and presented at national and international conferences. She regularly reviews for national and international journals in the fields of TLA in HE and professional learning of academics. [https://orcid.org/0000-0003-3990-5731] Email: nherman@sun.ac.za

Ms Jayseema Jagernath holds a Master of Commerce degree from the University of KwaZulu-Natal. Jayseema currently fulfils the role of Deputy Dean: School of Management Studies at the IIE's Varsity College, which is a brand of the Independent Institution of Education. She is responsible for academic management within the school, which runs across all campuses nationally. The author has specialised in finance, investments, banking, and management, and shares a passion for women's empowerment and gender equity. [https://orcid.org/0000-0002-6210-9592] Email: jjagernath@varsitycollege.co.za

Ms Dalene Joubert is a higher education advisor at the Centre for Teaching and Learning at Stellenbosch University and through her research she explores the intersection between generative AI and teaching, learning and assessment in higher education, and the unique South-African context specifically. She convenes the StellenboschX professional certificate programme titled *AI in Higher Education* and she is the author of the course "Higher education learning in the age of AI". Dalene advises on matters of GenAI in HE TLA regularly, and she also presents workshops and conference papers on the topic. Email: dvermeulen@sun.ac.za

Dr Jerome D. Kiley has over 25 years of experience in higher education. He is currently the postgraduate research coordinator for the CPUT Department of Human Resource Management, where he lectures on global business management and research methodology. He previously lectured for the UWC Department of Industrial Psychology, UJ's HRD (honours), and the Open University's Business School. He has authored chapters on generative AI in research, the organisational environment, training and development, motivation and emotion, and values, attitudes, and beliefs. His PhD examined the role of identity capital in graduate employment, and his current research interests are the impact of generative AI on work and research practices. [https://orcid.org/0000-0003-0187-0641] Email: kileyj@cput.ac.za

Dr Chris Mayer is a career US army officer and chair of the Department of English and Philosophy at the United States Military Academy (West Point). Prior to serving as Department Chair, Dr Mayer served as associate dean for strategy and initiatives. Dr Mayer teaches courses in the areas of ethical theory, military ethics, political philosophy, and philosophy of religion. He is a former Association of Professional Futurists Emerging Fellow and an advisor for the Quality Assurance Commons, where he works with colleges and universities to evaluate and strengthen their efforts to prepare students for the future of work. [https://orcid.org/0000-0001-5746-0356] Email: christopher.mayer@westpoint.edu

Dr Mantoa Mokhachane (MBBCh, FCPaeds, MMed Paeds, PGDip-Health Science Education, PhD Health Science Education) is the Director of the Unit of Undergraduate Medical Education at the University of the Witwatersrand, Johannesburg. Her interest in medical education is social justice and employing an African lens, *ubuntu*, in professionalism and professional identity formation. Dr Mokhachane's doctoral work produced three publications: 'Rethinking Professional Identity Formation Amidst Protests and Social Upheaval: A Journey in Africa', 'Medical Students' Views on What Professionalism Means: An Ubuntu Perspective', and 'Graduates' Reflections on Professionalism and Identity: Intersections of Race, Gender and Activism'. I AM because of OTHERS. [https://orcid.org/0000-0001-5596-3654] Email: mantoa.mokhachane@wits.ac.za

Dr Leigh Neethling is a senior research officer in the Development Policy Research Unit (DPRU) and a senior lecturer in the School of Economics at the University of Cape Town. She completed a PhD in Economics in 2023 with a focus on Higher Education in South Africa. She has more than 15 years of experience in the higher education sector. She lectures at the School of Economics and is regularly invited to teach at UCT's Graduate School of Business. [https://orcid.org/0009-0002-2846-6892] Email: leigh.neethling@uct.ac.za

Ms Dominique Marié Nupen is the Dean: School of Management Studies for the IIE's Varsity College. Dominique holds a Master of Commerce in Business Management (University of Pretoria) and is a doctoral candidate (University of Johannesburg). Dominique is responsible for the academic excellence of qualifications offered by the School of Management Studies. She contributes towards the management field through academic research and curricula, peer review, publications, conferences, lecturing, and postgraduate research supervision. [https://orcid.org/0000-0003-0977-8284] Email: dnupen@varsitycollege.co.za

Prof René Pellissier is professor of research and innovation and works as strategist, researcher, and systems engineer in the international arena based on her extensive international experience across the globe at universities in the United States, the United Kingdom, France, and across Africa. Her expertise lies in the world of future work based on developments in AI, technology advances, and digital transformation. She holds an MSc in Mathematical Statistics, and an MBA and a PhD in Systems Engineering. As Consultant: Regional Leadership and Management Development Programmes at Cape Higher Education Consortium (CHEC), her work involves the development of relevant leadership and management capacity programmes for academic and administrative leaders in higher education, a CHEC sponsored book on COVID-19 responses in HEIs, and the CHEC monthly Critical Conversations focusing on emerging issues in HEIs. [https://orcid.org/0000-0001-5275-2261] Email: rene.pellissier@chec.ac.za

Dr Antoinette Smith-Crous retired from a 20-year career at Stellenbosch University in 2018 after heading the Division for Social Impact since 2015 as Director and Senior Director: Social Impact. She is currently a research fellow at the Department of Sociology and Anthropology, Faculty of Arts and Social Sciences at the same university. She was recently appointed as an external professor at the University of Cologne in Germany. In addition, she is the project director of the Cape Higher Education Dual Higher Education project. She holds a Master of Philosophy degree in Sociology (Value and Policy Studies) and a PhD in Education (Curriculum Studies) from Stellenbosch University. Her fields of expertise are higher education curriculum studies and design, experiential learning pedagogies, sociology of development, and constructivist interpretive research methodologies. She has 15 years teaching experience in higher education, including undergraduate classes and graduate supervision of master and doctoral students. Her research record reflects several national and international publications in accredited journals and books. Email: asmi@sun.ac.za

Ms Lizl Steynberg, a seasoned academic, began her journey in 1994 at North-West University, transitioning to Tshwane University of Technology (TUT) in 2001. With a fervent commitment to education, she has led 14 undergraduate and three postgraduate courses while supervising postgraduate students. Lizl's influence extends globally, showcased by more than 70 conference papers, 25 published articles, and 20 book chapters, spanning topics like internationalisation of higher education and research methodology. Recognised with prestigious awards, including the TUT Vice-Chancellor Achievement Award, Women Researcher of the Year, and the Outstanding Teaching Award, Lizl remains a pivotal figure, inspiring students and colleagues with her dedication to advancing knowledge and learning. [https://orcid.org/0000-0003-2597-9406] Email: steynbergl@tut.ac.za

Dr Rika Swanzen has nearly 30 years' experience in child welfare, mental health, community development, residential care, and ecometric measurement. During her 14 years in academia, extensive engagement work led to a six-year term serving as ministerial appointee of the South African Council for Social Service Professions. She authored 24 peer-reviewed publications and delivered 26 conference presentations from 2007–2023. She conducted research in service-learning since 2013 and more recently in paediatric palliative care. After developing and managing qualifications for Child and Youth Care and other social science disciplines between 2009 and 2022, she currently holds the position of Deputy Dean of Research at The Independent Institute of Education, Varsity College, Waterfall. [https://orcid.org/0000-0002-3926-8579] Email: rswanzen@varsitycollege.co.za

AUTHOR BIOS

Dr. Rika Swanzen
Deputy Dean: Research
The Independent Institute of Education, Varsity College

Dr. Rika Swanzen holds a BA SocSc, MA SocSc (cum laude), and D.Lit.et Phil in Social Work from the University of Johannesburg, as well as a PGDip in Paediatric Palliative Care from the University of Cape Town. From mid-2016 to mid-2022, she served as a ministerial appointee on the South African Council for Social Service Professions to represent education and training. Her research interests include the development and standardization of assessment within the social service professions, Ecometric measurement scales (measuring person-in-environment fit), paediatric palliative care integration in child and youth care centers, optimal childhood development, and service-learning in higher education.
ORCID: https://orcid.org/0000-0002-3926-8579
Email: RSwanzen@varsitycollege.co.za

Dr. Chris Mayer
Director of Philosophy
United States Military Academy (West Point)

Dr. Chris Mayer is a career U.S. Army officer and Director of Philosophy in the Department of Law & Philosophy at the United States Military Academy (West Point). He holds a Ph.D. in Philosophy from the University of Virginia, an M.A. from Virginia Tech, an M.P.A. from Murray State University, and a B.S. from the United States Military Academy. His research interests include ethics, higher education leadership strategy, curriculum, and organizational strategic foresight.
ORCID: https://orcid.org/0000-0001-5746-0356
Email: christopher.mayer@westpoint.edu

Dr. Mantoa Mokhachane
Director of the Unit for Undergraduate Medical Education
University of Witwatersrand, Johannesburg

Dr. Mantoa Mokhachane holds an MBBCh, FCPaeds, MMed Paeds, PGDip-HSci Ed, and a Ph.D. She serves as Director of the Unit for Undergraduate Medical Education at the University of Witwatersrand. Her research interests focus on social justice in medical education, employing an African lens (Ubuntu) in professionalism and professional identity formation. Her doctoral work includes papers titled "Rethinking Professional Identity Formation Amidst Protests and Social Upheaval: A Journey in Africa," "Medical Students' Views

on Professionalism: An Ubuntu Perspective," and "Graduates' Reflections on Professionalism and Identity: Intersections of Race, Gender, and Activism."
ORCID: https://orcid.org/0000-0001-5596-3654
Email: Mantoa.Mokhachane@wits.ac.za

Me. Lizl Steynberg
Lecturer and Researcher, Department of Management and Entrepreneurship
Tshwane University of Technology (TUT), Pretoria, South Africa

Me. Lizl Steynberg is a lecturer and researcher in the Department of Management and Entrepreneurship at TUT. She began her academic career at North-West University in 1994, later joining TUT in 2001. Lizl holds a Master's degree with distinction from North-West University. Her research focuses on the internationalization of higher education and research methodology. She collaborates with researchers in entrepreneurship, small business management, and local economic development.
ORCID: 0000-0003-2597-9406
Email: steynbergl@tut.ac.za

Dominique Marie Nupen
Dean: School of Management Studies
The Independent Institute of Education, Varsity College

Dominique Marie Nupen holds a Bachelor of Commerce, a Bachelor of Commerce Honours, and a Master of Commerce in Business Management, all from the University of Pretoria. She is a doctoral candidate in Digital Transformation at the University of Johannesburg. As the Dean of the School of Management Studies, Dominique oversees the academic quality of qualifications and contributes nationally and internationally to the field of management through curriculum design, peer reviews, textbooks, articles, and conference presentations.
ORCID: 0000-0003-0977-8284

Ms. Jayseema Jagernath
Deputy Dean of Management Studies
The Independent Institute of Education, Varsity College

Ms. Jayseema Jagernath holds a Master of Commerce from the University of KwaZulu-Natal. Her career began in the corporate sector before transitioning to academia. She has also worked for a Non-Governmental Organization, helping rural communities develop and manage resources. As Deputy Dean, Jayseema manages the academic programs within the School of Management Studies across all campuses nationally. Her expertise lies in finance, investments, banking, and management, and she is passionate about women's empowerment and gender equity.
ORCID: https://orcid.org/0000-0002-6210-9592

AUTHOR BIOS

Dr. Shahieda Jansen
Regional Director (Acting), Western Cape Region
University of South Africa (UNISA)

Dr. Shahieda Jansen holds a Ph.D. in Psychology and serves as the Acting Regional Director for the Western Cape Region at UNISA. Her research focuses on models of social personhood and masculinities, particularly male-focused psychotherapy.
ORCID: 0000-0001-7566-6163
Email: janses@unisa.ac.za

Dr. Sharon Margaretta Auld
Postgraduate Academic Leader, Supervisor, and Senior Lecturer
The Independent Institute of Education, Varsity College, Durban North

Dr. Sharon Auld holds a Ph.D. in Clinical Psychology and has lectured at the University of KwaZulu-Natal, where she was also a Postdoctoral Fellow with the National Institute for the Humanities and Social Sciences. A clinical psychologist, her research interests include the social construction of psychopathology, critical identity studies, and the transformation of higher education.
ORCID: https://orcid.org/0000-0002-3057-3921
Email: sauld@varsitycollege.co.za

Dr. Jerome Kiley
HRM Department Research Coordinator
Cape Peninsula University of Technology (CPUT)

Dr. Jerome Kiley holds a Ph.D. in Organisational Psychology from the University of Cape Town and an M.A. in Research Psychology from UNISA. His research interests include artificial intelligence in higher education and graduate employability.
ORCID: 0000-0003-0187-0641
Email: kileyj@cput.ac.za

Dr. Nicoline Herman
Director, Centre for Teaching and Learning
Stellenbosch University

Dr. Nicoline Herman holds a Ph.D. in Higher Education and has 25 years of experience as an academic developer in higher education institutions. Her research focuses on educational leadership, teaching-learning-assessment (TLA), and professional learning of academics with an emphasis on ethics of care.
ORCID: https://orcid.org/0000-0003-3990-5731
Email: nherman@sun.ac.za

Dr. Hanelie Adendorff
Senior Advisor, Centre for Teaching and Learning
Stellenbosch University

Dr. Hanelie Adendorff holds a Ph.D. in Chemistry and has been working in professional development since 2002. Her research focuses on blended learning, collaborative learning, decolonization of the science curriculum, and the role of AI in teaching, learning, and assessment.
ORCID: https://orcid.org/0000-0002-6405-1507
Email: hja@sun.ac.za

Ms. Dalene Joubert
Higher Education Advisor
Centre for Teaching and Learning, Stellenbosch University

Ms. Dalene Joubert's research explores the intersection between generative AI and teaching, learning, and assessment in higher education within the South African context. She convenes the StellenboschX professional certificate program on AI in higher education and advises on AI-related matters.
Email: dvermeulen@sun.ac.za

Dr Antoinette Smith-Crous
Director: Dual Higher Education Project
Cape Higher Education Consortium

Dr Antoinette Smith-Crous holds a PhD in Education (Curriculum Studies) from Stellenbosch University She has fifteen years teaching experience in Sociology and Education, including undergraduate, graduate and supervision of master and doctoral students. Her fields of expertise are higher education curriculum studies and design, experiential learning pedagogies, sociology of development and constructivist interpretive research methodologies. Her research record reflects several national and international publications in accredited journals and books.
ORCHID: https://orcid.org/0009-0007-7597-8205
Email: asmi@chec.ac.za

www.ingramcontent.com/pod-product-compliance
Lightning Source LLC
Chambersburg PA
CBHW080222170426
43192CB00015B/2721